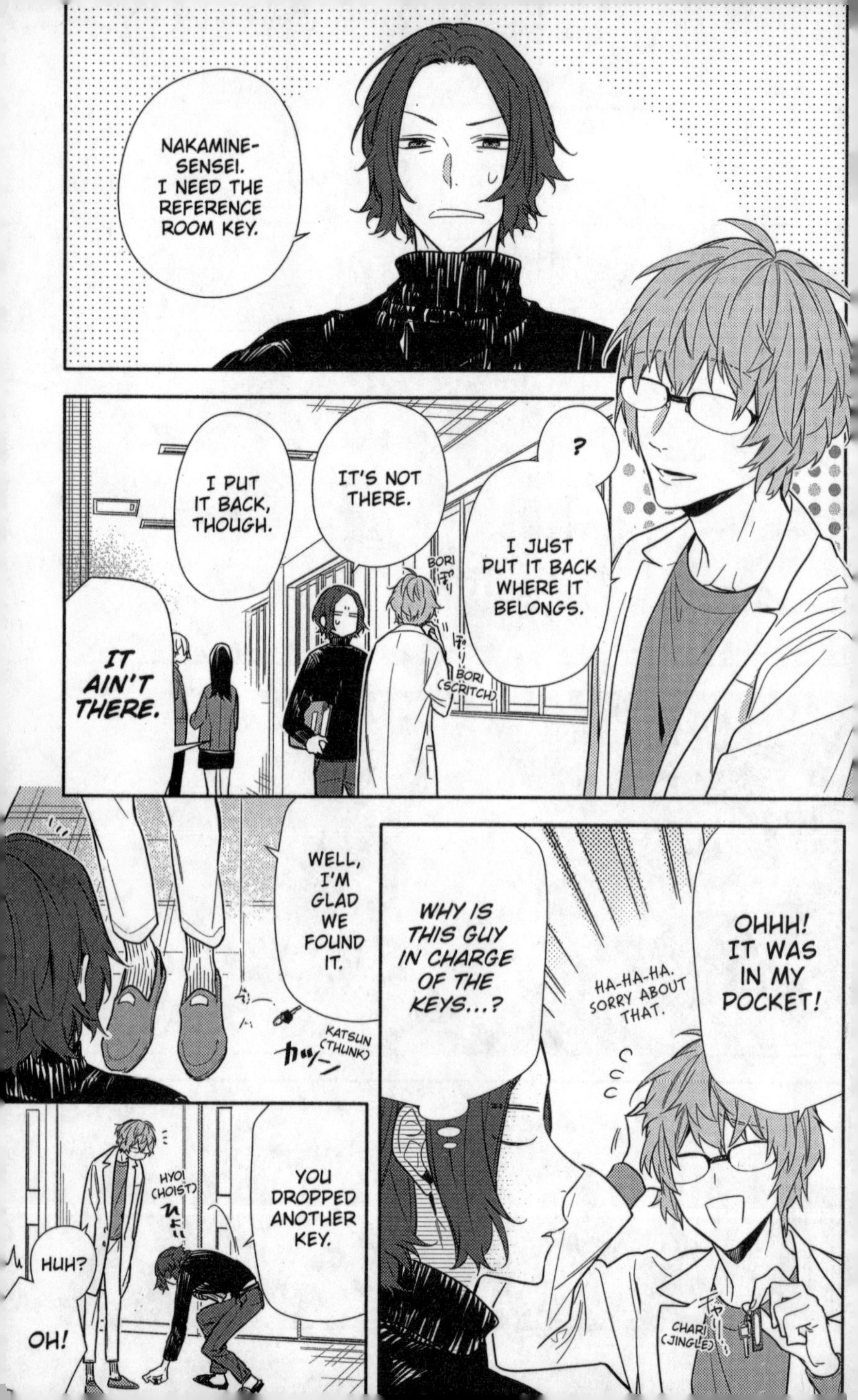
NAKAMINE-SENSEI. I NEED THE REFERENCE ROOM KEY.
?
I JUST PUT IT BACK WHERE IT BELONGS.
BORI BORI (SCRITCH)
IT'S NOT THERE.
I PUT IT BACK, THOUGH.
IT AIN'T THERE.
OHHH! IT WAS IN MY POCKET!
HA-HA-HA. SORRY ABOUT THAT.
CHARI (JINGLE)
WHY IS THIS GUY IN CHARGE OF THE KEYS...?
WELL, I'M GLAD WE FOUND IT.
KATSUN (THUNK)
YOU DROPPED ANOTHER KEY.
HYOI (HOIST)
HUH?
OH!

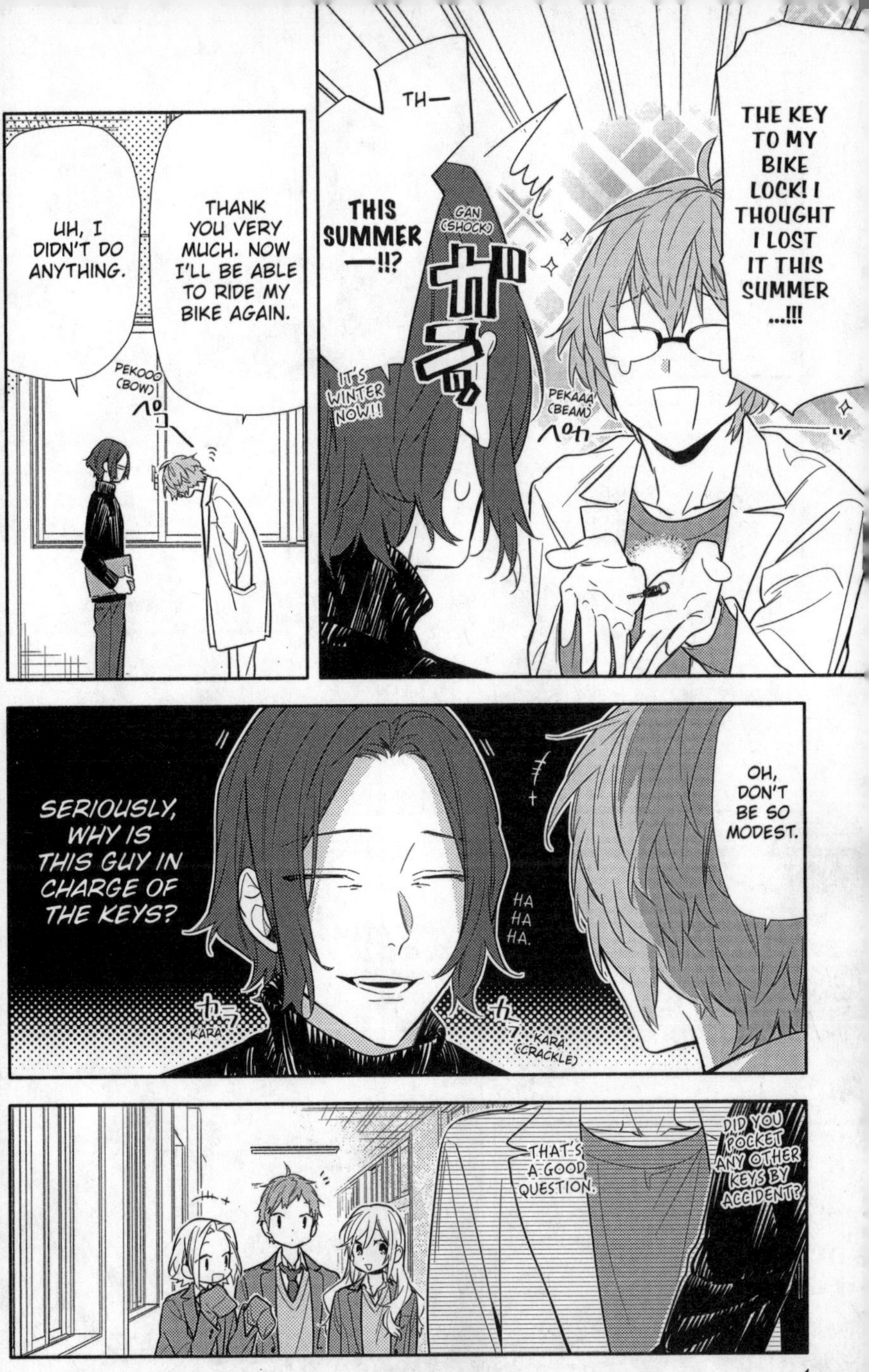
THE KEY TO MY BIKE LOCK!! I THOUGHT I LOST IT THIS SUMMER ...!!!
PEKAAA (BEAM)
TH—
GAN (SHOCK)
THIS SUMMER—!!?
IT'S WINTER NOW!!
THANK YOU VERY MUCH. NOW I'LL BE ABLE TO RIDE MY BIKE AGAIN.
UH, I DIDN'T DO ANYTHING.
PEKOOO (BOW)
OH, DON'T BE SO MODEST.
HA HA HA.
KARA (CRACKLE)
KARA
SERIOUSLY, WHY IS THIS GUY IN CHARGE OF THE KEYS?
DID YOU POCKET ANY OTHER KEYS BY ACCIDENT?
THAT'S A GOOD QUESTION.

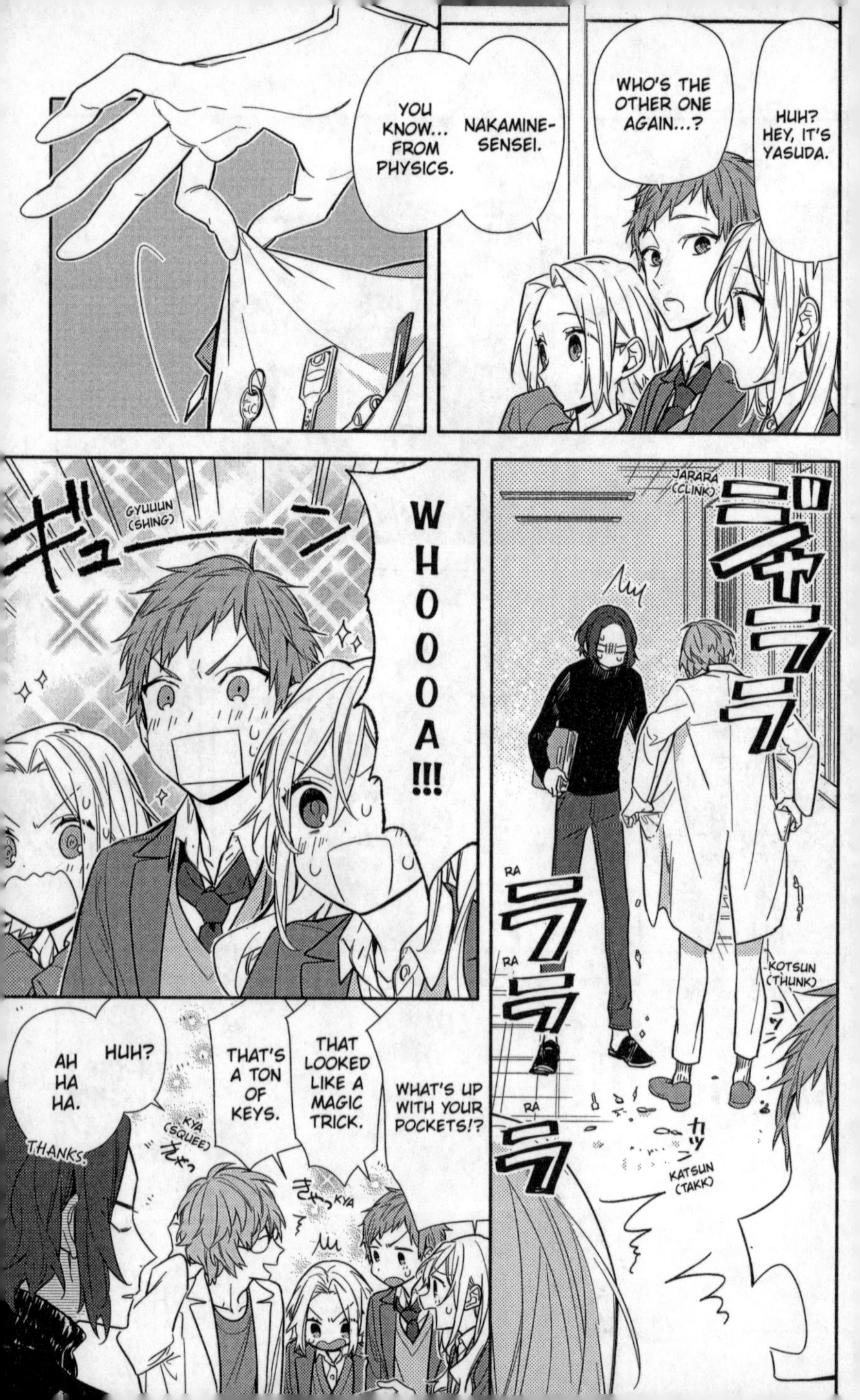
HUH? HEY, IT'S YASUDA.
WHO'S THE OTHER ONE AGAIN...?
NAKAMINE-SENSEI.
YOU KNOW... FROM PHYSICS.
JARARA (CLINK)
RA
RA
RA
KOTSUN (THUNK)
KATSUN (TAKK)
GYUUUN (SHING)
WHOOOOA!!!
WHAT'S UP WITH YOUR POCKETS!?
THAT LOOKED LIKE A MAGIC TRICK.
THAT'S A TON OF KEYS.
KYA (SQUEE)
KYA
HUH?
AH HA HA.
THANKS.

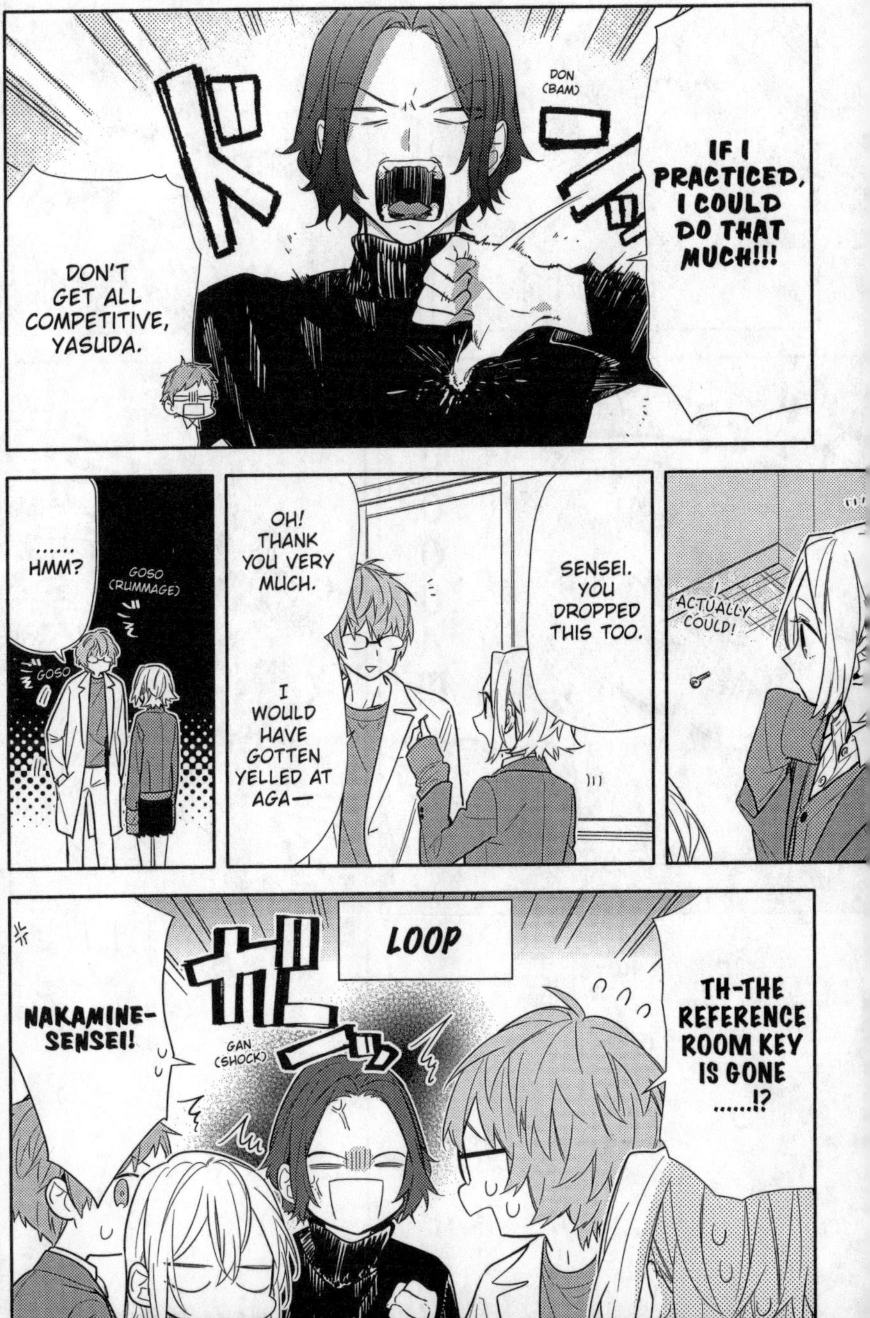
IF I PRACTICED, I COULD DO THAT MUCH!!!
DON (BAM)
DON'T GET ALL COMPETITIVE, YASUDA.
I ACTUALLY COULD!
SENSEI. YOU DROPPED THIS TOO.
OH! THANK YOU VERY MUCH.
I WOULD HAVE GOTTEN YELLED AT AGA—
......HMM?
GOSO (RUMMAGE)
GOSO
LOOP
TH-THE REFERENCE ROOM KEY IS GONE ......!?
GAN (SHOCK)
NAKAMINE-SENSEI!

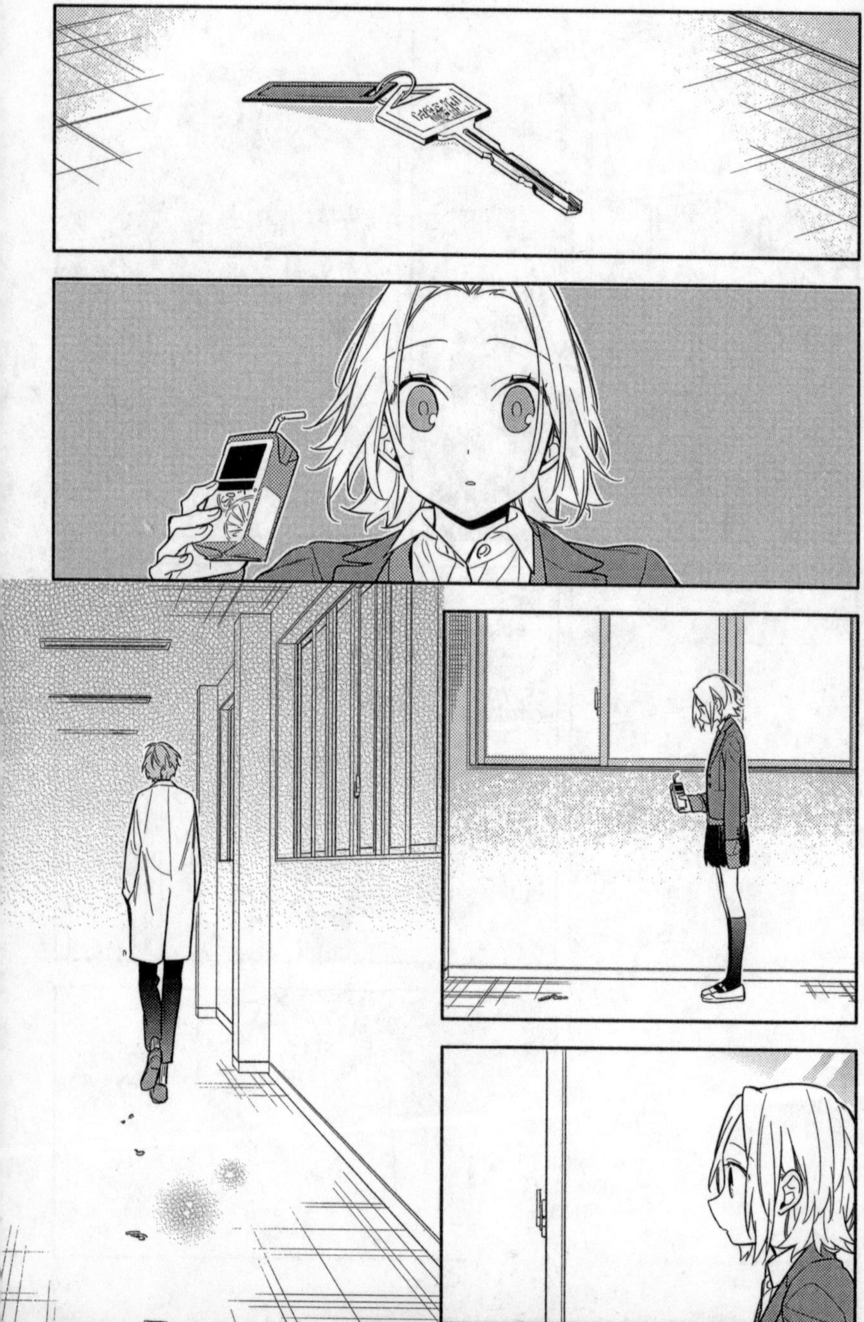

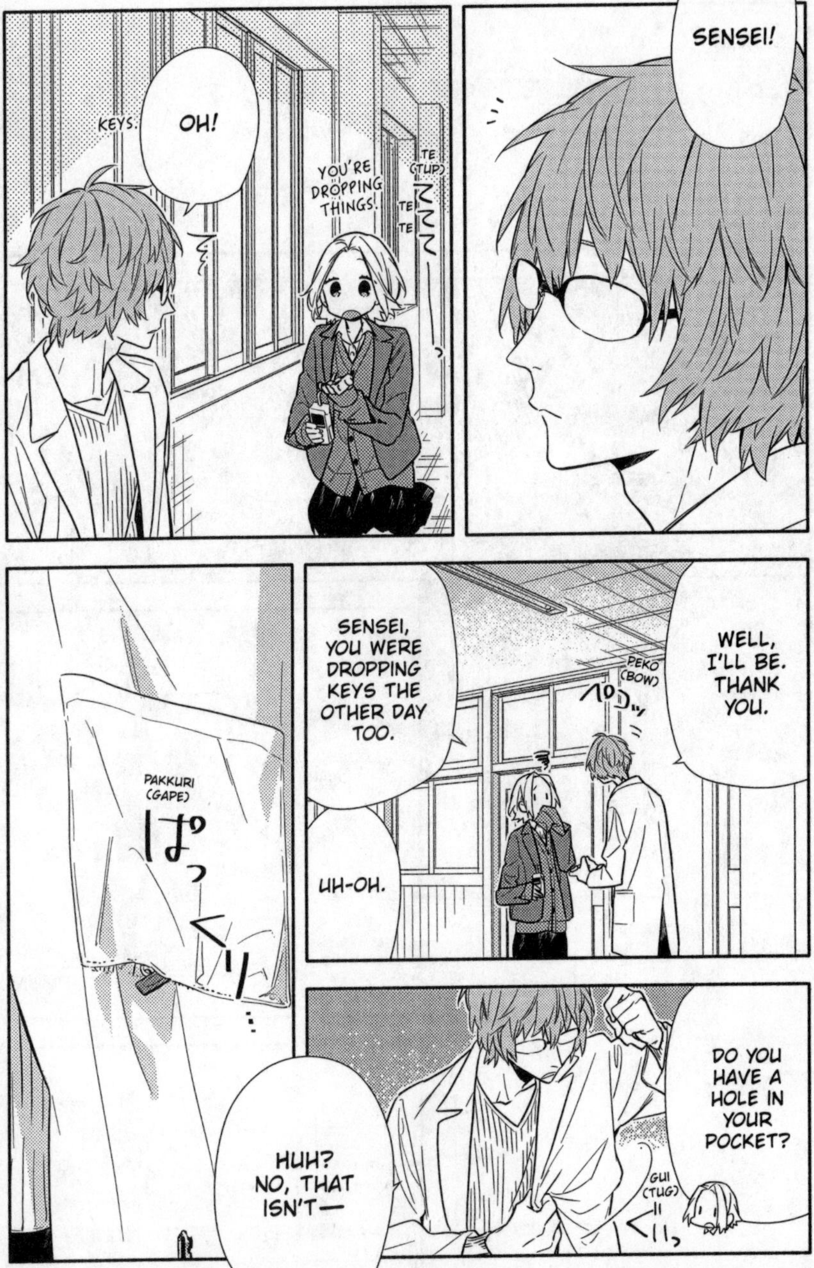
SENSEI!
OH!
KEYS.
YOU'RE DROPPING THINGS!
TE (TUP)
TE
TE
WELL, I'LL BE. THANK YOU.
PEKO (BOW)
SENSEI, YOU WERE DROPPING KEYS THE OTHER DAY TOO.
UH-OH.
DO YOU HAVE A HOLE IN YOUR POCKET?
GUI (TUG)
HUH? NO, THAT ISN'T—
PAKKURI (GAPE)

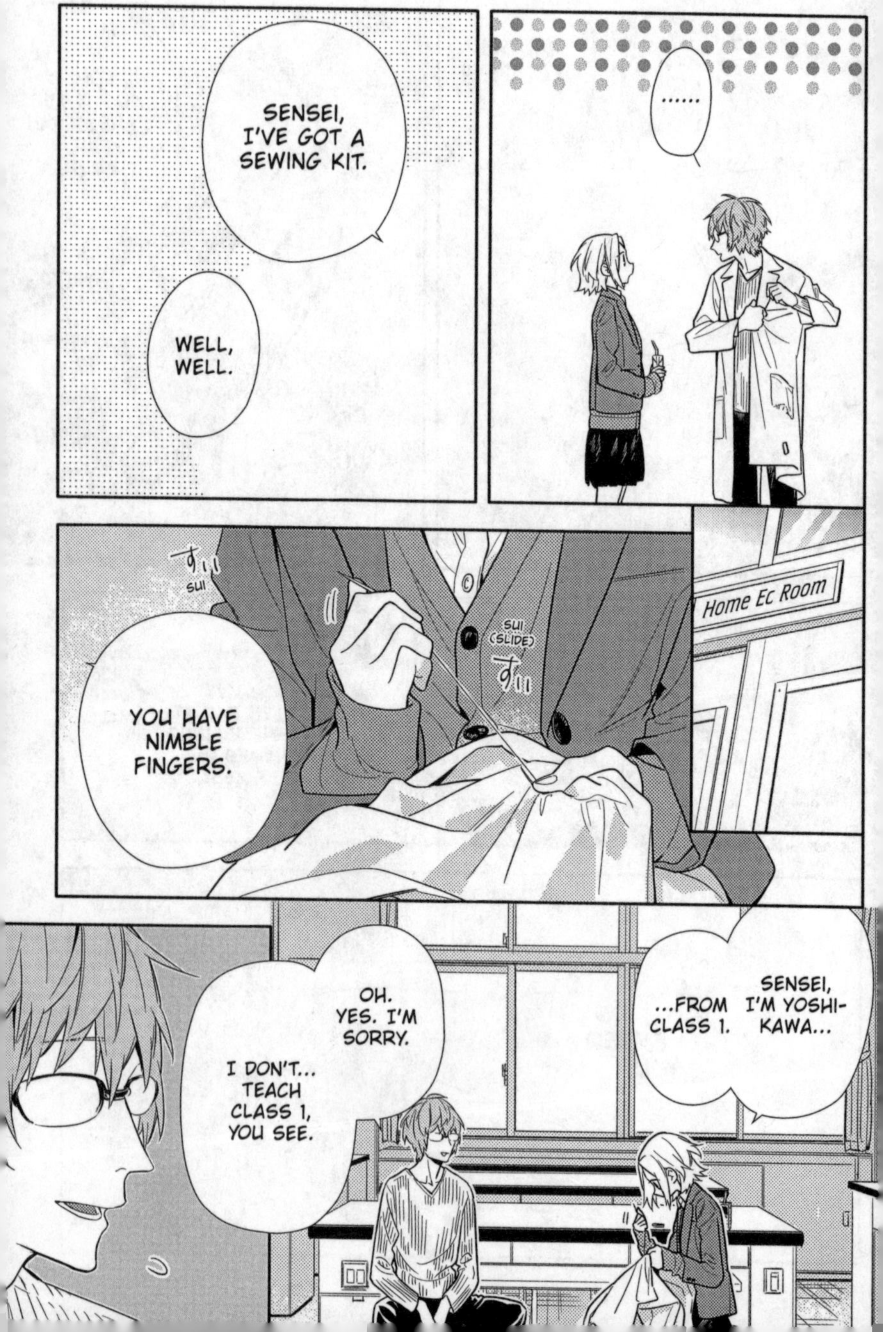
......
SENSEI, I'VE GOT A SEWING KIT.
WELL, WELL.
Home Ec Room
SUI (SLIDE) すい
すい SUI
YOU HAVE NIMBLE FINGERS.
SENSEI, I'M YOSHI-KAWA...
...FROM CLASS 1.
OH. YES. I'M SORRY.
I DON'T... TEACH CLASS 1, YOU SEE.

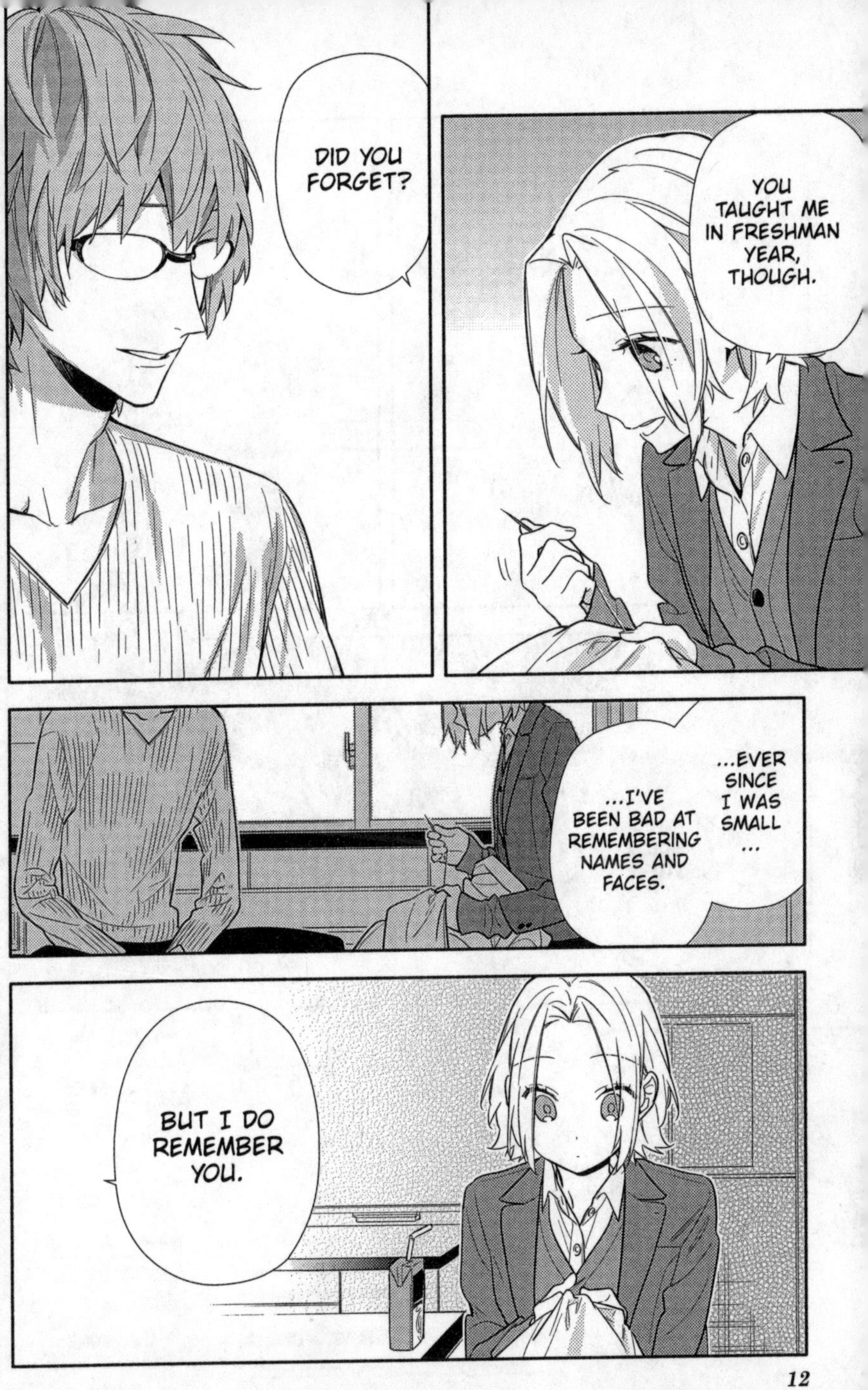
YOU TAUGHT ME IN FRESHMAN YEAR, THOUGH.
DID YOU FORGET?
...EVER SINCE I WAS SMALL...
...I'VE BEEN BAD AT REMEMBERING NAMES AND FACES.
BUT I DO REMEMBER YOU.

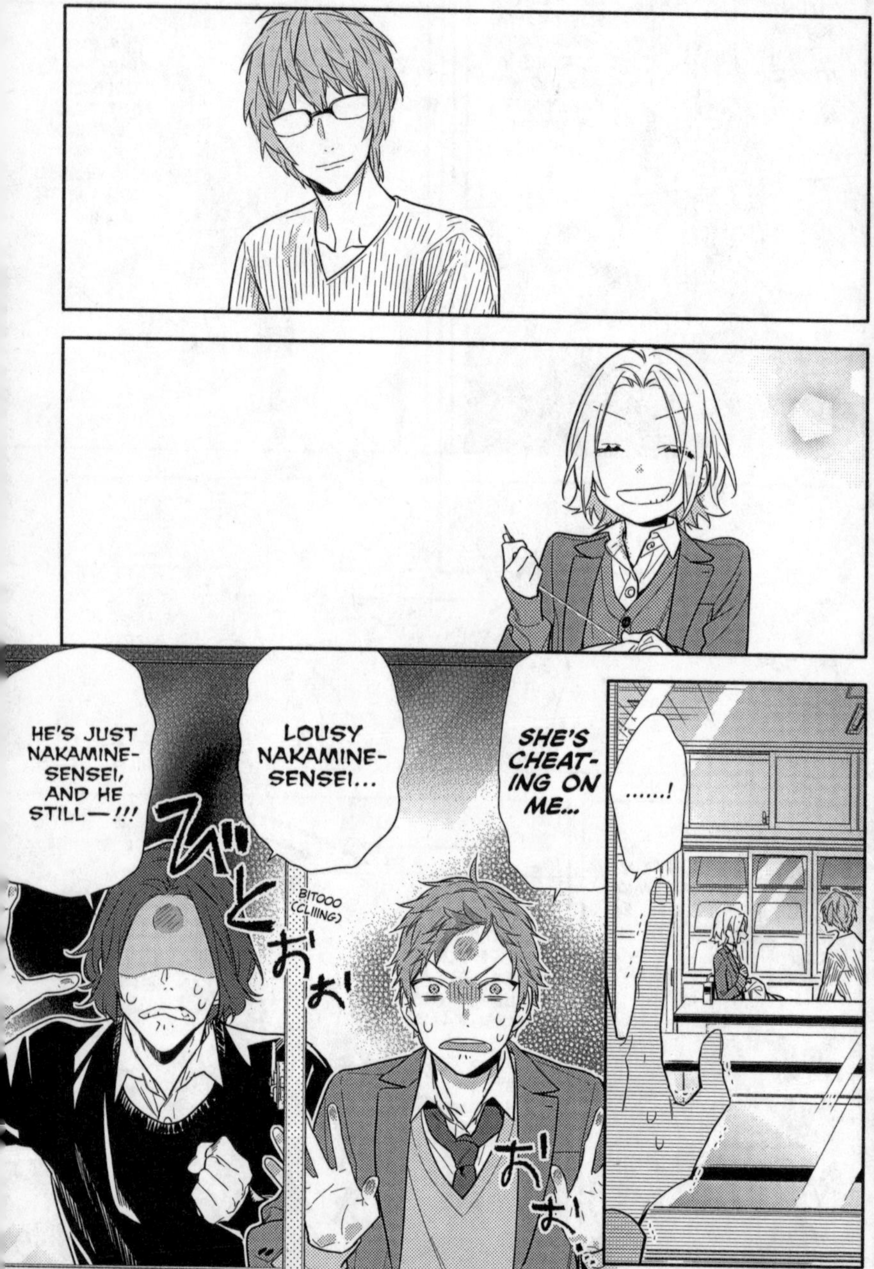
......!
SHE'S CHEATING ON ME...
LOUSY NAKAMINE-SENSEI...
HE'S JUST NAKAMINE-SENSEI, AND HE STILL—!!!
BITOOO (CLIIING)

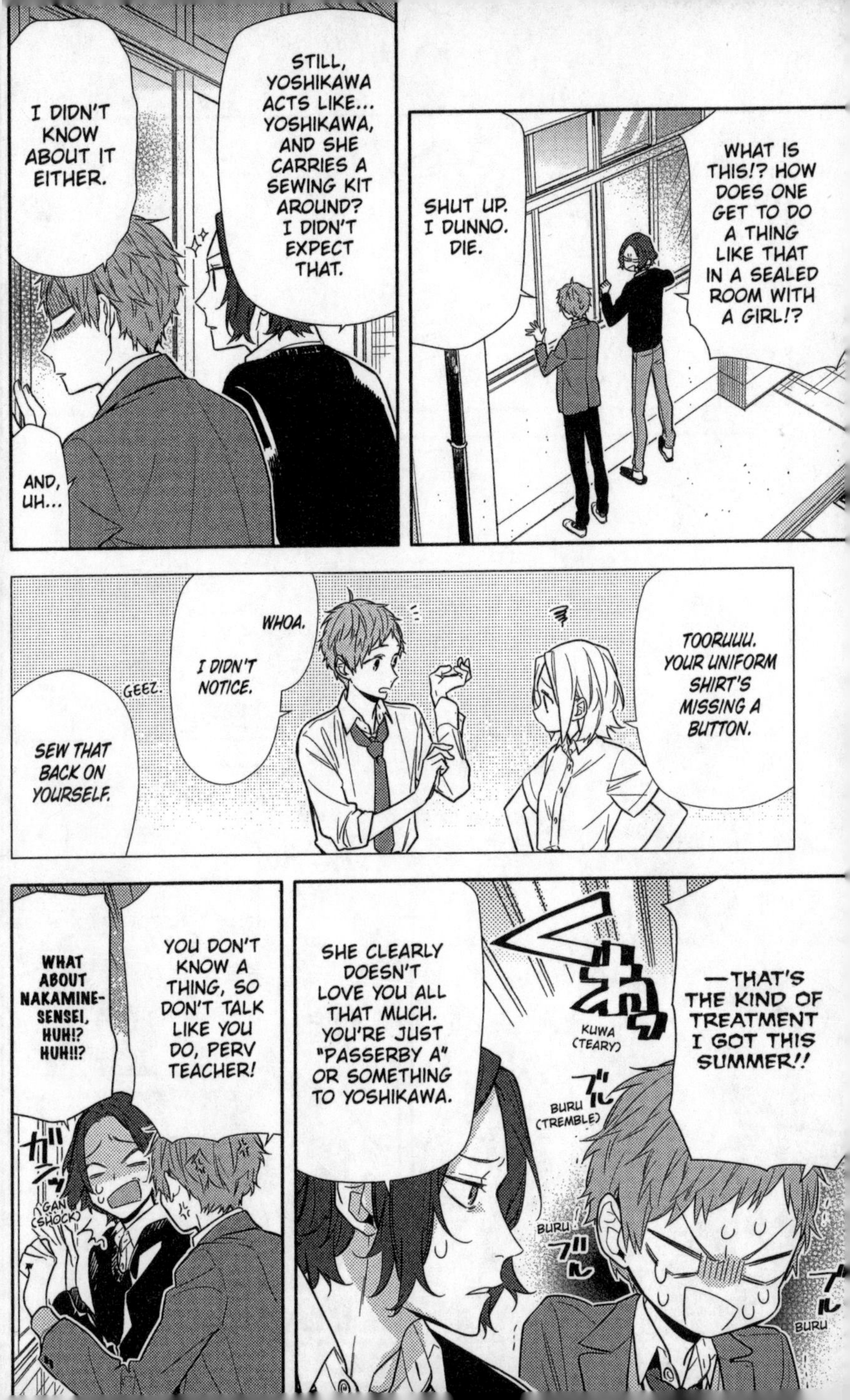
WHAT IS THIS!? HOW DOES ONE GET TO DO A THING LIKE THAT IN A SEALED ROOM WITH A GIRL!?
SHUT UP. I DUNNO. DIE.
STILL, YOSHIKAWA ACTS LIKE... YOSHIKAWA, AND SHE CARRIES A SEWING KIT AROUND? I DIDN'T EXPECT THAT.
I DIDN'T KNOW ABOUT IT EITHER.
AND, UH...
TOORUUU. YOUR UNIFORM SHIRT'S MISSING A BUTTON.
WHOA.
I DIDN'T NOTICE.
GEEZ.
SEW THAT BACK ON YOURSELF.
—THAT'S THE KIND OF TREATMENT I GOT THIS SUMMER!!
KUWA (TEARY)
BURU (TREMBLE)
SHE CLEARLY DOESN'T LOVE YOU ALL THAT MUCH. YOU'RE JUST "PASSERBY A" OR SOMETHING TO YOSHIKAWA.
BURU
BURU
YOU DON'T KNOW A THING, SO DON'T TALK LIKE YOU DO, PERV TEACHER!
WHAT ABOUT NAKAMINE-SENSEI, HUH!? HUH!!?
GAN (SHOCK)

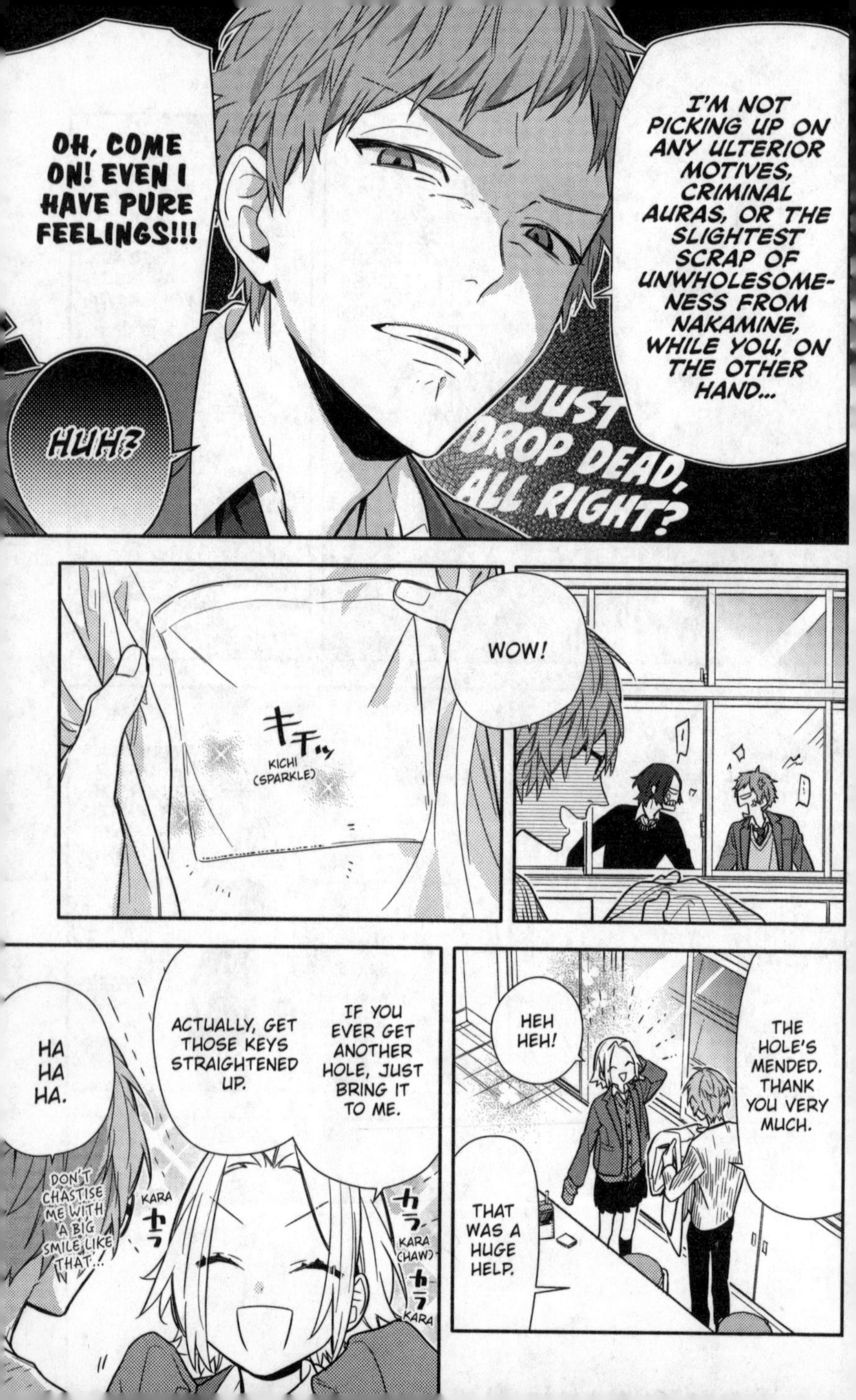
I'M NOT PICKING UP ON ANY ULTERIOR MOTIVES, CRIMINAL AURAS, OR THE SLIGHTEST SCRAP OF UNWHOLESOMENESS FROM NAKAMINE, WHILE YOU, ON THE OTHER HAND...
JUST DROP DEAD, ALL RIGHT?
HUH?
OH, COME ON! EVEN I HAVE PURE FEELINGS!!!
WOW!
KICHI (SPARKLE)
THE HOLE'S MENDED. THANK YOU VERY MUCH.
HEH HEH!
THAT WAS A HUGE HELP.
IF YOU EVER GET ANOTHER HOLE, JUST BRING IT TO ME.
ACTUALLY, GET THOSE KEYS STRAIGHTENED UP.
KARA (CHAW) KARA
KARA
DON'T CHASTISE ME WITH A BIG SMILE LIKE THAT...
HA HA HA.

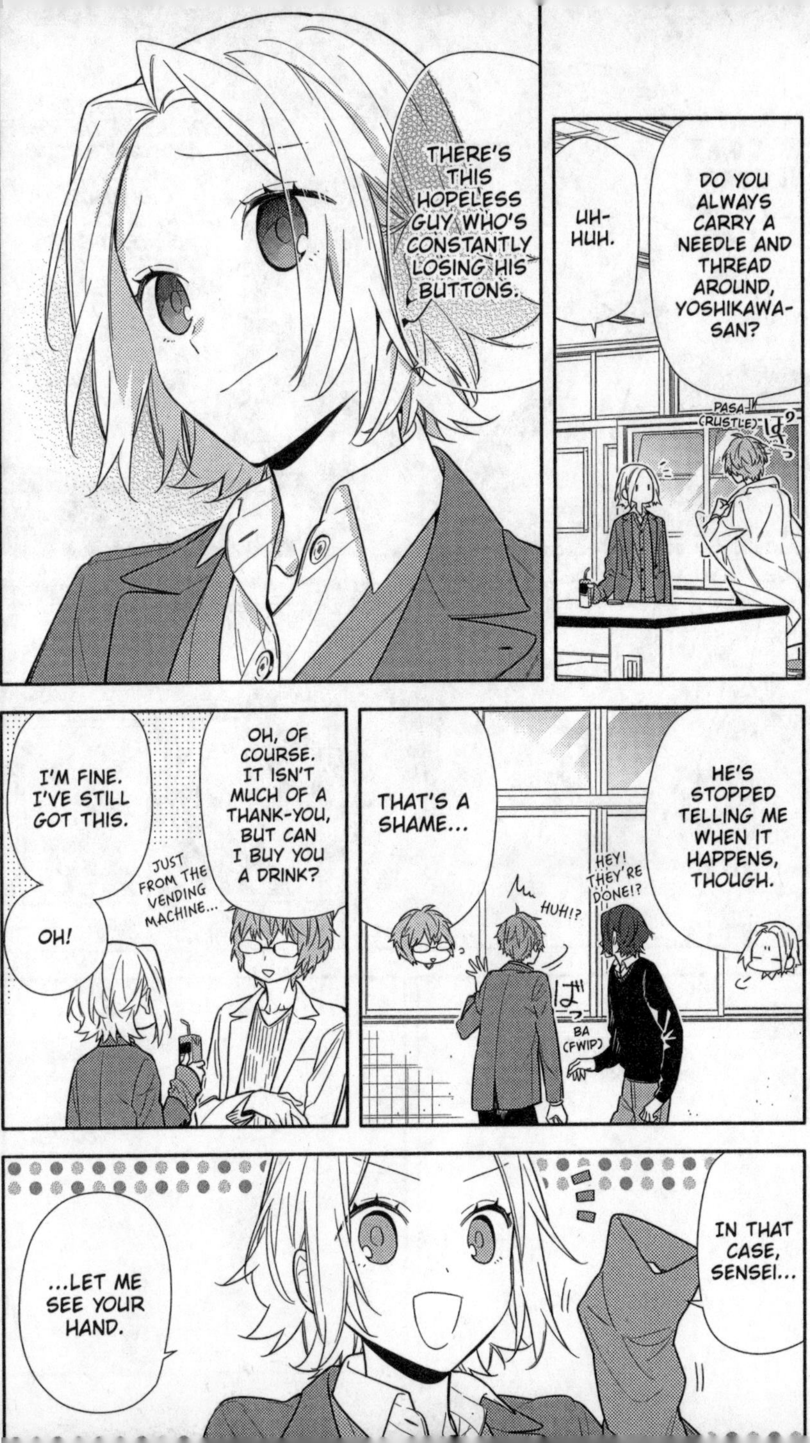
DO YOU ALWAYS CARRY A NEEDLE AND THREAD AROUND, YOSHIKAWA-SAN?
UH-HUH.
PASA (RUSTLE)
THERE'S THIS HOPELESS GUY WHO'S CONSTANTLY LOSING HIS BUTTONS.
HE'S STOPPED TELLING ME WHEN IT HAPPENS, THOUGH.
HEY! THEY'RE DONE!?
HUH!?
BA (FWIP)
THAT'S A SHAME...
OH, OF COURSE. IT ISN'T MUCH OF A THANK-YOU, BUT CAN I BUY YOU A DRINK?
JUST FROM THE VENDING MACHINE...
I'M FINE. I'VE STILL GOT THIS.
OH!
IN THAT CASE, SENSEI...
...LET ME SEE YOUR HAND.

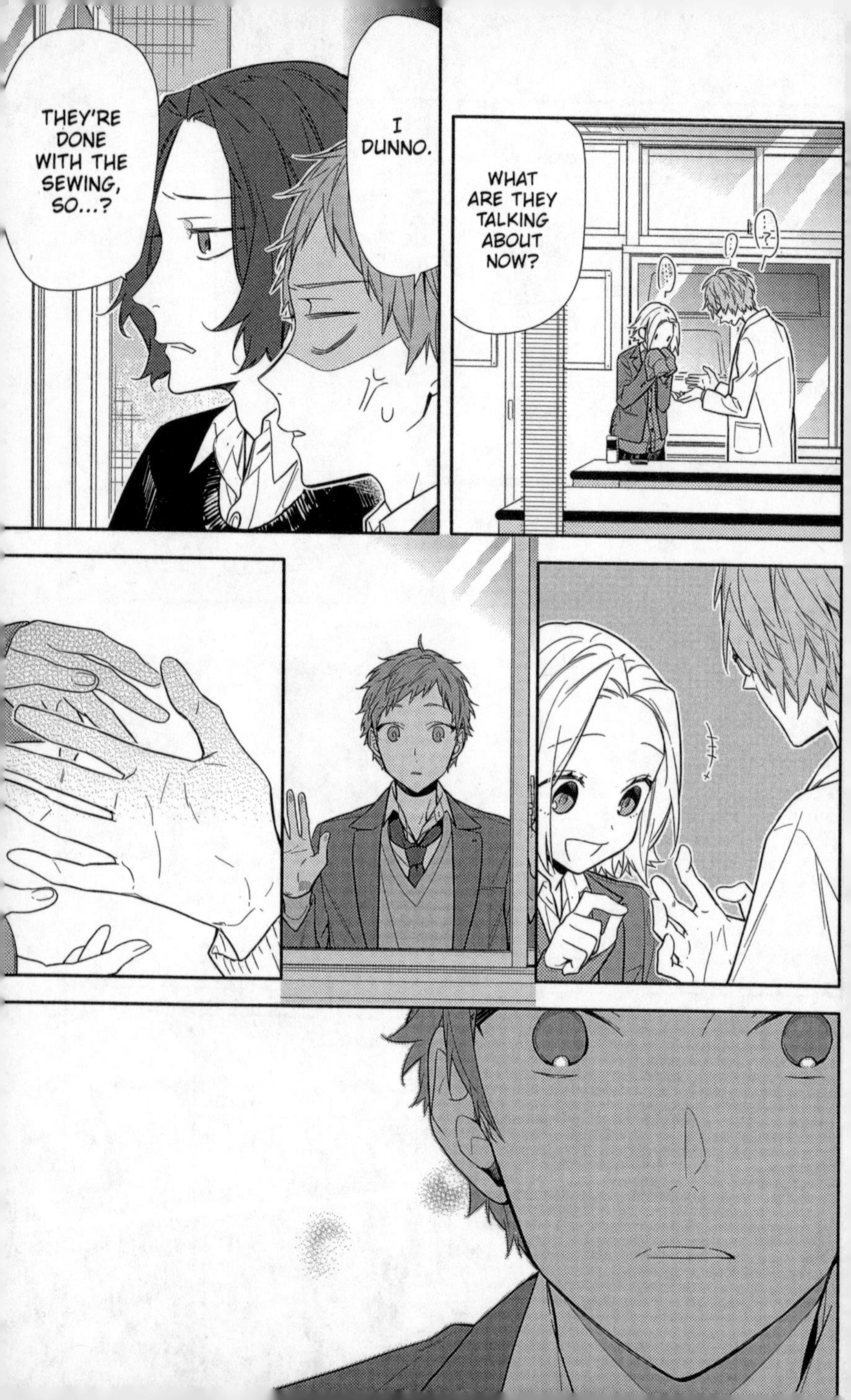
WHAT ARE THEY TALKING ABOUT NOW?
I DUNNO.
THEY'RE DONE WITH THE SEWING, SO...?

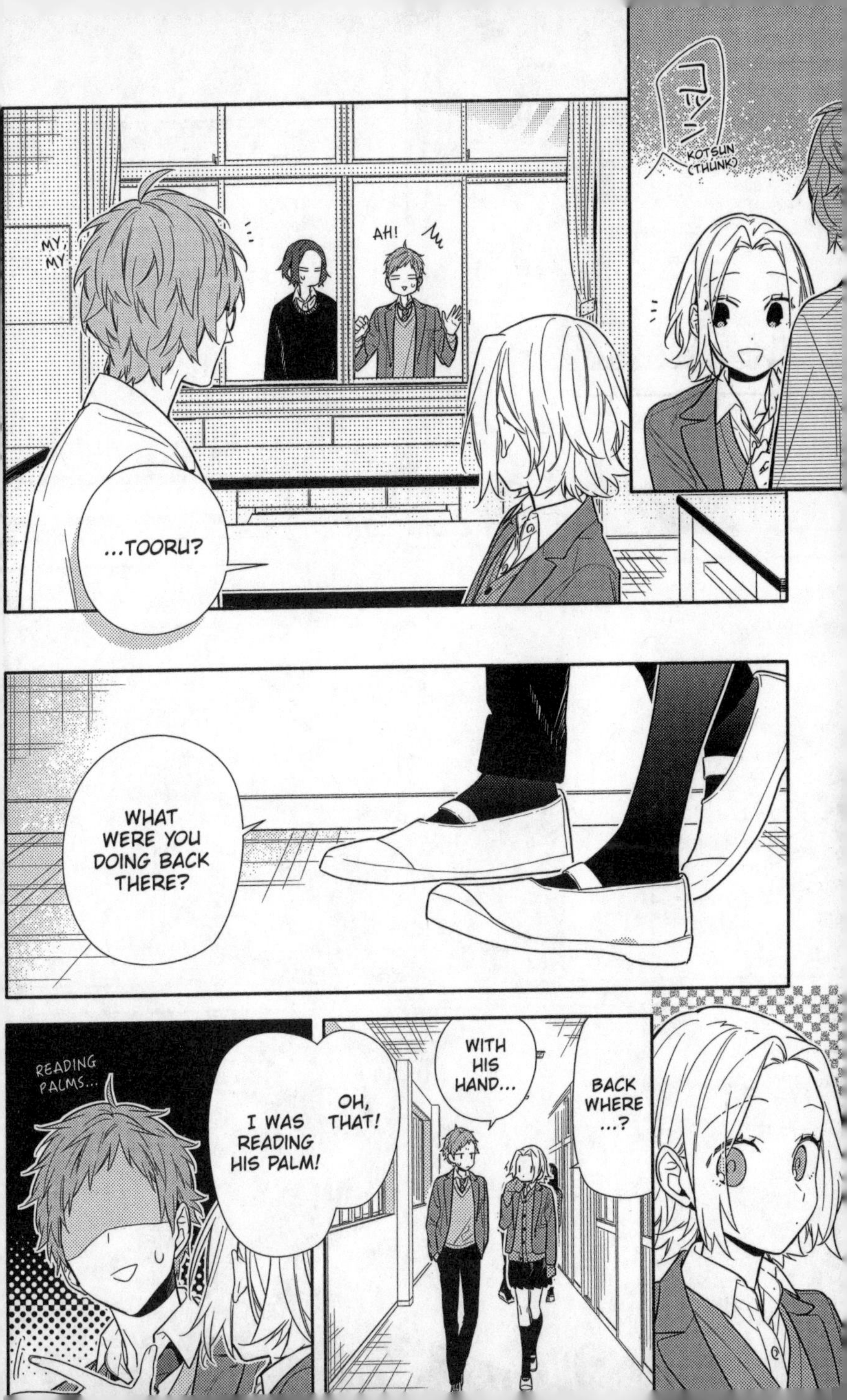

コツン
KOTSUN (THUNK)
AH!
MY, MY
...TOORU?
WHAT WERE YOU DOING BACK THERE?
BACK WHERE ...?
WITH HIS HAND...
OH, THAT!
I WAS READING HIS PALM!
READING PALMS...

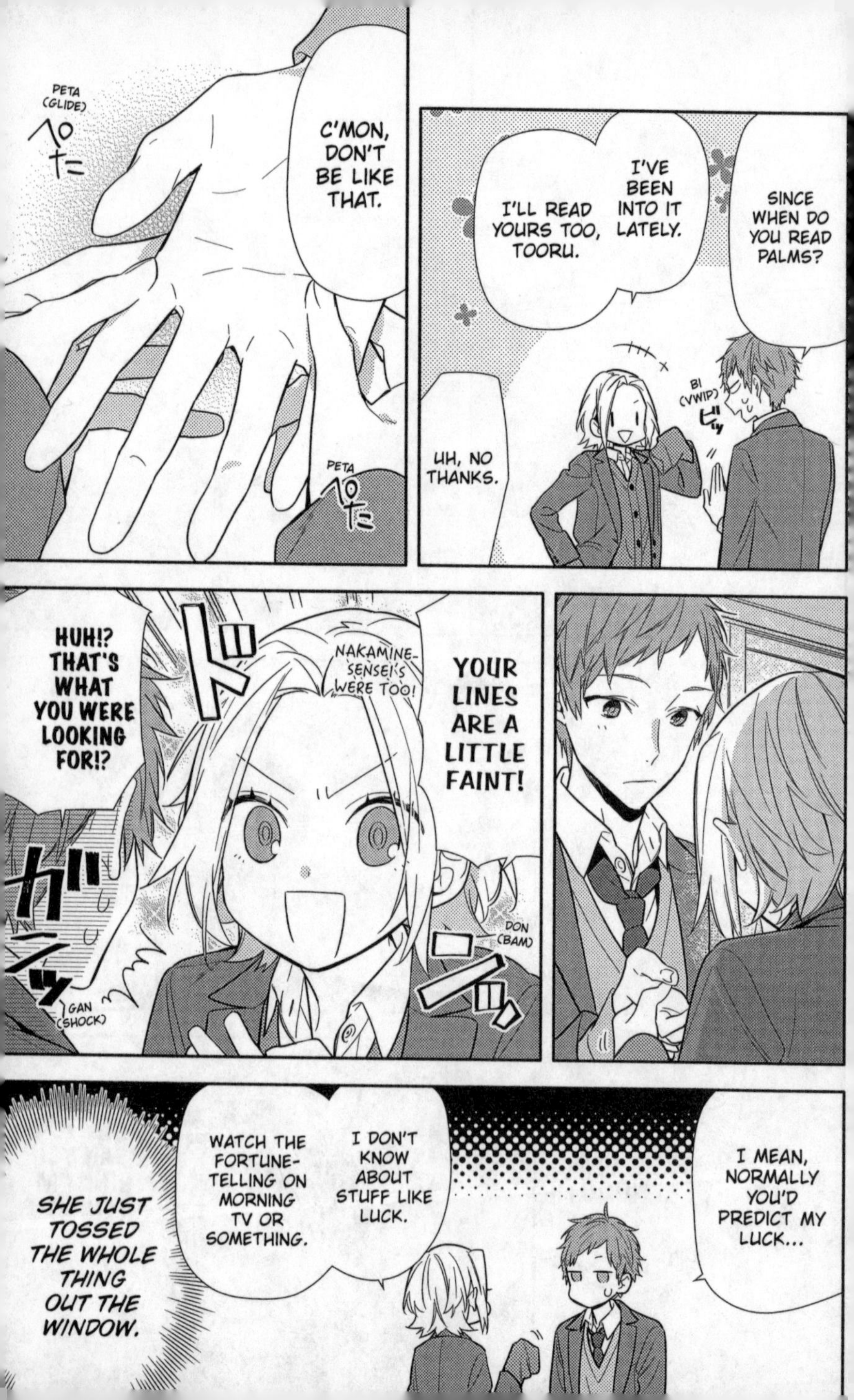
SINCE WHEN DO YOU READ PALMS?
I'VE BEEN INTO IT LATELY.
I'LL READ YOURS TOO, TOORU.
BI (VWIP)
UH, NO THANKS.
C'MON, DON'T BE LIKE THAT.
PETA (GLIDE)
PETA
YOUR LINES ARE A LITTLE FAINT!
NAKAMINE-SENSEI'S WERE TOO!
DON (BAM)
HUH!? THAT'S WHAT YOU WERE LOOKING FOR!?
GAN (SHOCK)
I MEAN, NORMALLY YOU'D PREDICT MY LUCK...
I DON'T KNOW ABOUT STUFF LIKE LUCK.
WATCH THE FORTUNE-TELLING ON MORNING TV OR SOMETHING.
SHE JUST TOSSED THE WHOLE THING OUT THE WINDOW.

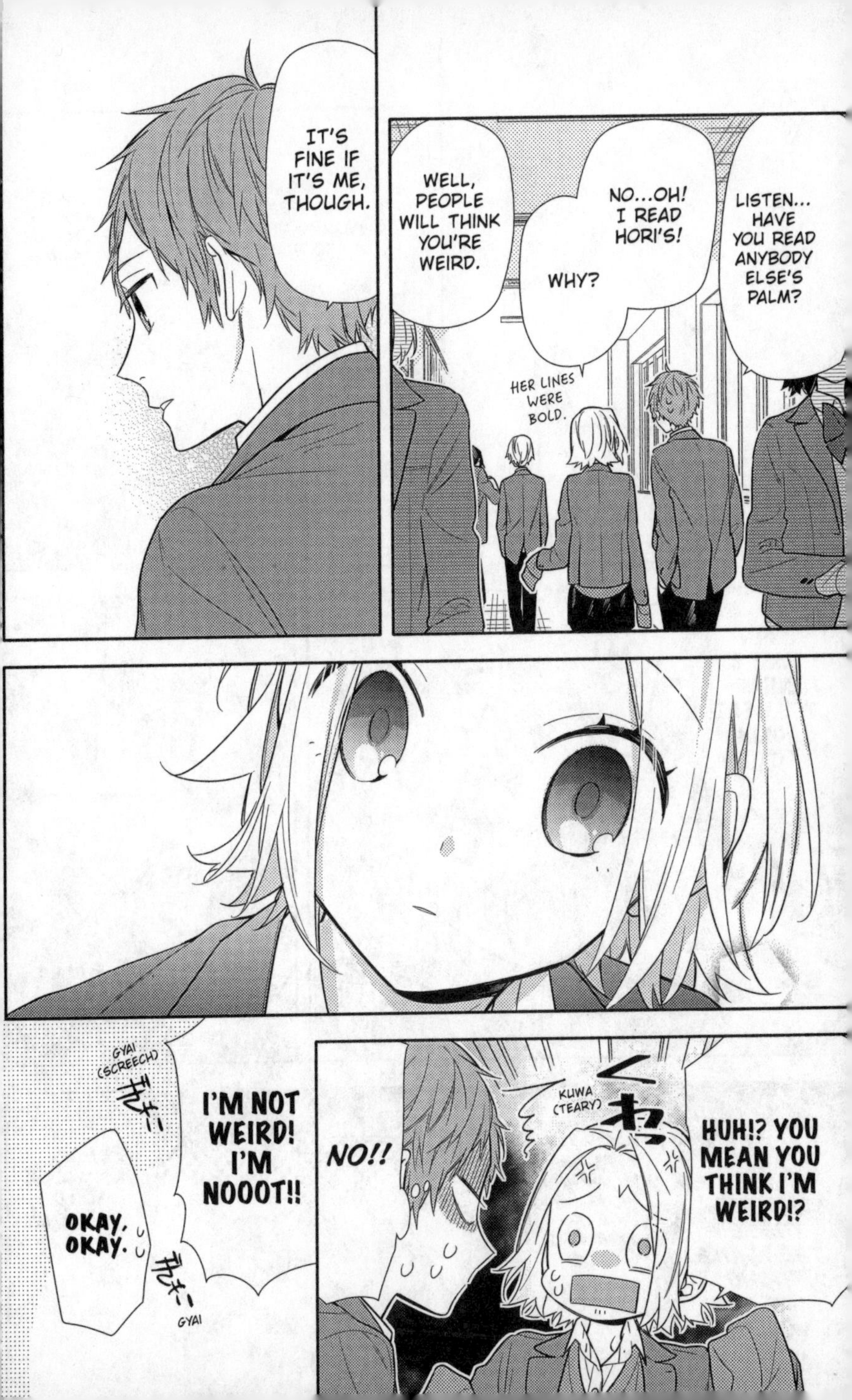
LISTEN... HAVE YOU READ ANYBODY ELSE'S PALM?
NO...OH! I READ HORI'S!
HER LINES WERE BOLD.
WHY?
WELL, PEOPLE WILL THINK YOU'RE WEIRD.
IT'S FINE IF IT'S ME, THOUGH.
HUH!? YOU MEAN YOU THINK I'M WEIRD!?
KUWA (TEARY)
NO!!
GYAI (SCREECH)
I'M NOT WEIRD! I'M NOOOT!!
GYAI
OKAY. OKAY.

HORIMIYA

HORIMIYA

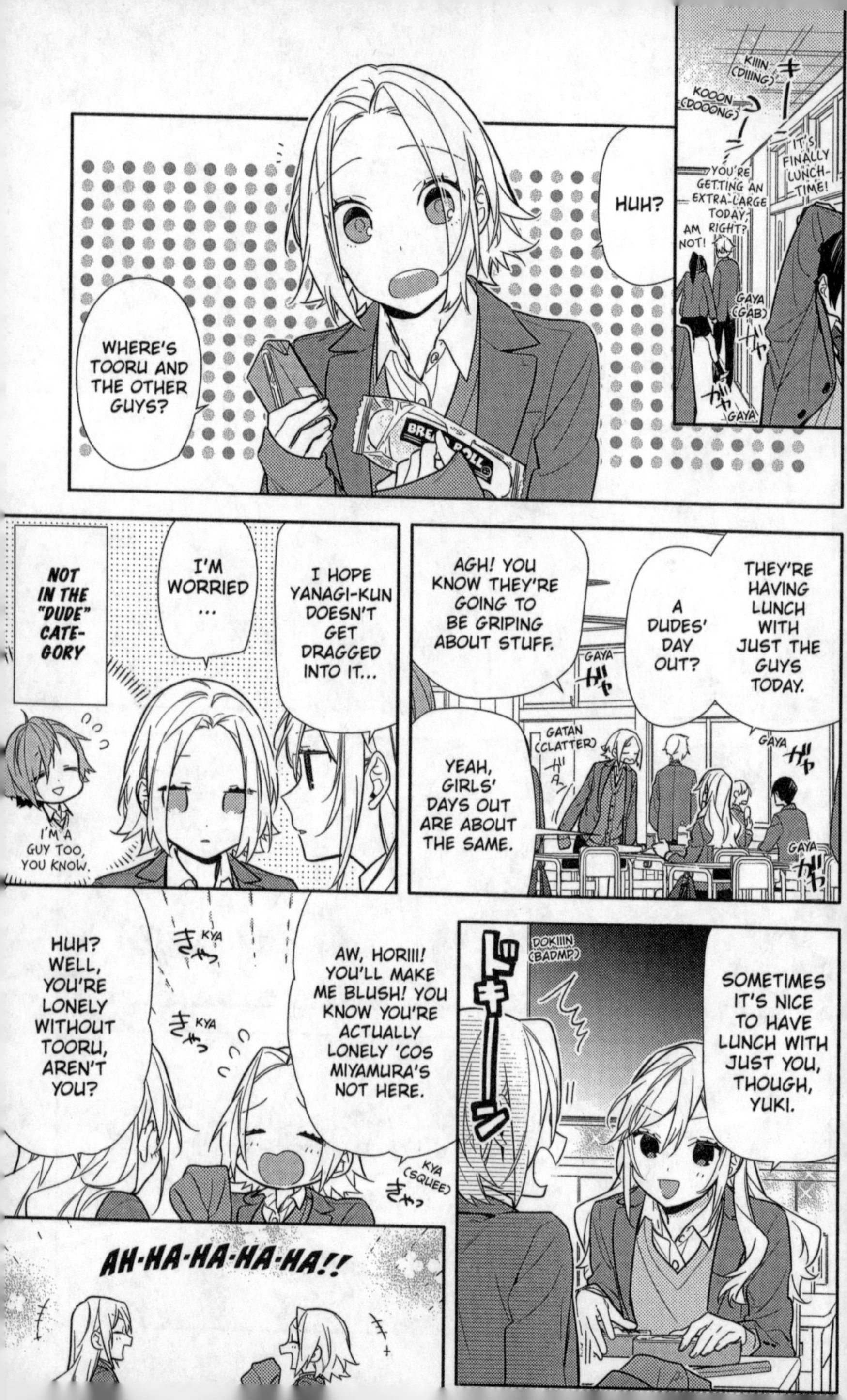

KIIIN (DIIING)
KOOON (DOOONG)
IT'S FINALLY LUNCHTIME!
YOU'RE GETTING AN EXTRA-LARGE TODAY, RIGHT?
AM NOT!
GAYA (GAB)
GAYA
HUH?
WHERE'S TOORU AND THE OTHER GUYS?
THEY'RE HAVING LUNCH WITH JUST THE GUYS TODAY.
A DUDES' DAY OUT?
AGH! YOU KNOW THEY'RE GOING TO BE GRIPING ABOUT STUFF.
GAYA
GATAN (CLATTER)
GAYA
YEAH, GIRLS' DAYS OUT ARE ABOUT THE SAME.
GAYA
I HOPE YANAGI-KUN DOESN'T GET DRAGGED INTO IT...
I'M WORRIED...
NOT IN THE "DUDE" CATEGORY
I'M A GUY TOO, YOU KNOW.
DOKIIIN (BADMP)
SOMETIMES IT'S NICE TO HAVE LUNCH WITH JUST YOU, THOUGH, YUKI.
AW, HORIII! YOU'LL MAKE ME BLUSH! YOU KNOW YOU'RE ACTUALLY LONELY 'COS MIYAMURA'S NOT HERE.
HUH? WELL, YOU'RE LONELY WITHOUT TOORU, AREN'T YOU?
KYA
KYA
KYA (SQUEE)
AH-HA-HA-HA-HA!!

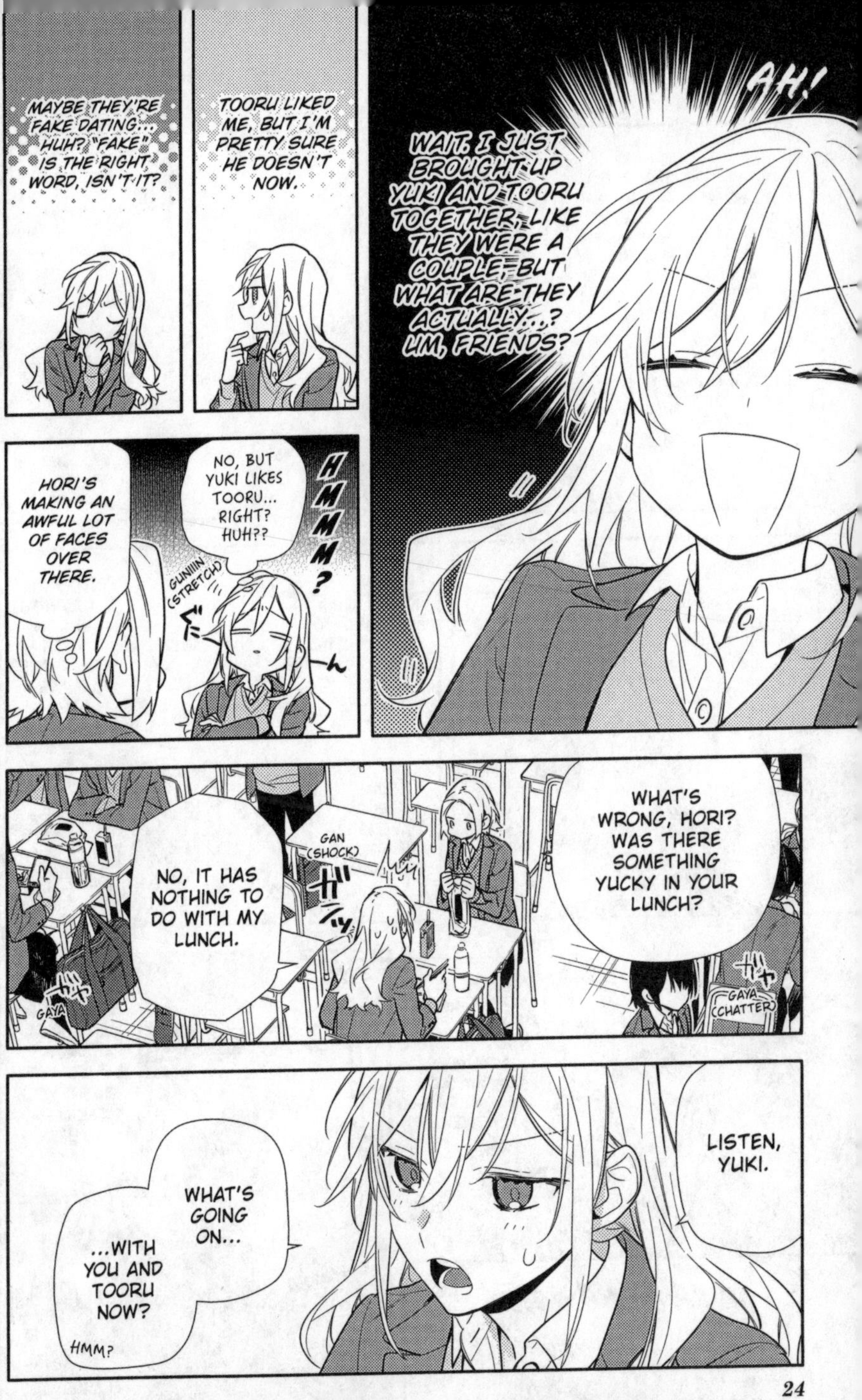

AH!
WAIT. I JUST BROUGHT UP YUKI AND TOORU TOGETHER, LIKE THEY WERE A COUPLE, BUT WHAT ARE THEY ACTUALLY...? UM, FRIENDS?
TOORU LIKED ME, BUT I'M PRETTY SURE HE DOESN'T NOW.
MAYBE THEY'RE FAKE DATING... HUH? "FAKE" IS THE RIGHT WORD, ISN'T IT?
HMMMM?
NO, BUT YUKI LIKES TOORU... RIGHT? HUH??
GUNIIIN (STRETCH)
HORI'S MAKING AN AWFUL LOT OF FACES OVER THERE.
WHAT'S WRONG, HORI? WAS THERE SOMETHING YUCKY IN YOUR LUNCH?
GAYA (CHATTER)
GAN (SHOCK)
NO, IT HAS NOTHING TO DO WITH MY LUNCH.
GAYA
LISTEN, YUKI.
WHAT'S GOING ON...
...WITH YOU AND TOORU NOW?
HMM?

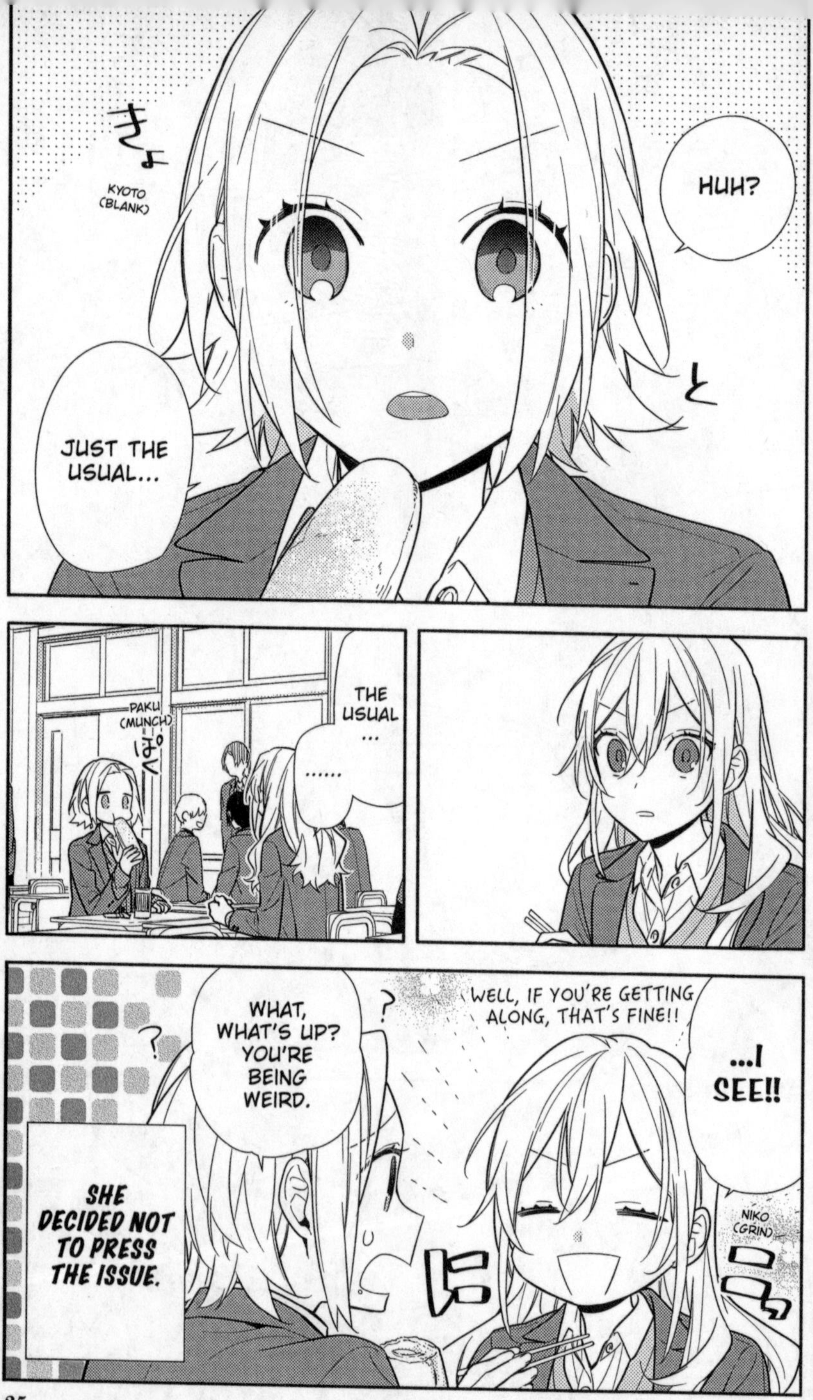

HUH?
きょ
KYOTO (BLANK)
と
JUST THE USUAL...
THE USUAL ...
......
PAKU (MUNCH)
ぱく
...I SEE!!
NIKO (GRIN)
にこっ
WELL, IF YOU'RE GETTING ALONG, THAT'S FINE!!
?
WHAT, WHAT'S UP? YOU'RE BEING WEIRD.
?
SHE DECIDED NOT TO PRESS THE ISSUE.

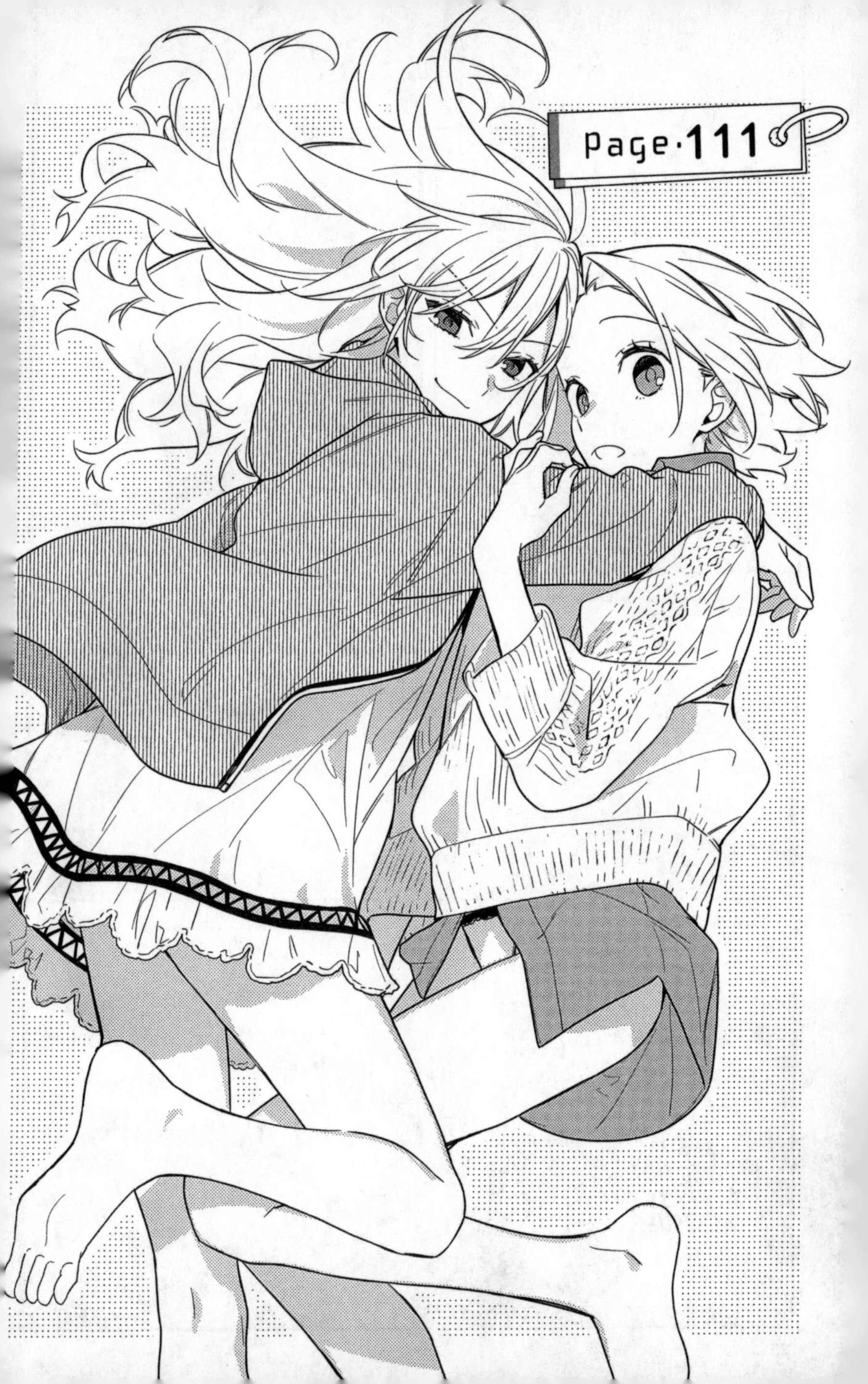
Page·111

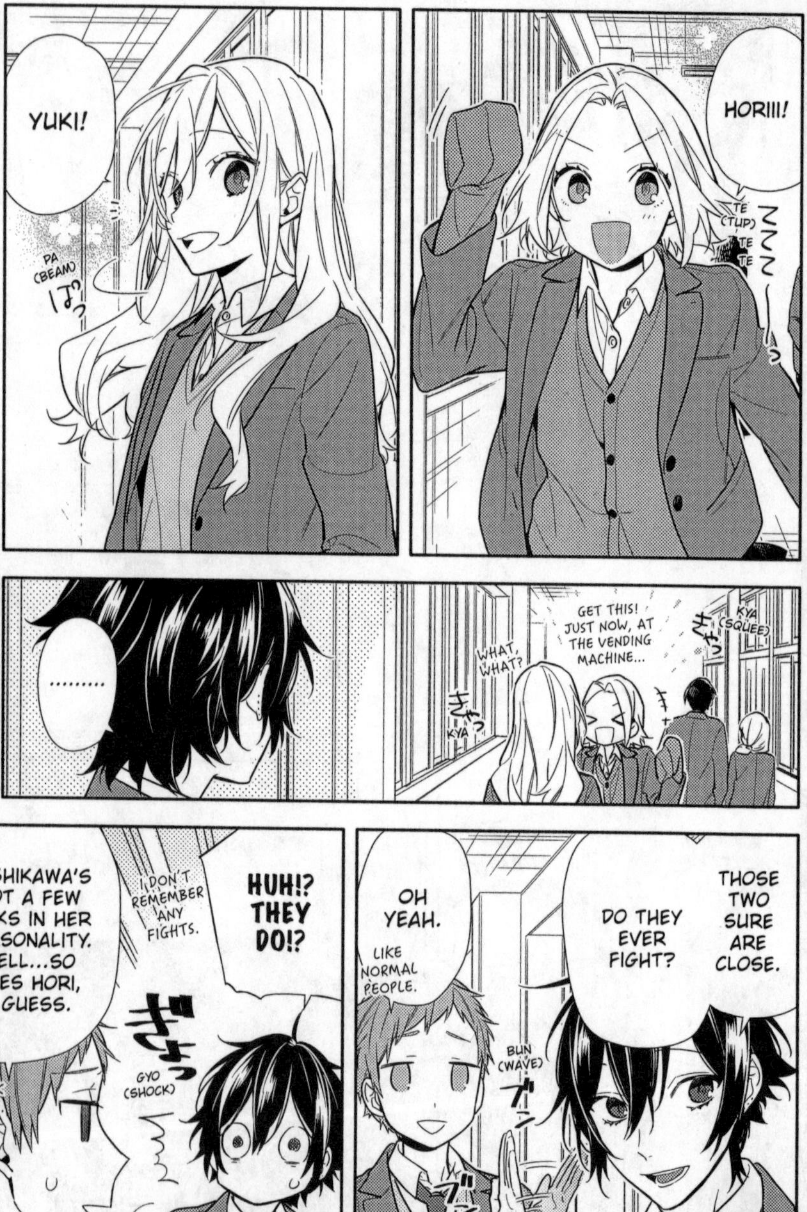

HORIII!
TE (TUP) TE TE
YUKI!
PA (BEAM)
GET THIS! JUST NOW, AT THE VENDING MACHINE...
KYA (SQUEE)
WHAT, WHAT?
KYA
....
THOSE TWO SURE ARE CLOSE.
DO THEY EVER FIGHT?
OH YEAH.
LIKE NORMAL PEOPLE.
BUN (WAVE)
BUN
HUH!? THEY DO!?
I DON'T REMEMBER ANY FIGHTS.
GYO (SHOCK)
YOSHIKAWA'S GOT A FEW KINKS IN HER PERSONALITY. WELL...SO DOES HORI, I GUESS.
COME TO THINK OF IT.

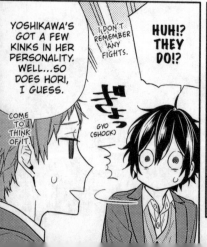

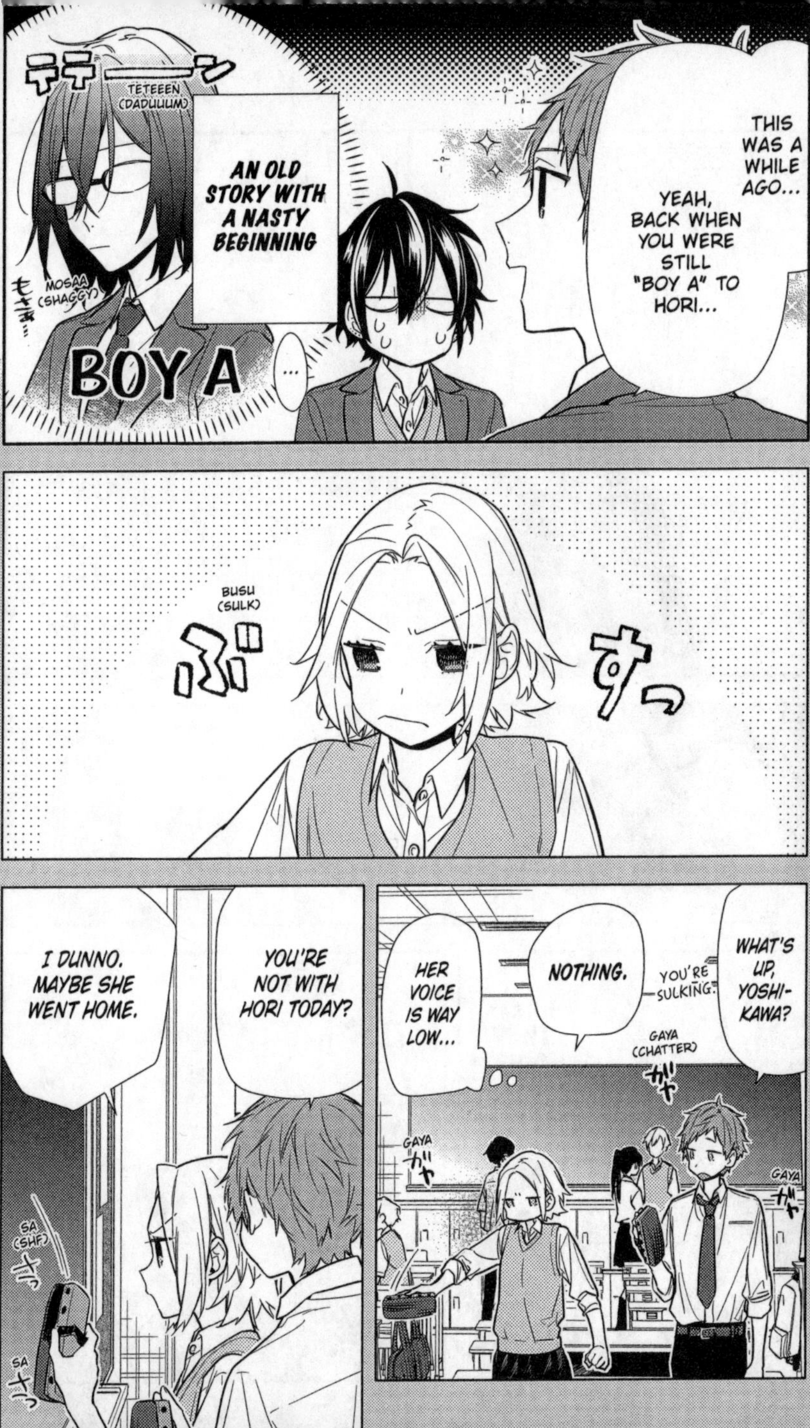
THIS WAS A WHILE AGO...
YEAH, BACK WHEN YOU WERE STILL "BOY A" TO HORI...
AN OLD STORY WITH A NASTY BEGINNING
テテーーン
TETEEEN (DADUUUM)
...
BOY A
もさぁ…
MOSAA (SHAGGY)
すっ
ぶ
BUSU (SULK)
WHAT'S UP, YOSHI-KAWA?
YOU'RE SULKING.
GAYA (CHATTER)
がや
NOTHING.
HER VOICE IS WAY LOW...
GAYA
がや
GAYA
がや
YOU'RE NOT WITH HORI TODAY?
I DUNNO. MAYBE SHE WENT HOME.
SA (SHF)
さっ
SA
さっ

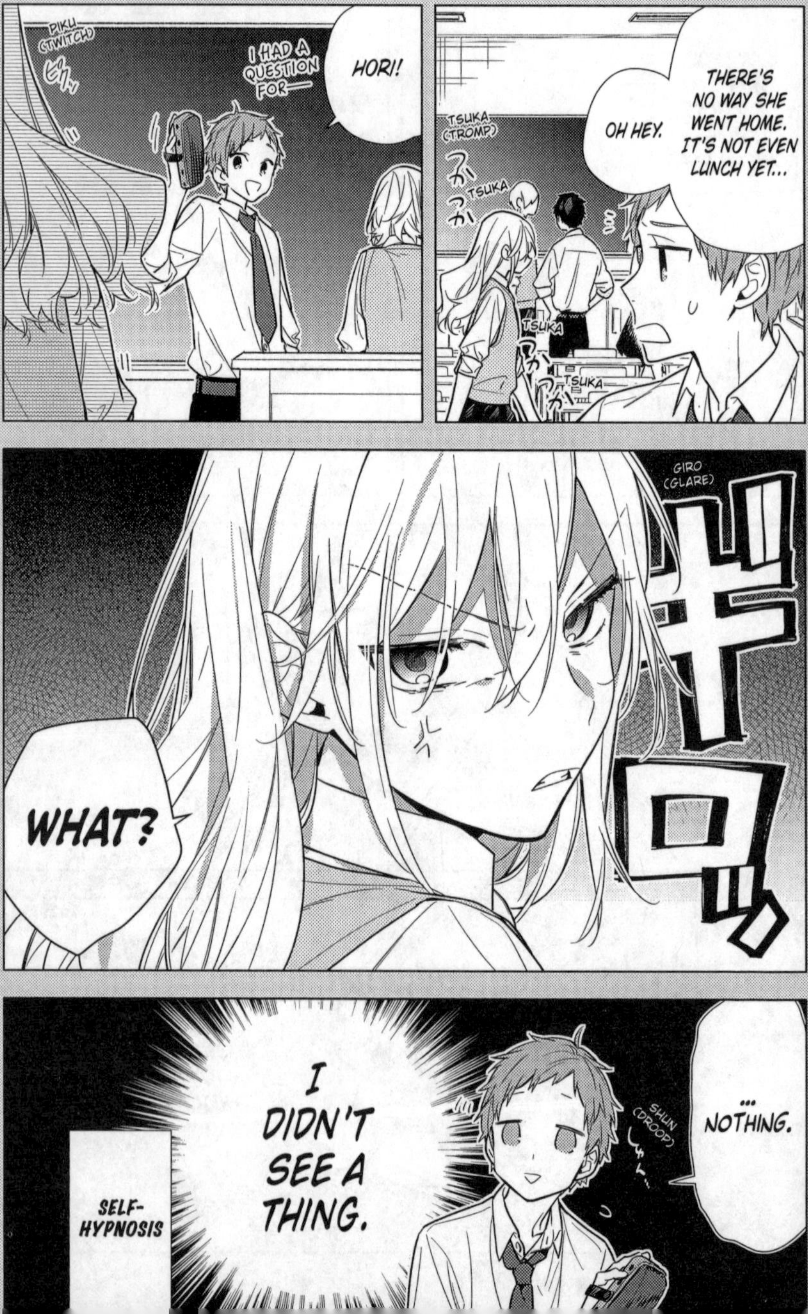
THERE'S NO WAY SHE WENT HOME. IT'S NOT EVEN LUNCH YET...
OH HEY.
TSUKA (TROMP)
TSUKA
TSUKA
TSUKA
HORI!
I HAD A QUESTION FOR—
PIKU (TWITCH)
GIRO (GLARE)
WHAT?
...NOTHING.
SHUN (DROOP)
I DIDN'T SEE A THING.
SELF-HYPNOSIS

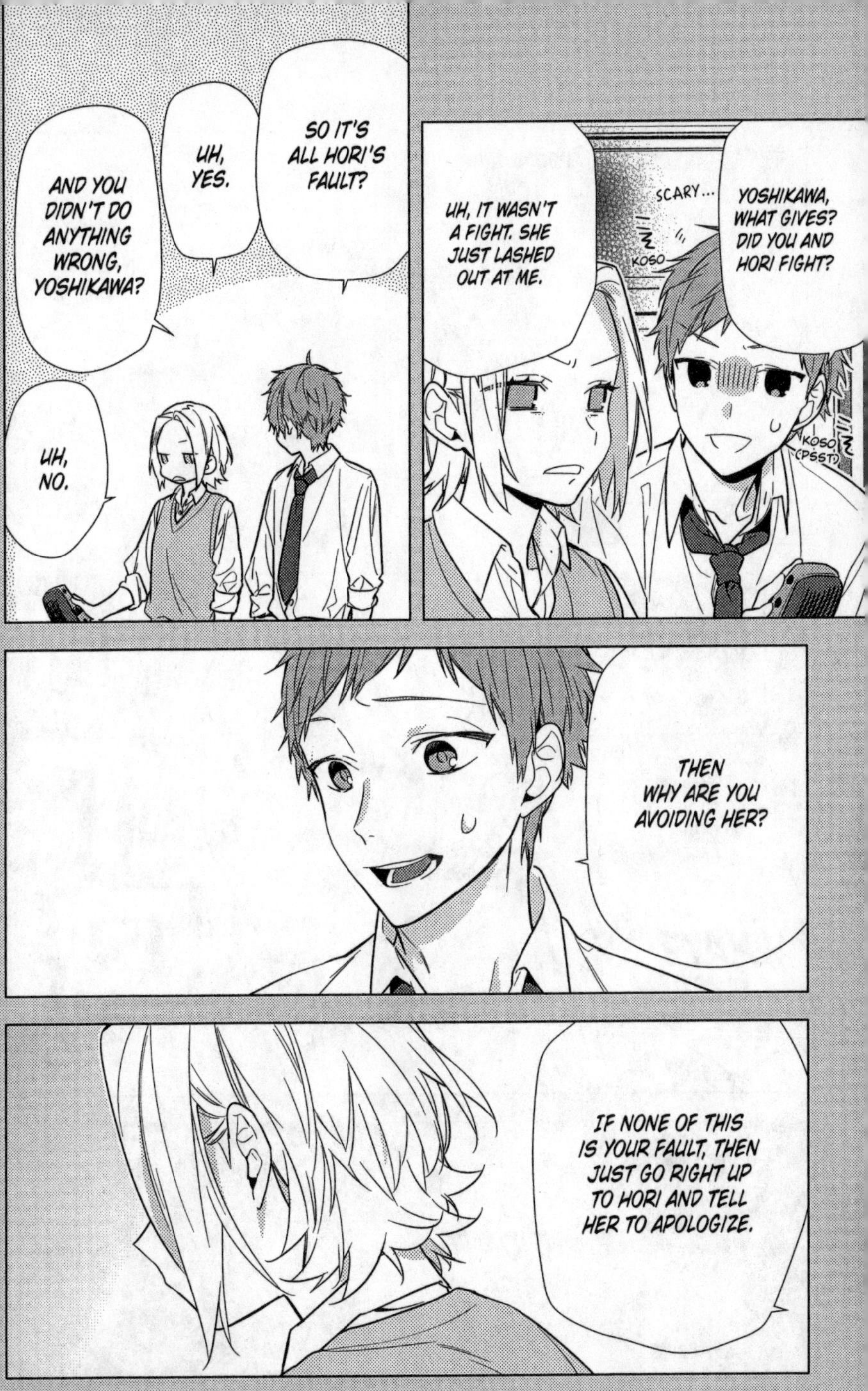
KOSO (PSST)
YOSHIKAWA, WHAT GIVES? DID YOU AND HORI FIGHT?
SCARY...
KOSO
UH, IT WASN'T A FIGHT. SHE JUST LASHED OUT AT ME.
SO IT'S ALL HORI'S FAULT?
UH, YES.
AND YOU DIDN'T DO ANYTHING WRONG, YOSHIKAWA?
UH, NO.
THEN WHY ARE YOU AVOIDING HER?
IF NONE OF THIS IS YOUR FAULT, THEN JUST GO RIGHT UP TO HORI AND TELL HER TO APOLOGIZE.

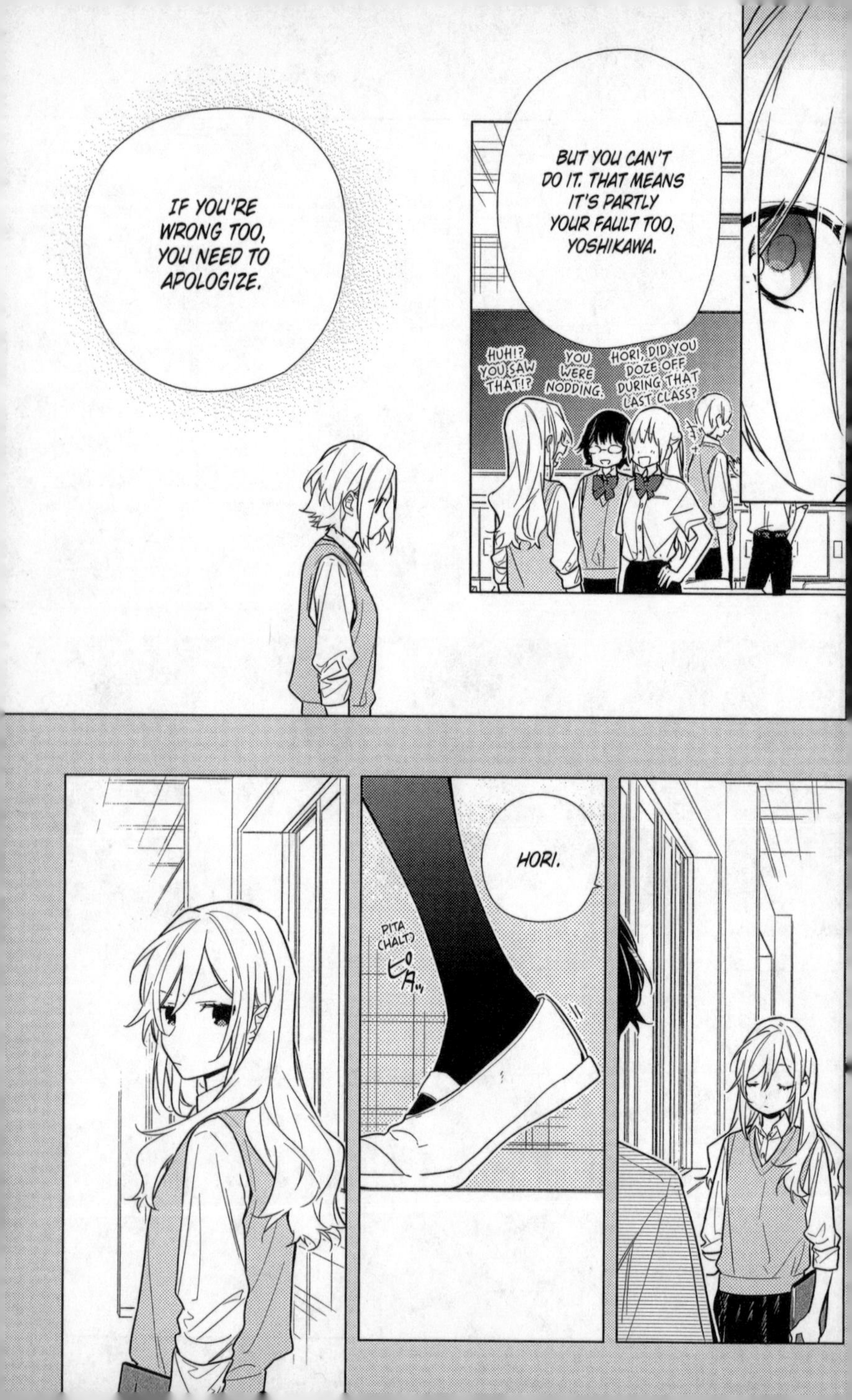
BUT YOU CAN'T DO IT. THAT MEANS IT'S PARTLY YOUR FAULT TOO, YOSHIKAWA.
HORI, DID YOU DOZE OFF DURING THAT LAST CLASS?
YOU WERE NODDING.
HUH!? YOU SAW THAT!?
IF YOU'RE WRONG TOO, YOU NEED TO APOLOGIZE.
HORI.
PITA (HALT)
ピタ…

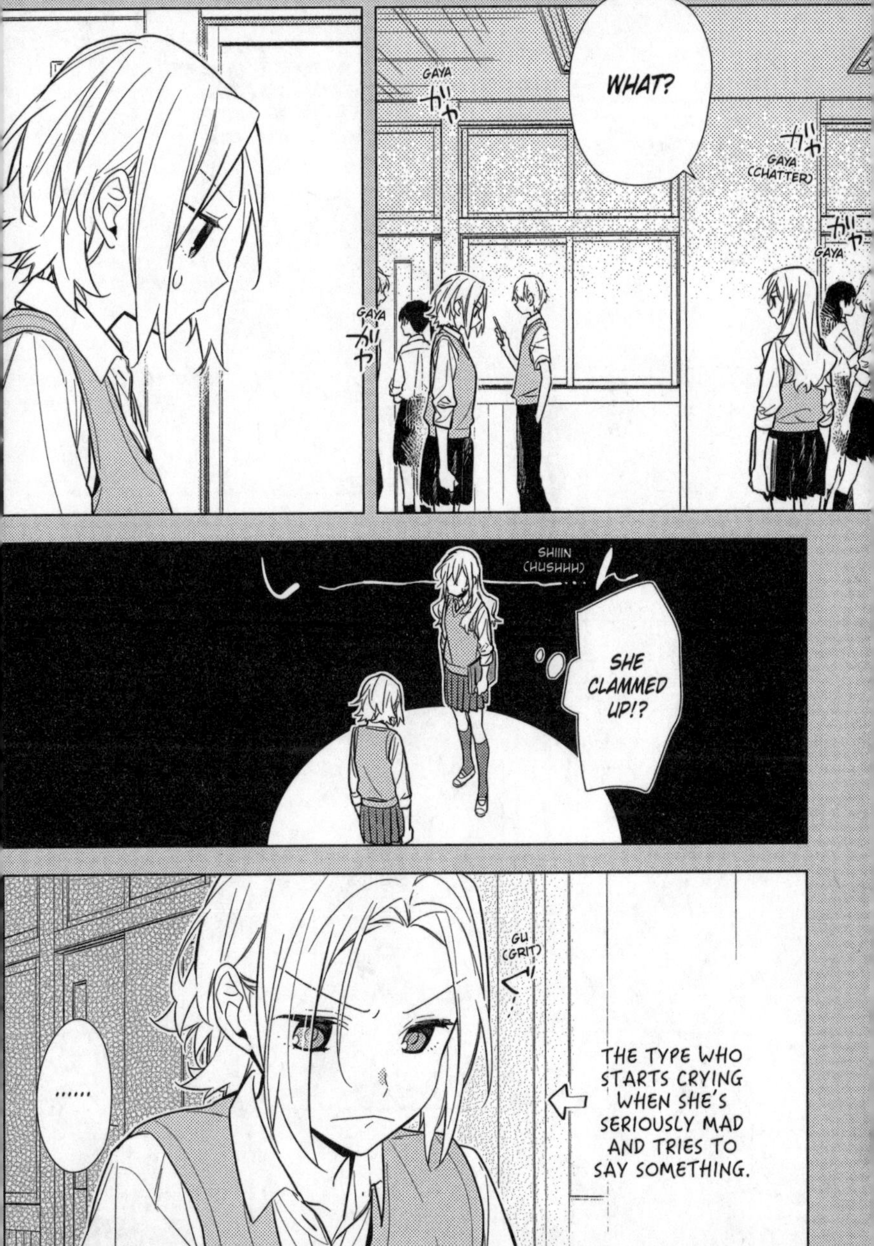
GAYA (CHATTER)
WHAT?
GAYA
GAYA
GAYA
SHIIN (HUSHHH)
SHE CLAMMED UP!?
GU (GRIT)
THE TYPE WHO STARTS CRYING WHEN SHE'S SERIOUSLY MAD AND TRIES TO SAY SOMETHING.
......

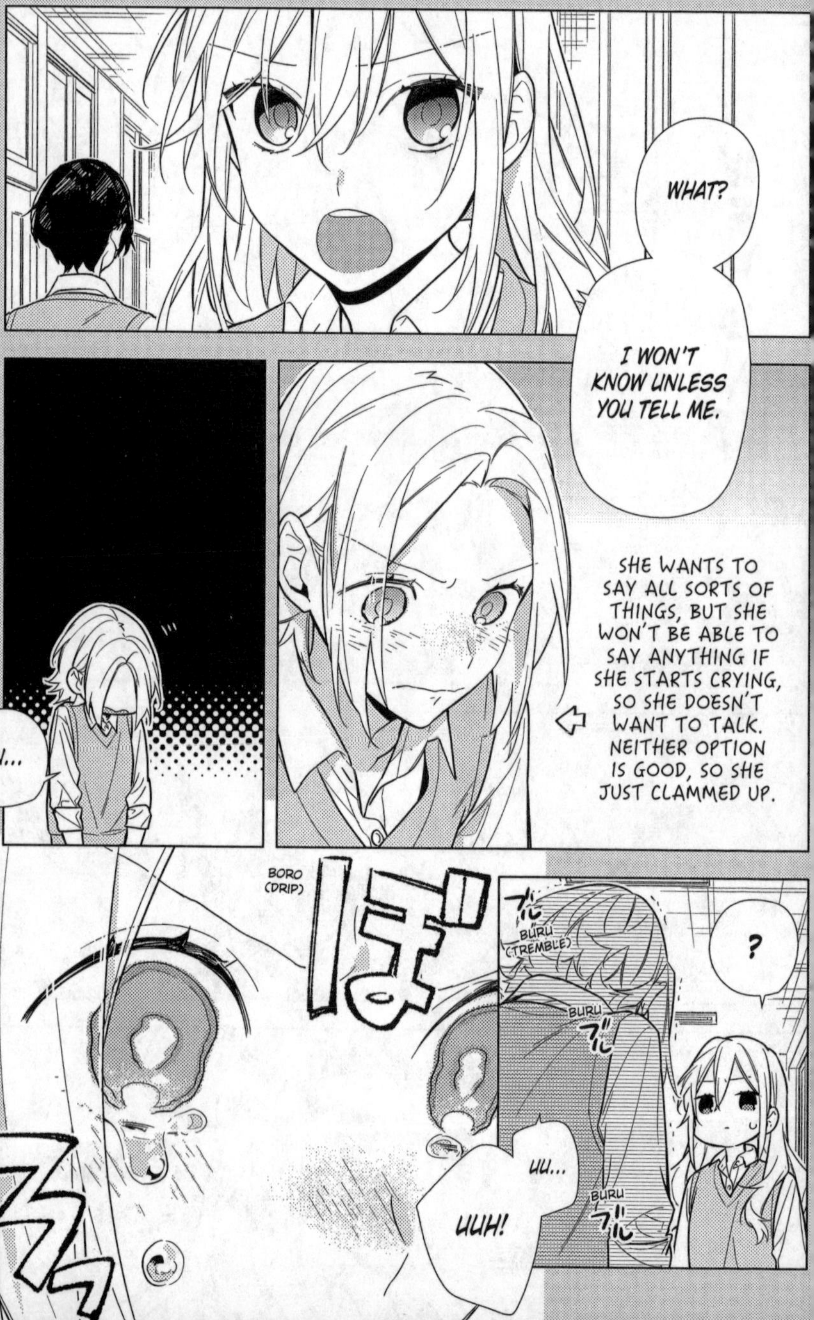
WHAT?
I WON'T KNOW UNLESS YOU TELL ME.
SHE WANTS TO SAY ALL SORTS OF THINGS, BUT SHE WON'T BE ABLE TO SAY ANYTHING IF SHE STARTS CRYING, SO SHE DOESN'T WANT TO TALK. NEITHER OPTION IS GOOD, SO SHE JUST CLAMMED UP.
UU...
ぶる
BURU (TREMBLE)
?
BURU
ぶる
BURU
ぶる
BORO (DRIP)
ぼ
UU...
UUH!

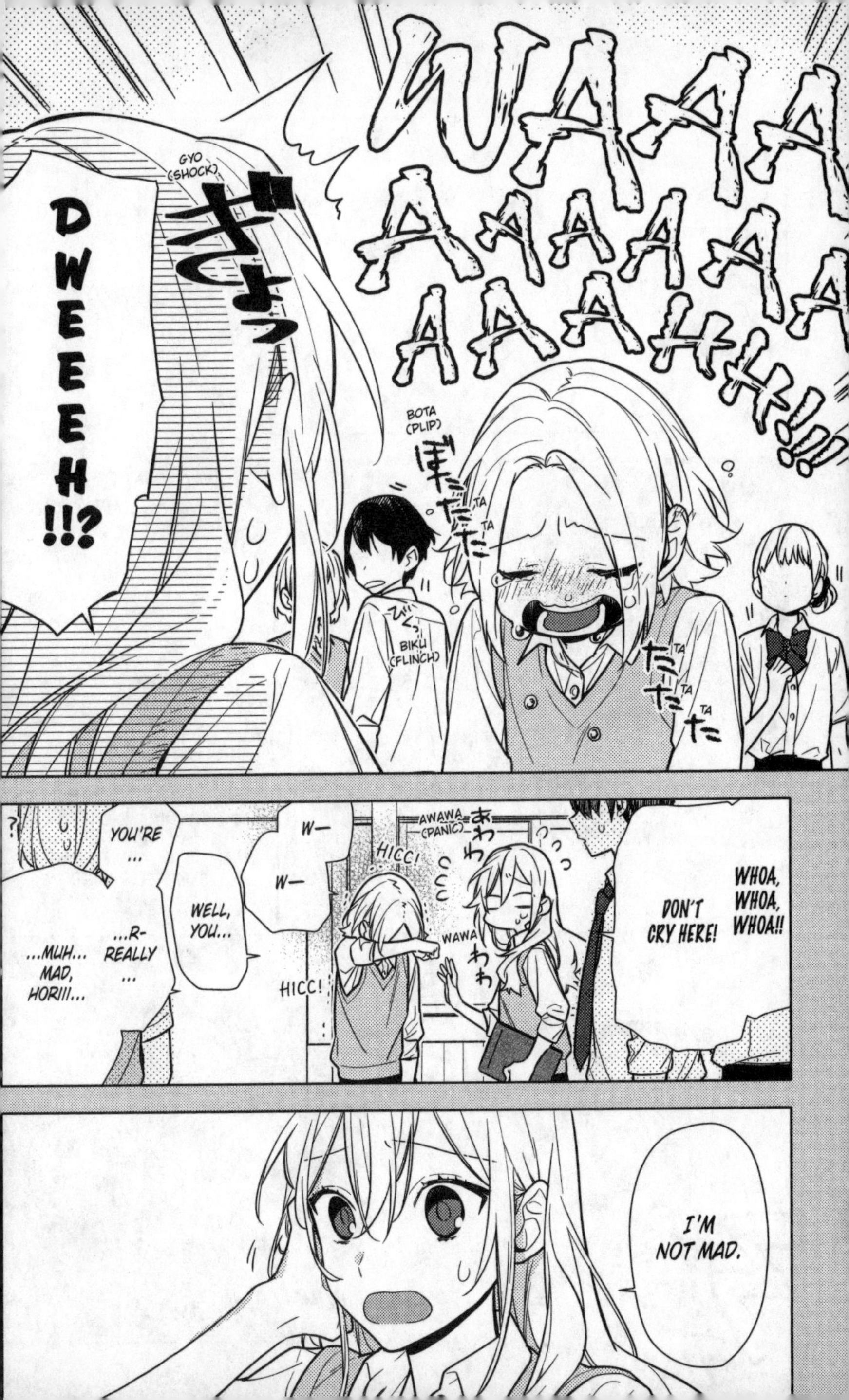
WAAAAAAAAAAAHH!!!!
GYO (SHOCK)
ぎょっ
DWEEEEH!!?
BOTA (PLIP)
ぼた
TA TA
たた
BIKU (FLINCH)
びくっ
TA TA TA
たたた
WHOA, WHOA, WHOA!!
DON'T CRY HERE!
AWAWA (PANIC)
あわわ
HICC!
W—
W—
WAWA
わわ
HICC!
YOU'RE ...
WELL, YOU...
...R- REALLY ...
...MUH... MAD, HORIII...
I'M NOT MAD.

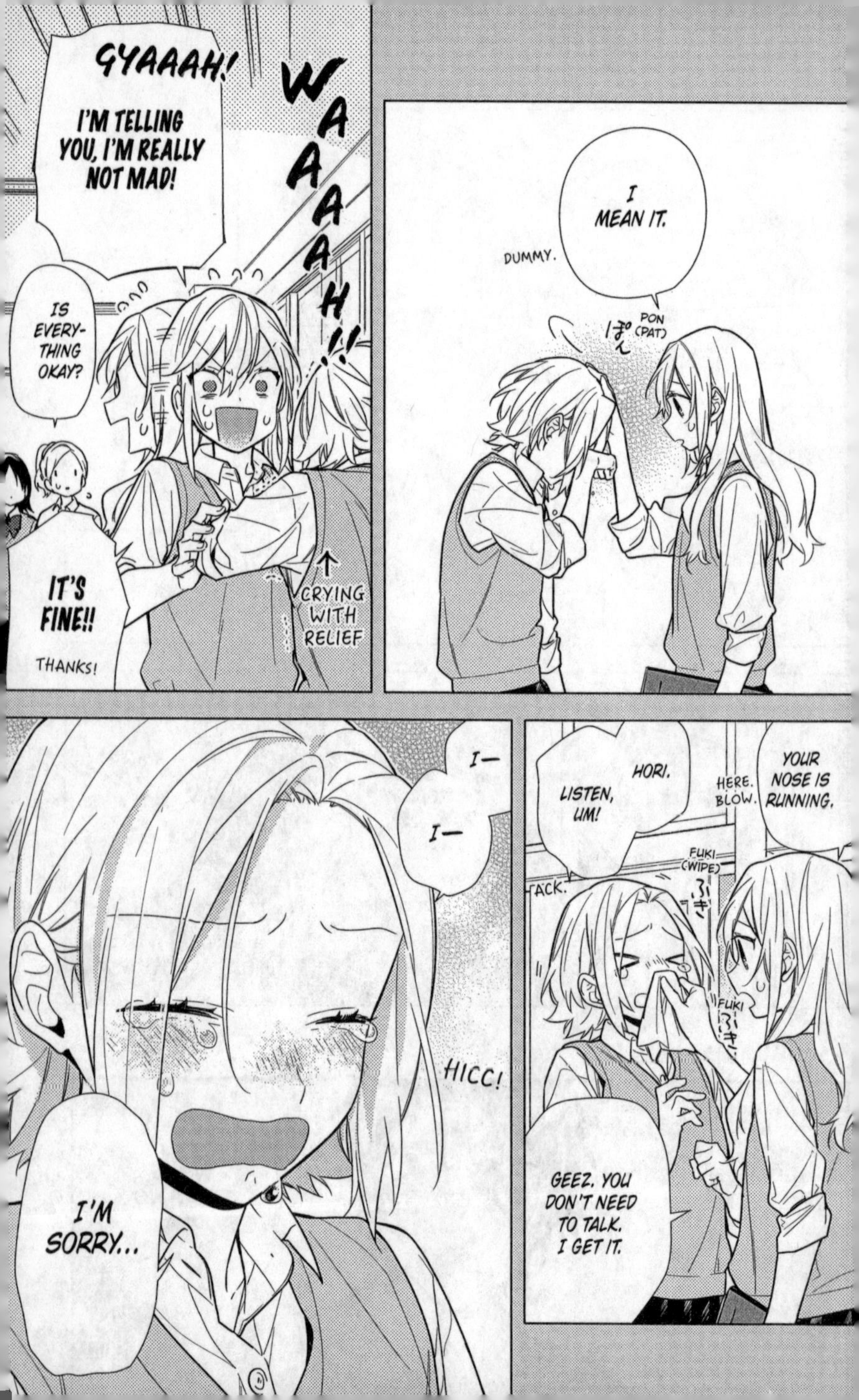
I MEAN IT.
DUMMY.
ぽん
PON (PAT)
WAAAAAH!!
GYAAAH!
I'M TELLING YOU, I'M REALLY NOT MAD!
IS EVERYTHING OKAY?
↑ CRYING WITH RELIEF
IT'S FINE!!
THANKS!
YOUR NOSE IS RUNNING.
HERE. BLOW.
HORI.
LISTEN, UM!
FUKI (WIPE)
ふき
ACK.
FUKI
ふき
GEEZ. YOU DON'T NEED TO TALK. I GET IT.
I—
I—
HICC!
I'M SORRY...

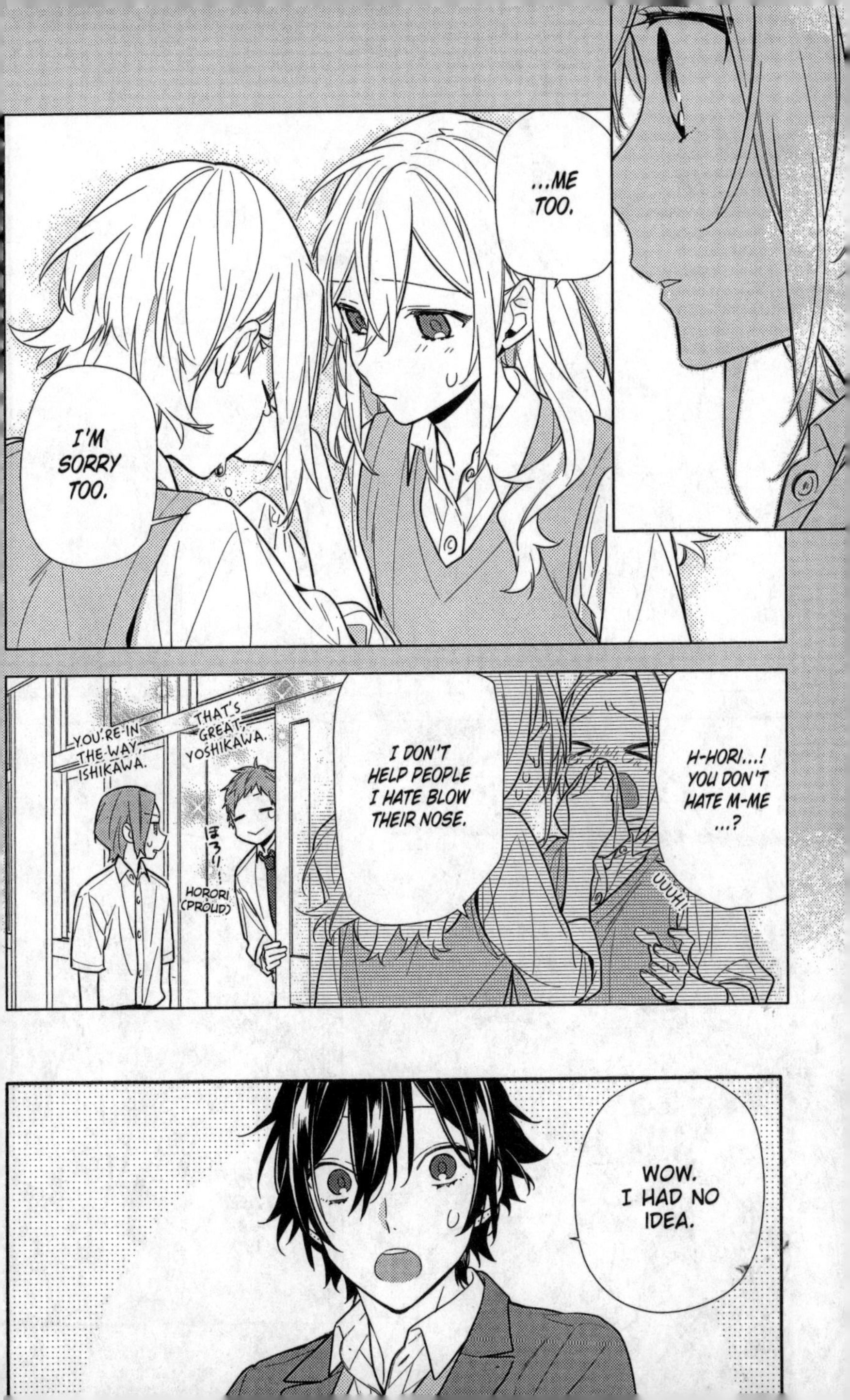
...ME TOO.
I'M SORRY TOO.
H-HORI...! YOU DON'T HATE M-ME ...?
UUUH!
I DON'T HELP PEOPLE I HATE BLOW THEIR NOSE.
THAT'S GREAT, YOSHIKAWA.
ほろり
HORORI (PROUD)
YOU'RE IN THE WAY, ISHIKAWA.
WOW. I HAD NO IDEA.

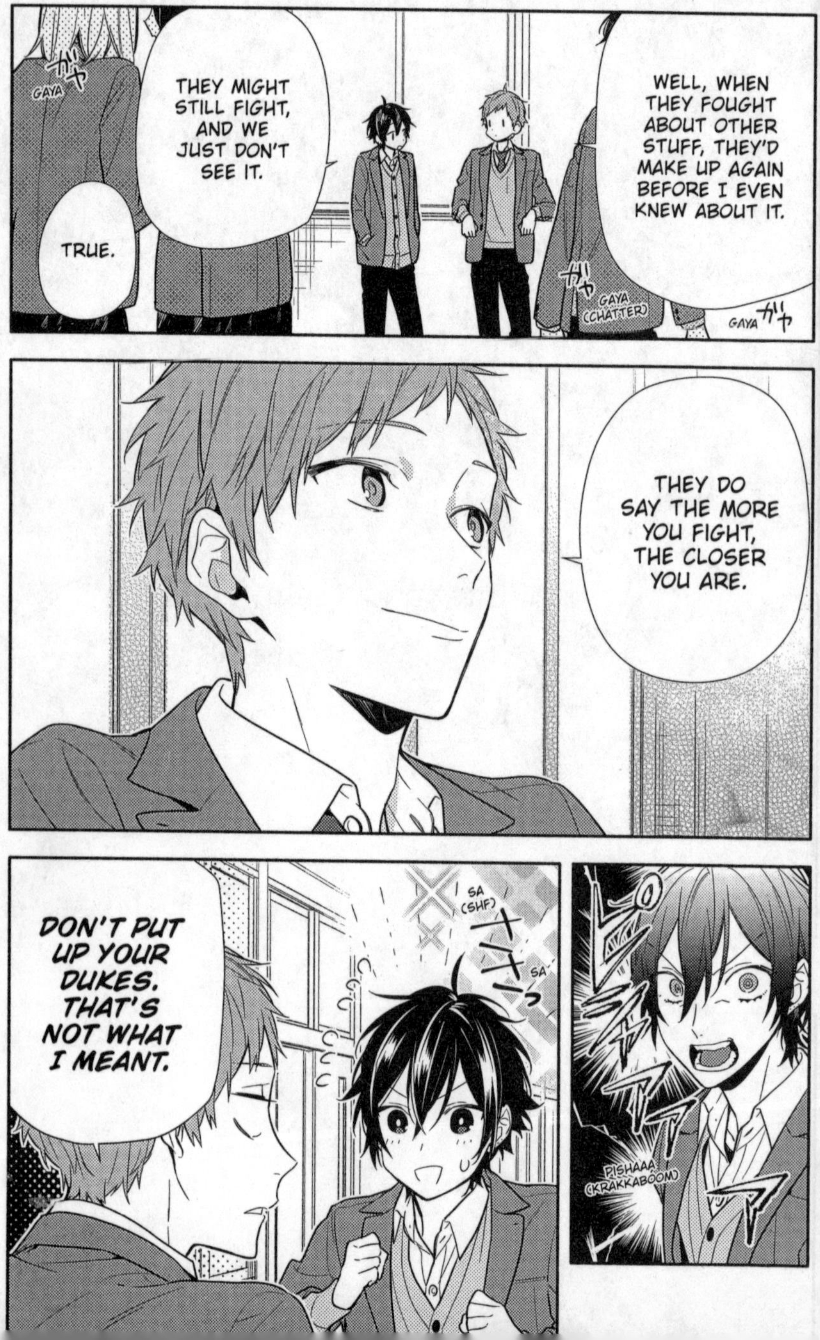
WELL, WHEN THEY FOUGHT ABOUT OTHER STUFF, THEY'D MAKE UP AGAIN BEFORE I EVEN KNEW ABOUT IT.
GAYA
GAYA (CHATTER)
THEY MIGHT STILL FIGHT, AND WE JUST DON'T SEE IT.
GAYA
TRUE.
THEY DO SAY THE MORE YOU FIGHT, THE CLOSER YOU ARE.
PISHAAA (KRAKKABOOM)
SA (SHF)
SA
DON'T PUT UP YOUR DUKES. THAT'S NOT WHAT I MEANT.

HORIMIYA

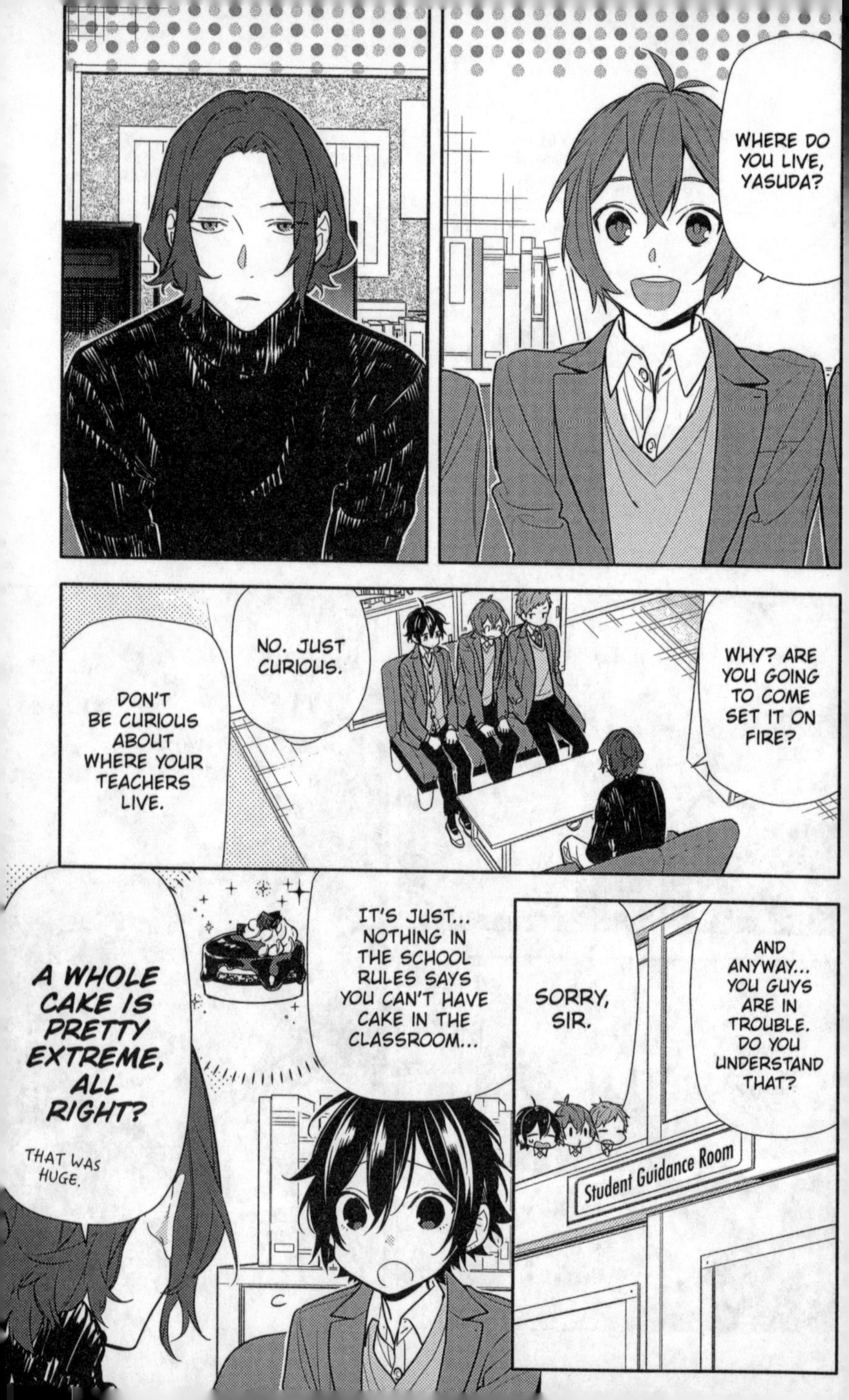
WHERE DO YOU LIVE, YASUDA?
WHY? ARE YOU GOING TO COME SET IT ON FIRE?
NO. JUST CURIOUS.
DON'T BE CURIOUS ABOUT WHERE YOUR TEACHERS LIVE.
AND ANYWAY... YOU GUYS ARE IN TROUBLE. DO YOU UNDERSTAND THAT?
SORRY, SIR.
Student Guidance Room
IT'S JUST... NOTHING IN THE SCHOOL RULES SAYS YOU CAN'T HAVE CAKE IN THE CLASSROOM...
A WHOLE CAKE IS PRETTY EXTREME, ALL RIGHT?
THAT WAS HUGE.

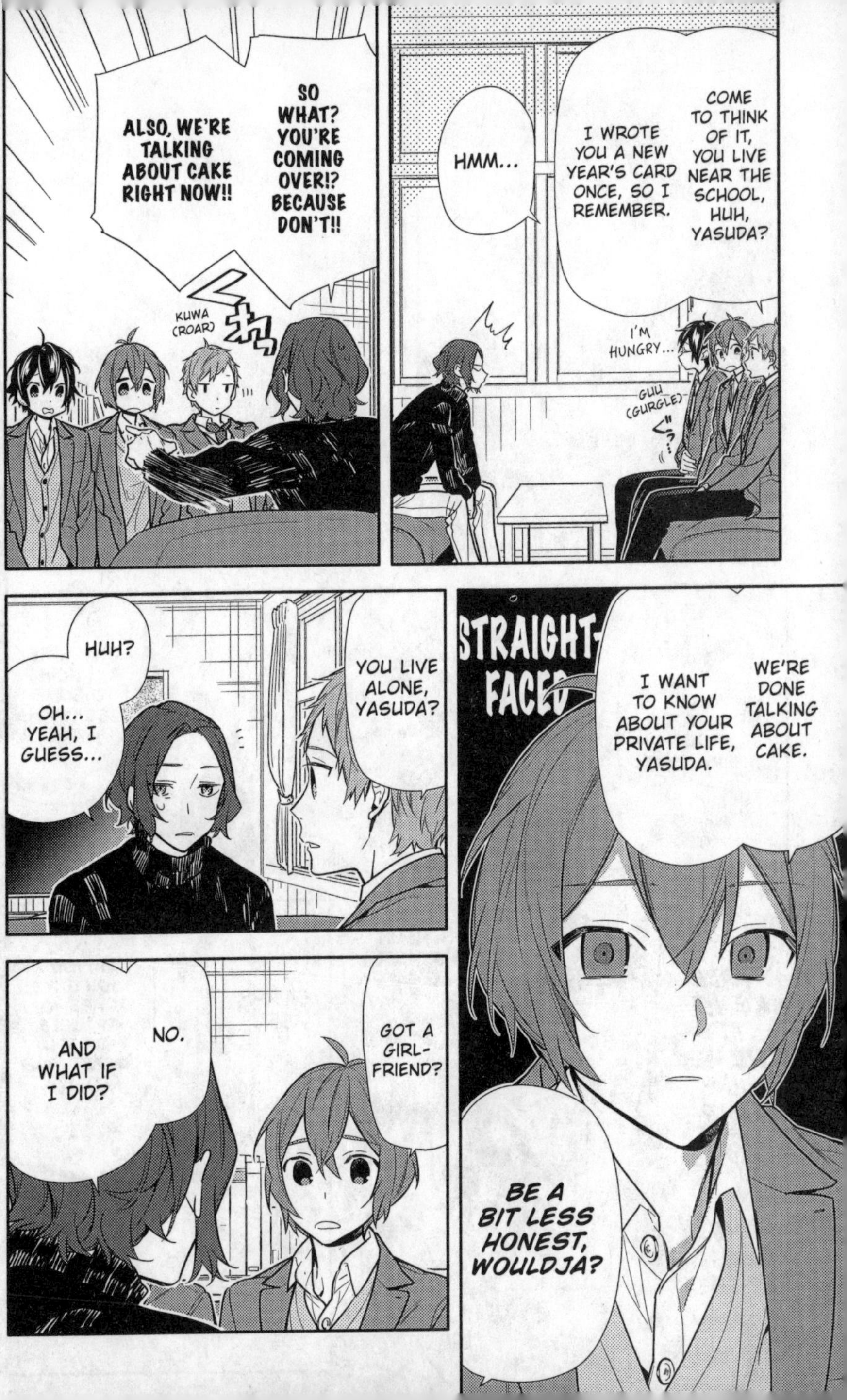
COME TO THINK OF IT, YOU LIVE NEAR THE SCHOOL, HUH, YASUDA?
I WROTE YOU A NEW YEAR'S CARD ONCE, SO I REMEMBER.
HMM...
I'M HUNGRY...
GUU (GURGLE)
SO WHAT? YOU'RE COMING OVER!? BECAUSE DON'T!!
ALSO, WE'RE TALKING ABOUT CAKE RIGHT NOW!!
KUWA (ROAR)
WE'RE DONE TALKING ABOUT CAKE.
I WANT TO KNOW ABOUT YOUR PRIVATE LIFE, YASUDA.
STRAIGHT-FACED
BE A BIT LESS HONEST, WOULDJA?
YOU LIVE ALONE, YASUDA?
HUH?
OH... YEAH, I GUESS...
GOT A GIRL-FRIEND?
NO.
AND WHAT IF I DID?

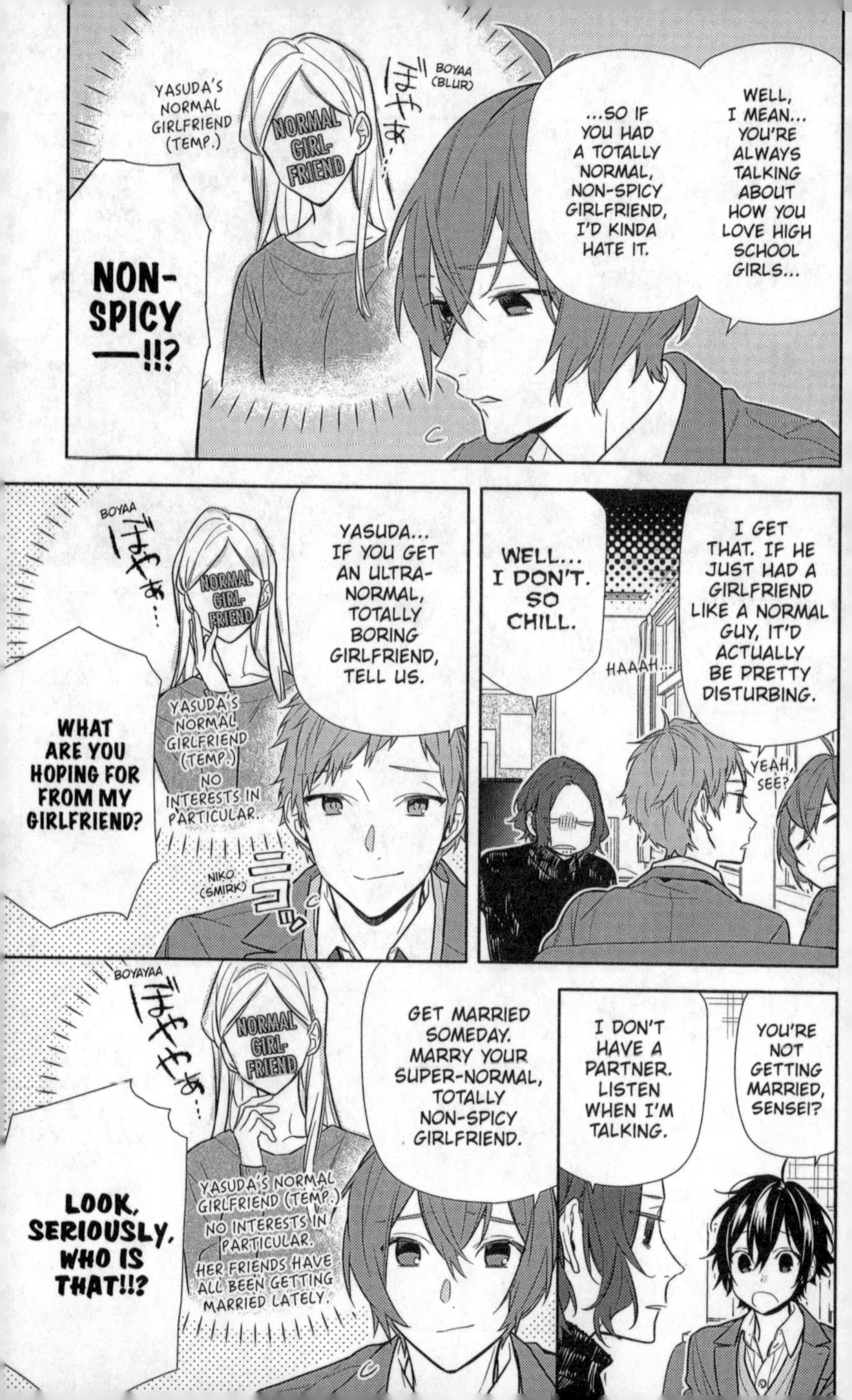
WELL, I MEAN... YOU'RE ALWAYS TALKING ABOUT HOW YOU LOVE HIGH SCHOOL GIRLS...
...SO IF YOU HAD A TOTALLY NORMAL, NON-SPICY GIRLFRIEND, I'D KINDA HATE IT.
BOYAA (BLUR)
NORMAL GIRL-FRIEND
YASUDA'S NORMAL GIRLFRIEND (TEMP.)
NON-SPICY—!!?
I GET THAT. IF HE JUST HAD A GIRLFRIEND LIKE A NORMAL GUY, IT'D ACTUALLY BE PRETTY DISTURBING.
YEAH, SEE?
WELL... I DON'T. SO CHILL.
HAAAH...
YASUDA... IF YOU GET AN ULTRA-NORMAL, TOTALLY BORING GIRLFRIEND, TELL US.
BOYAA
NORMAL GIRL-FRIEND
YASUDA'S NORMAL GIRLFRIEND (TEMP.) NO INTERESTS IN PARTICULAR.
NIKO (SMIRK)
WHAT ARE YOU HOPING FOR FROM MY GIRLFRIEND?
YOU'RE NOT GETTING MARRIED, SENSEI?
I DON'T HAVE A PARTNER. LISTEN WHEN I'M TALKING.
GET MARRIED SOMEDAY. MARRY YOUR SUPER-NORMAL, TOTALLY NON-SPICY GIRLFRIEND.
BOYAYAA
NORMAL GIRL-FRIEND
YASUDA'S NORMAL GIRLFRIEND (TEMP.) NO INTERESTS IN PARTICULAR. HER FRIENDS HAVE ALL BEEN GETTING MARRIED LATELY.
LOOK. SERIOUSLY. WHO IS THAT!!?

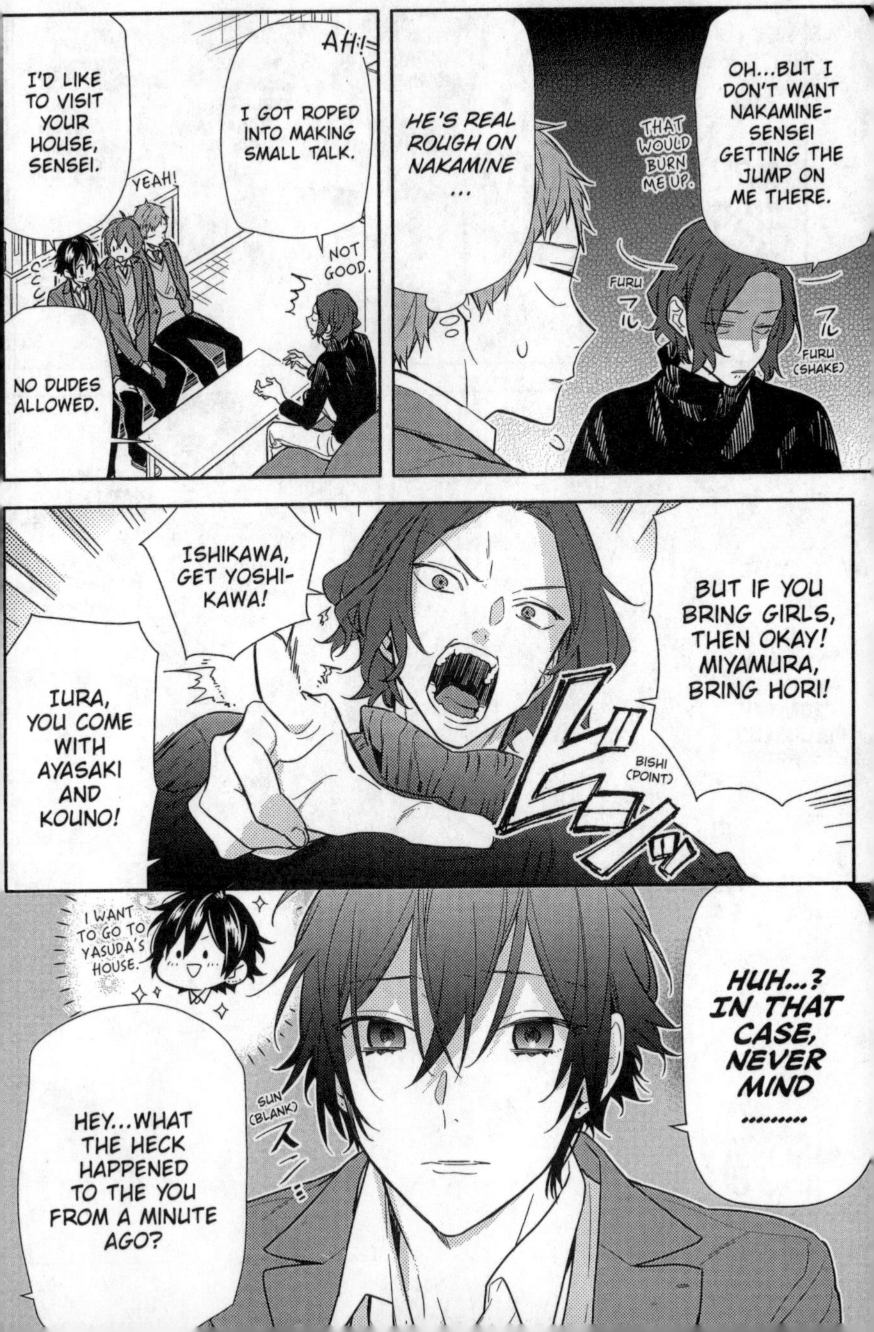
OH...BUT I DON'T WANT NAKAMINE-SENSEI GETTING THE JUMP ON ME THERE.
THAT WOULD BURN ME UP.
FURU
FURU (SHAKE)
HE'S REAL ROUGH ON NAKAMINE ...
AH!
I GOT ROPED INTO MAKING SMALL TALK.
NOT GOOD.
I'D LIKE TO VISIT YOUR HOUSE, SENSEI.
YEAH!
NO DUDES ALLOWED.
BUT IF YOU BRING GIRLS, THEN OKAY! MIYAMURA, BRING HORI!
BISHI (POINT)
ISHIKAWA, GET YOSHI-KAWA!
IURA, YOU COME WITH AYASAKI AND KOUNO!
HUH...? IN THAT CASE, NEVER MIND ....
SUN (BLANK)
HEY...WHAT THE HECK HAPPENED TO THE YOU FROM A MINUTE AGO?
I WANT TO GO TO YASUDA'S HOUSE.

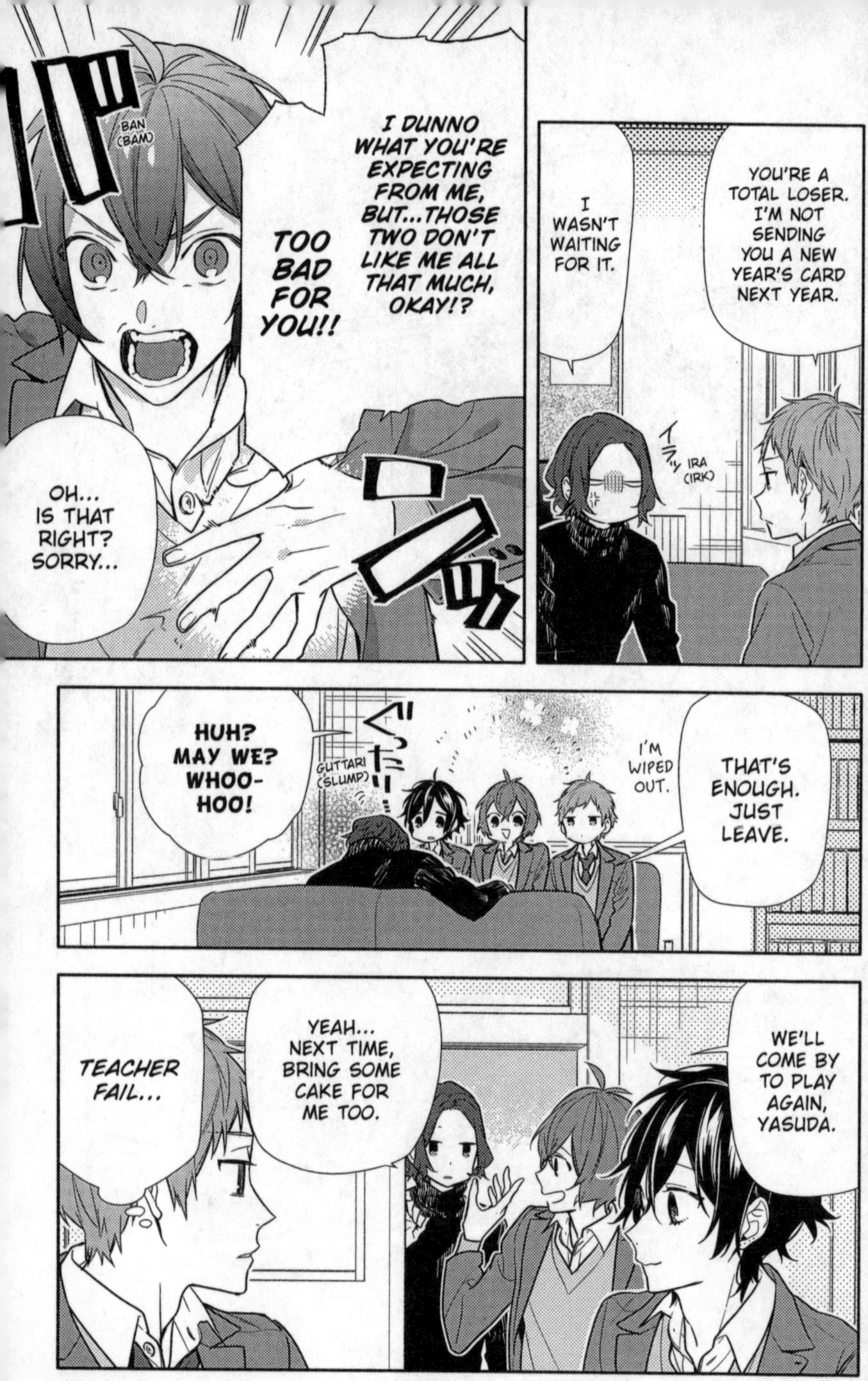
YOU'RE A TOTAL LOSER. I'M NOT SENDING YOU A NEW YEAR'S CARD NEXT YEAR.
I WASN'T WAITING FOR IT.
IRA (IRK)
BAN (BAM)
I DUNNO WHAT YOU'RE EXPECTING FROM ME, BUT...THOSE TWO DON'T LIKE ME ALL THAT MUCH, OKAY!?
TOO BAD FOR YOU!!
OH... IS THAT RIGHT? SORRY...
THAT'S ENOUGH. JUST LEAVE.
I'M WIPED OUT.
GUTTARI (SLUMP)
HUH? MAY WE? WHOO-HOO!
WE'LL COME BY TO PLAY AGAIN, YASUDA.
YEAH... NEXT TIME, BRING SOME CAKE FOR ME TOO.
TEACHER FAIL...

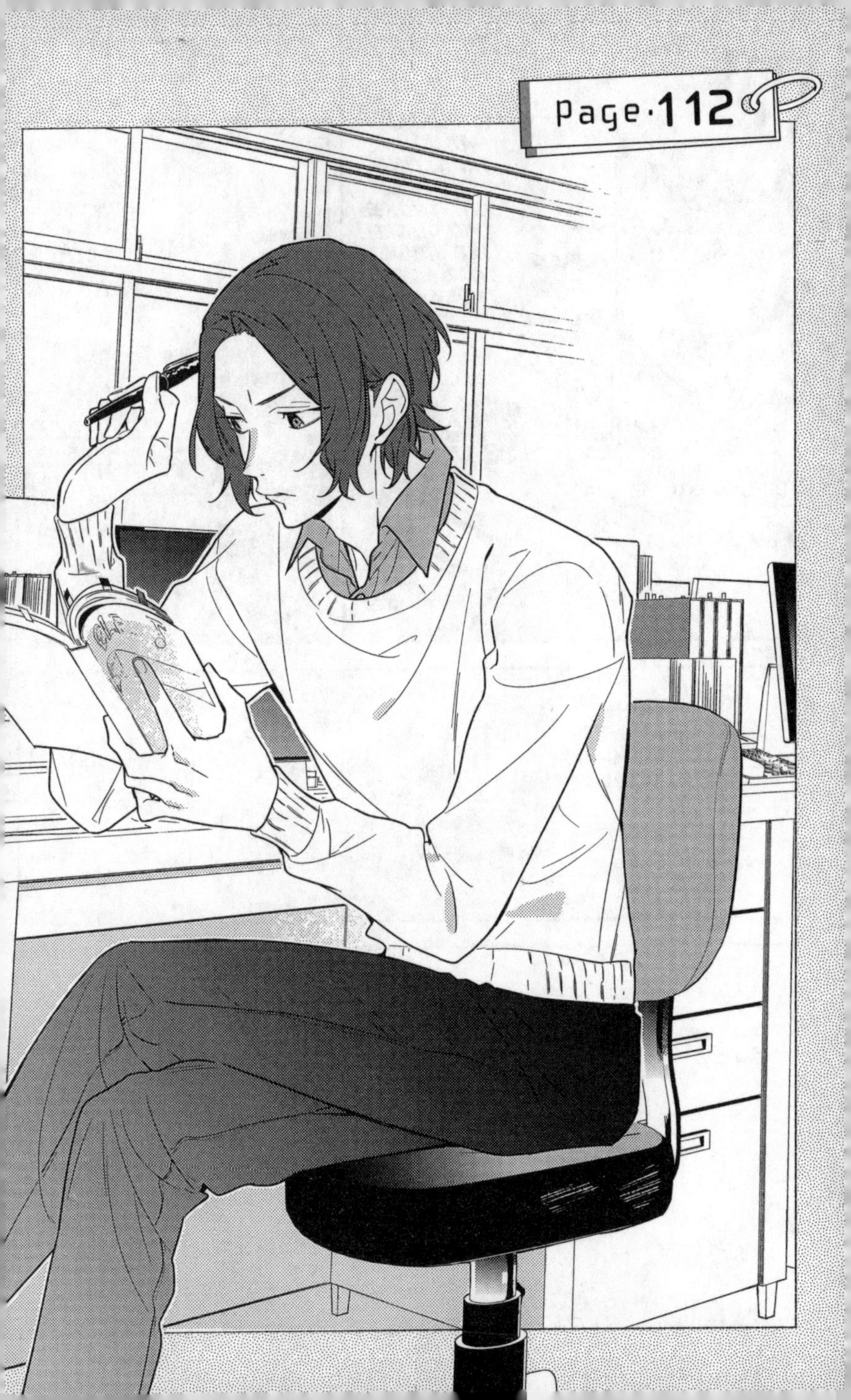
Page·112

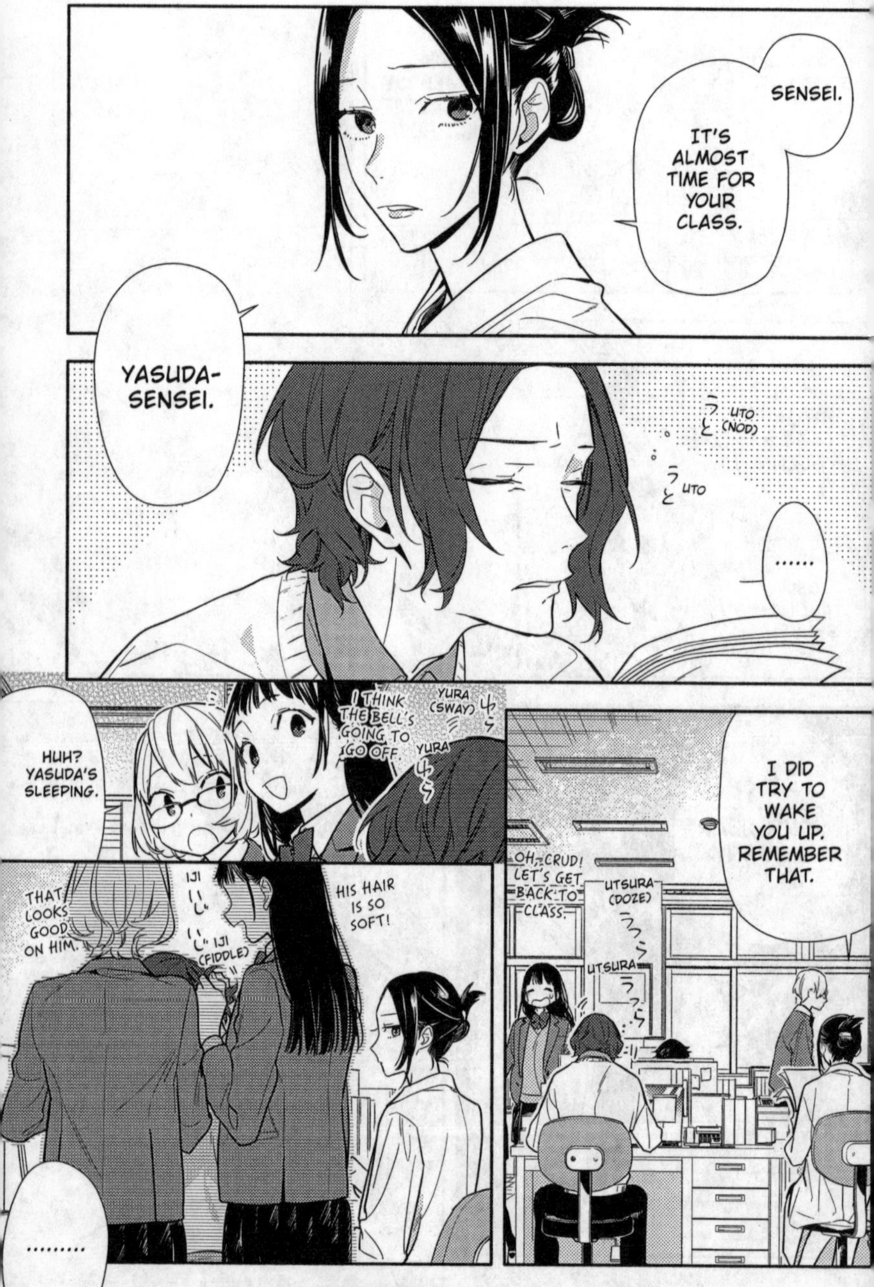
SENSEI.
IT'S ALMOST TIME FOR YOUR CLASS.
YASUDA-SENSEI.
UTO (NOD)
UTO
......
I DID TRY TO WAKE YOU UP. REMEMBER THAT.
OH, CRUD! LET'S GET BACK TO CLASS.
UTSURA (DOZE)
UTSURA
I THINK THE BELL'S GOING TO GO OFF.
YURA (SWAY)
YURA
HUH? YASUDA'S SLEEPING.
HIS HAIR IS SO SOFT!
IJI
IJI (FIDDLE)
THAT LOOKS GOOD ON HIM.
....

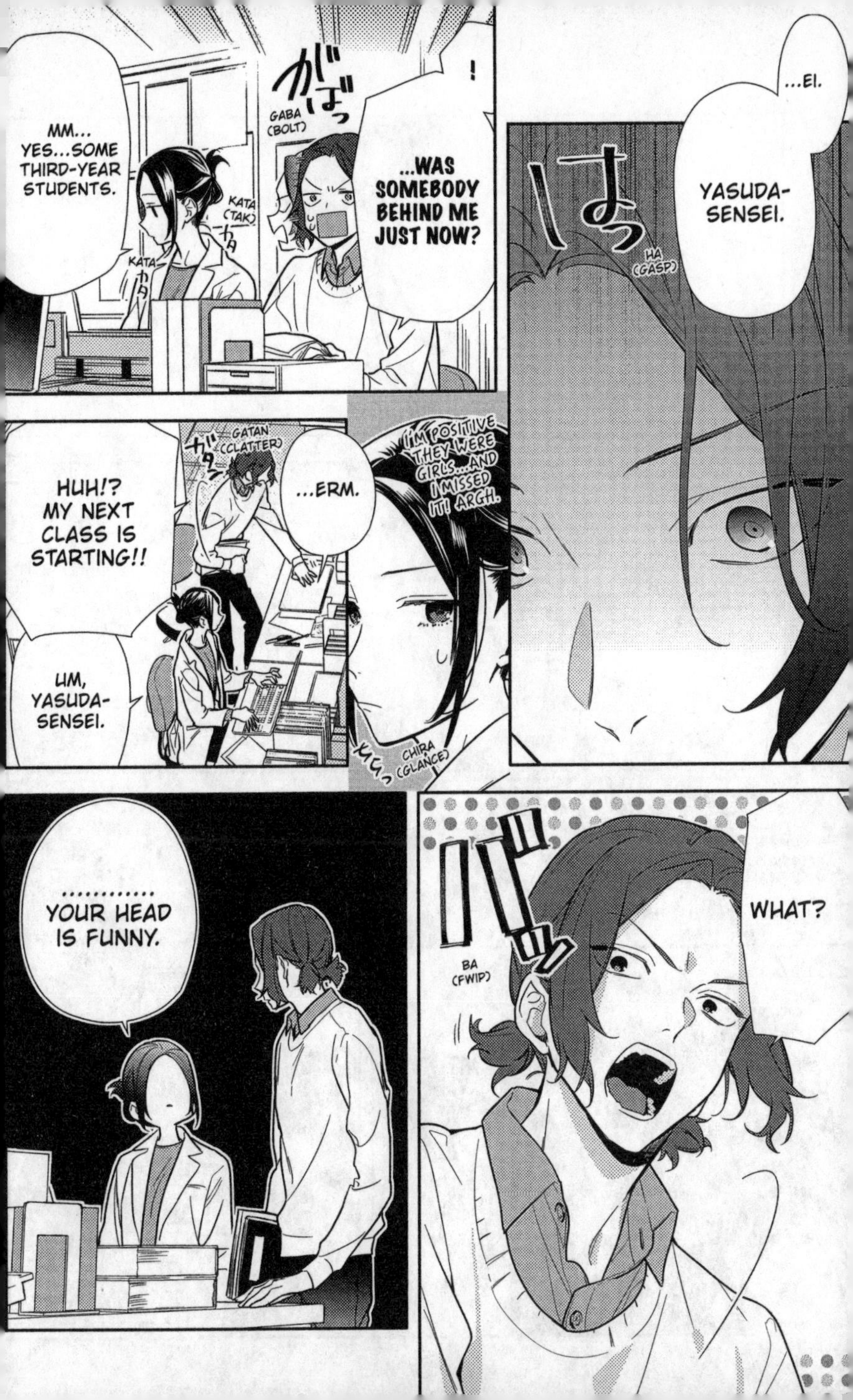
...EI.
YASUDA-SENSEI.
はっ
HA (GASP)
!
...WAS SOMEBODY BEHIND ME JUST NOW?
がばっ
GABA (BOLT)
KATA (TAK)
MM... YES...SOME THIRD-YEAR STUDENTS.
KATA
I'M POSITIVE THEY WERE GIRLS...AND I MISSED IT! ARGH.
CHIRA (GLANCE)
...ERM.
GATAN (CLATTER)
HUH!? MY NEXT CLASS IS STARTING!!
UM, YASUDA-SENSEI.
WHAT?
BA (FWIP)
.... YOUR HEAD IS FUNNY.

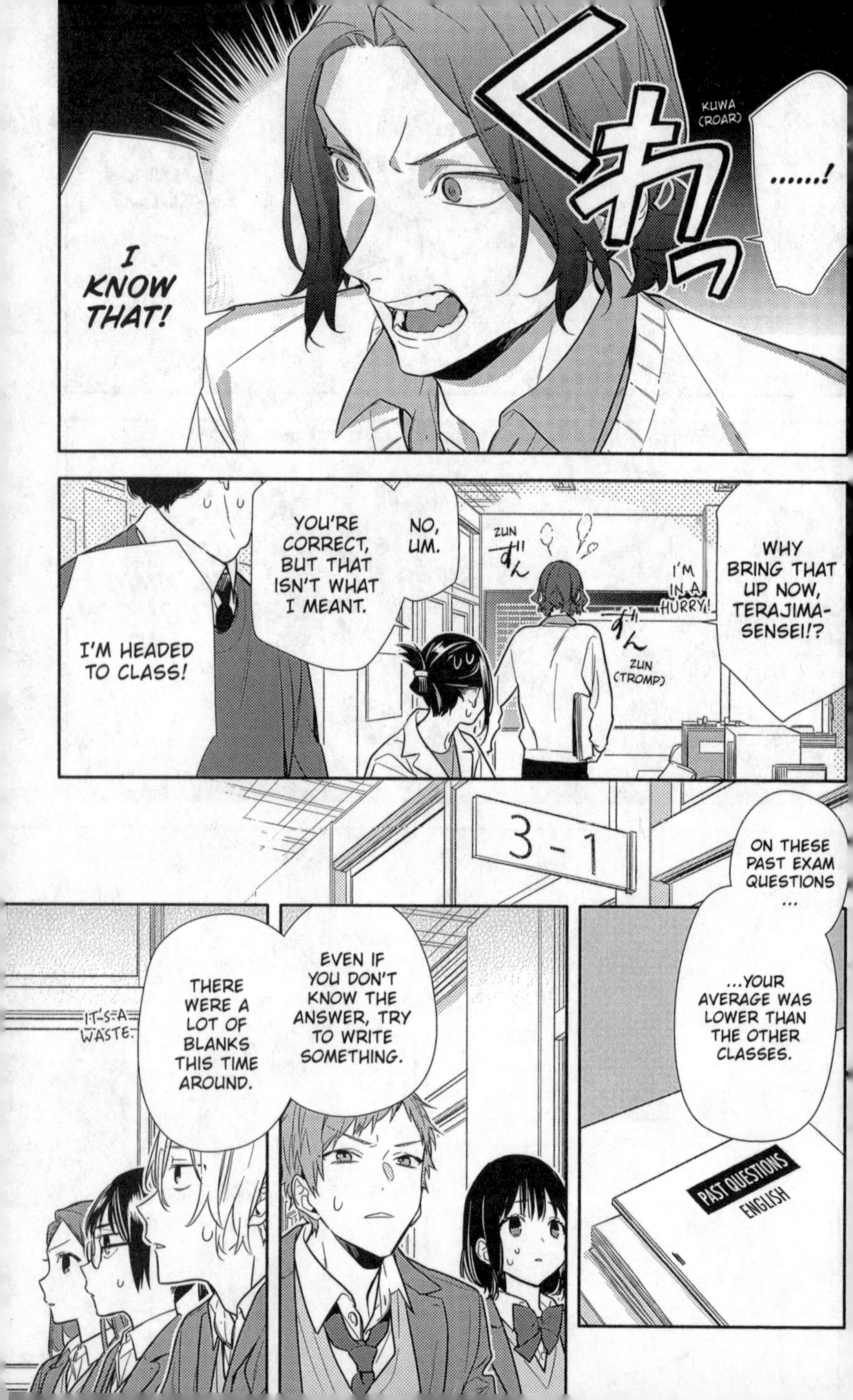
......!
KUWA (ROAR)
I KNOW THAT!
WHY BRING THAT UP NOW, TERAJIMA-SENSEI!?
I'M IN A HURRY!
ZUN
ZUN (TROMP)
NO, UM.
YOU'RE CORRECT, BUT THAT ISN'T WHAT I MEANT.
I'M HEADED TO CLASS!
3-1
ON THESE PAST EXAM QUESTIONS ...
...YOUR AVERAGE WAS LOWER THAN THE OTHER CLASSES.
PAST QUESTIONS
ENGLISH
EVEN IF YOU DON'T KNOW THE ANSWER, TRY TO WRITE SOMETHING.
THERE WERE A LOT OF BLANKS THIS TIME AROUND.
IT'S A WASTE.

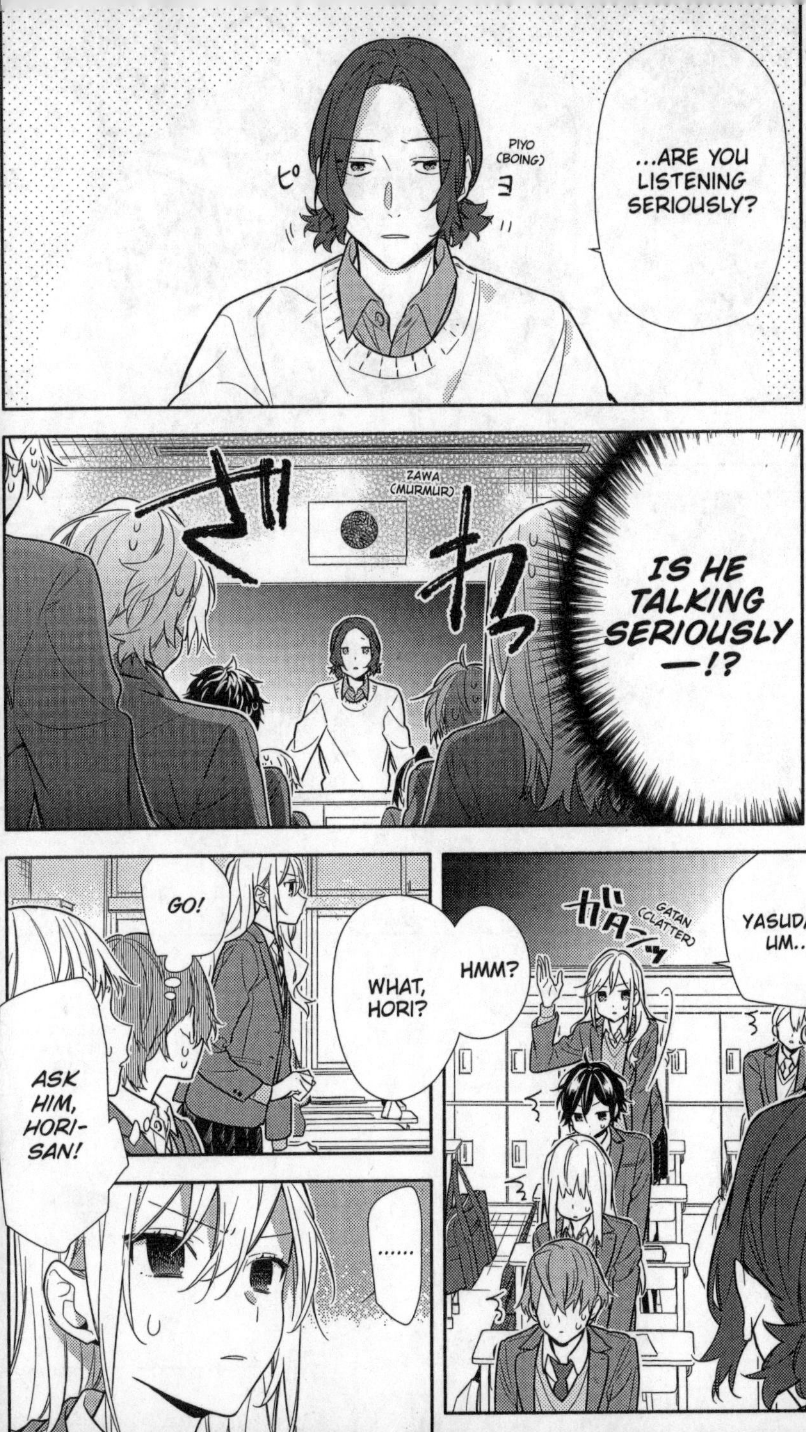
...ARE YOU LISTENING SERIOUSLY?
PIYO (BOING)
IS HE TALKING SERIOUSLY—!?
ZAWA (MURMUR)
YASUDA... UM...
GATAN (CLATTER)
HMM? WHAT, HORI?
GO!
ASK HIM, HORI-SAN!
......

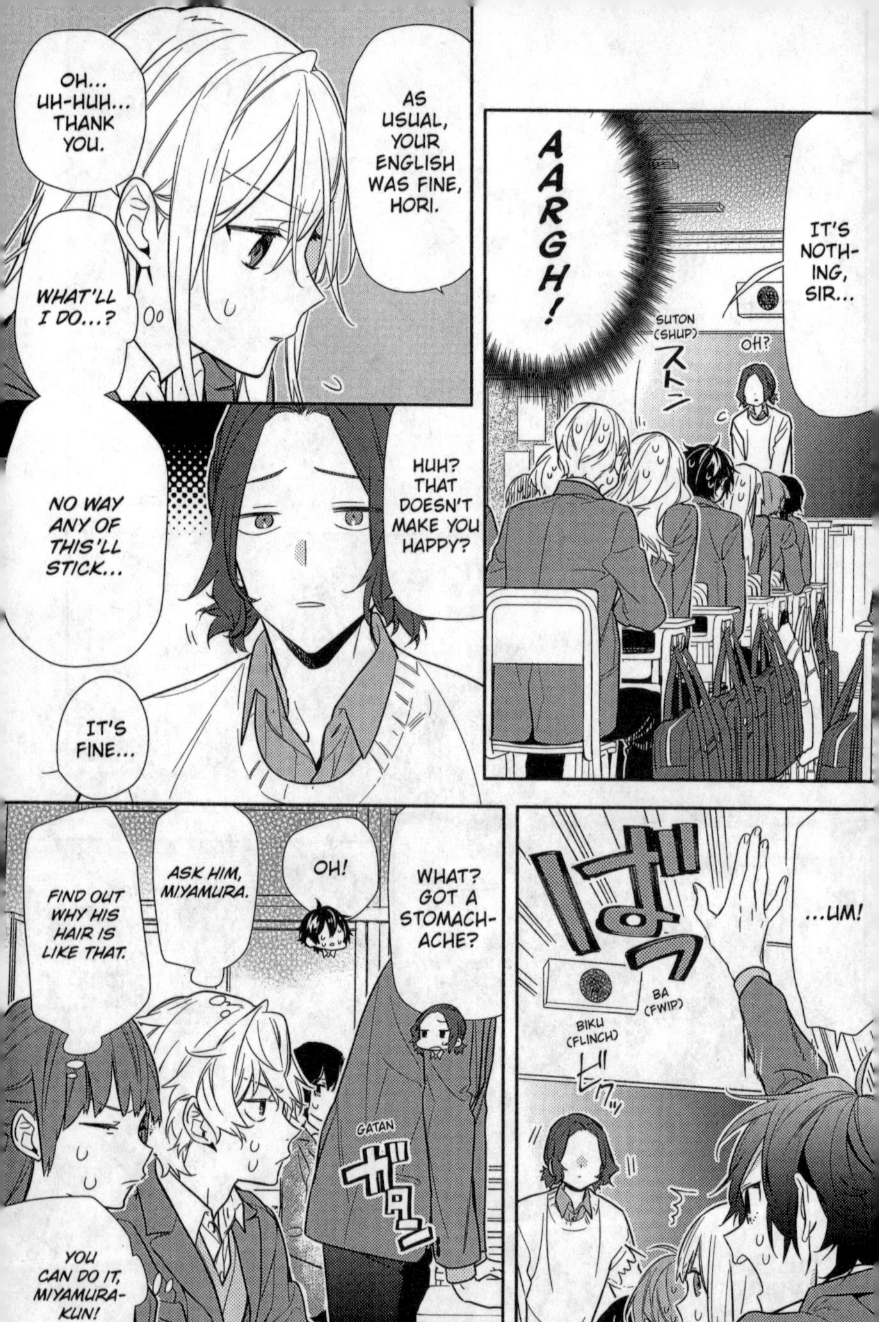
AARGH!
IT'S NOTHING, SIR...
OH?
SUTON (SHUP)
ストン
AS USUAL, YOUR ENGLISH WAS FINE, HORI.
OH... UH-HUH... THANK YOU.
WHAT'LL I DO...?
HUH? THAT DOESN'T MAKE YOU HAPPY?
IT'S FINE...
NO WAY ANY OF THIS'LL STICK...
...UM!
ばっ
BA (FWIP)
BIKU (FLINCH)
ビクッ
WHAT? GOT A STOMACH-ACHE?
OH!
ASK HIM, MIYAMURA.
FIND OUT WHY HIS HAIR IS LIKE THAT.
GATAN
ガタン
YOU CAN DO IT, MIYAMURA-KUN!

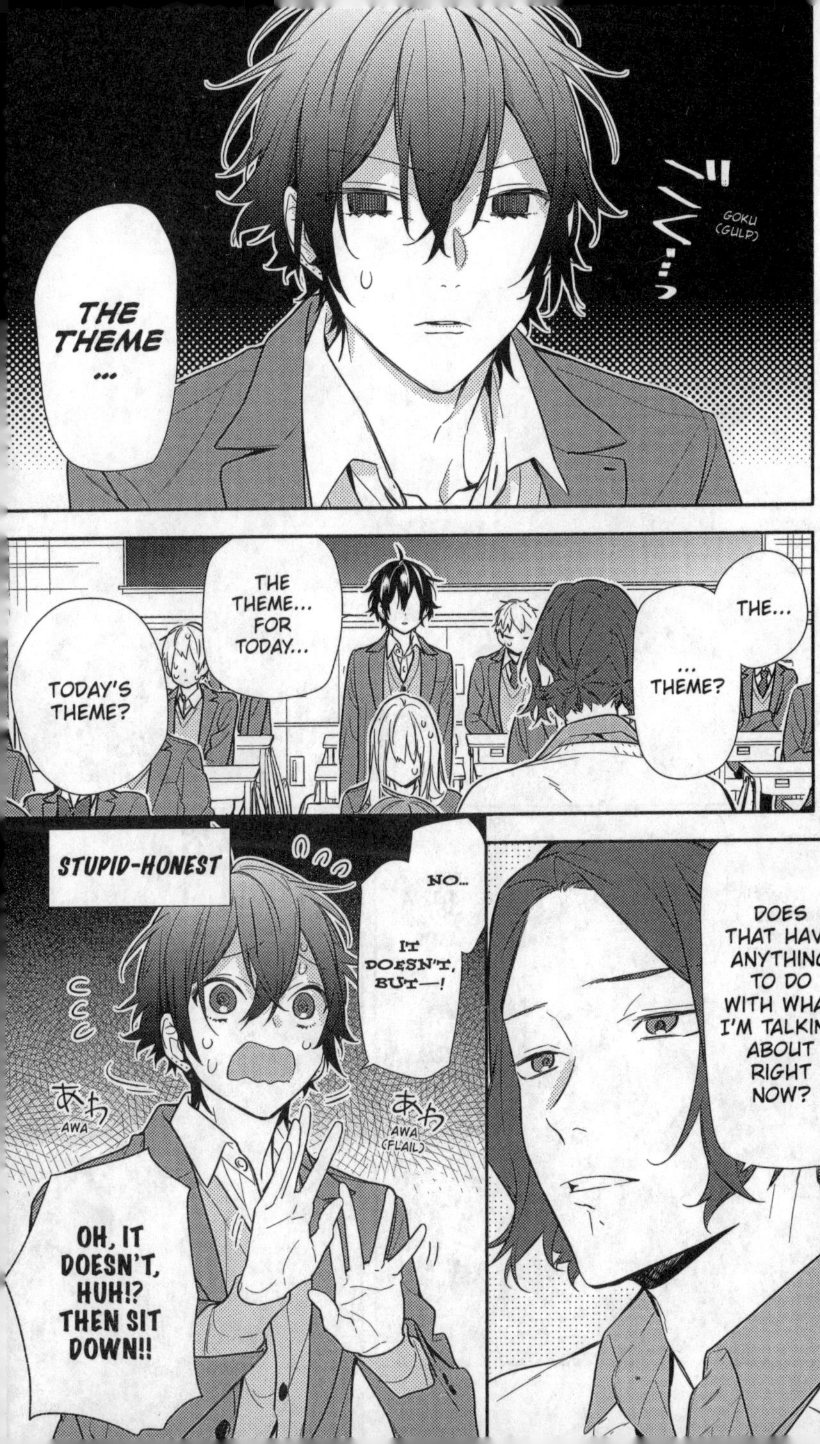
GOKU (GULP)
THE THEME...
THE... ...THEME?
THE THEME... FOR TODAY...
TODAY'S THEME?
DOES THAT HAVE ANYTHING TO DO WITH WHAT I'M TALKING ABOUT RIGHT NOW?
NO... IT DOESN'T, BUT—!
STUPID-HONEST
あわ AWA (FLAIL)
あわ AWA
OH, IT DOESN'T, HUH!? THEN SIT DOWN!!

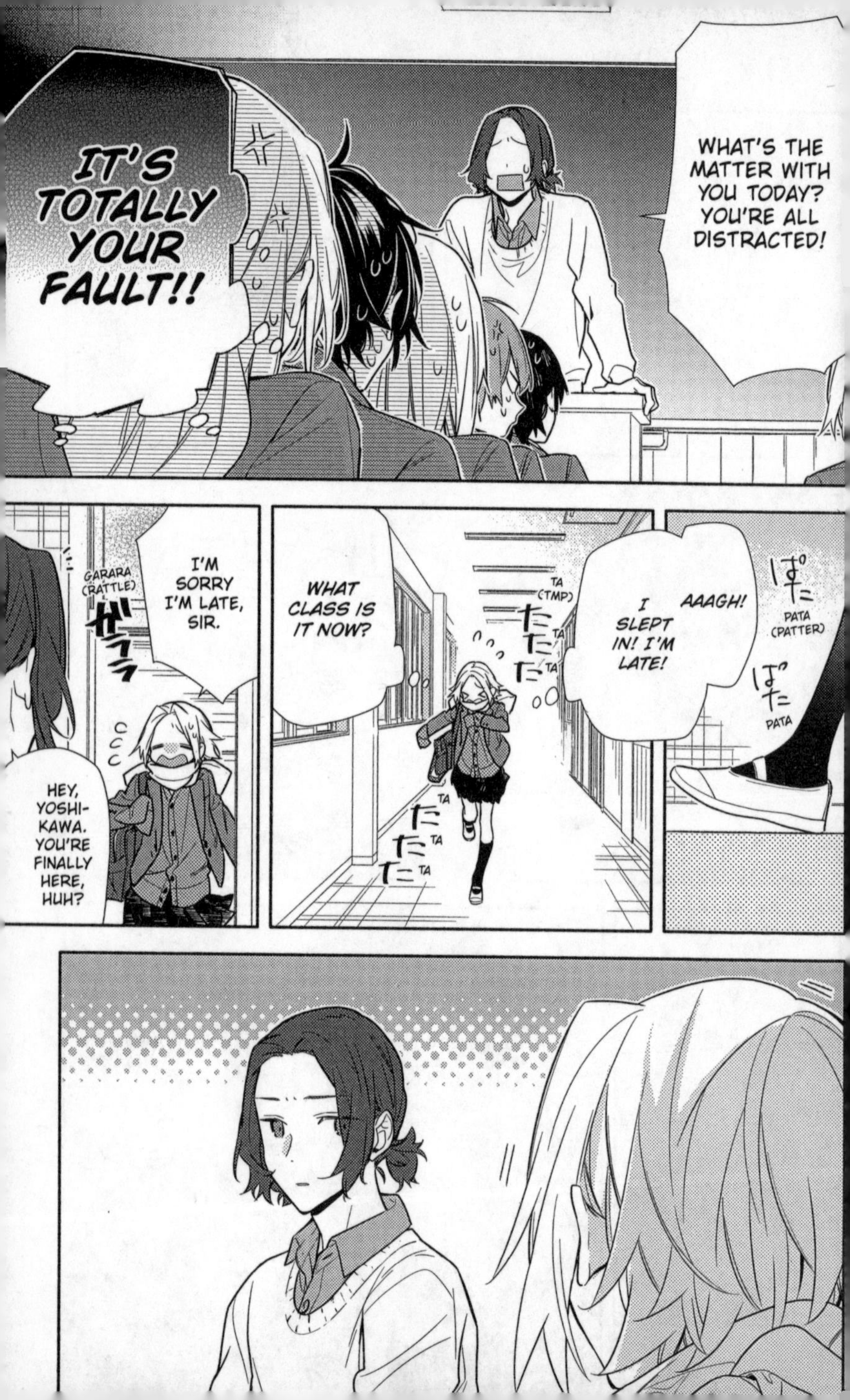
WHAT'S THE MATTER WITH YOU TODAY? YOU'RE ALL DISTRACTED!
IT'S TOTALLY YOUR FAULT!!
ぱた
PATA (PATTER)
ぱた
PATA
AAAGH! I SLEPT IN! I'M LATE!
たたた
TA (TMP) TA TA
WHAT CLASS IS IT NOW?
たたた
TA TA TA
I'M SORRY I'M LATE, SIR.
GARARA (RATTLE)
HEY, YOSHIKAWA. YOU'RE FINALLY HERE, HUH?

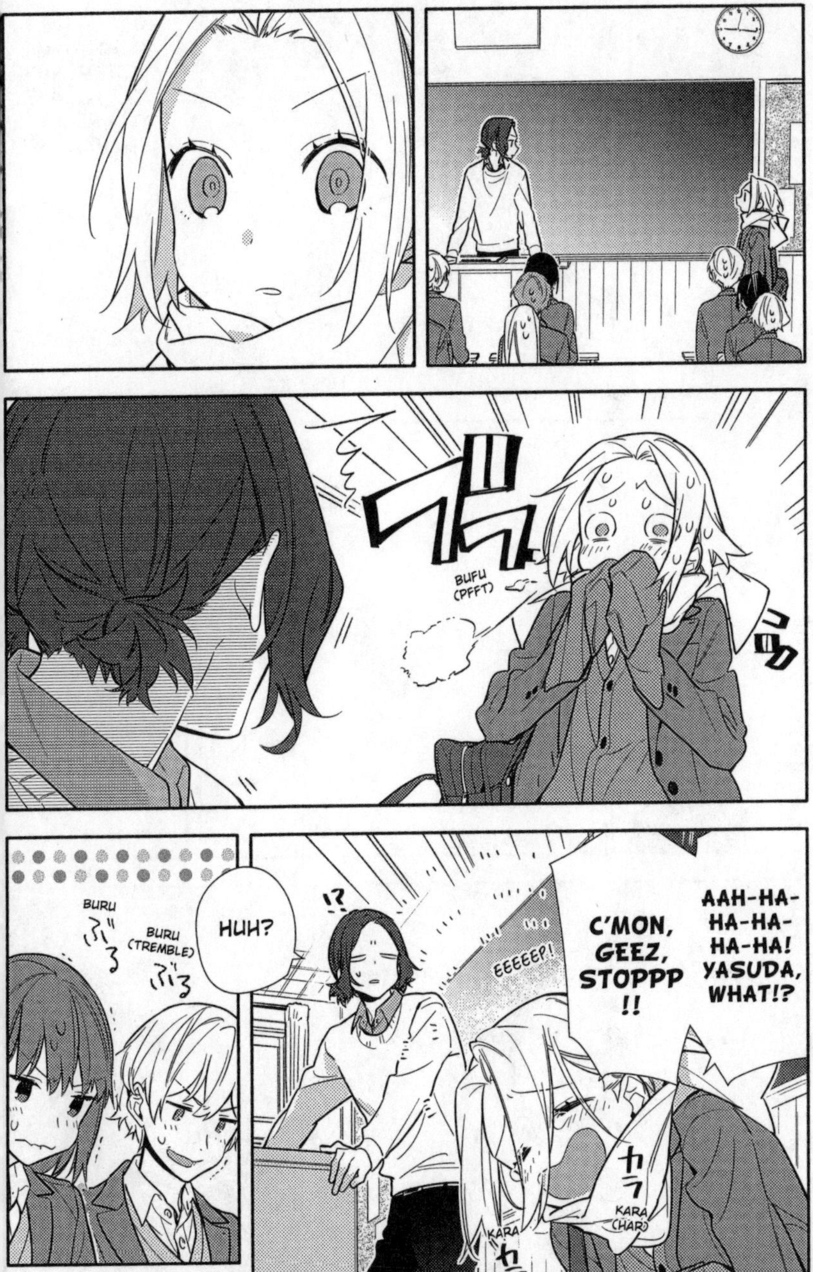
BUFU
(PFFT)
AAH-HA-HA-HA-HA-HA! YASUDA, WHAT!?
C'MON, GEEZ, STOPPP!!
EEEEEP!
!?
KARA
(HAR)
カラ
KARA
カラ
HUH?
BURU
(TREMBLE)
ぶる
BURU
ぶる

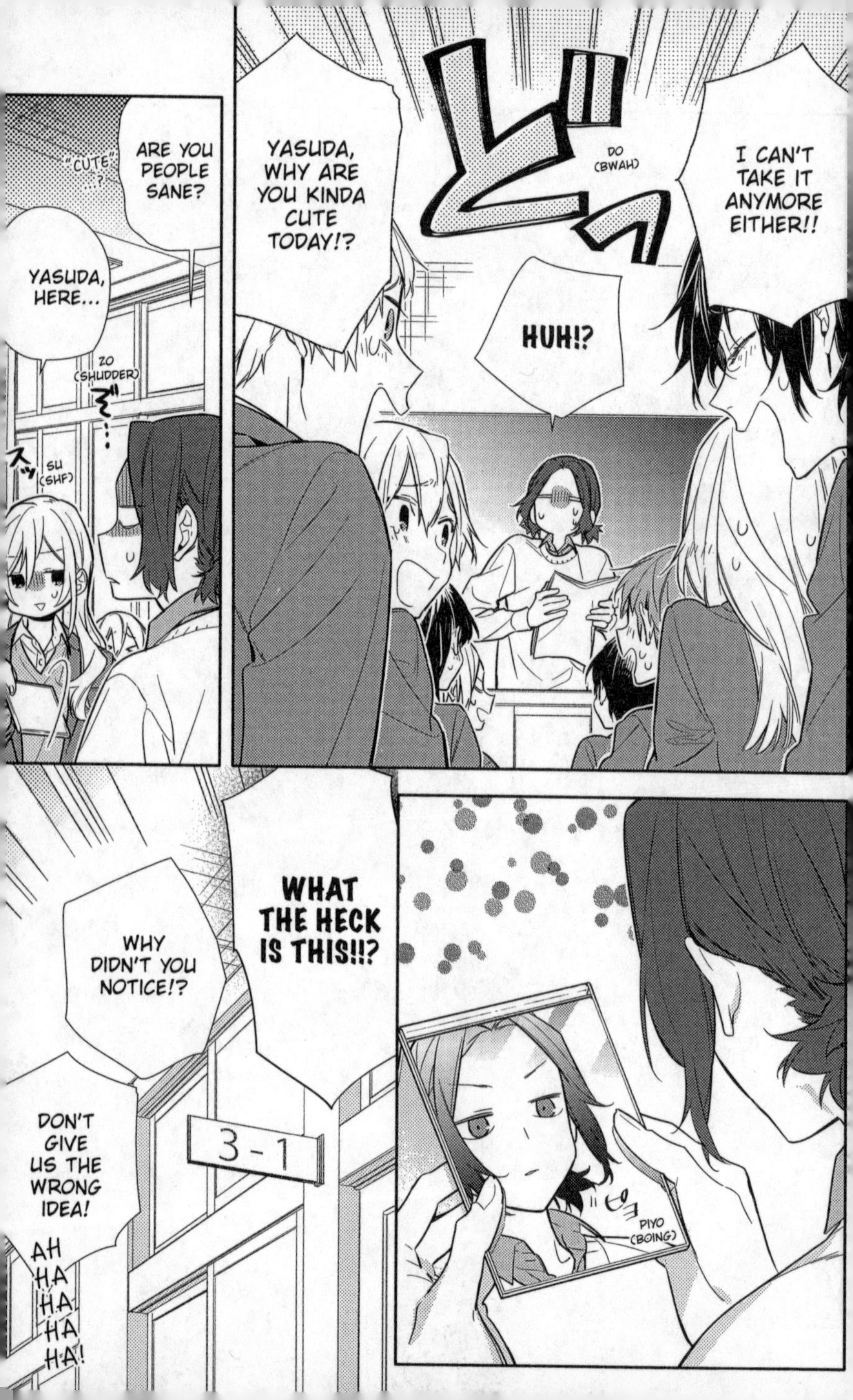
I CAN'T TAKE IT ANYMORE EITHER!!
DO (BWAH)
YASUDA, WHY ARE YOU KINDA CUTE TODAY!?
HUH!?
ARE YOU PEOPLE SANE?
"CUTE"...?
YASUDA, HERE...
ZO (SHUDDER)
SU (SHF)
PIYO (BOING)
WHAT THE HECK IS THIS!!!?
WHY DIDN'T YOU NOTICE!?
DON'T GIVE US THE WRONG IDEA!
AH HA HA HA HA!
3-1

HORIMIYA

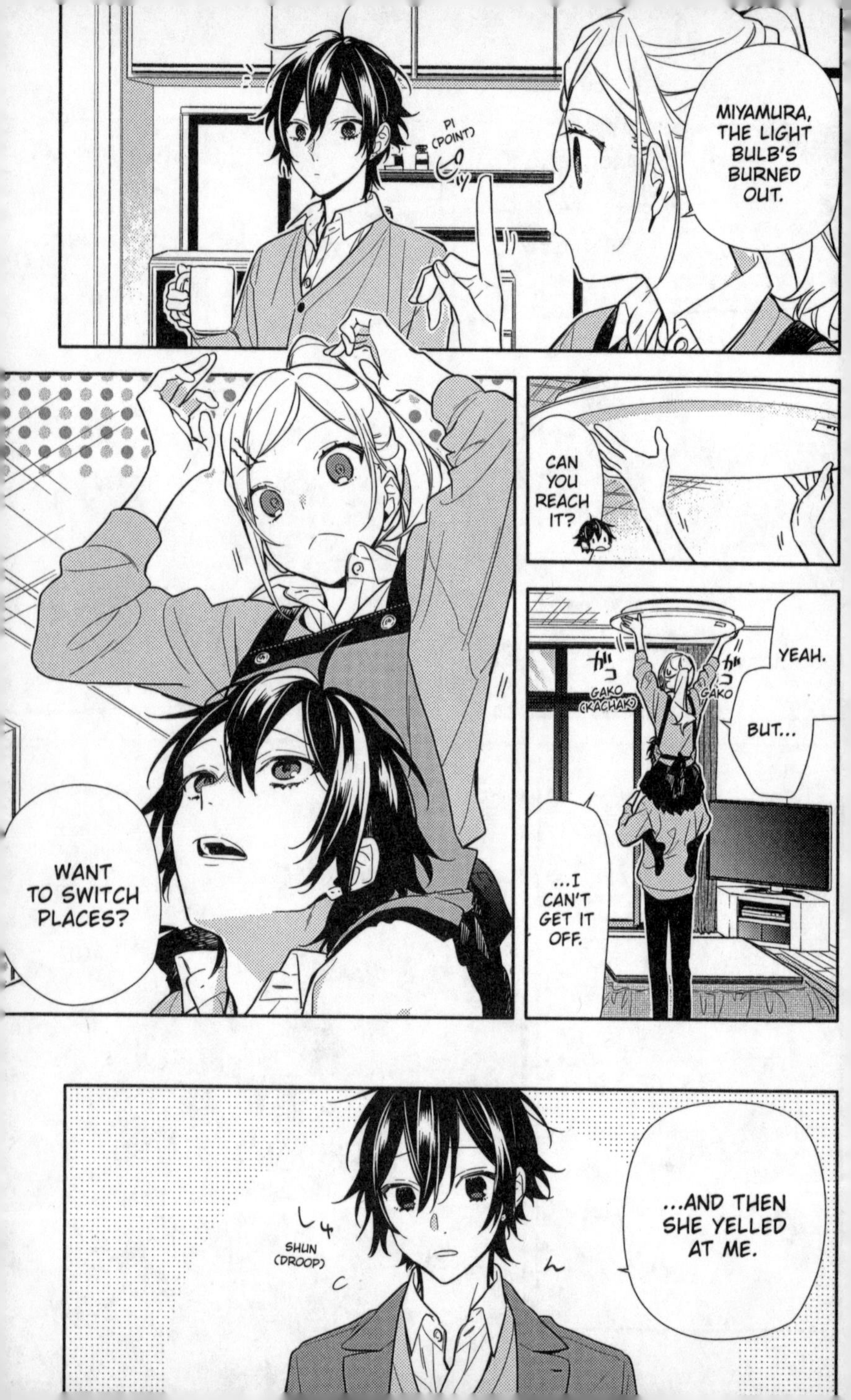
MIYAMURA, THE LIGHT BULB'S BURNED OUT.
PI (POINT)
CAN YOU REACH IT?
WANT TO SWITCH PLACES?
GAKO GAKO (KACHAK)
YEAH.
BUT...
...I CAN'T GET IT OFF.
...AND THEN SHE YELLED AT ME.
SHUN (DROOP)

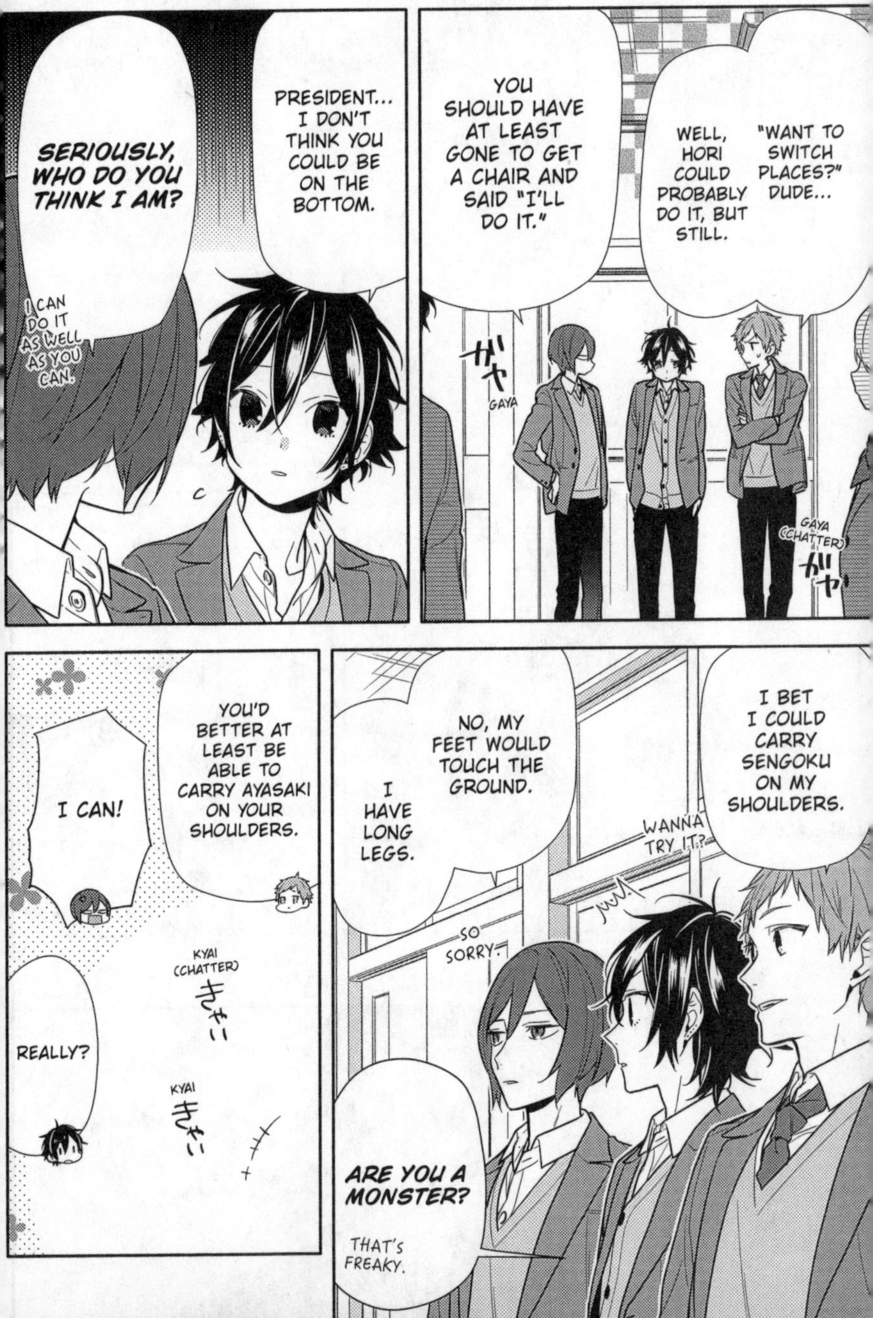
"WANT TO SWITCH PLACES?" DUDE...
WELL, HORI COULD PROBABLY DO IT, BUT STILL.
YOU SHOULD HAVE AT LEAST GONE TO GET A CHAIR AND SAID "I'LL DO IT."
ガヤ GAYA
GAYA (CHATTER) ガヤ
PRESIDENT... I DON'T THINK YOU COULD BE ON THE BOTTOM.
SERIOUSLY, WHO DO YOU THINK I AM?
I CAN DO IT AS WELL AS YOU CAN.
I BET I COULD CARRY SENGOKU ON MY SHOULDERS.
WANNA TRY IT?
NO, MY FEET WOULD TOUCH THE GROUND.
I HAVE LONG LEGS.
SO SORRY.
ARE YOU A MONSTER?
THAT'S FREAKY.
YOU'D BETTER AT LEAST BE ABLE TO CARRY AYASAKI ON YOUR SHOULDERS.
I CAN!
KYAI (CHATTER) きゃい
REALLY?
KYAI きゃい

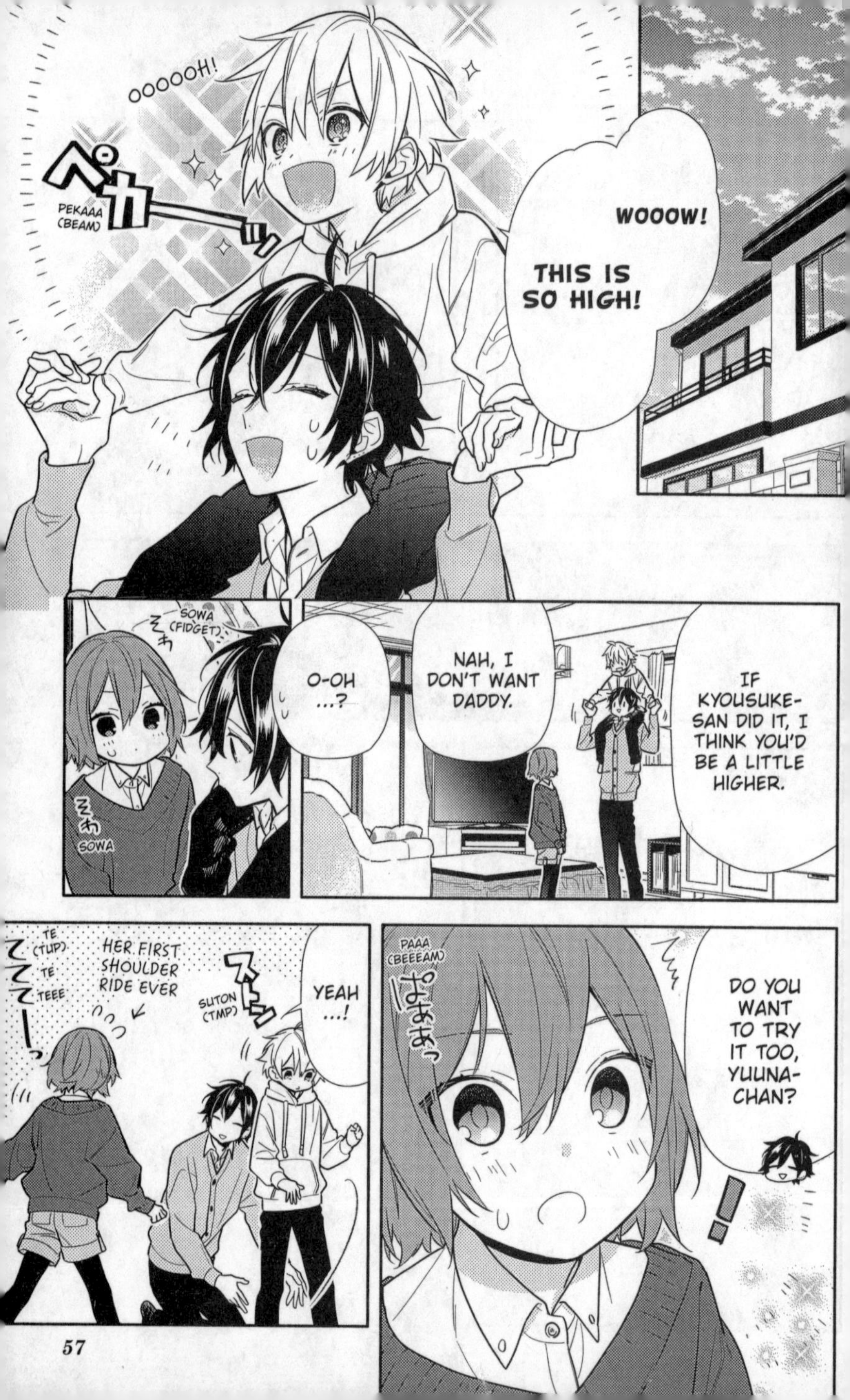
WOOOW!
THIS IS SO HIGH!
OOOOOH!
ペカー
PEKAAA (BEAM)
IF KYOUSUKE-SAN DID IT, I THINK YOU'D BE A LITTLE HIGHER.
NAH, I DON'T WANT DADDY.
O-OH ...?
SOWA (FIDGET)
SOWA
DO YOU WANT TO TRY IT TOO, YUUNA-CHAN?
PAAA (BEEEAM)
ぱあっ
YEAH ...!
SUTON (TMP)
HER FIRST SHOULDER RIDE EVER
TE (TUP) TE TEEE

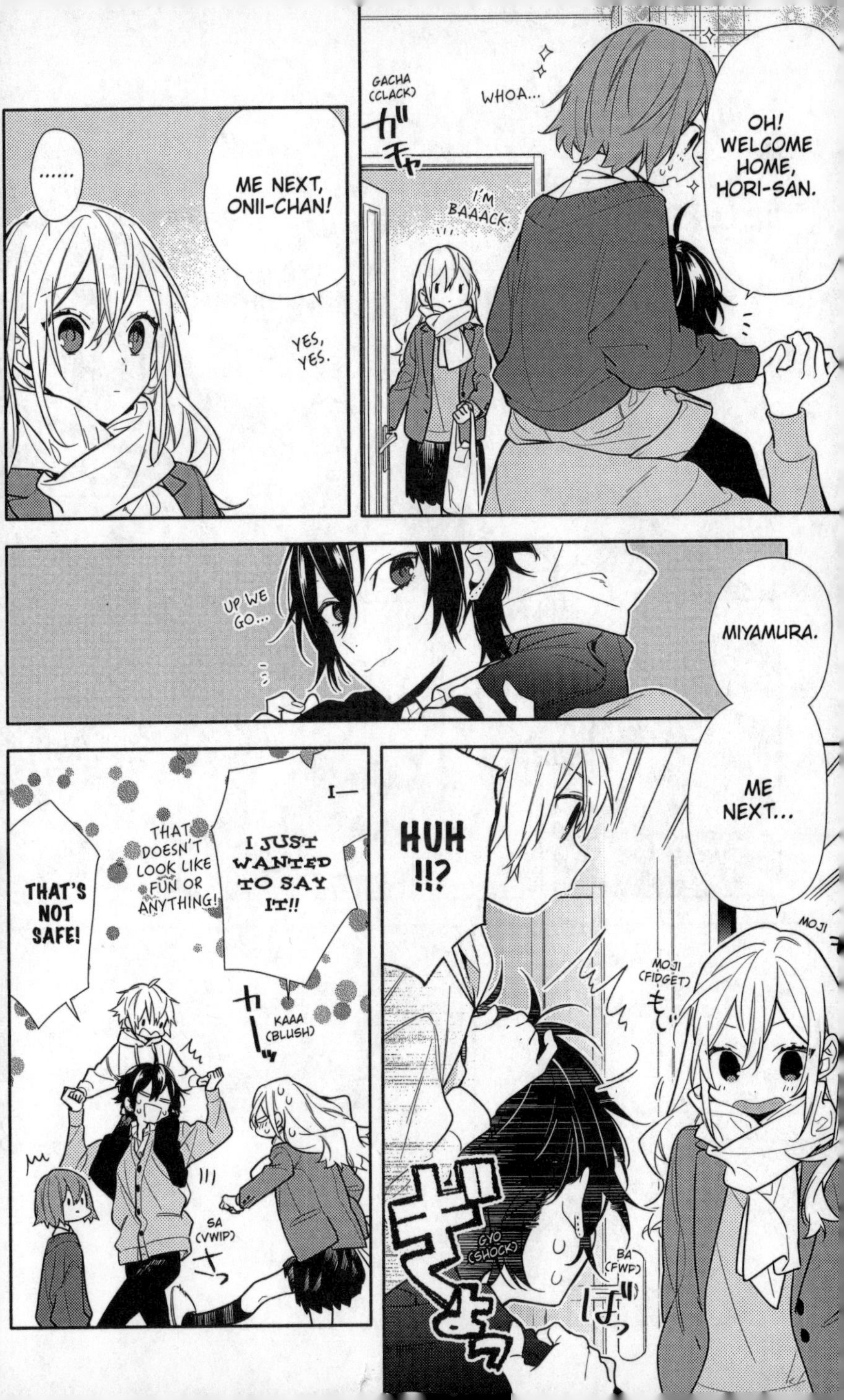
OH! WELCOME HOME, HORI-SAN.
WHOA...
GACHA (CLACK)
ガチャ
I'M BAAACK.
ME NEXT, ONII-CHAN!
......
YES, YES.
MIYAMURA.
UP WE GO...
ME NEXT...
MOJI
HUH!!?
MOJI (FIDGET)
BA (FWP)
GYO (SHOCK)
I—
I JUST WANTED TO SAY IT!!
KAAA (BLUSH)
カーッ
THAT DOESN'T LOOK LIKE FUN OR ANYTHING!
THAT'S NOT SAFE!
SA (VWIP)

Page·113

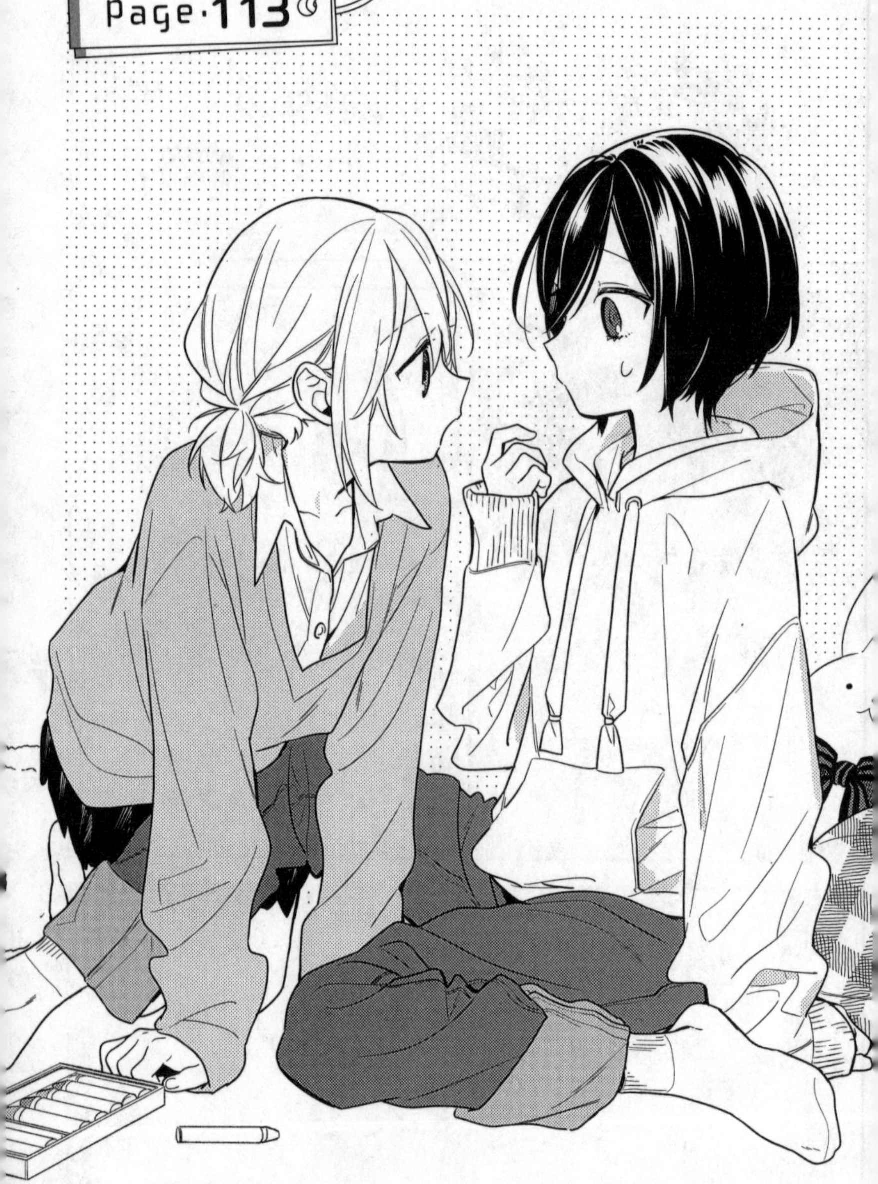

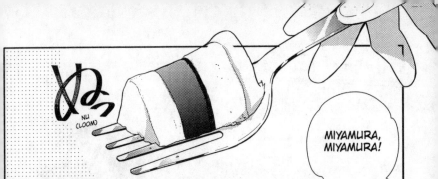

ぬっ
NU
(LOOM)

MIYAMURA, MIYAMURA!

HERE, I'LL FEED YOU!

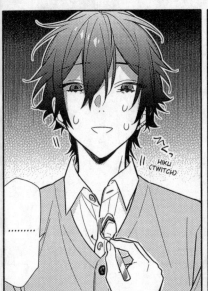

SAY "AAAH."

HIKU
(TWITCH)

....

SU
(SHF)

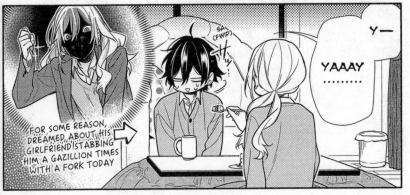

SA
(FWIP)

Y—

YAAAY
....

FOR SOME REASON, DREAMED ABOUT HIS GIRLFRIEND STABBING HIM A GAZILLION TIMES WITH A FORK TODAY

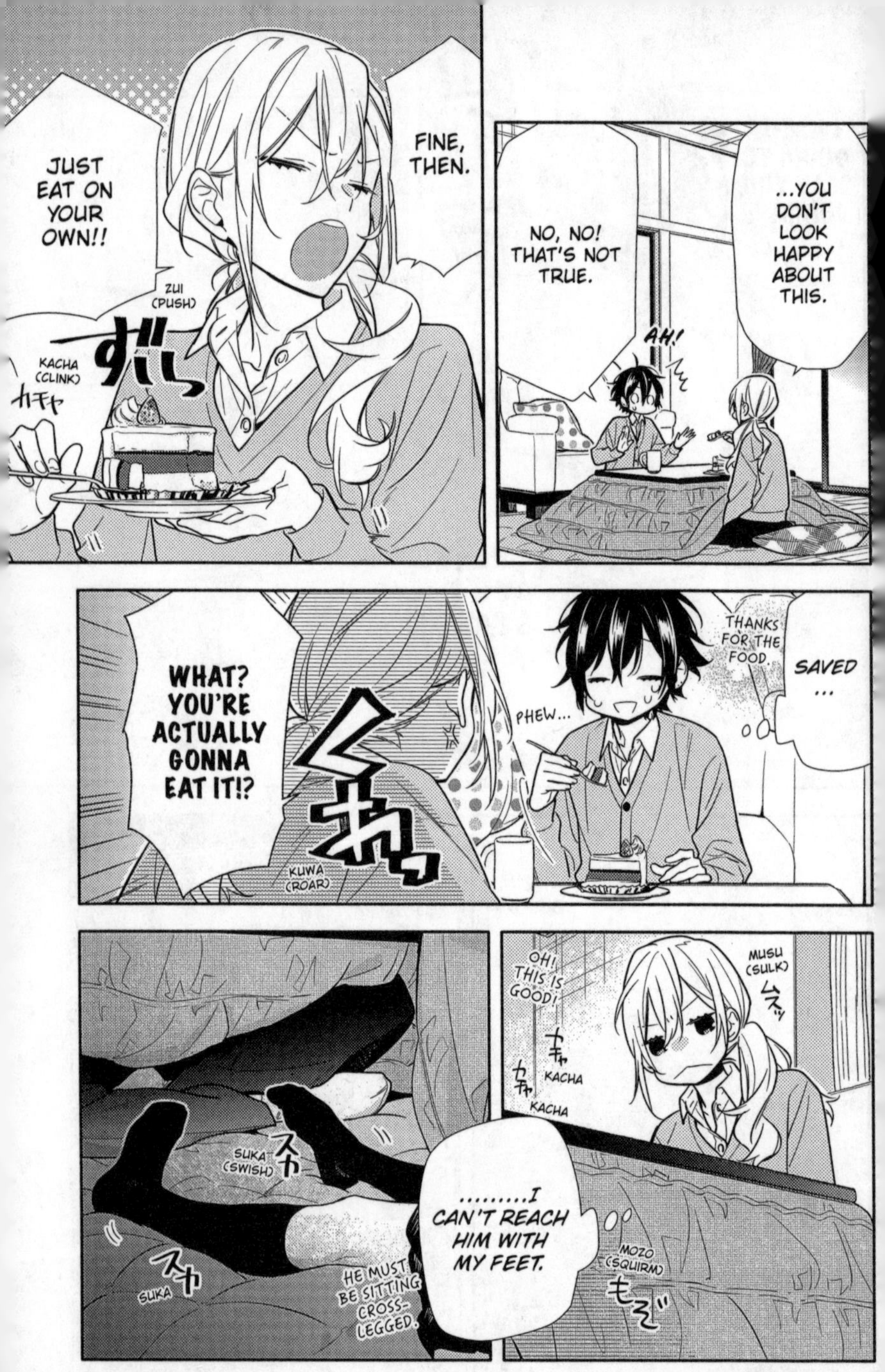

...YOU DON'T LOOK HAPPY ABOUT THIS.
NO, NO! THAT'S NOT TRUE.
AH!
FINE, THEN.
JUST EAT ON YOUR OWN!!
ZUI (PUSH)
KACHA (CLINK)
SAVED...
THANKS FOR THE FOOD.
PHEW...
WHAT? YOU'RE ACTUALLY GONNA EAT IT!?
KUWA (ROAR)
MUSU (SULK)
OH! THIS IS GOOD!
KACHA
KACHA
MOZO (SQUIRM)
.........I CAN'T REACH HIM WITH MY FEET.
HE MUST BE SITTING CROSS-LEGGED.
SUKA (SWISH)
SUKA

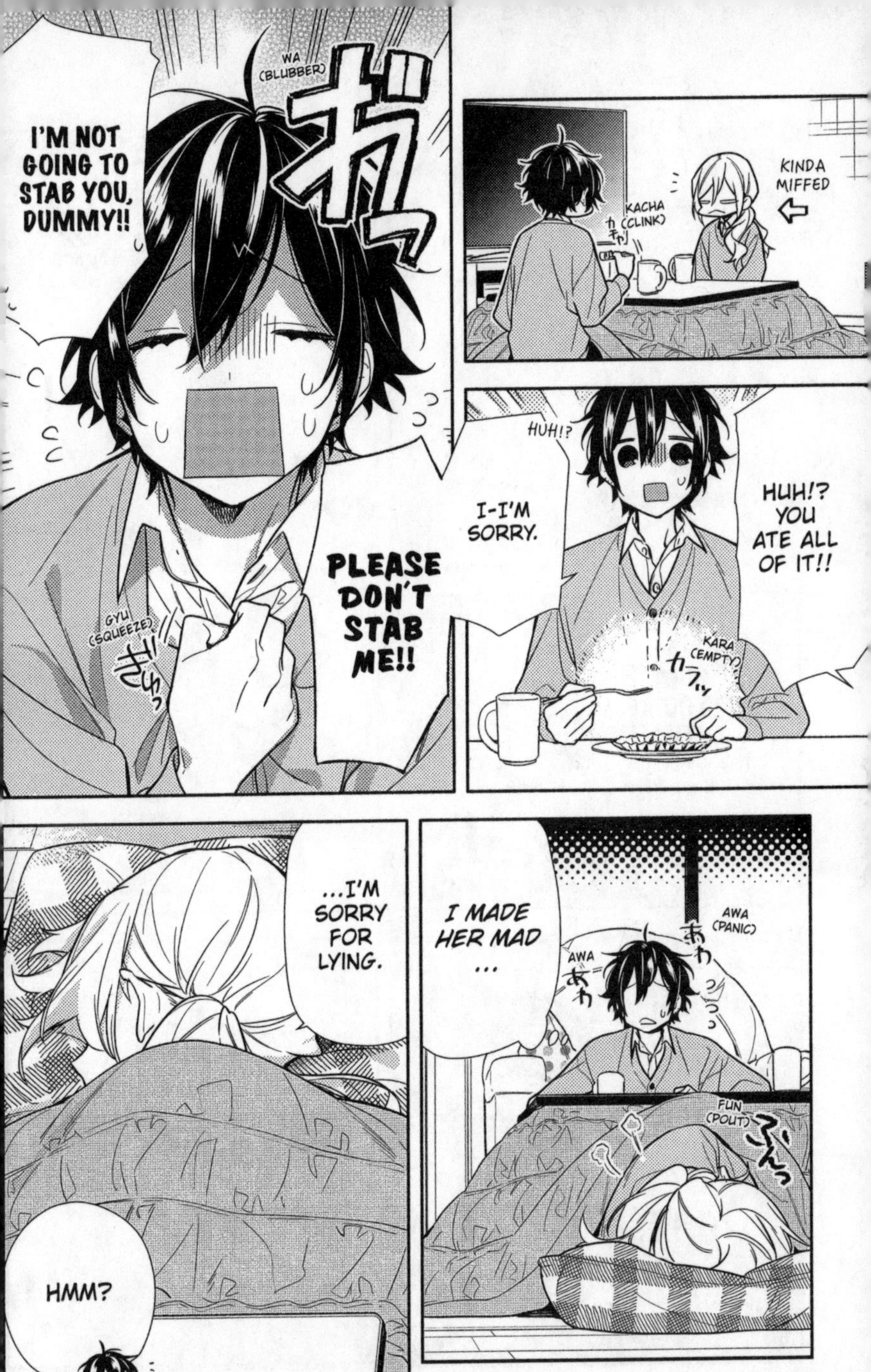
KACHA (CLINK)
KINDA MIFFED
HUH!? YOU ATE ALL OF IT!!
HUH!?
I-I'M SORRY.
KARA (EMPTY)
PLEASE DON'T STAB ME!!
WA (BLUBBER)
I'M NOT GOING TO STAB YOU, DUMMY!!
GYU (SQUEEZE)
AWA (PANIC)
AWA
I MADE HER MAD ...
FUN (POUT)
...I'M SORRY FOR LYING.
HMM?

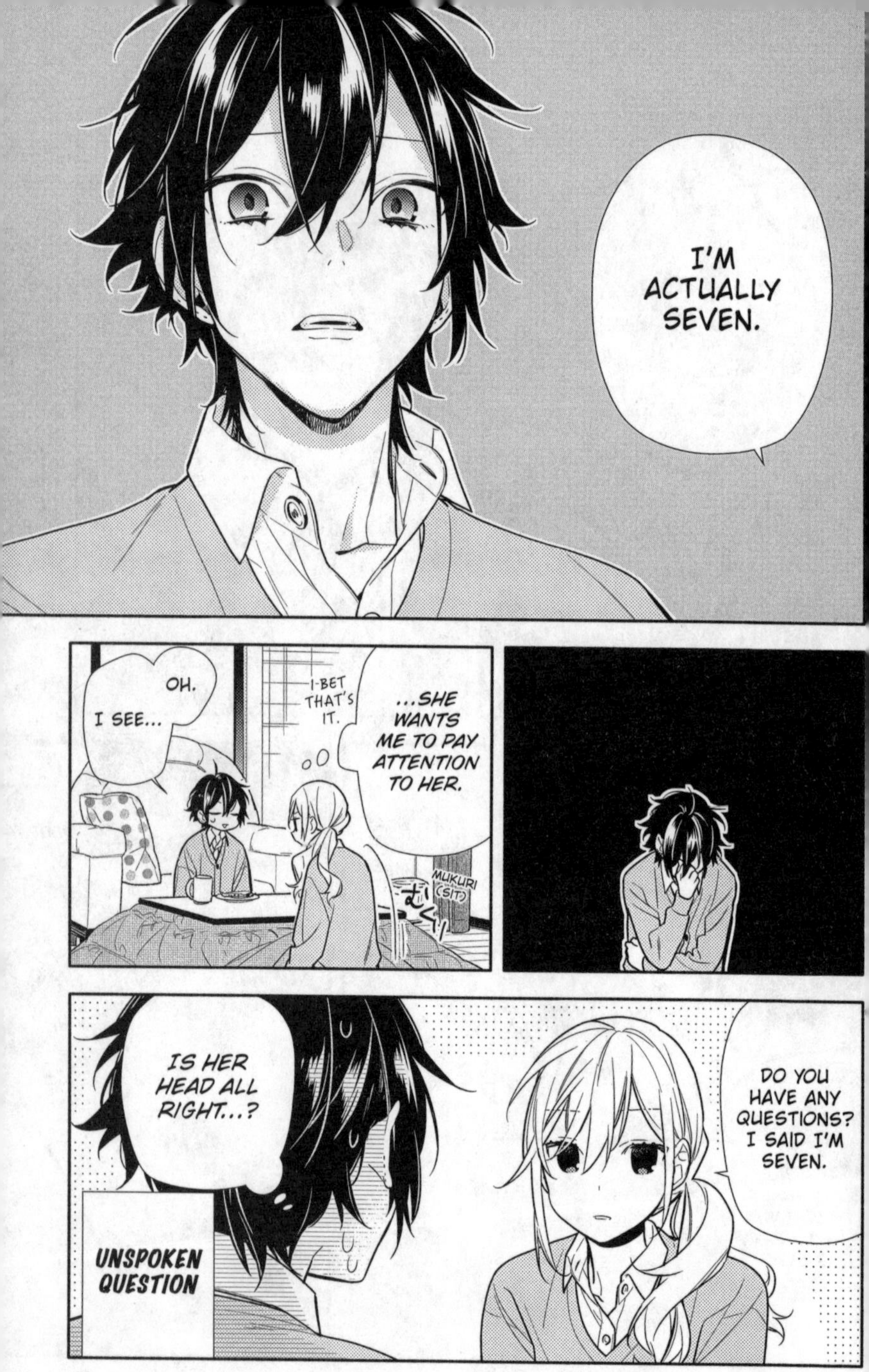
I'M ACTUALLY SEVEN.
...SHE WANTS ME TO PAY ATTENTION TO HER.
I BET THAT'S IT.
MUKURI (SIT)
OH. I SEE...
DO YOU HAVE ANY QUESTIONS? I SAID I'M SEVEN.
IS HER HEAD ALL RIGHT...?
UNSPOKEN QUESTION

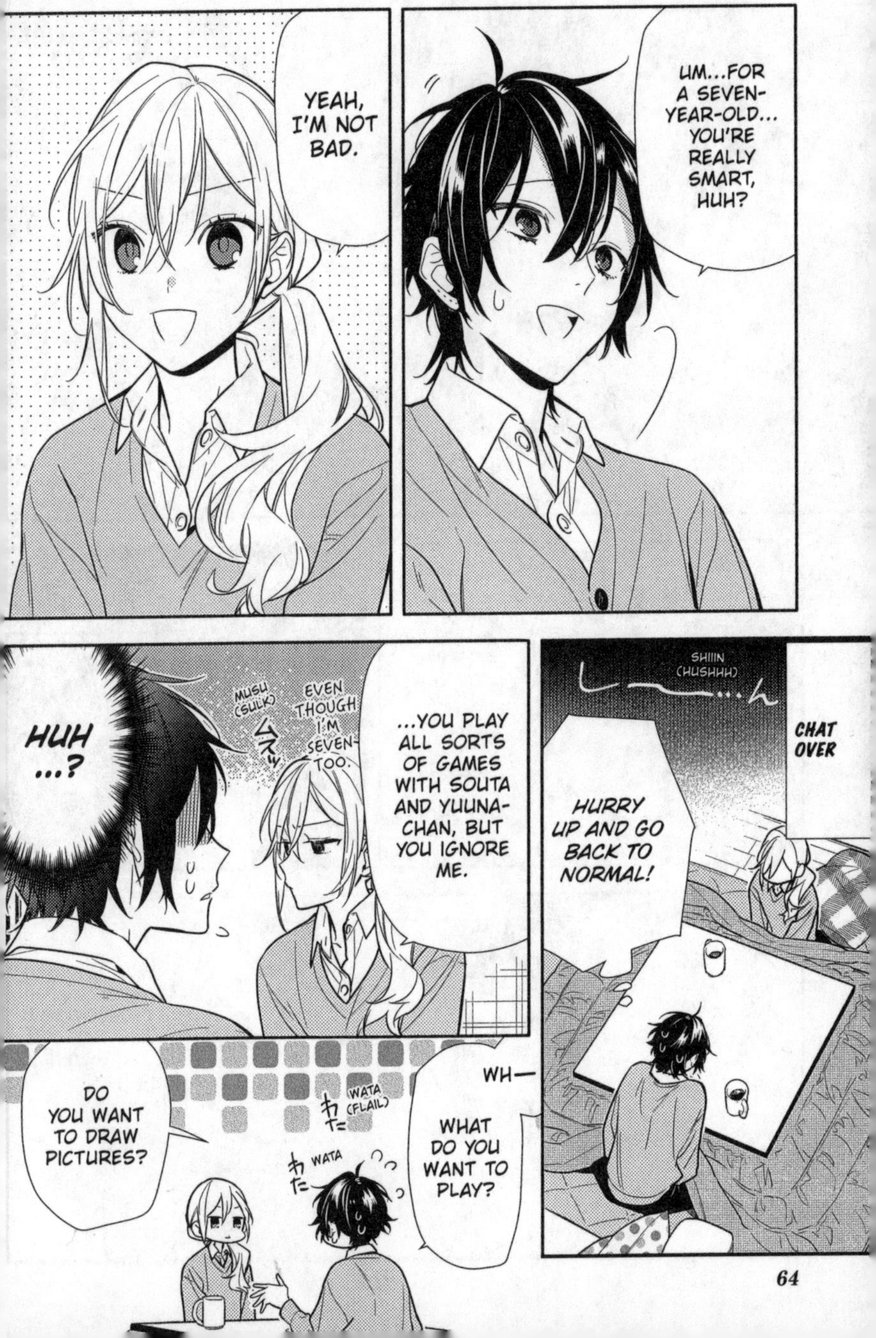
UM...FOR A SEVEN-YEAR-OLD... YOU'RE REALLY SMART, HUH?
YEAH, I'M NOT BAD.
SHIIN (HUSHHH)
CHAT OVER
HURRY UP AND GO BACK TO NORMAL!
EVEN THOUGH I'M SEVEN TOO.
...YOU PLAY ALL SORTS OF GAMES WITH SOUTA AND YUUNA-CHAN, BUT YOU IGNORE ME.
MUSU (SULK)
HUH ...?
WH—
WHAT DO YOU WANT TO PLAY?
WATA (FLAIL)
WATA
DO YOU WANT TO DRAW PICTURES?

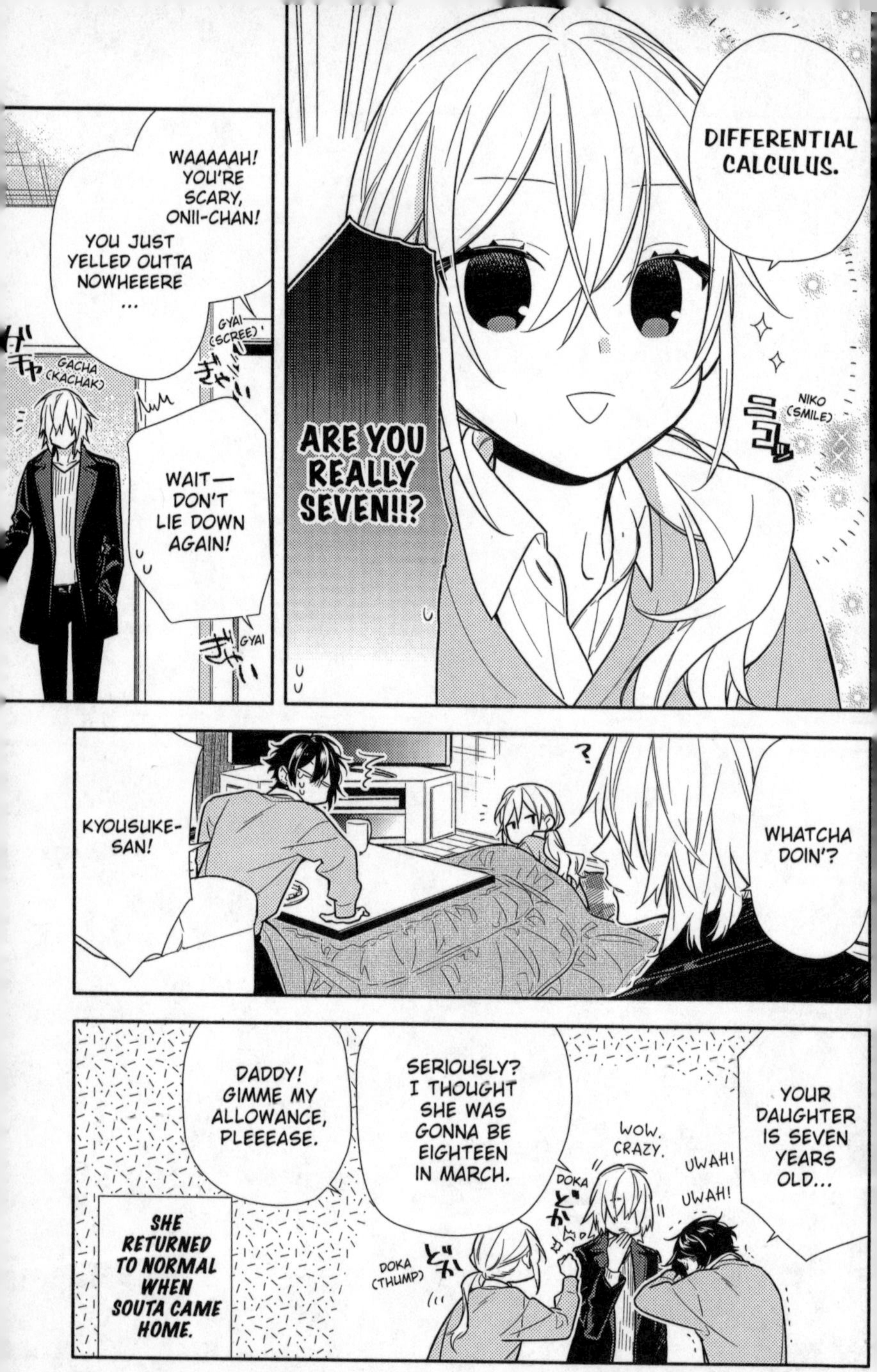
DIFFERENTIAL CALCULUS.
NIKO (SMILE)
ARE YOU REALLY SEVEN!!?
WAAAAAH! YOU'RE SCARY, ONII-CHAN!
YOU JUST YELLED OUTTA NOWHEEERE ...
GYAI (SCREE)
GACHA (KACHAK)
WAIT— DON'T LIE DOWN AGAIN!
GYAI
WHATCHA DOIN'?
?
KYOUSUKE-SAN!
YOUR DAUGHTER IS SEVEN YEARS OLD...
UWAH!
UWAH!
WOW. CRAZY.
DOKA
SERIOUSLY? I THOUGHT SHE WAS GONNA BE EIGHTEEN IN MARCH.
DADDY! GIMME MY ALLOWANCE, PLEEEASE.
DOKA (THUMP)
SHE RETURNED TO NORMAL WHEN SOUTA CAME HOME.

HORIMIYA

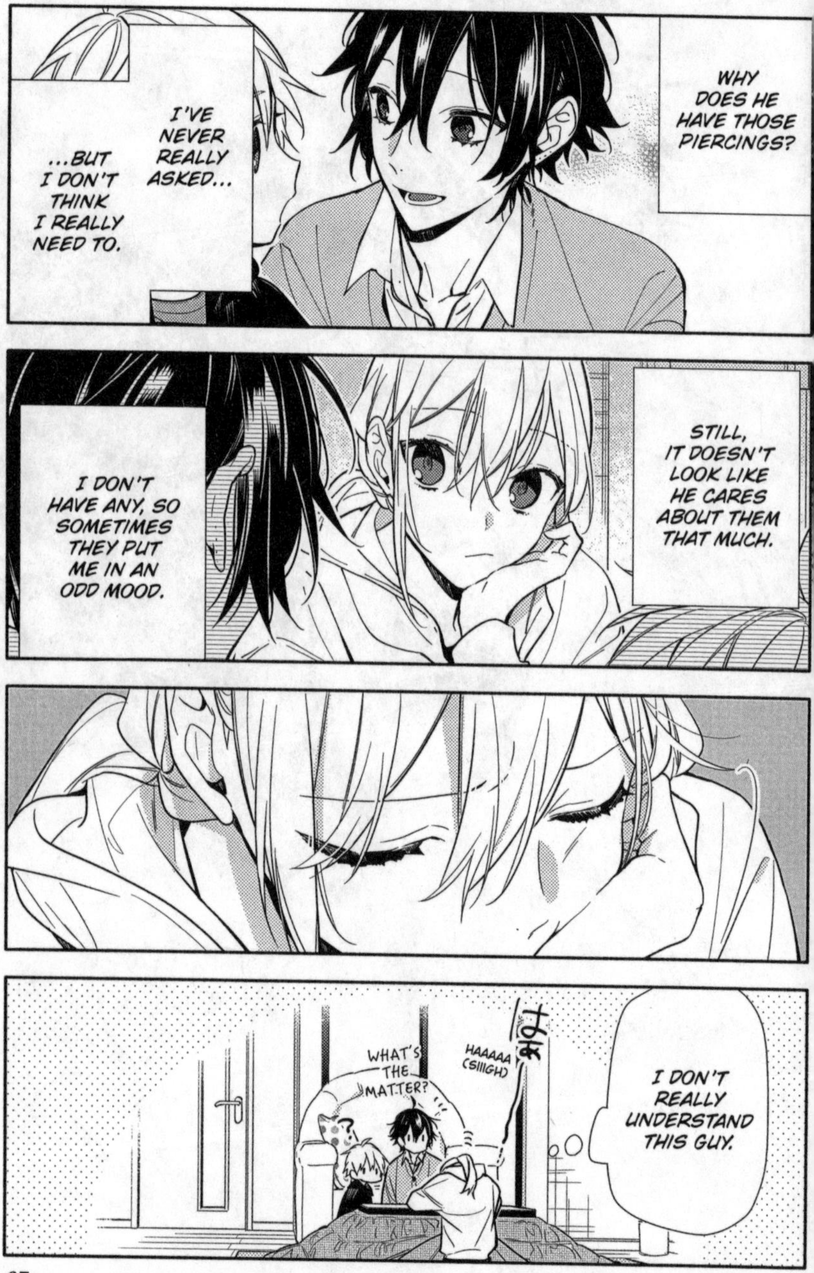
WHY DOES HE HAVE THOSE PIERCINGS?
I'VE NEVER REALLY ASKED...
...BUT I DON'T THINK I REALLY NEED TO.
STILL, IT DOESN'T LOOK LIKE HE CARES ABOUT THEM THAT MUCH.
I DON'T HAVE ANY, SO SOMETIMES THEY PUT ME IN AN ODD MOOD.
I DON'T REALLY UNDERSTAND THIS GUY.
はぁ
HAAAAA (SIIIGH)
WHAT'S THE MATTER?

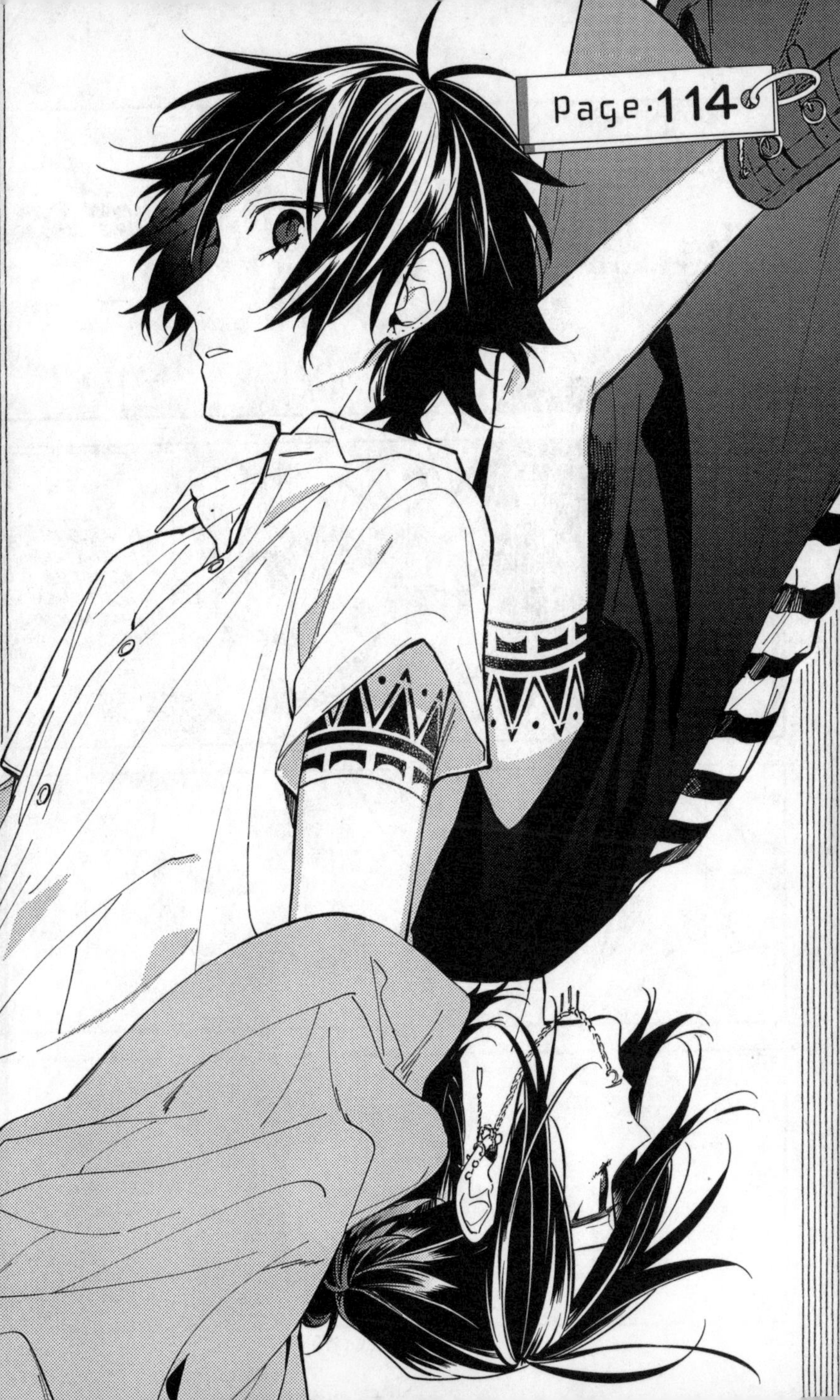
Page.114

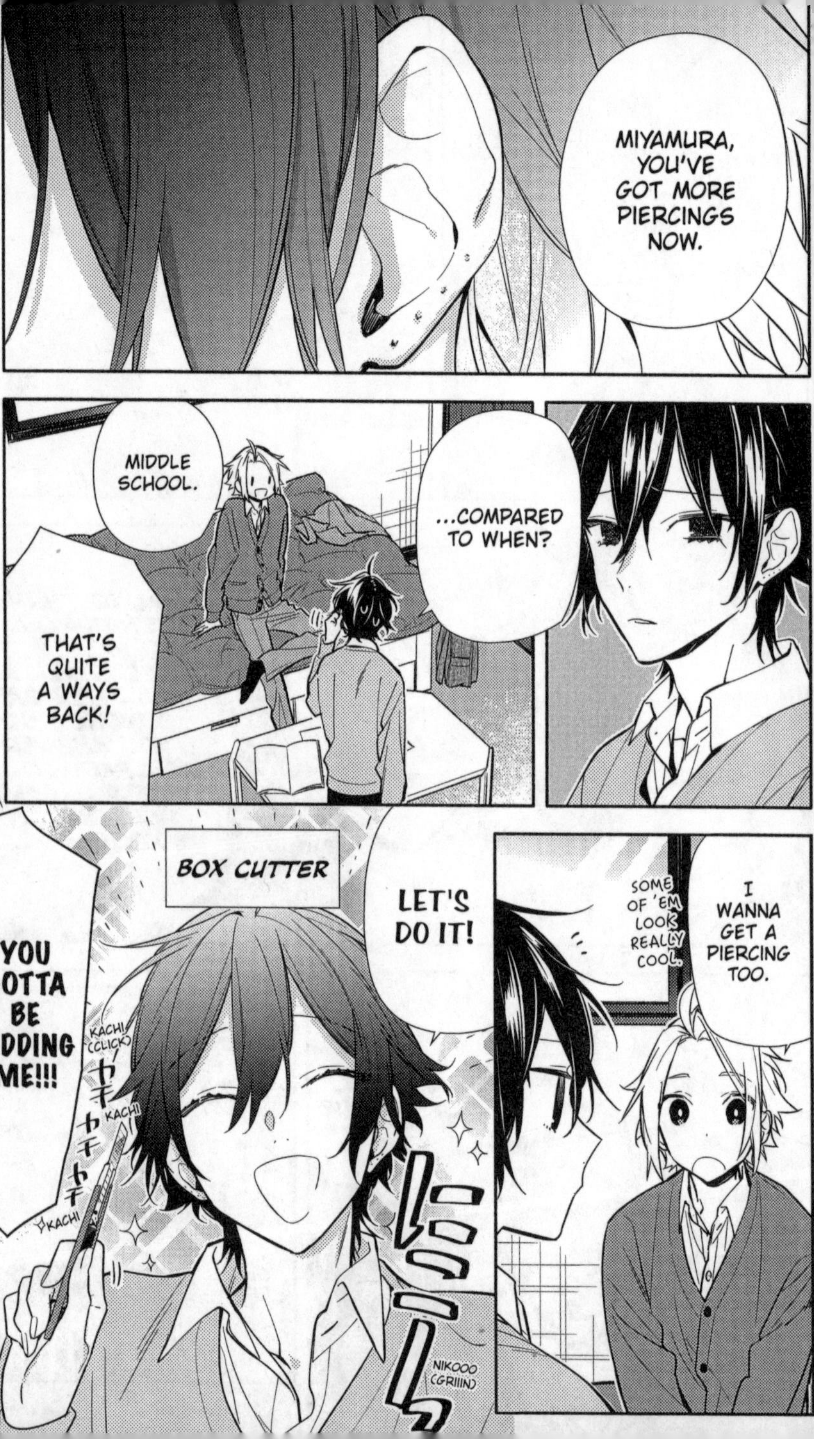
MIYAMURA, YOU'VE GOT MORE PIERCINGS NOW.
...COMPARED TO WHEN?
MIDDLE SCHOOL.
THAT'S QUITE A WAYS BACK!
I WANNA GET A PIERCING TOO.
SOME OF 'EM LOOK REALLY COOL.
LET'S DO IT!
BOX CUTTER
KACHI (CLICK)
KACHI
KACHI
NIKOOO (GRIIIN)
YOU GOTTA BE KIDDING ME!!!

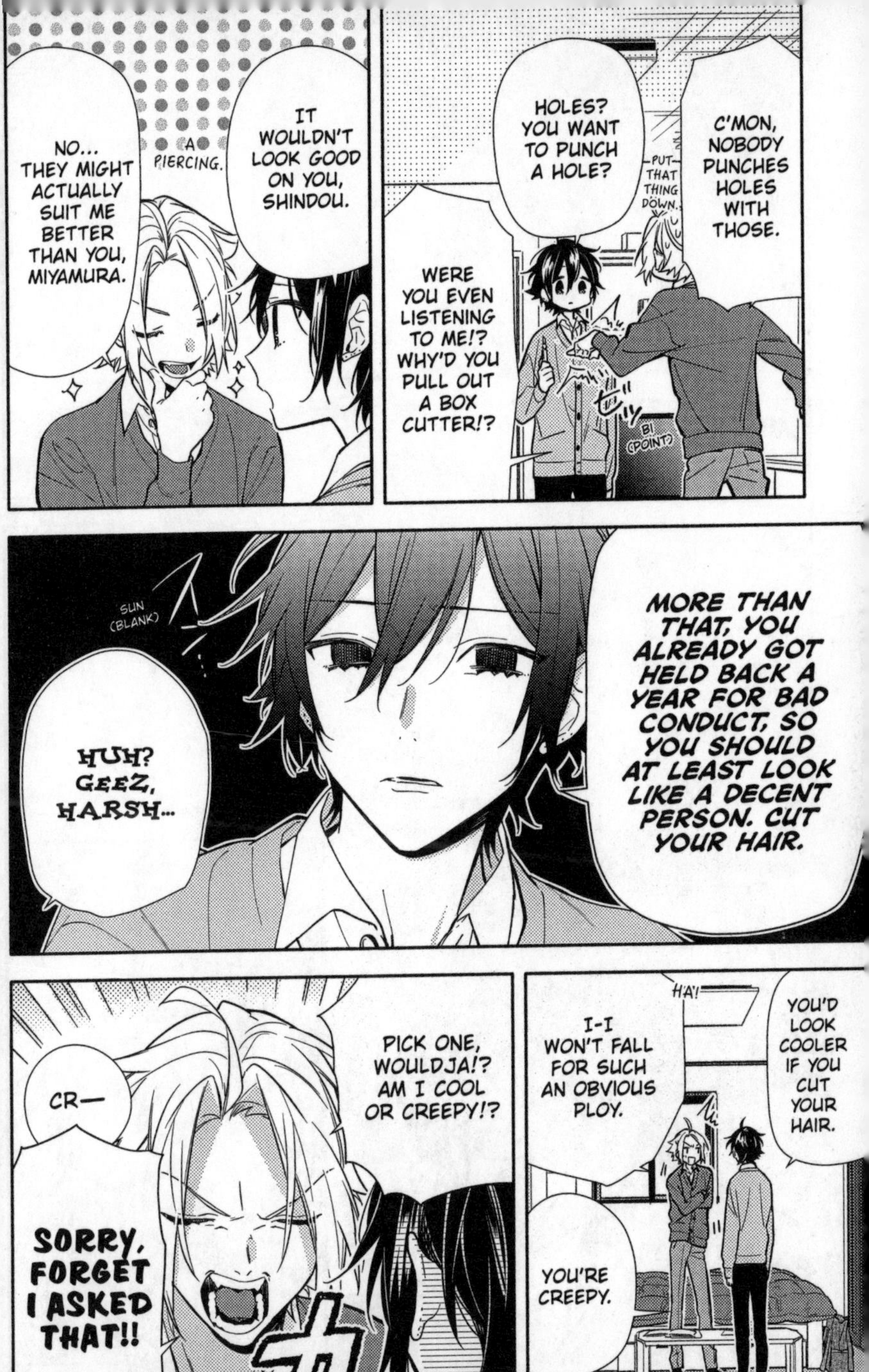
C'MON, NOBODY PUNCHES HOLES WITH THOSE.
PUT THAT THING DOWN.
HOLES? YOU WANT TO PUNCH A HOLE?
WERE YOU EVEN LISTENING TO ME!? WHY'D YOU PULL OUT A BOX CUTTER!?
BI (POINT)
IT WOULDN'T LOOK GOOD ON YOU, SHINDOU.
A PIERCING.
NO... THEY MIGHT ACTUALLY SUIT ME BETTER THAN YOU, MIYAMURA.
MORE THAN THAT, YOU ALREADY GOT HELD BACK A YEAR FOR BAD CONDUCT, SO YOU SHOULD AT LEAST LOOK LIKE A DECENT PERSON. CUT YOUR HAIR.
SUN (BLANK)
HUH? GEEZ, HARSH...
YOU'D LOOK COOLER IF YOU CUT YOUR HAIR.
HA!
I-I WON'T FALL FOR SUCH AN OBVIOUS PLOY.
YOU'RE CREEPY.
PICK ONE, WOULDJA!? AM I COOL OR CREEPY!?
CR—
SORRY. FORGET I ASKED THAT!!
KA (GRAR)

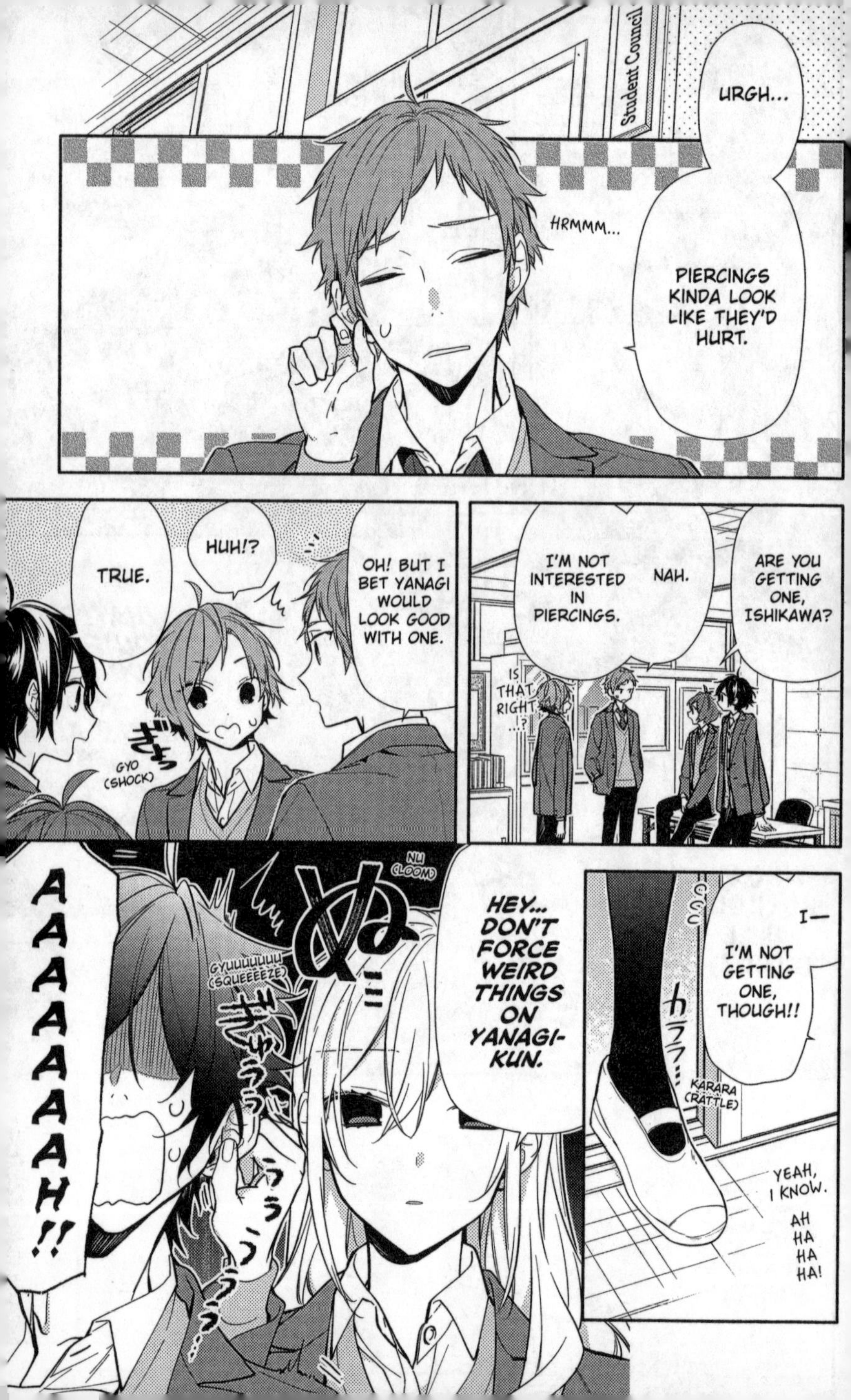
Student Council
URGH...
PIERCINGS KINDA LOOK LIKE THEY'D HURT.
HRMMM...
ARE YOU GETTING ONE, ISHIKAWA?
NAH.
I'M NOT INTERESTED IN PIERCINGS.
IS THAT RIGHT...!?
OH! BUT I BET YANAGI WOULD LOOK GOOD WITH ONE.
HUH!?
TRUE.
GYO (SHOCK)
I—
I'M NOT GETTING ONE, THOUGH!!
KARARA (RATTLE)
YEAH, I KNOW.
AH HA HA HA!
HEY... DON'T FORCE WEIRD THINGS ON YANAGI-KUN.
NU (LOOM)
GYUUUUUUU (SQUEEEEZE)
AAAAAAAAH!!

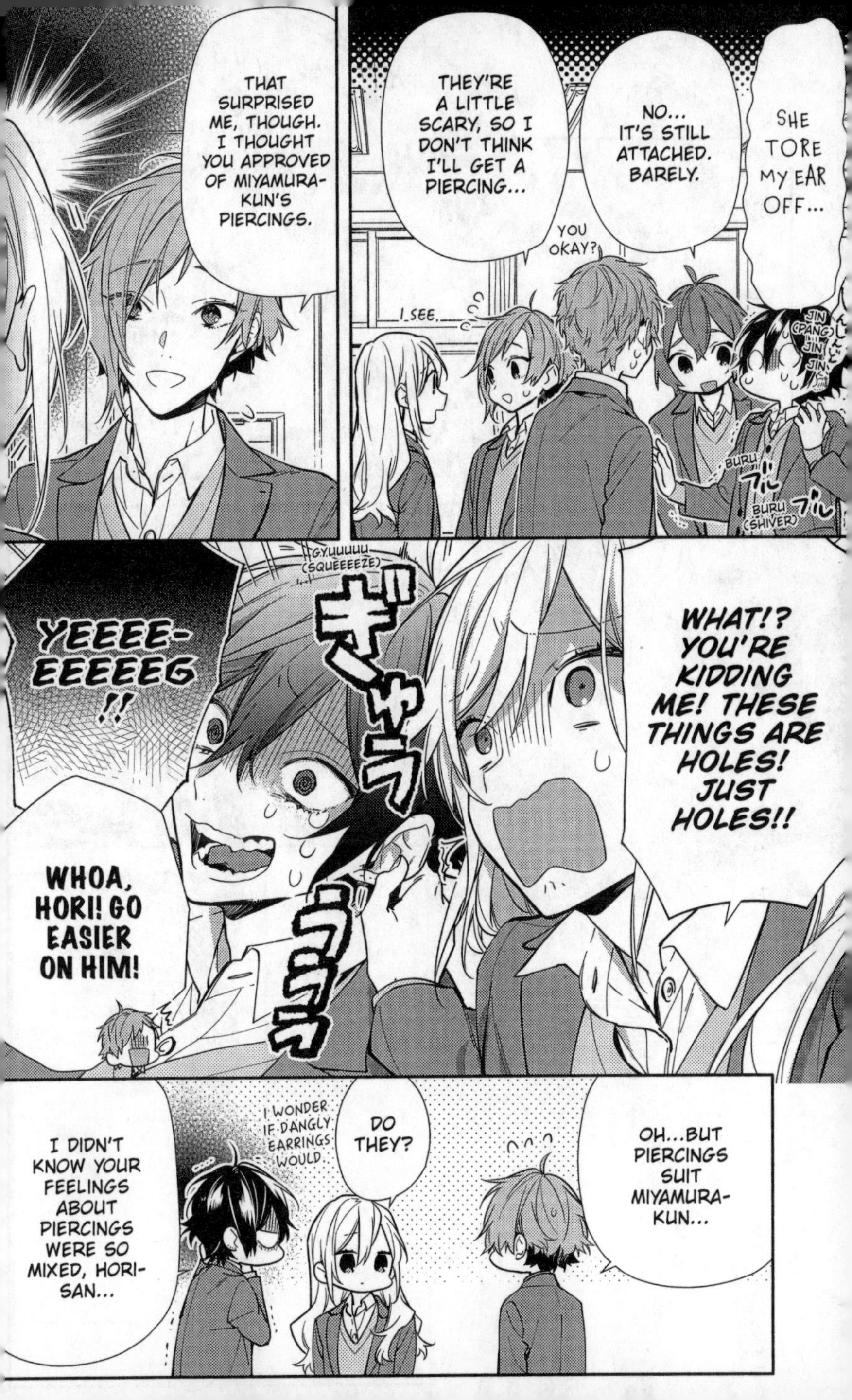
SHE TORE MY EAR OFF...
NO... IT'S STILL ATTACHED. BARELY.
THEY'RE A LITTLE SCARY, SO I DON'T THINK I'LL GET A PIERCING...
YOU OKAY?
JIN (PANG) JIN JIN
I SEE.
BURU BURU (SHIVER)
THAT SURPRISED ME, THOUGH. I THOUGHT YOU APPROVED OF MIYAMURA-KUN'S PIERCINGS.
WHAT!? YOU'RE KIDDING ME! THESE THINGS ARE HOLES! JUST HOLES!!
GYUUUUU (SQUEEEEZE)
YEEEEE-EEEEEG!!
WHOA, HORI! GO EASIER ON HIM!
OH...BUT PIERCINGS SUIT MIYAMURA-KUN...
DO THEY?
I WONDER IF DANGLY EARRINGS WOULD.
I DIDN'T KNOW YOUR FEELINGS ABOUT PIERCINGS WERE SO MIXED, HORI-SAN...

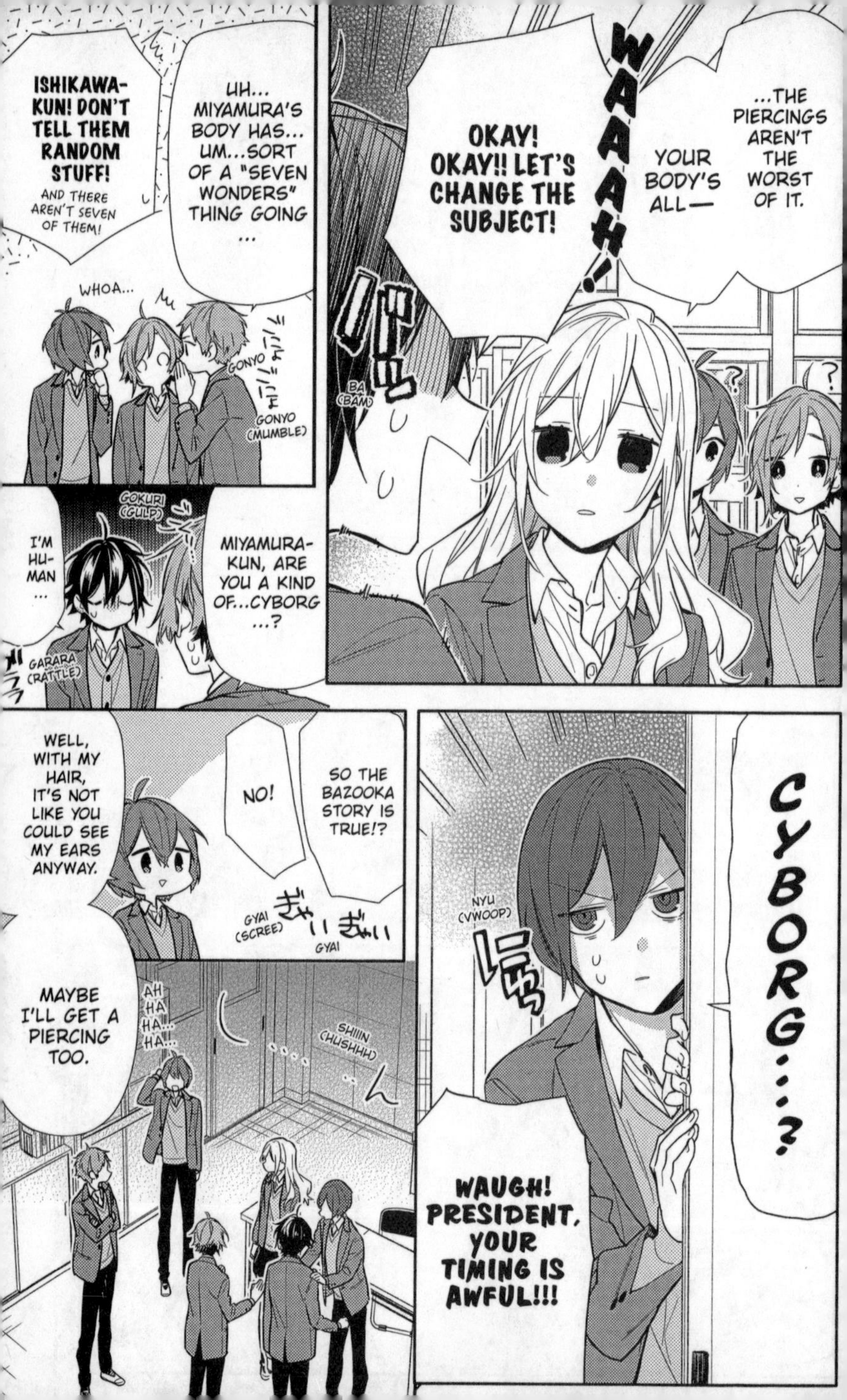
...THE PIERCINGS AREN'T THE WORST OF IT.
YOUR BODY'S ALL—
WAAAAH!
OKAY! OKAY!! LET'S CHANGE THE SUBJECT!
BA (BAM)
UH... MIYAMURA'S BODY HAS... UM...SORT OF A "SEVEN WONDERS" THING GOING...
ISHIKAWA-KUN! DON'T TELL THEM RANDOM STUFF!
AND THERE AREN'T SEVEN OF THEM!
GONYO GONYO (MUMBLE)
WHOA...
MIYAMURA-KUN, ARE YOU A KIND OF...CYBORG...?
GOKURI (GULP)
I'M HU-MAN...
GARARA (RATTLE)
CYBORG...?
NYU (VWOOP)
WAUGH! PRESIDENT, YOUR TIMING IS AWFUL!!!
SO THE BAZOOKA STORY IS TRUE!?
NO!
WELL, WITH MY HAIR, IT'S NOT LIKE YOU COULD SEE MY EARS ANYWAY.
GYAI (SCREE) GYAI
SHIIIN (HUSHHH)
AH HA HA... HA...
MAYBE I'LL GET A PIERCING TOO.

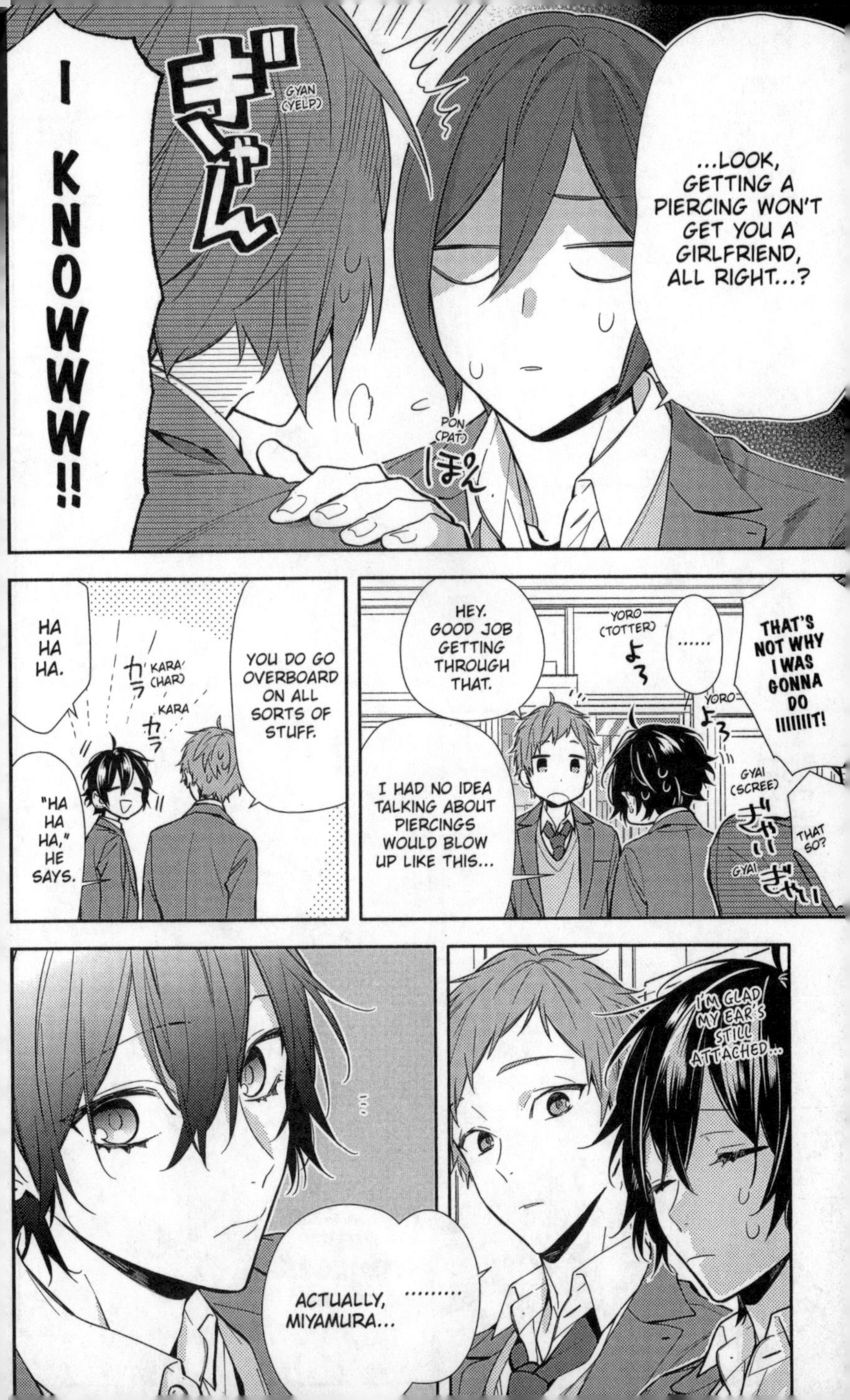
...LOOK, GETTING A PIERCING WON'T GET YOU A GIRLFRIEND, ALL RIGHT...?
PON (PAT)
ぽん
GYAN (YELP)
ぎゃん
I KNOWWWW!!
THAT'S NOT WHY I WAS GONNA DO IIIIIIIT!
......
YORO (TOTTER)
よろ
YORO
よろ
HEY. GOOD JOB GETTING THROUGH THAT.
GYAI (SCREE)
ぎゃー
GYAI
ぎゃー
THAT SO?
I HAD NO IDEA TALKING ABOUT PIERCINGS WOULD BLOW UP LIKE THIS...
YOU DO GO OVERBOARD ON ALL SORTS OF STUFF.
KARA (HAR)
カラ
KARA
カラ
HA HA HA.
"HA HA HA," HE SAYS.
I'M GLAD MY EAR'S STILL ATTACHED...
....
...
ACTUALLY, MIYAMURA...

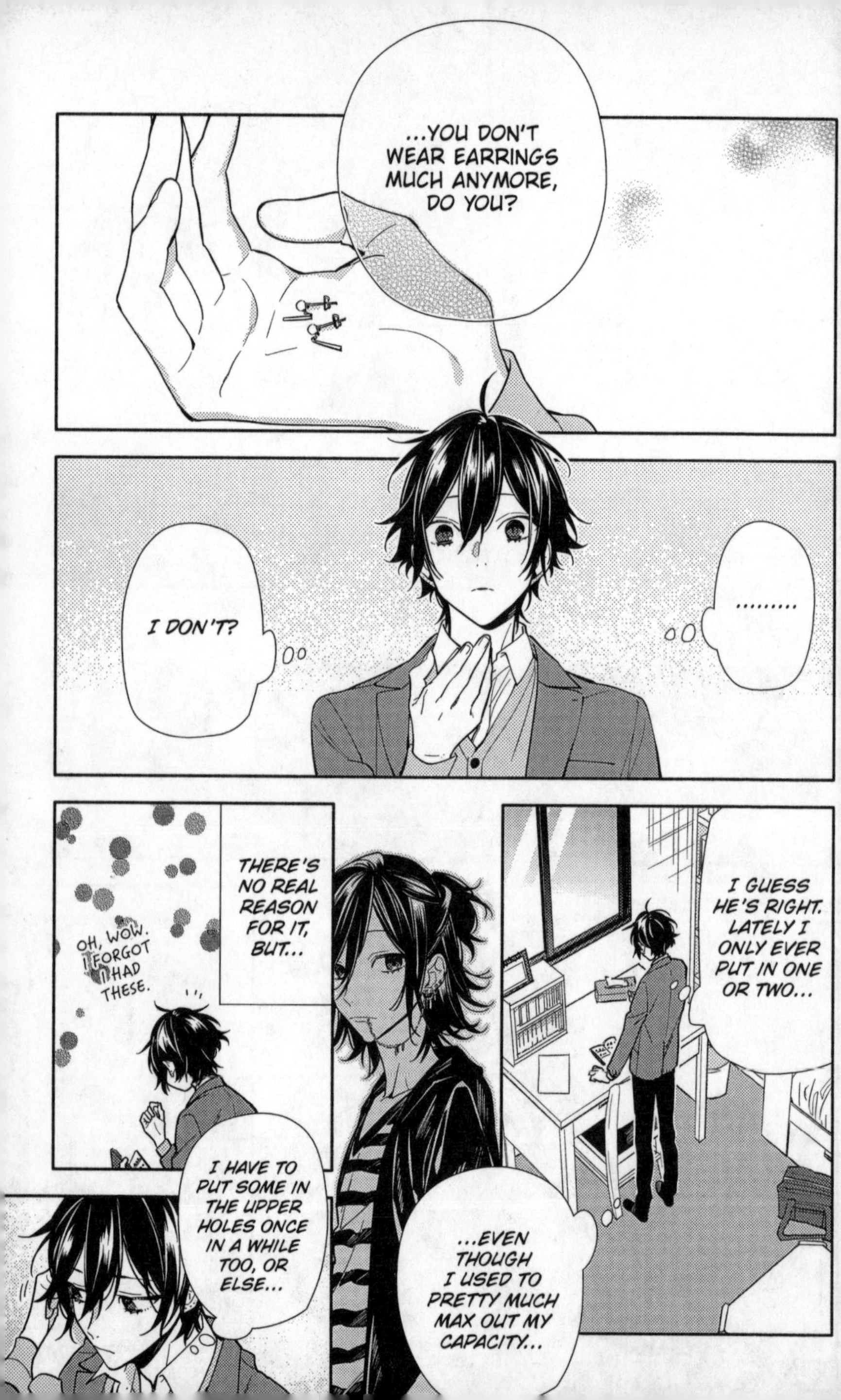
...YOU DON'T WEAR EARRINGS MUCH ANYMORE, DO YOU?
....
I DON'T?
I GUESS HE'S RIGHT. LATELY I ONLY EVER PUT IN ONE OR TWO...
...EVEN THOUGH I USED TO PRETTY MUCH MAX OUT MY CAPACITY...
THERE'S NO REAL REASON FOR IT, BUT...
OH, WOW. I FORGOT I HAD THESE.
I HAVE TO PUT SOME IN THE UPPER HOLES ONCE IN A WHILE TOO, OR ELSE...

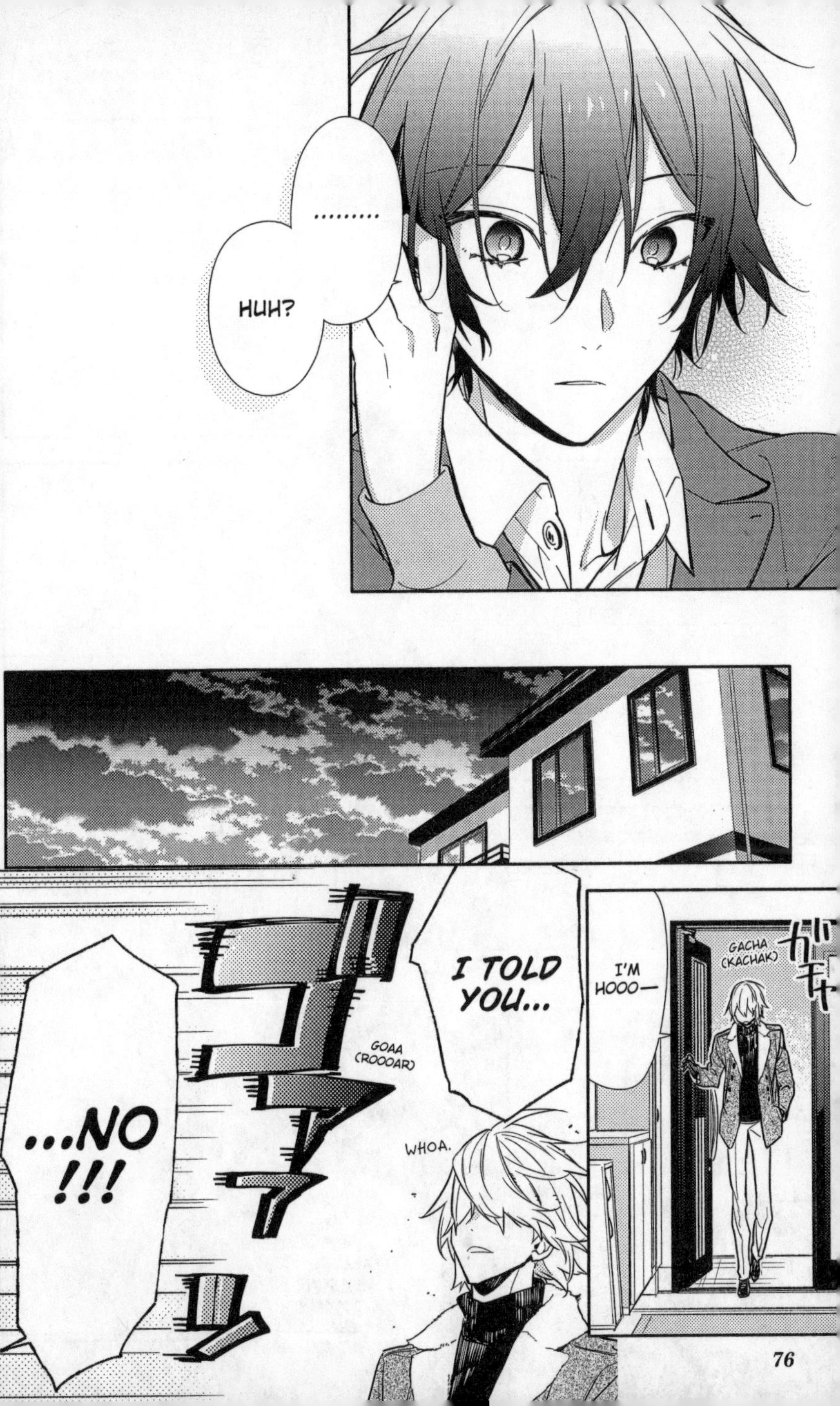
....
HUH?
GACHA (KACHAK)
ガチャ
I'M HOOO—
I TOLD YOU...
GOAA (ROOOAR)
WHOA.
...NO !!!

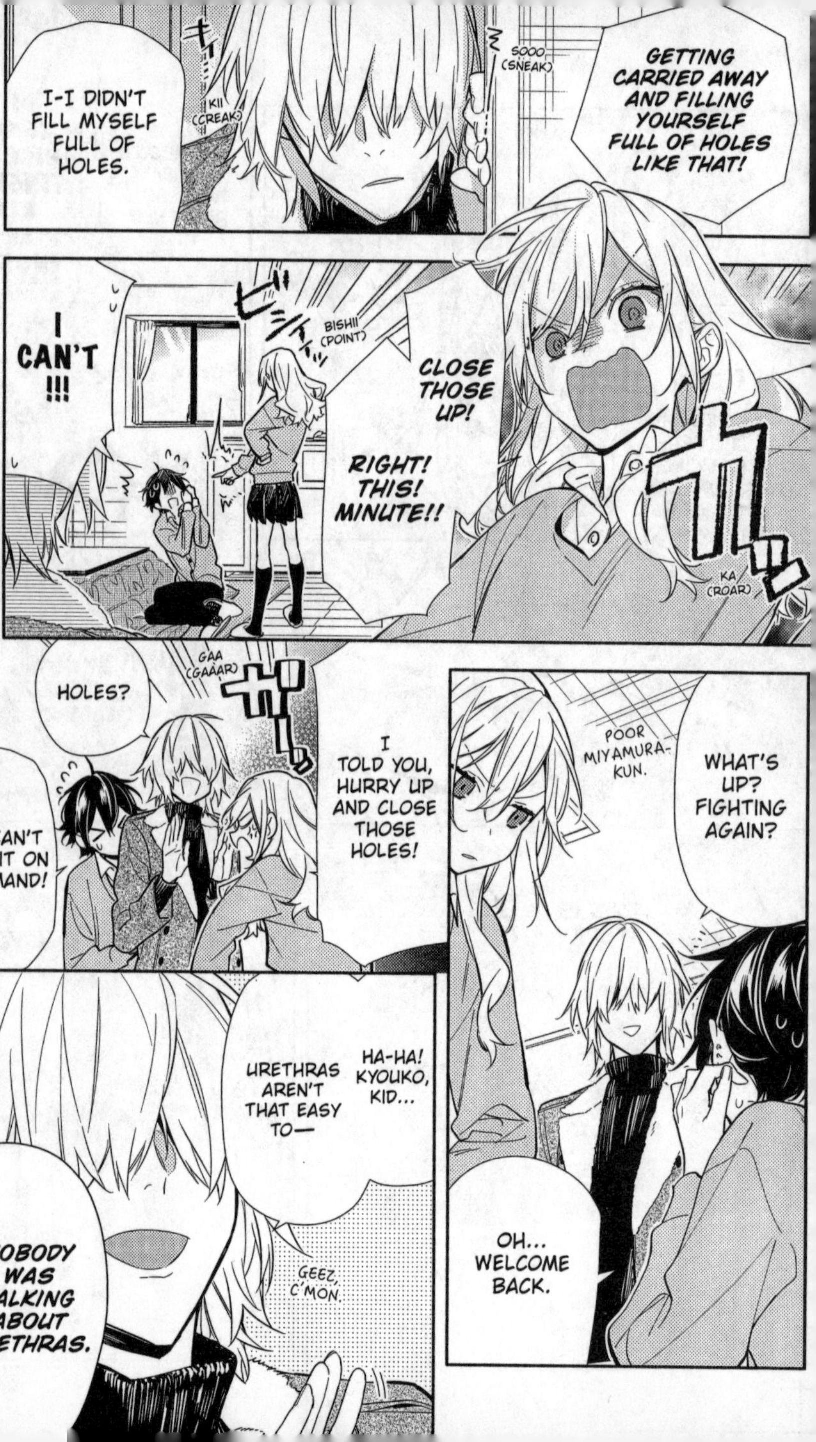
GETTING CARRIED AWAY AND FILLING YOURSELF FULL OF HOLES LIKE THAT!
SOOO (SNEAK)
KII (CREAK)
I-I DIDN'T FILL MYSELF FULL OF HOLES.
CLOSE THOSE UP!
RIGHT! THIS! MINUTE!!
KA (ROAR)
BISHII (POINT)
I CAN'T!!!
WHAT'S UP? FIGHTING AGAIN?
POOR MIYAMURA-KUN.
OH... WELCOME BACK.
I TOLD YOU, HURRY UP AND CLOSE THOSE HOLES!
GAA (GAAAR)
HOLES?
I CAN'T DO IT ON DEMAND!
HA-HA! KYOUKO, KID...
URETHRAS AREN'T THAT EASY TO—
GEEZ, C'MON.
NOBODY WAS TALKING ABOUT URETHRAS.

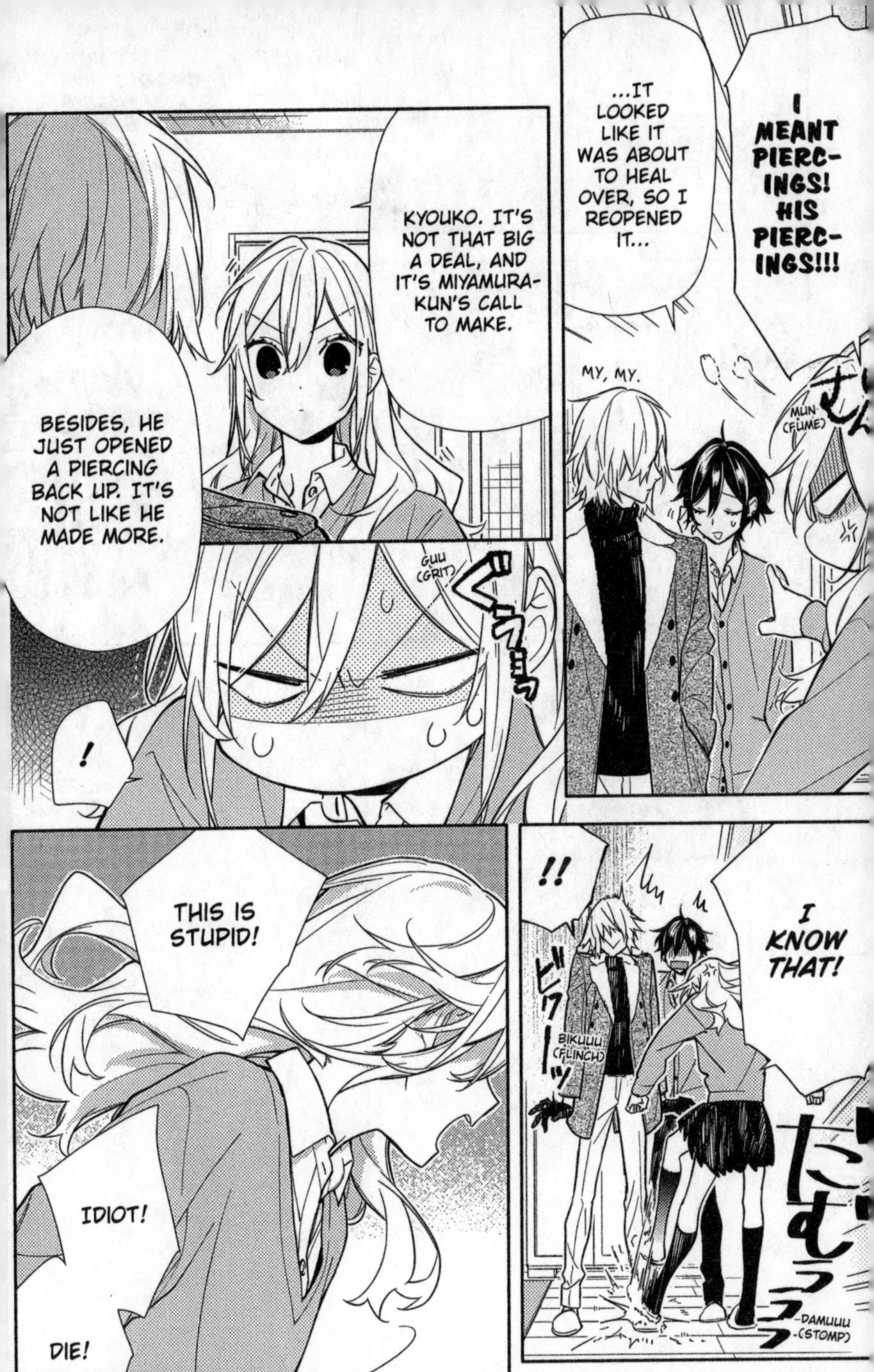
I MEANT PIERC-INGS! HIS PIERC-INGS!!!
...IT LOOKED LIKE IT WAS ABOUT TO HEAL OVER, SO I REOPENED IT...
MUN (FUME)
MY, MY.
KYOUKO. IT'S NOT THAT BIG A DEAL, AND IT'S MIYAMURA-KUN'S CALL TO MAKE.
BESIDES, HE JUST OPENED A PIERCING BACK UP. IT'S NOT LIKE HE MADE MORE.
GUU (GRIT)
!
I KNOW THAT!
!!
BIKUUU (FLINCH)
DAMUUU (STOMP)
THIS IS STUPID!
IDIOT!
DIE!

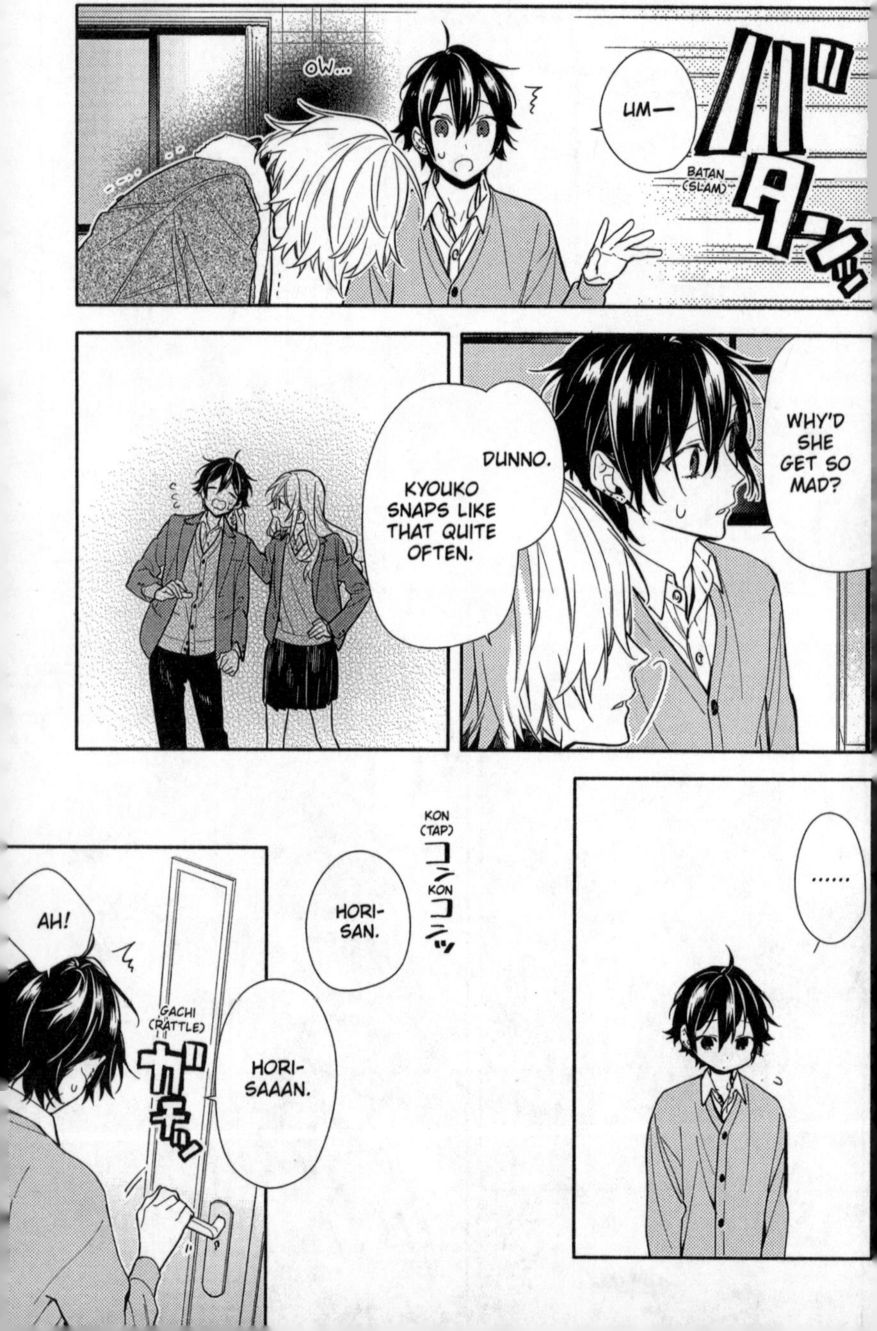
BATAN (SLAM)
UM—
OW...
WHY'D SHE GET SO MAD?
DUNNO.
KYOUKO SNAPS LIKE THAT QUITE OFTEN.
......
KON (TAP) KON
HORI-SAN.
HORI-SAAAN.
GACHI (RATTLE)
AH!

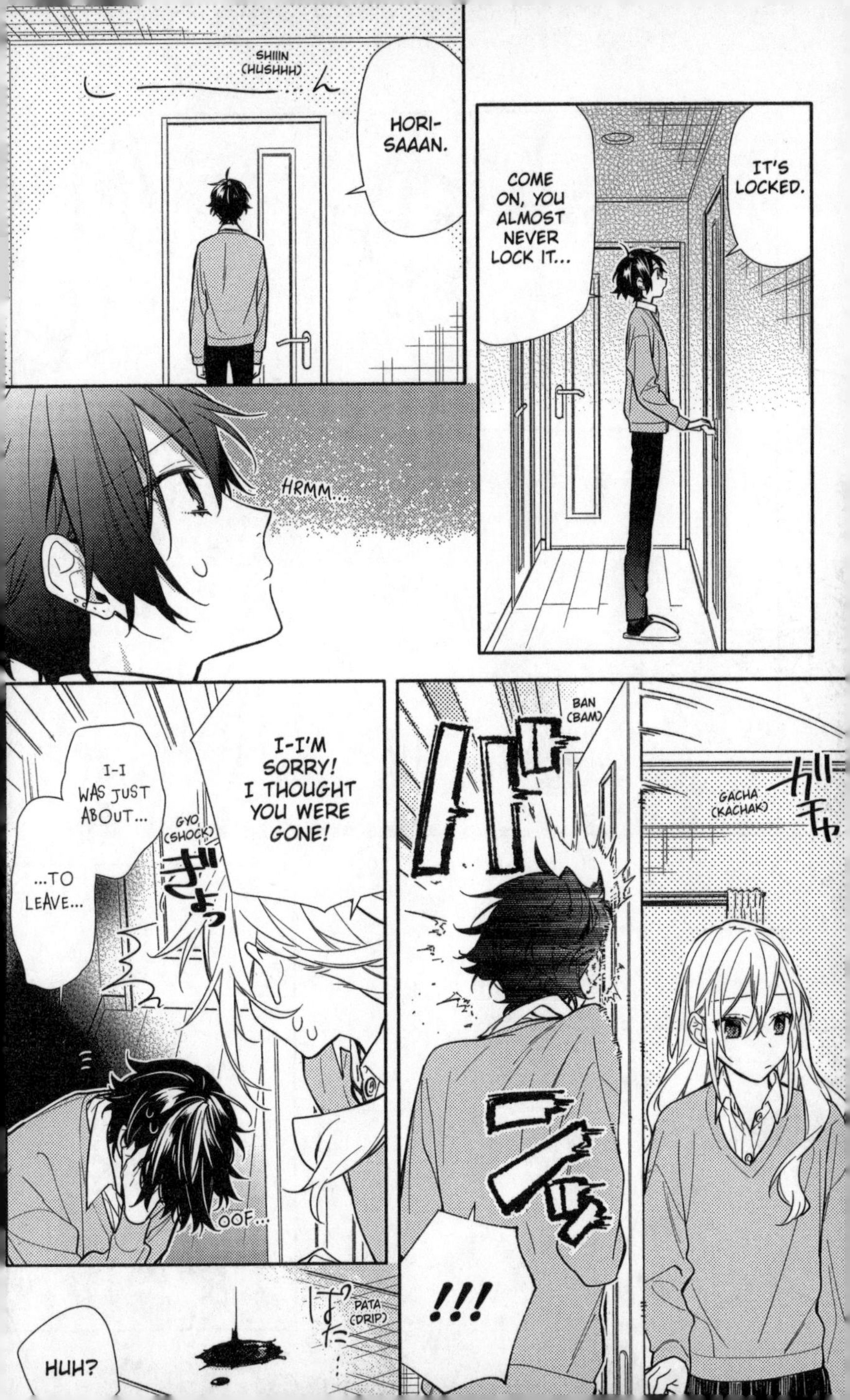
SHIIIN (HUSHHH)
HORI-SAAAN.
IT'S LOCKED.
COME ON, YOU ALMOST NEVER LOCK IT...
HRMM...
GACHA (KACHAK)
BAN (BAM)
!!!
I-I'M SORRY! I THOUGHT YOU WERE GONE!
GYO (SHOCK)
I-I WAS JUST ABOUT...
...TO LEAVE...
OOF...
PATA (DRIP)
HUH?

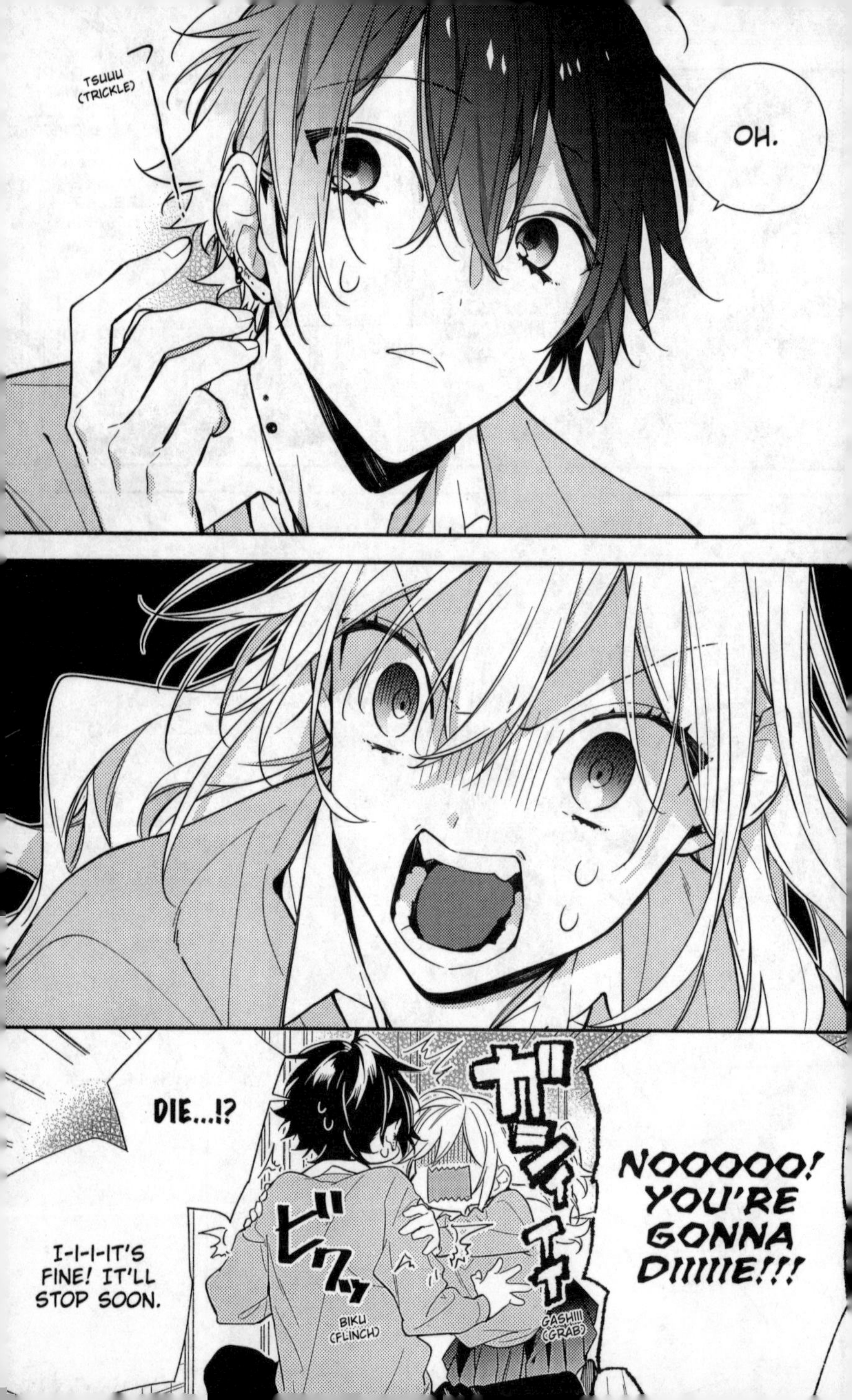
OH.
TSUUU (TRICKLE)
NOOOOO! YOU'RE GONNA DIIIIIE!!!
ガシィィ
GASHIII (GRAB)
ビクッ
BIKU (FLINCH)
DIE...!?
I-I-I-IT'S FINE! IT'LL STOP SOON.

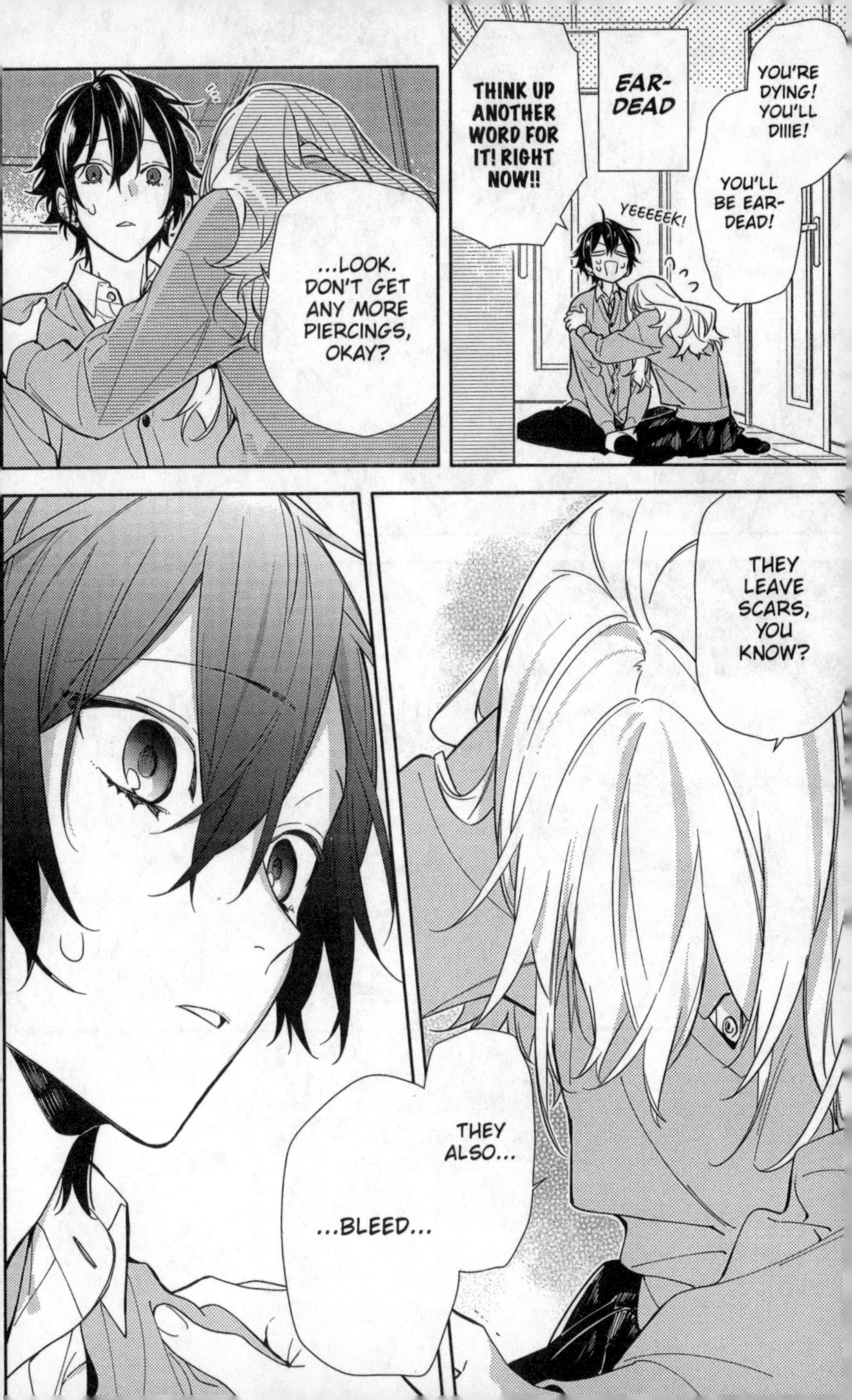
YOU'RE DYING! YOU'LL DIIIE!
EAR-DEAD
THINK UP ANOTHER WORD FOR IT! RIGHT NOW!!
YOU'LL BE EAR-DEAD!
YEEEEEK!
...LOOK. DON'T GET ANY MORE PIERCINGS, OKAY?
THEY LEAVE SCARS, YOU KNOW?
THEY ALSO...
...BLEED...

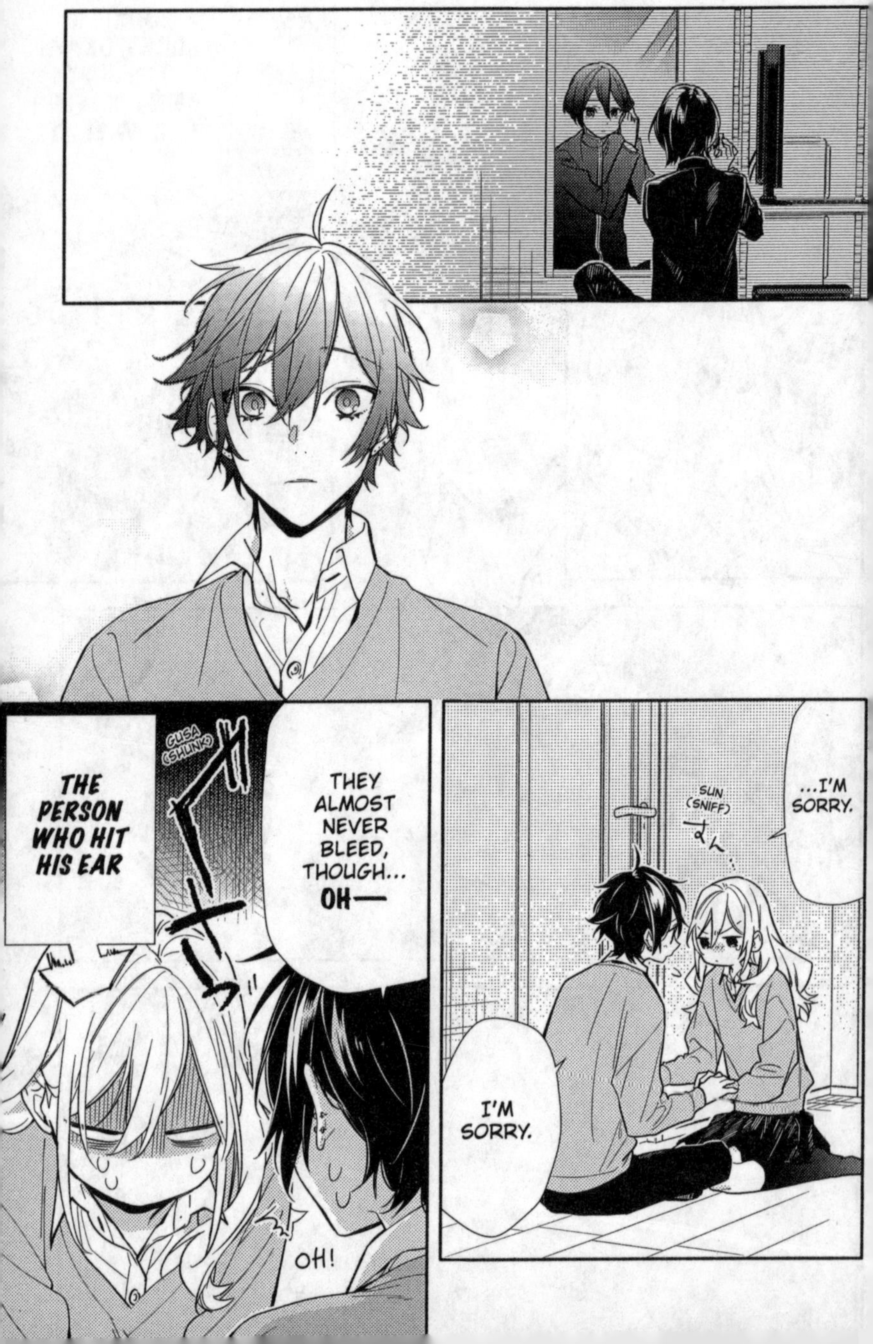
...I'M SORRY.
SUN (SNIFF)
すん
I'M SORRY.
THEY ALMOST NEVER BLEED, THOUGH... OH—
GUSA (SHLINK)
THE PERSON WHO HIT HIS EAR
OH!

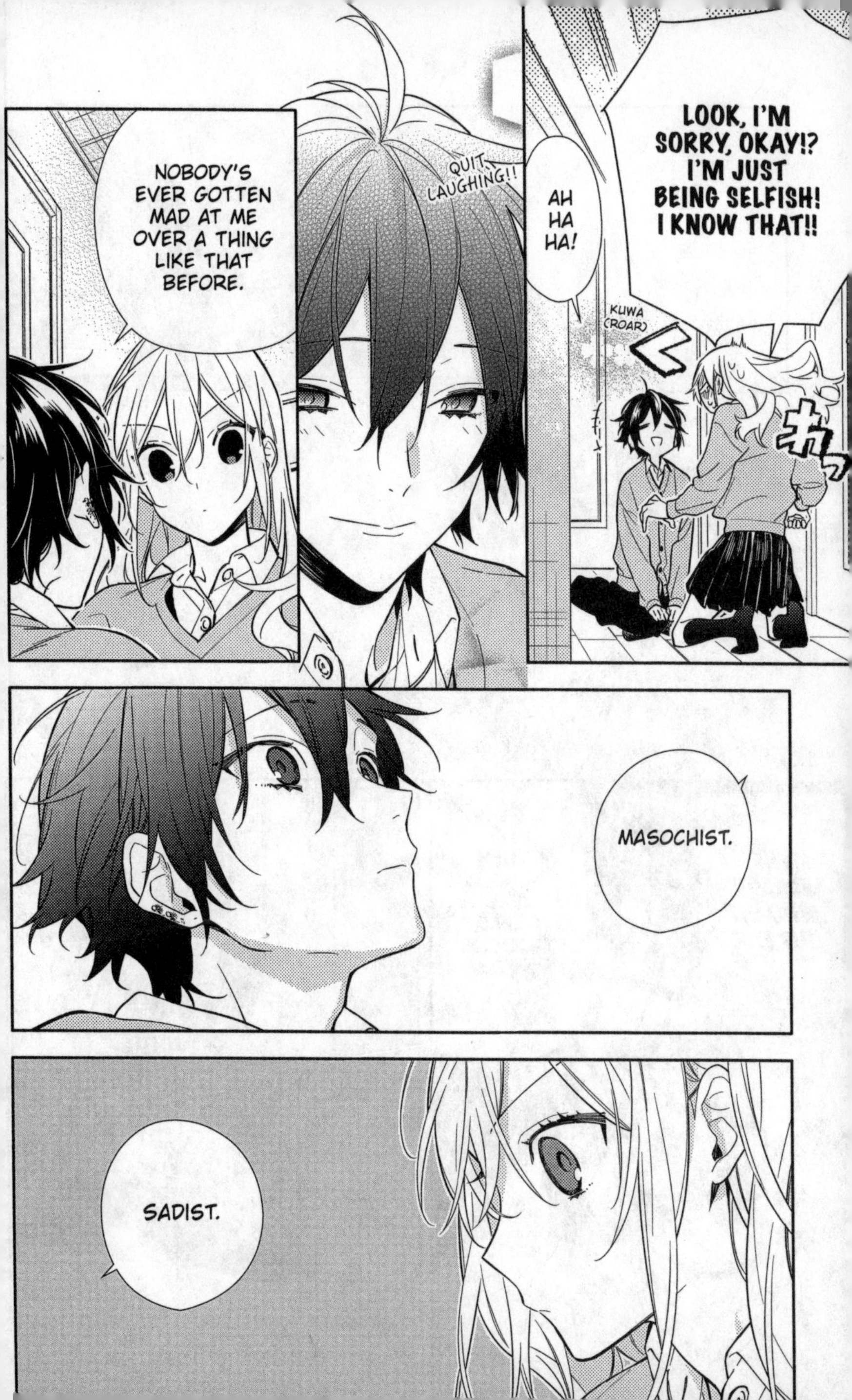
LOOK, I'M SORRY, OKAY!? I'M JUST BEING SELFISH! I KNOW THAT!!
AH HA HA!
QUIT LAUGHING!!
KUWA (ROAR)
NOBODY'S EVER GOTTEN MAD AT ME OVER A THING LIKE THAT BEFORE.
MASOCHIST.
SADIST.

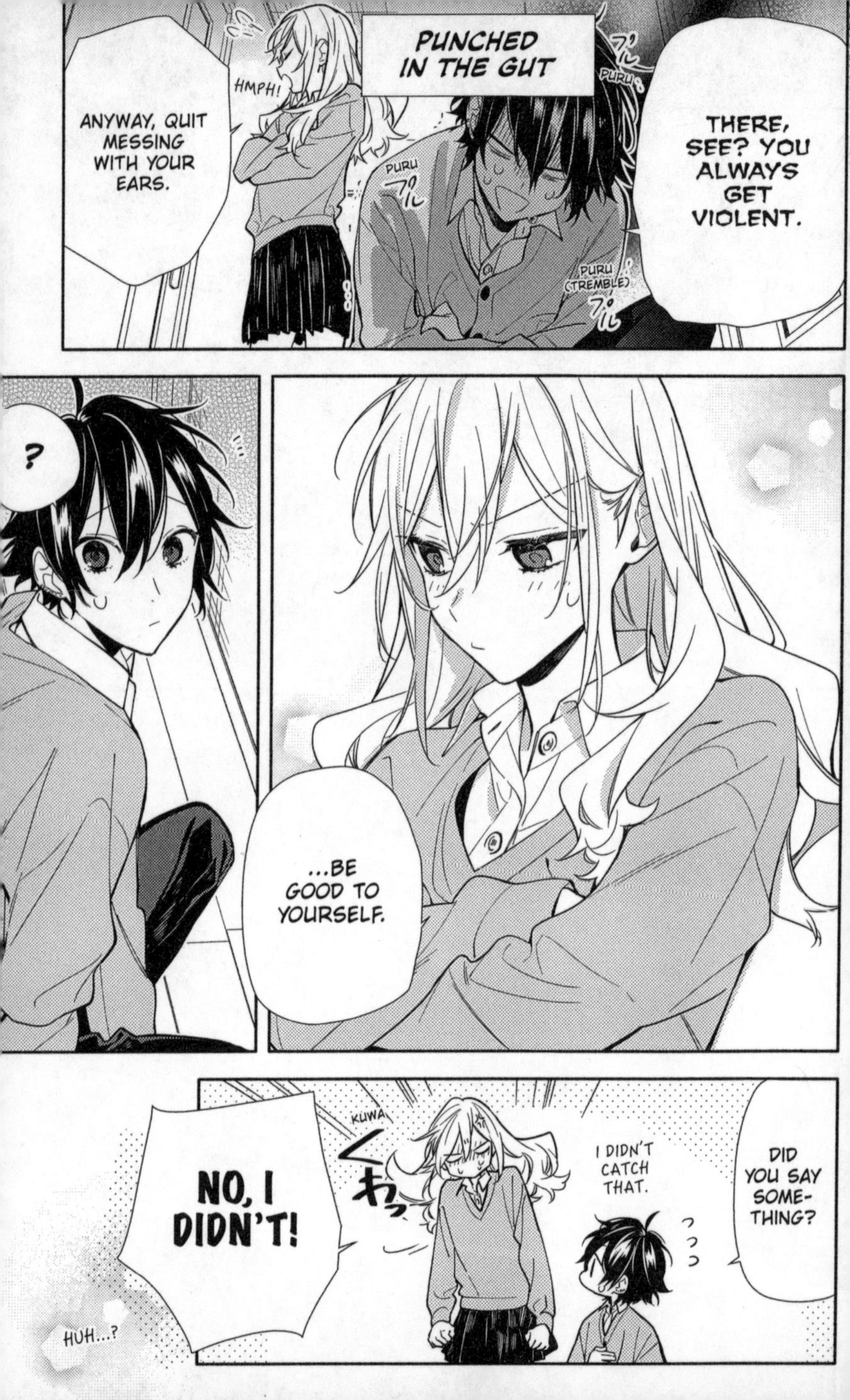
PURU
THERE, SEE? YOU ALWAYS GET VIOLENT.
PUNCHED IN THE GUT
PURU (TREMBLE)
PURU
HMPH!
ANYWAY, QUIT MESSING WITH YOUR EARS.
...BE GOOD TO YOURSELF.
?
DID YOU SAY SOME-THING?
I DIDN'T CATCH THAT.
KUWA
NO, I DIDN'T!
HUH...?

HORIMIYA

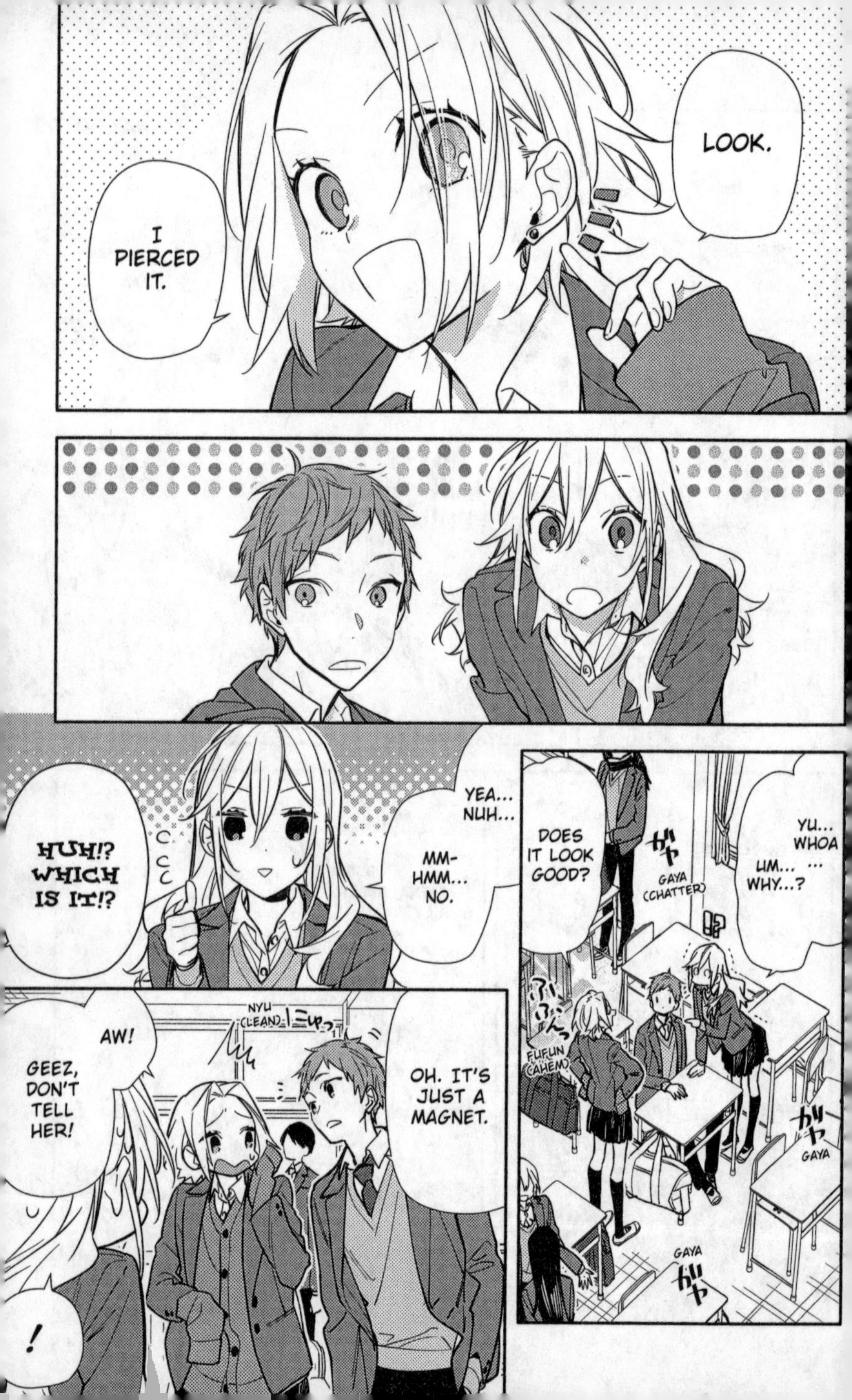

LOOK.
I PIERCED IT.
YU... WHOA ...
UM... WHY...?
DOES IT LOOK GOOD?
GAYA (CHATTER)
GAYA
GAYA
FUFUN (AHEM)
YEA... NUH...
MM-HMM... NO.
HUH!? WHICH IS IT!?
OH. IT'S JUST A MAGNET.
NYU (CLEAN)
AW!
GEEZ, DON'T TELL HER!
!

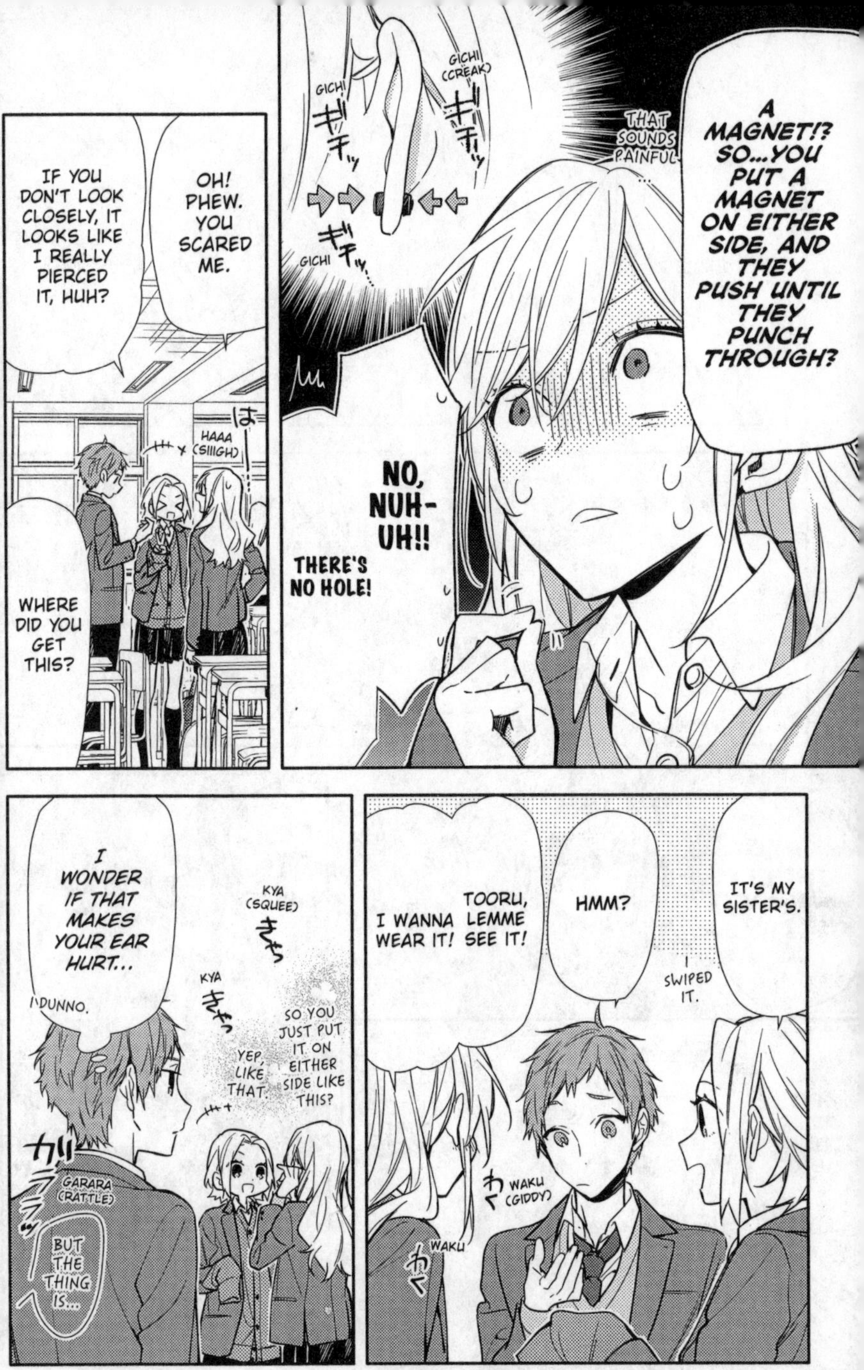

A MAGNET!? SO...YOU PUT A MAGNET ON EITHER SIDE, AND THEY PUSH UNTIL THEY PUNCH THROUGH?
THAT SOUNDS PAINFUL...
GICHI (CREAK)
GICHI
GICHI
NO, NUH-UH!!
THERE'S NO HOLE!
OH! PHEW. YOU SCARED ME.
IF YOU DON'T LOOK CLOSELY, IT LOOKS LIKE I REALLY PIERCED IT, HUH?
HAAA (SIIIGH)
WHERE DID YOU GET THIS?
IT'S MY SISTER'S.
I SWIPED IT.
HMM?
TOORU, LEMME SEE IT!
I WANNA WEAR IT!
WAKU (GIDDY)
WAKU
KYA (SQUEE)
KYA
SO YOU JUST PUT IT ON EITHER SIDE LIKE THIS?
YEP, LIKE THAT.
I WONDER IF THAT MAKES YOUR EAR HURT...
I DUNNO.
GARARA (RATTLE)
BUT THE THING IS...

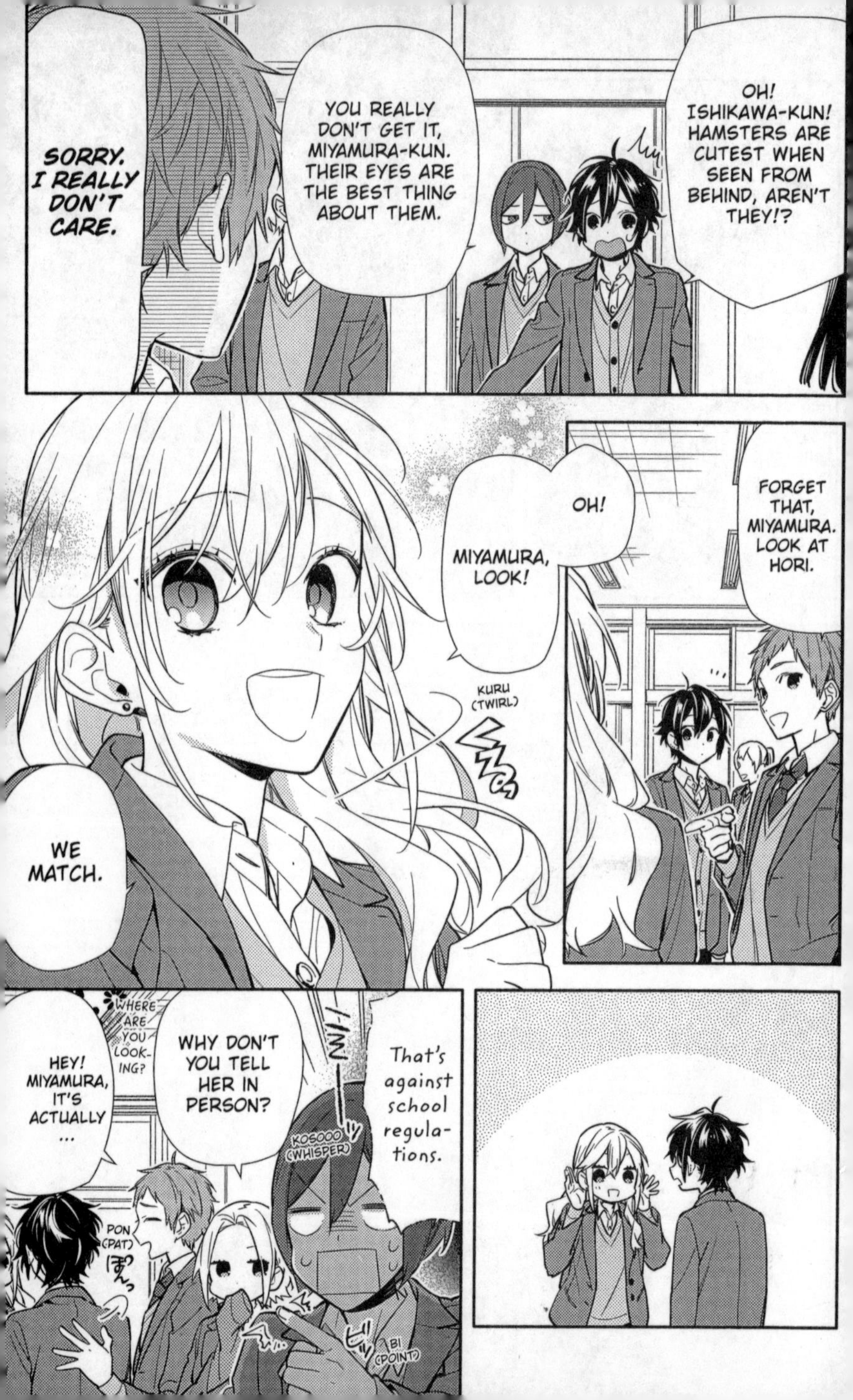
OH! ISHIKAWA-KUN! HAMSTERS ARE CUTEST WHEN SEEN FROM BEHIND, AREN'T THEY!?
YOU REALLY DON'T GET IT, MIYAMURA-KUN. THEIR EYES ARE THE BEST THING ABOUT THEM.
SORRY. I REALLY DON'T CARE.
FORGET THAT, MIYAMURA. LOOK AT HORI.
OH! MIYAMURA, LOOK!
KURU (TWIRL)
WE MATCH.
That's against school regulations.
KOSOOO (WHISPER)
WHY DON'T YOU TELL HER IN PERSON?
WHERE ARE YOU LOOKING?
HEY! MIYAMURA, IT'S ACTUALLY ...
PON (PAT)
BI (POINT)

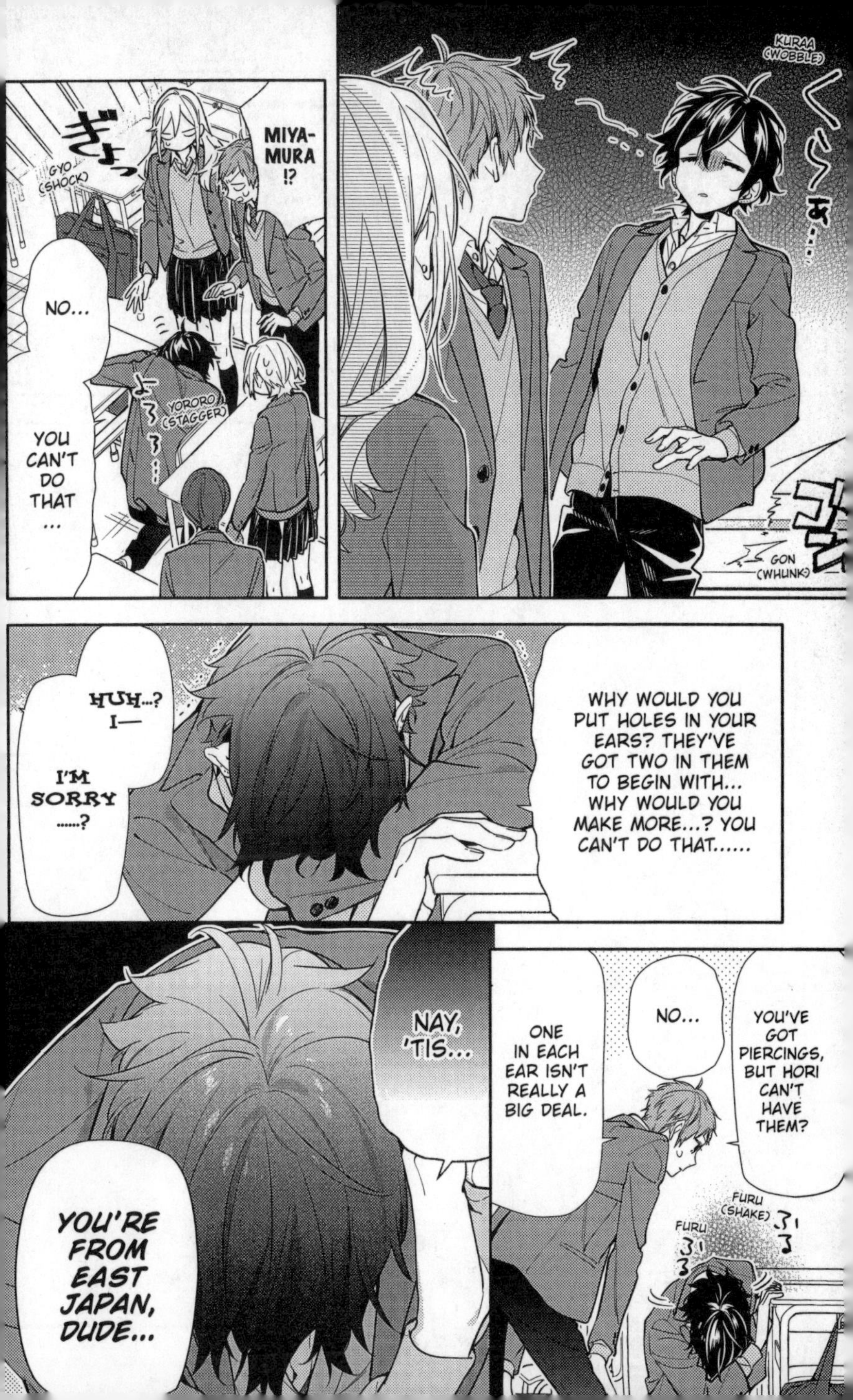
KURAA (WOBBLE)
くらぁ…
GON (WHUNK)
ぎょっ
GYO (SHOCK)
MIYA-MURA!?
NO…
YORORO (STAGGER)
YOU CAN'T DO THAT…
WHY WOULD YOU PUT HOLES IN YOUR EARS? THEY'VE GOT TWO IN THEM TO BEGIN WITH… WHY WOULD YOU MAKE MORE…? YOU CAN'T DO THAT……
HUH…? I—
I'M SORRY……?
YOU'VE GOT PIERCINGS, BUT HORI CAN'T HAVE THEM?
NO…
ONE IN EACH EAR ISN'T REALLY A BIG DEAL.
FURU (SHAKE)
FURU
NAY, 'TIS…
YOU'RE FROM EAST JAPAN, DUDE…

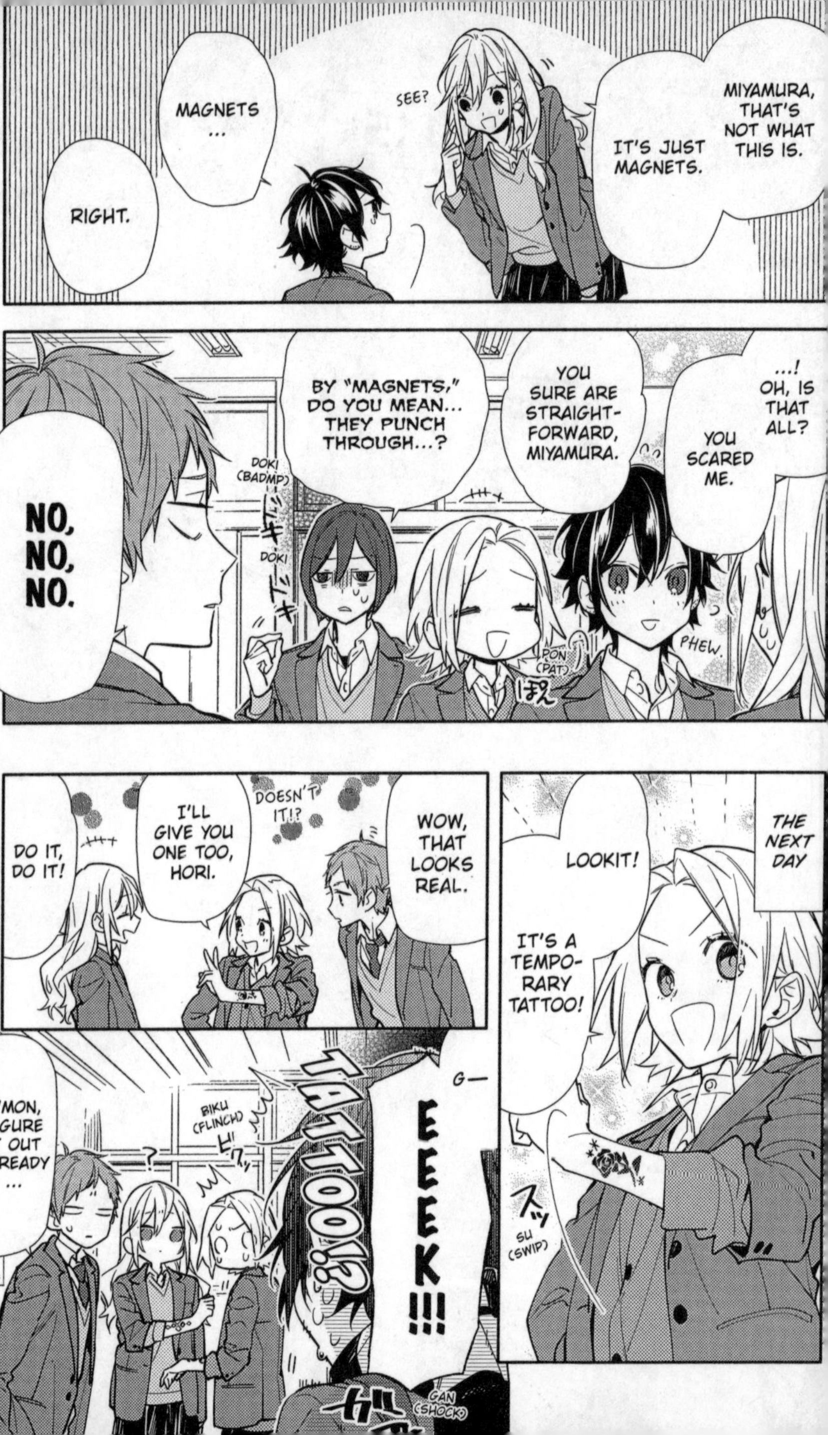
MIYAMURA, THAT'S NOT WHAT THIS IS.
IT'S JUST MAGNETS.
SEE?
MAGNETS ...
RIGHT.
...! OH, IS THAT ALL?
YOU SCARED ME.
PHEW.
PON (PAT)
ぽん
YOU SURE ARE STRAIGHT-FORWARD, MIYAMURA.
BY "MAGNETS," DO YOU MEAN... THEY PUNCH THROUGH...?
DOKI (BADMP)
DOKI
NO, NO, NO.
THE NEXT DAY
LOOKIT!
IT'S A TEMPORARY TATTOO!
スッ
SU (SWIP)
WOW, THAT LOOKS REAL.
DOESN'T IT!?
I'LL GIVE YOU ONE TOO, HORI.
DO IT, DO IT!
G—
EEEK!!!
TATTOO!?
BIKU (FLINCH)
ビクッ
GAN (SHOCK)
C'MON, FIGURE IT OUT ALREADY ...

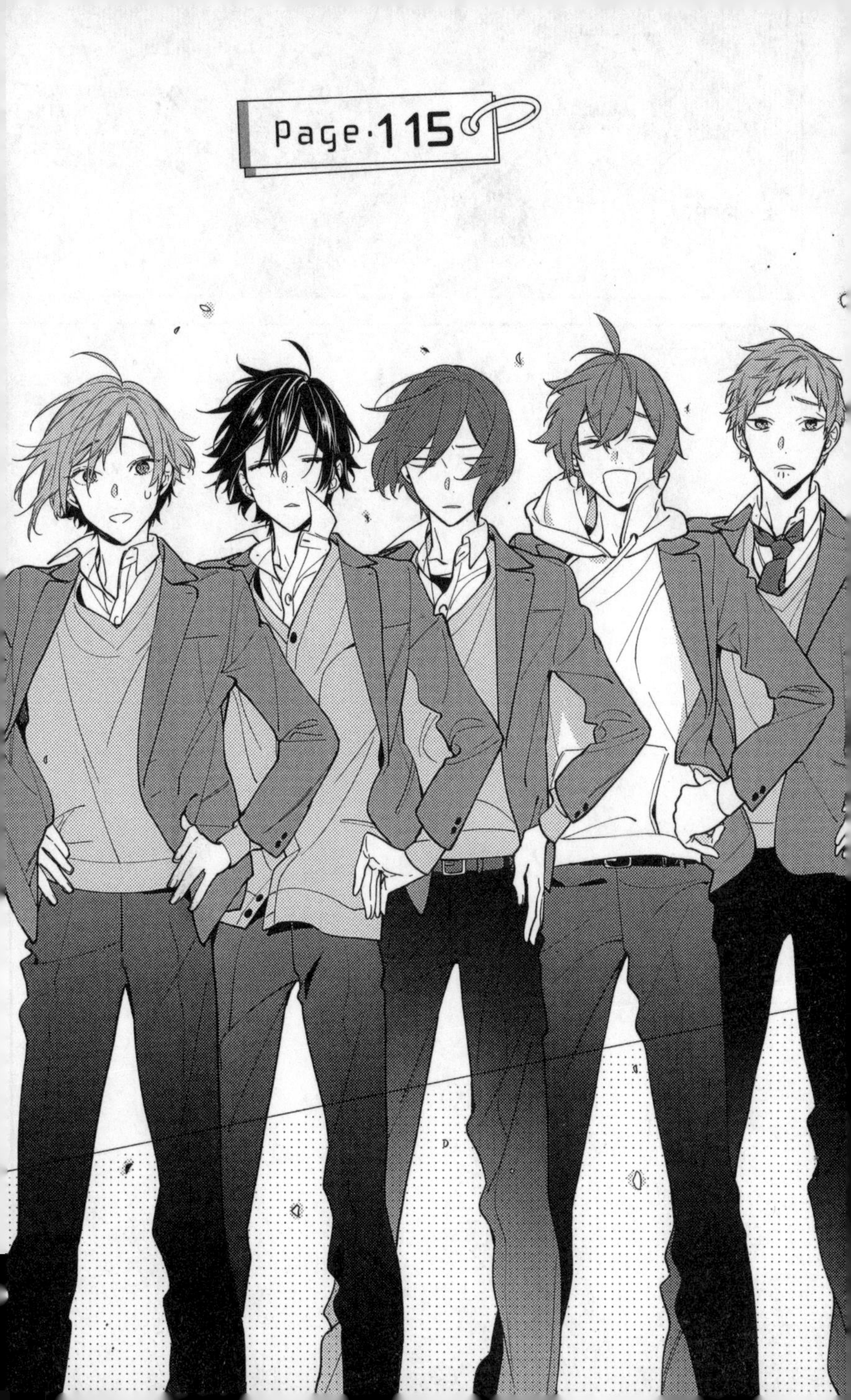
Page·115

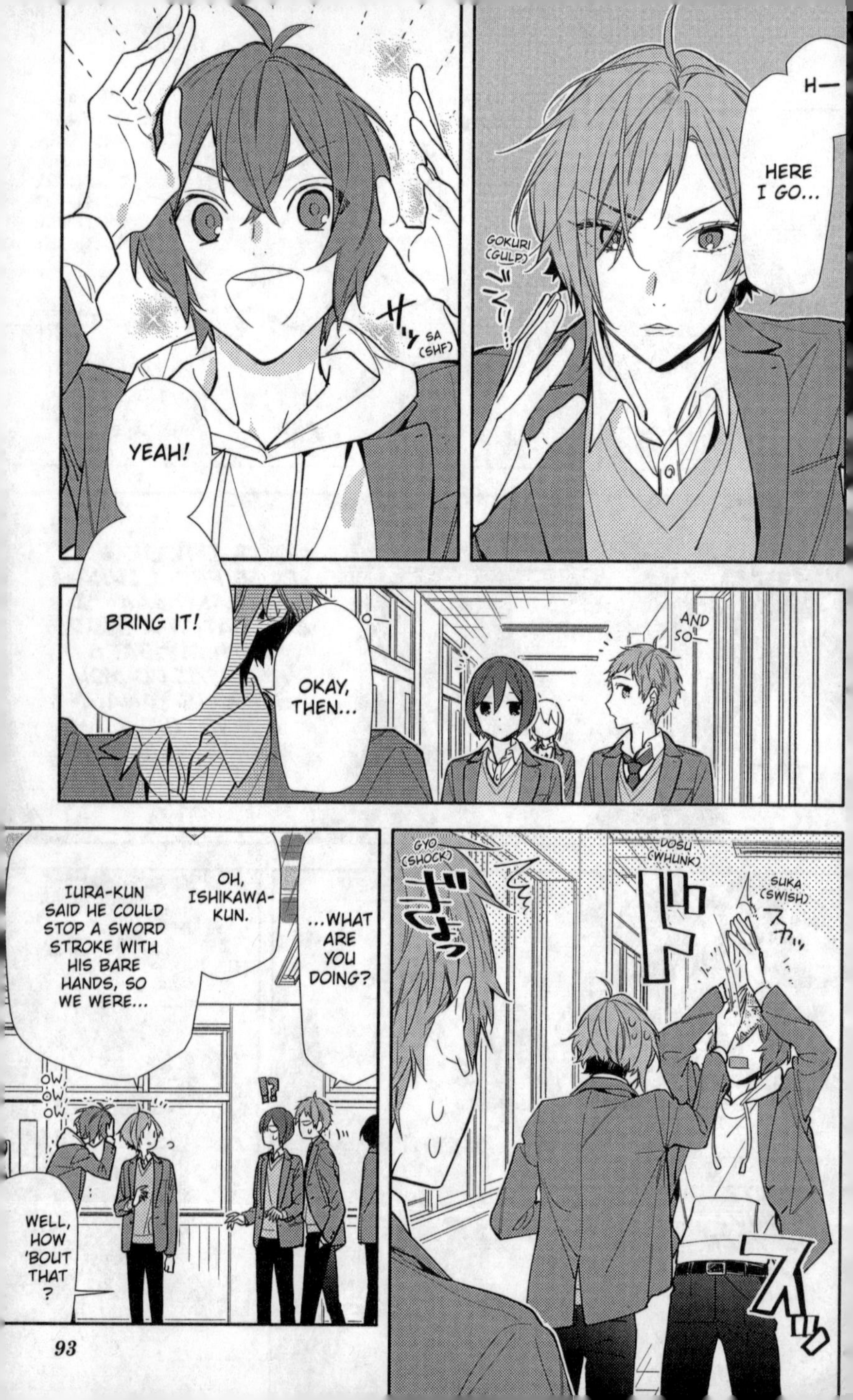
H—
HERE I GO...
GOKURI (GULP)
SA (SHF)
YEAH!
BRING IT!
AND SO—
OKAY, THEN...
SUKA (SWISH)
DOSU (WHUNK)
GYO (SHOCK)
...WHAT ARE YOU DOING?
OH, ISHIKAWA-KUN.
IURA-KUN SAID HE COULD STOP A SWORD STROKE WITH HIS BARE HANDS, SO WE WERE...
OW OW OW
WELL, HOW 'BOUT THAT?

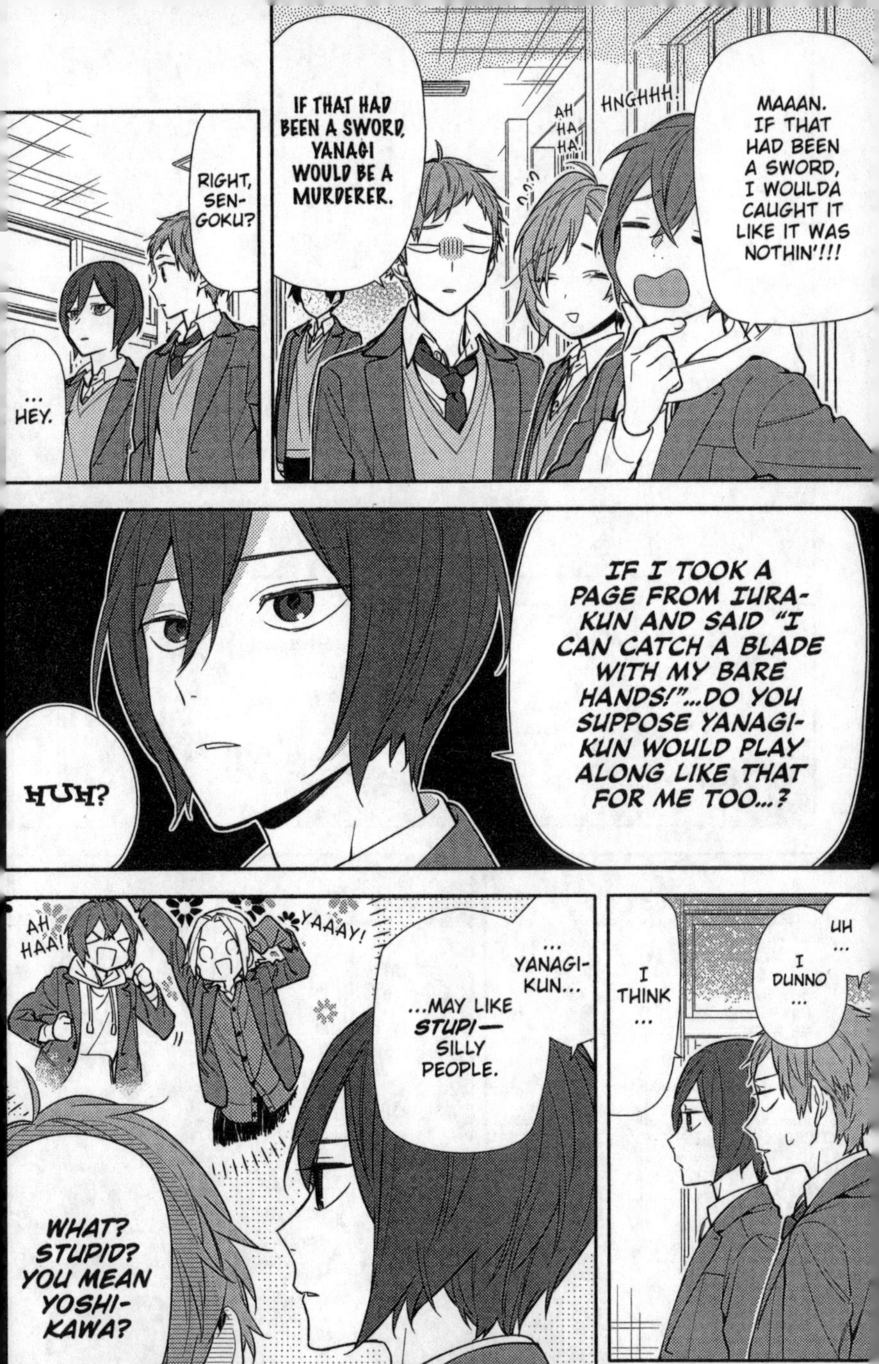
MAAAN. IF THAT HAD BEEN A SWORD, I WOULDA CAUGHT IT LIKE IT WAS NOTHIN'!!!
HNGHHH!
AH HA HA!
IF THAT HAD BEEN A SWORD, YANAGI WOULD BE A MURDERER.
RIGHT, SEN-GOKU?
... HEY.
IF I TOOK A PAGE FROM IURA-KUN AND SAID "I CAN CATCH A BLADE WITH MY BARE HANDS!"...DO YOU SUPPOSE YANAGI-KUN WOULD PLAY ALONG LIKE THAT FOR ME TOO...?
HUH?
UH ... I DUNNO ...
I THINK ...
... YANAGI-KUN...
...MAY LIKE STUPI— SILLY PEOPLE.
AH HAA!
YAAAY!
WHAT? STUPID? YOU MEAN YOSHI-KAWA?

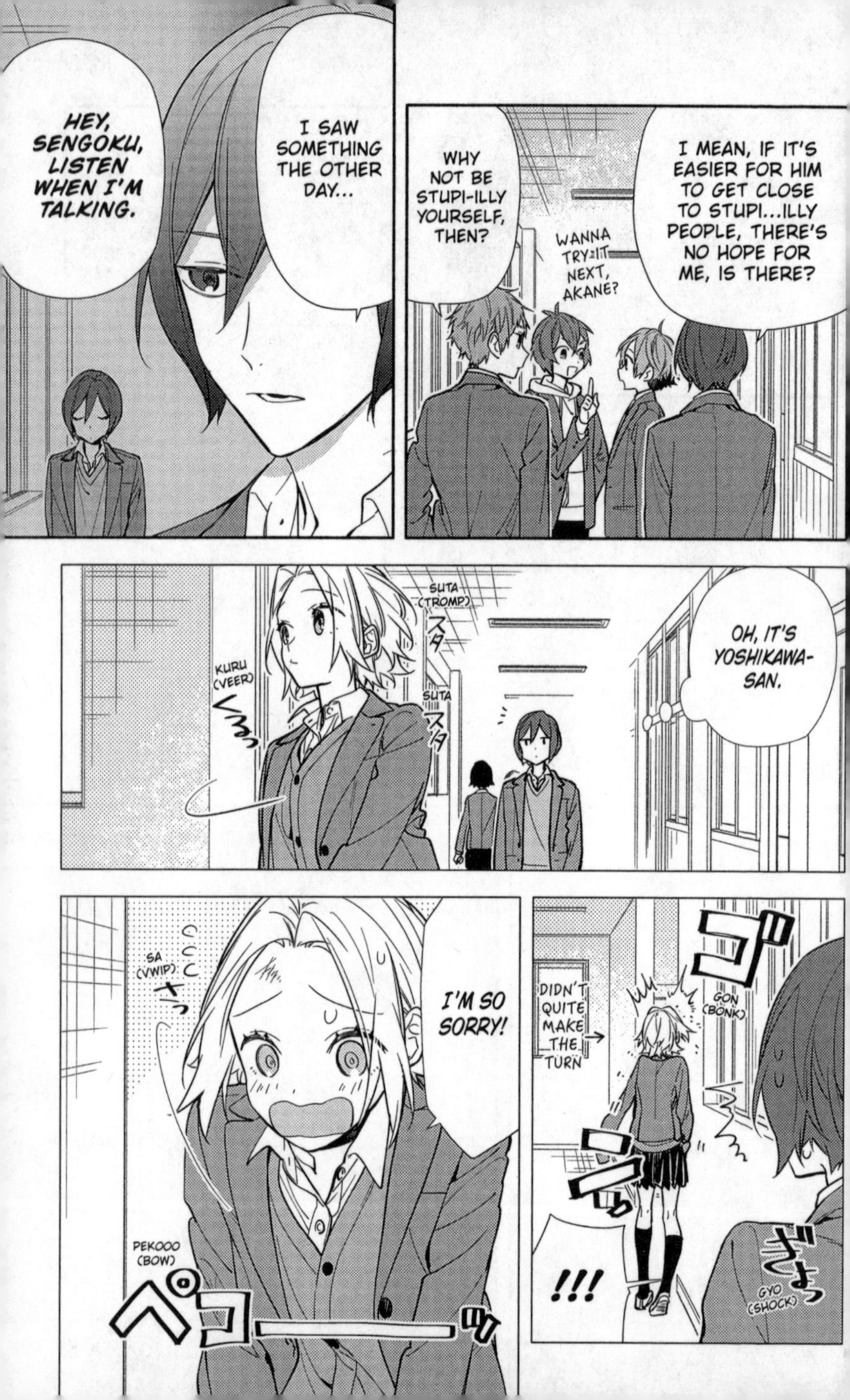
I MEAN, IF IT'S EASIER FOR HIM TO GET CLOSE TO STUPI...ILLY PEOPLE, THERE'S NO HOPE FOR ME, IS THERE?
WHY NOT BE STUPI-ILLY YOURSELF, THEN?
WANNA TRY IT NEXT, AKANE?
I SAW SOMETHING THE OTHER DAY...
HEY, SENGOKU, LISTEN WHEN I'M TALKING.
OH, IT'S YOSHIKAWA-SAN.
SUTA (TROMP)
SUTA
KURU (VEER)
GON (BONK)
DIDN'T QUITE MAKE THE TURN
!!!
GYO (SHOCK)
I'M SO SORRY!
SA (VWIP)
PEKOOO (BOW)

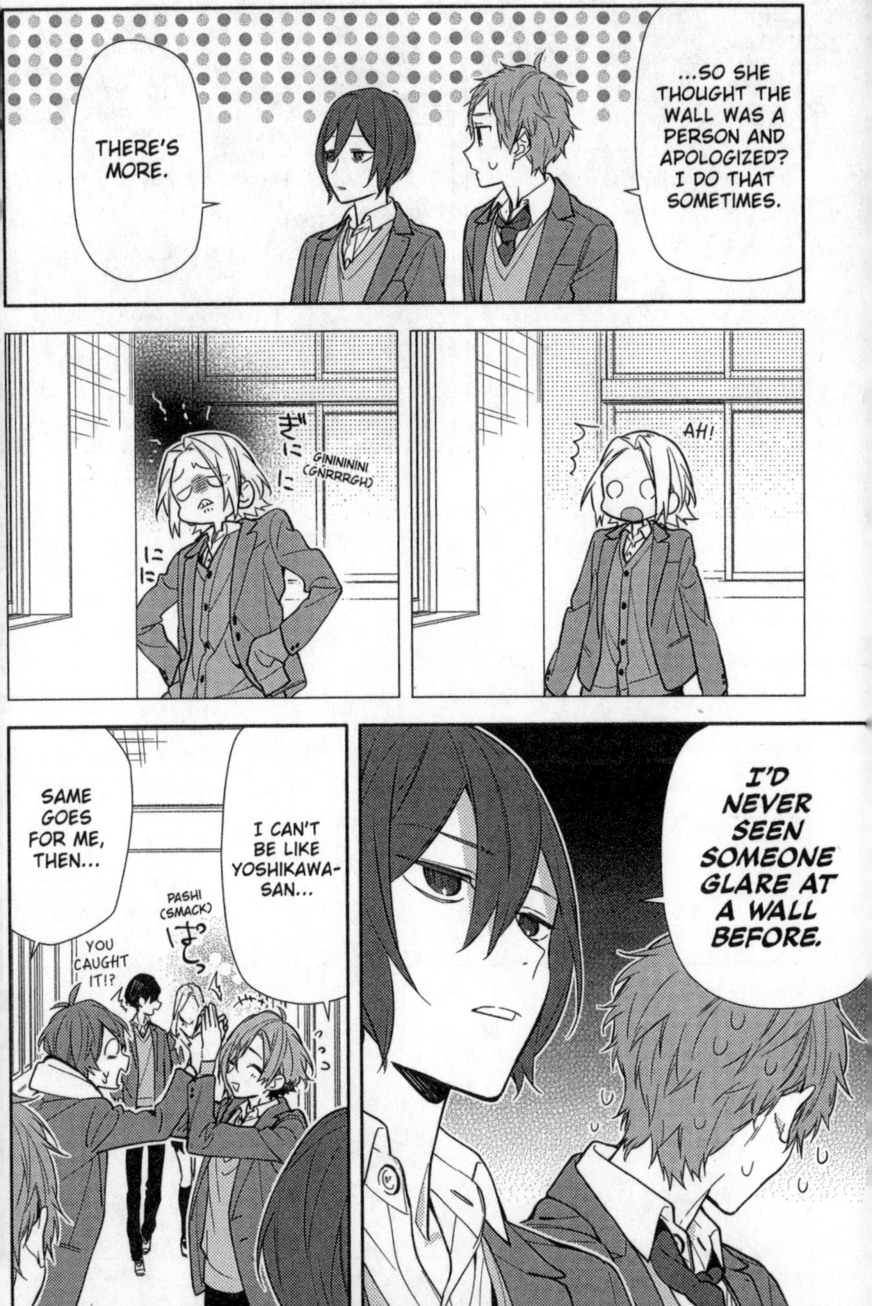
...SO SHE THOUGHT THE WALL WAS A PERSON AND APOLOGIZED? I DO THAT SOMETIMES.
THERE'S MORE.
AH!
GINININI (GNRRRGH)
I'D NEVER SEEN SOMEONE GLARE AT A WALL BEFORE.
I CAN'T BE LIKE YOSHIKAWA-SAN...
SAME GOES FOR ME, THEN...
PASHI (SMACK)
YOU CAUGHT IT!?

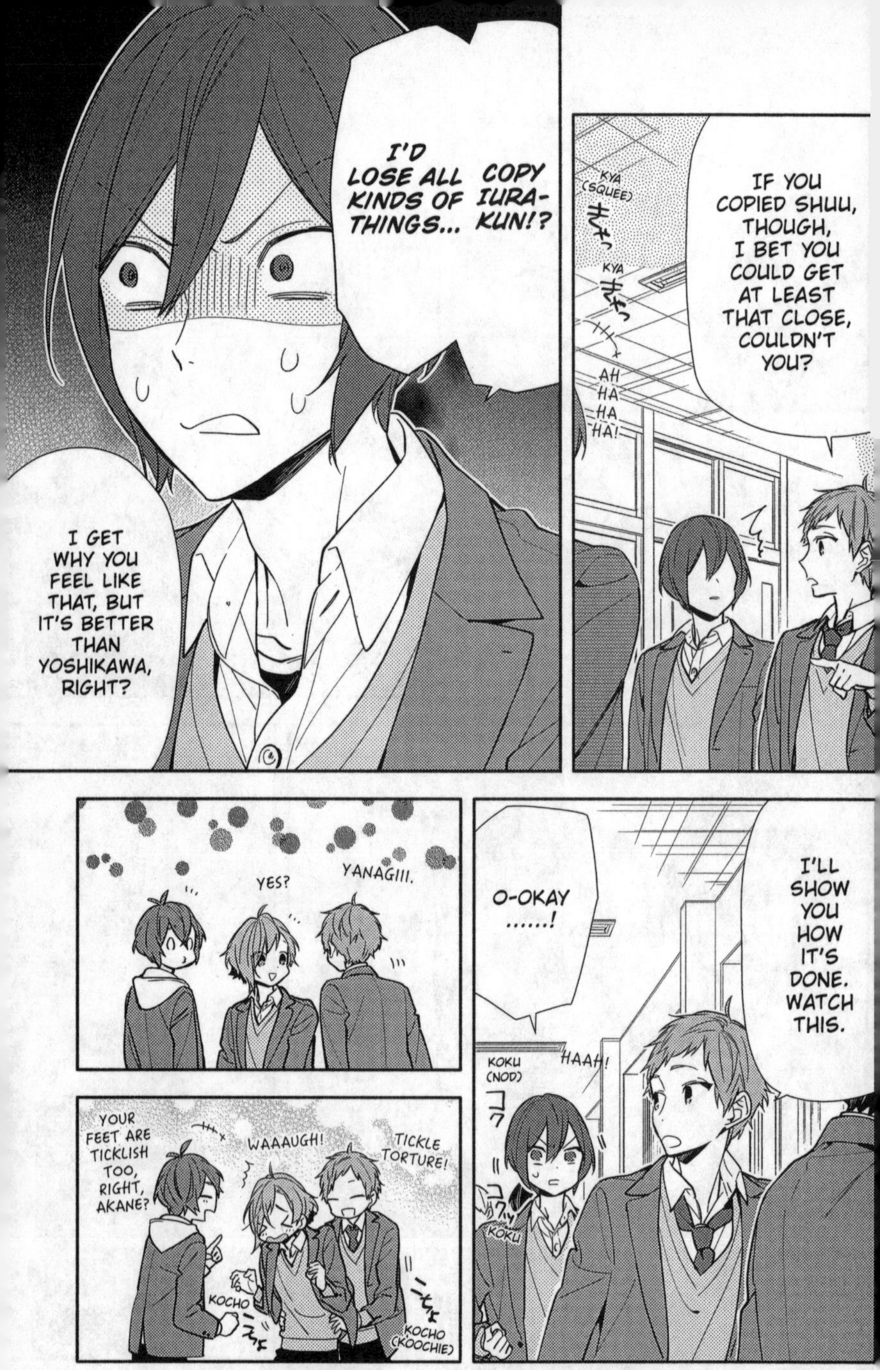
IF YOU COPIED SHUU, THOUGH, I BET YOU COULD GET AT LEAST THAT CLOSE, COULDN'T YOU?
KYA (SQUEE)
KYA
AH HA HA HA!
COPY IURA-KUN!?
I'D LOSE ALL KINDS OF THINGS...
I GET WHY YOU FEEL LIKE THAT, BUT IT'S BETTER THAN YOSHIKAWA, RIGHT?
I'LL SHOW YOU HOW IT'S DONE. WATCH THIS.
O-OKAY ......!
HAAH!
KOKU (NOD)
KOKU
YANAGIII.
YES?
TICKLE TORTURE!
WAAAUGH!
YOUR FEET ARE TICKLISH TOO, RIGHT, AKANE?
KOCHO (KOOCHIE)
KOCHO

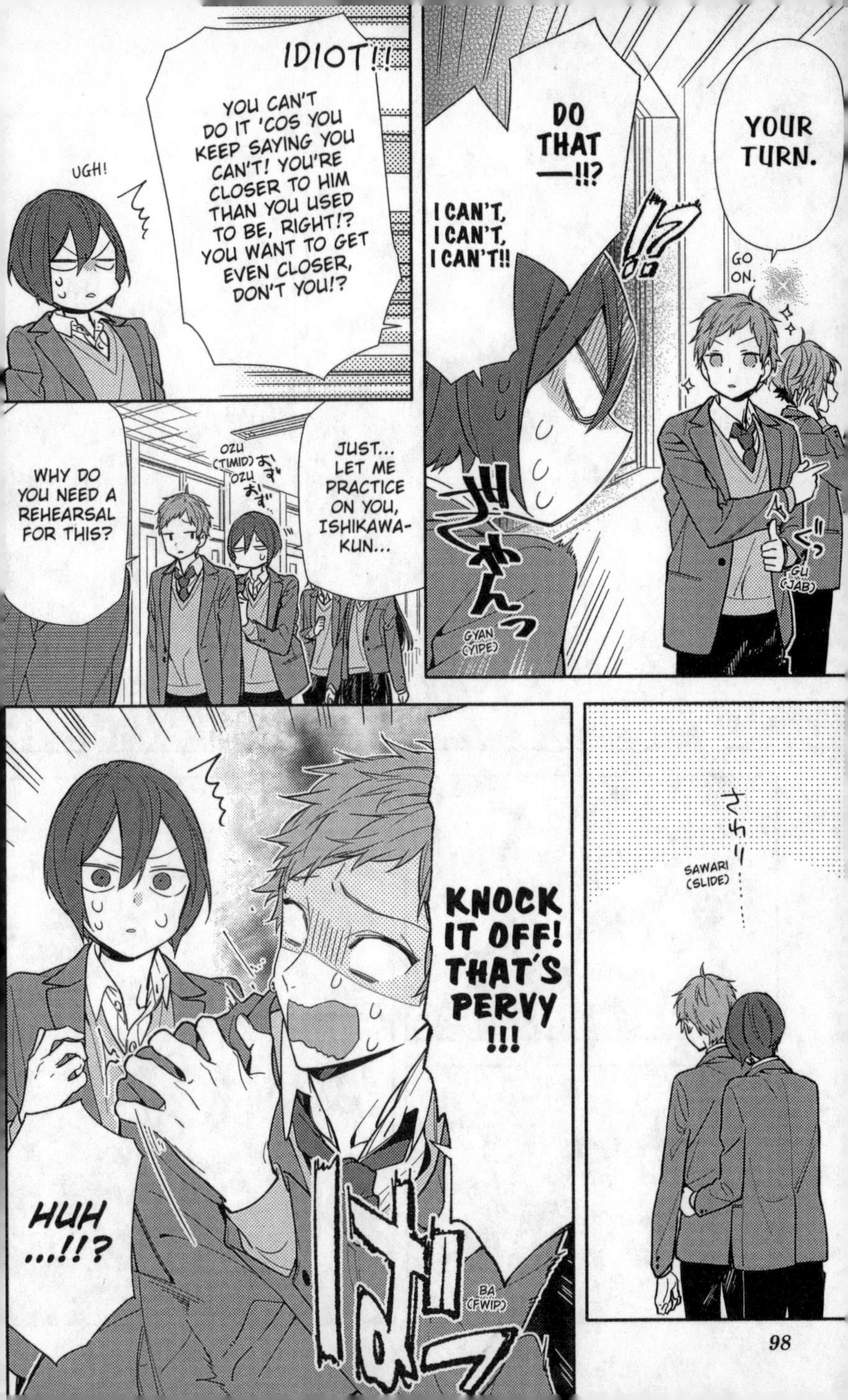
YOUR TURN.
GO ON.
GU (JAB)
DO THAT—!!?
I CAN'T, I CAN'T, I CAN'T!!
GYAN (YIPE)
IDIOT!!
YOU CAN'T DO IT 'COS YOU KEEP SAYING YOU CAN'T! YOU'RE CLOSER TO HIM THAN YOU USED TO BE, RIGHT!? YOU WANT TO GET EVEN CLOSER, DON'T YOU!?
UGH!
JUST... LET ME PRACTICE ON YOU, ISHIKAWA-KUN...
OZU (TIMID) OZU
WHY DO YOU NEED A REHEARSAL FOR THIS?
SAWARI (SLIDE)
KNOCK IT OFF! THAT'S PERVY!!!
BA (FWIP)
HUH ...!!?

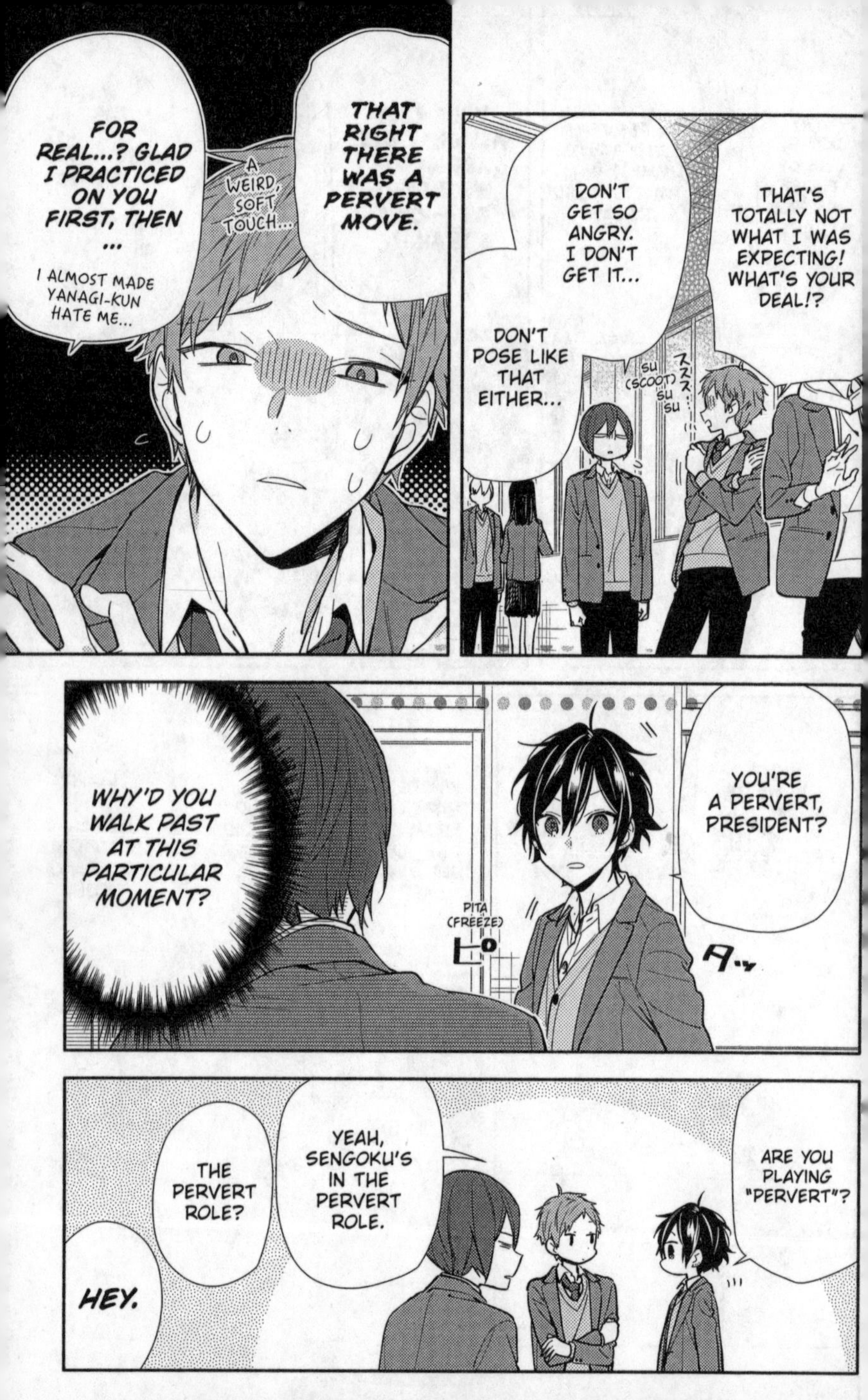
THAT'S TOTALLY NOT WHAT I WAS EXPECTING! WHAT'S YOUR DEAL!?
DON'T GET SO ANGRY. I DON'T GET IT...
DON'T POSE LIKE THAT EITHER...
SU (SCOOT) SU SU
THAT RIGHT THERE WAS A PERVERT MOVE.
A WEIRD, SOFT TOUCH...
FOR REAL...? GLAD I PRACTICED ON YOU FIRST, THEN ...
I ALMOST MADE YANAGI-KUN HATE ME...
YOU'RE A PERVERT, PRESIDENT?
PITA (FREEZE)
WHY'D YOU WALK PAST AT THIS PARTICULAR MOMENT?
ARE YOU PLAYING "PERVERT"?
YEAH, SENGOKU'S IN THE PERVERT ROLE.
THE PERVERT ROLE?
HEY.

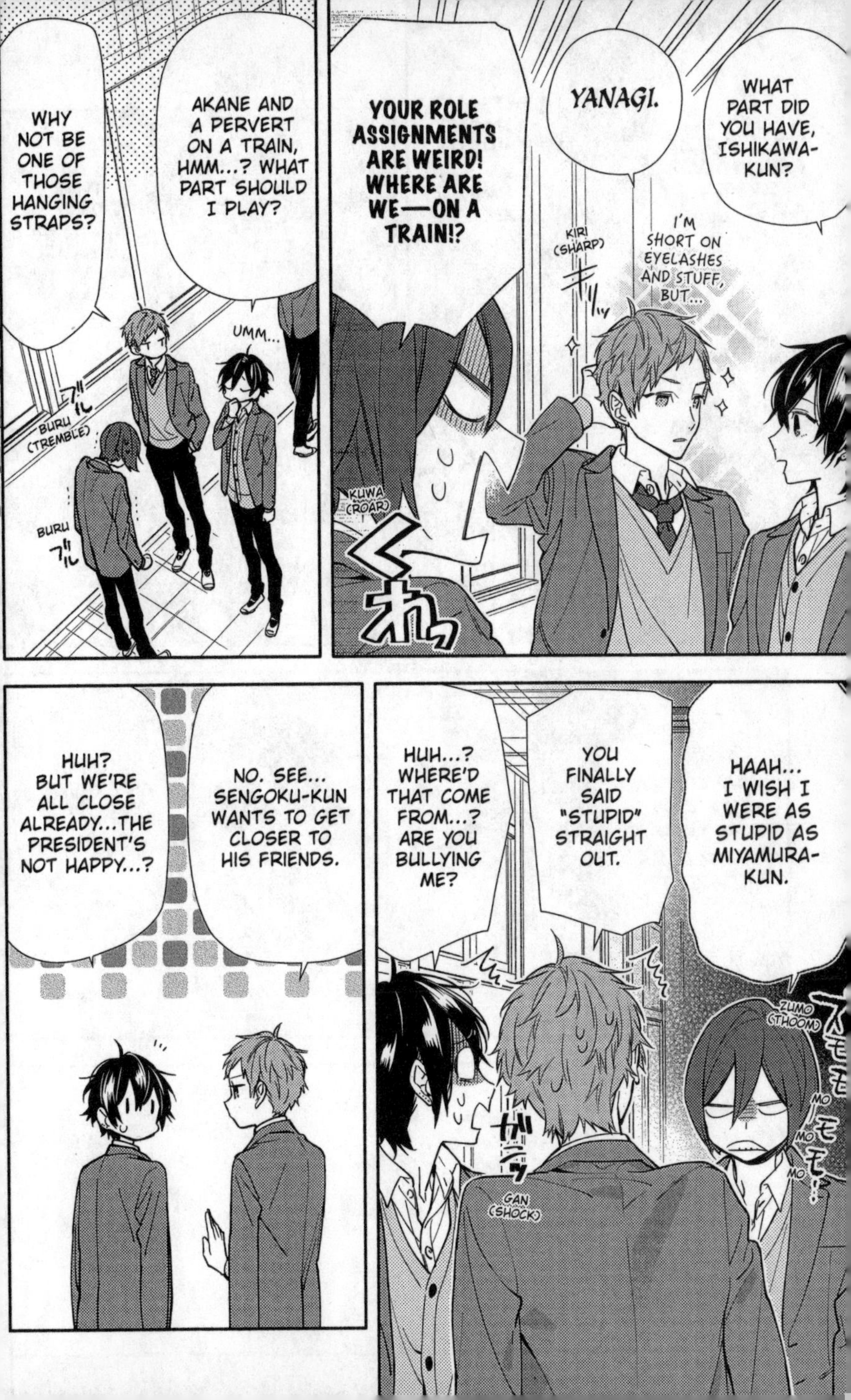
WHAT PART DID YOU HAVE, ISHIKAWA-KUN?
YANAGI.
I'M SHORT ON EYELASHES AND STUFF, BUT...
KIRI (SHARP)
YOUR ROLE ASSIGNMENTS ARE WEIRD! WHERE ARE WE—ON A TRAIN!?
KUWA (ROAR)
AKANE AND A PERVERT ON A TRAIN, HMM...? WHAT PART SHOULD I PLAY?
WHY NOT BE ONE OF THOSE HANGING STRAPS?
UMM...
BURU (TREMBLE)
BURU
HAAH... I WISH I WERE AS STUPID AS MIYAMURA-KUN.
YOU FINALLY SAID "STUPID" STRAIGHT OUT.
HUH...? WHERE'D THAT COME FROM...? ARE YOU BULLYING ME?
ZUMO (THOOM)
MO
MO
MO
GAN (SHOCK)
NO. SEE... SENGOKU-KUN WANTS TO GET CLOSER TO HIS FRIENDS.
HUH? BUT WE'RE ALL CLOSE ALREADY...THE PRESIDENT'S NOT HAPPY...?

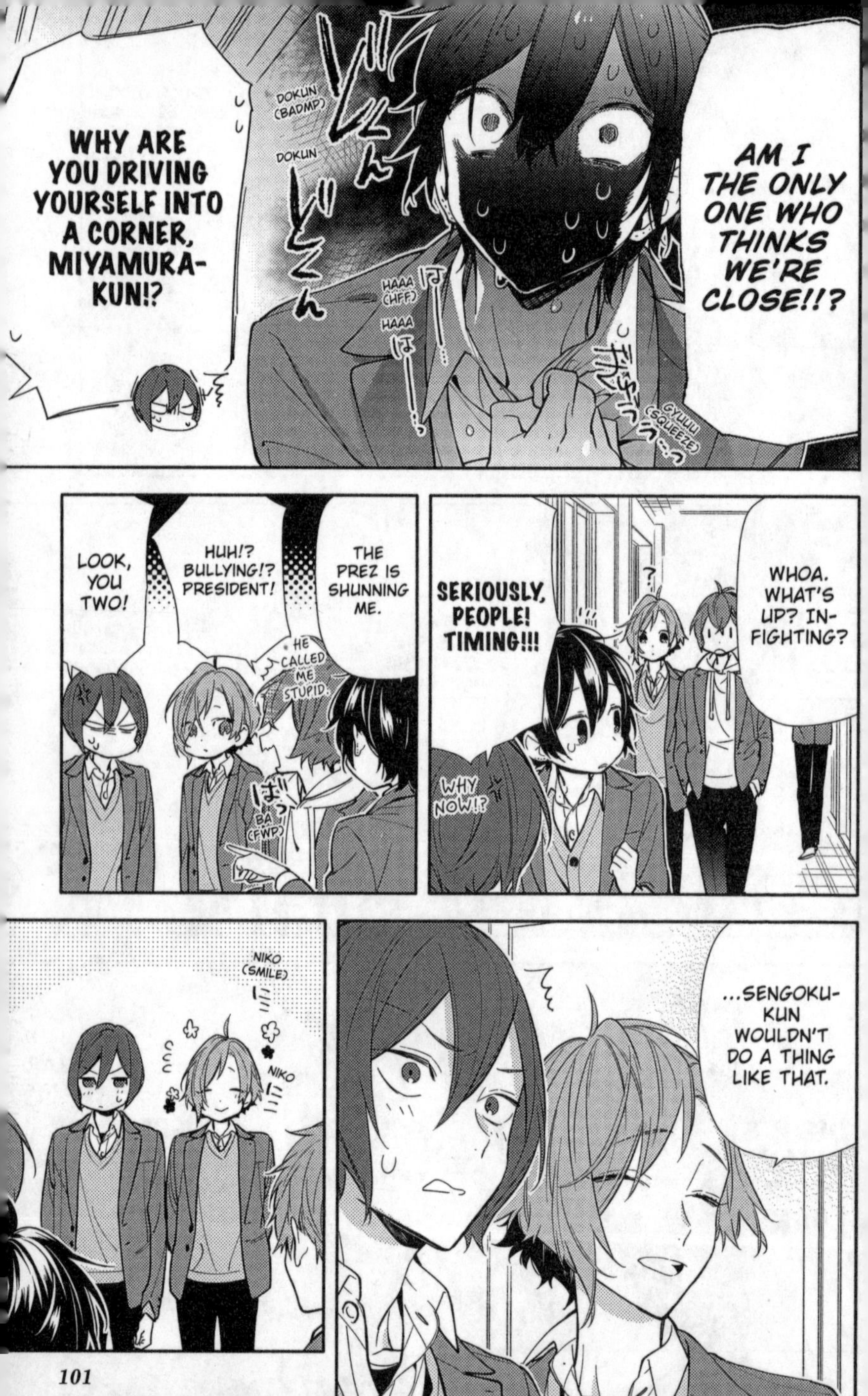
AM I THE ONLY ONE WHO THINKS WE'RE CLOSE!!?
DOKUN (BADMP)
DOKUN
HAAA (CHFF)
HAAA
GYUUU (SQUEEZE)
WHY ARE YOU DRIVING YOURSELF INTO A CORNER, MIYAMURA-KUN!?
WHOA. WHAT'S UP? IN-FIGHTING?
?
SERIOUSLY, PEOPLE! TIMING!!!
WHY NOW!?
THE PREZ IS SHUNNING ME.
HE CALLED ME STUPID.
BA (FWP)
HUH!? BULLYING!? PRESIDENT!
LOOK, YOU TWO!
...SENGOKU-KUN WOULDN'T DO A THING LIKE THAT.
NIKO (SMILE)
NIKO

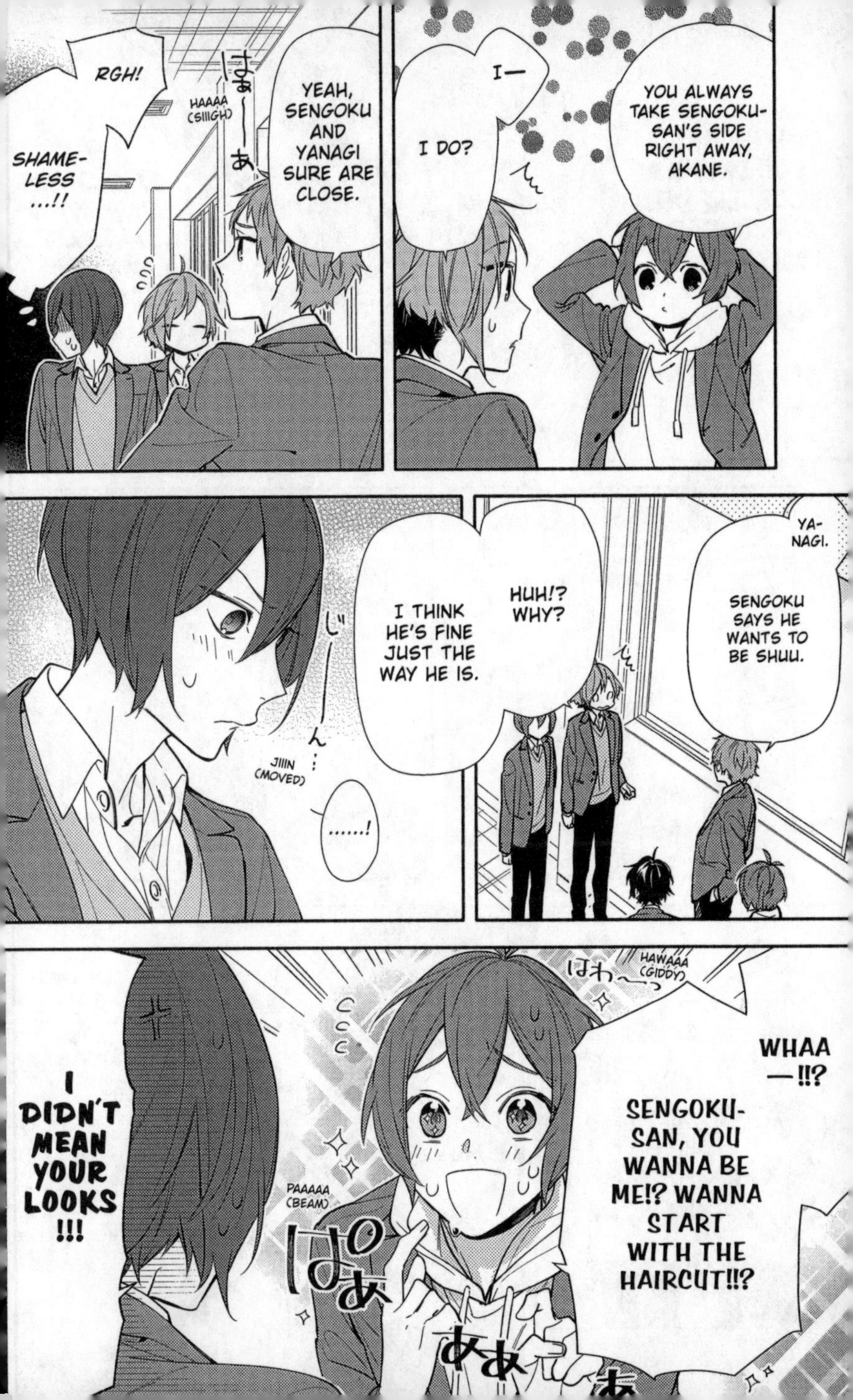
YOU ALWAYS TAKE SENGOKU-SAN'S SIDE RIGHT AWAY, AKANE.
I—
I DO?
YEAH, SENGOKU AND YANAGI SURE ARE CLOSE.
HAAAA (SIIIGH)
RGH!
SHAME-LESS ...!!
YA-NAGI.
SENGOKU SAYS HE WANTS TO BE SHUU.
HUH!? WHY?
I THINK HE'S FINE JUST THE WAY HE IS.
JIIIN (MOVED)
......!
WHAA—!!?
SENGOKU-SAN, YOU WANNA BE ME!? WANNA START WITH THE HAIRCUT!!?
HAWAAA (GIDDY)
PAAAAA (BEAM)
I DIDN'T MEAN YOUR LOOKS!!!

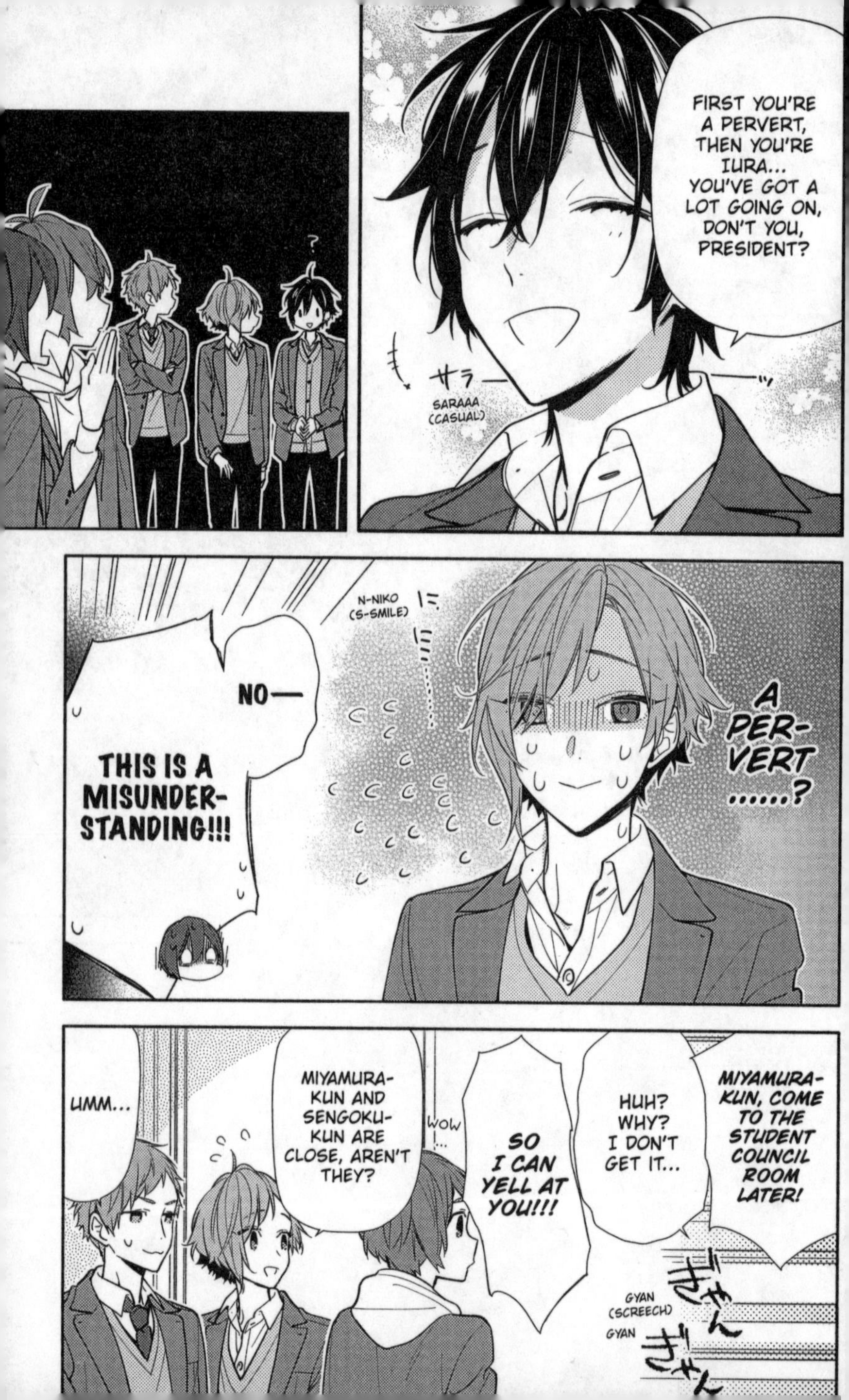
FIRST YOU'RE A PERVERT, THEN YOU'RE IURA... YOU'VE GOT A LOT GOING ON, DON'T YOU, PRESIDENT?
SARAAA (CASUAL)
?
A PERVERT......?
N-NIKO (S-SMILE)
NO—
THIS IS A MISUNDERSTANDING!!!
GYAN (SCREECH) GYAN
MIYAMURA-KUN, COME TO THE STUDENT COUNCIL ROOM LATER!
HUH? WHY? I DON'T GET IT...
SO I CAN YELL AT YOU!!!
WOW!...
MIYAMURA-KUN AND SENGOKU-KUN ARE CLOSE, AREN'T THEY?
UMM...

HORIMIYA

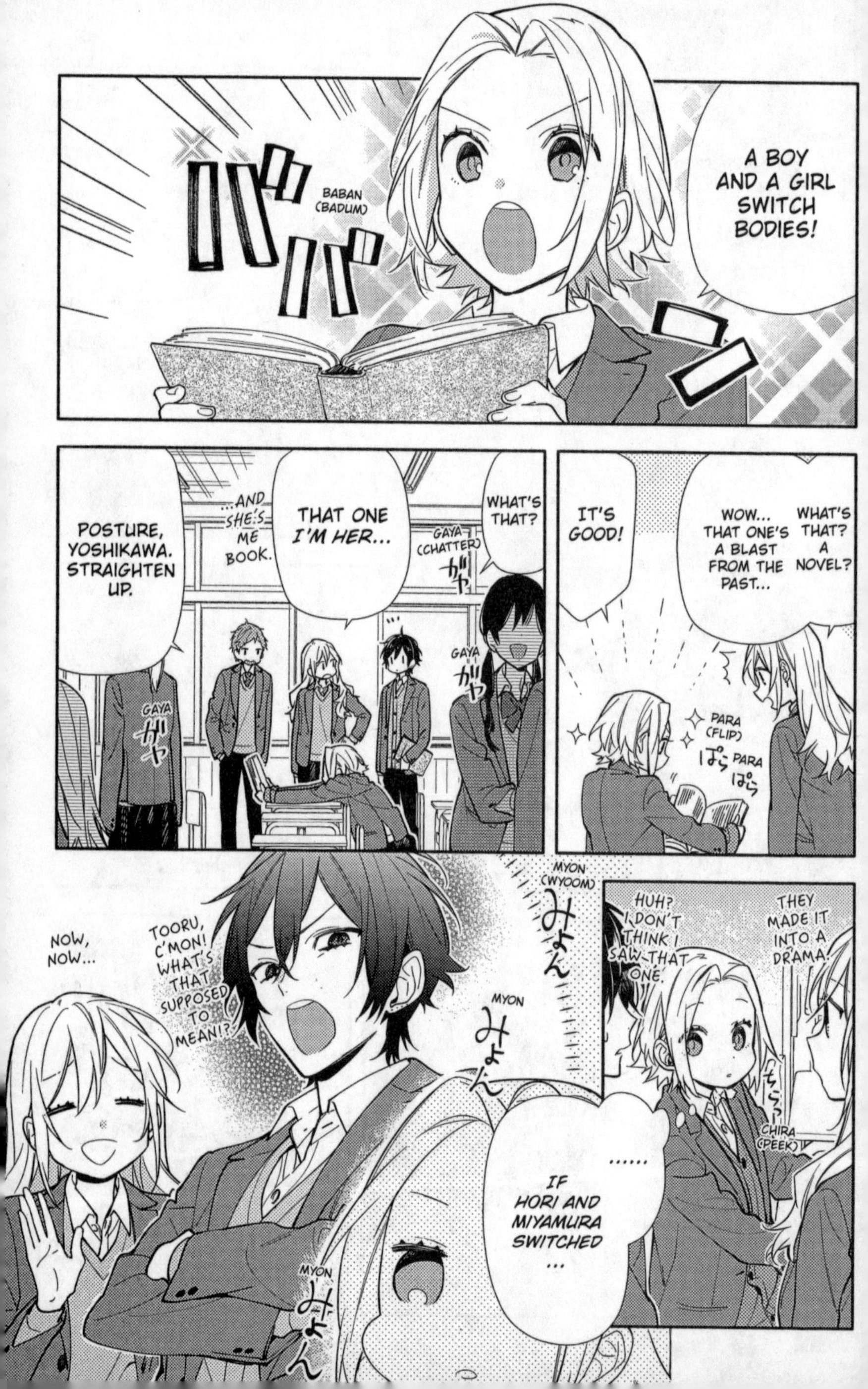
A BOY AND A GIRL SWITCH BODIES!
BABAN (BADUM)
WHAT'S THAT? A NOVEL?
WOW... THAT ONE'S A BLAST FROM THE PAST...
IT'S GOOD!
PARA (FLIP)
PARA
WHAT'S THAT?
GAYA (CHATTER)
THAT ONE *I'M HER...*
...AND SHE'S ME BOOK.
GAYA
POSTURE, YOSHIKAWA. STRAIGHTEN UP.
GAYA
THEY MADE IT INTO A DRAMA.
HUH? I DON'T THINK I SAW THAT ONE.
CHIRA (PEEK)
MYON (WYOOM)
TOORU, C'MON! WHAT'S THAT SUPPOSED TO MEAN!?
NOW, NOW...
MYON
...... IF HORI AND MIYAMURA SWITCHED ...
MYON

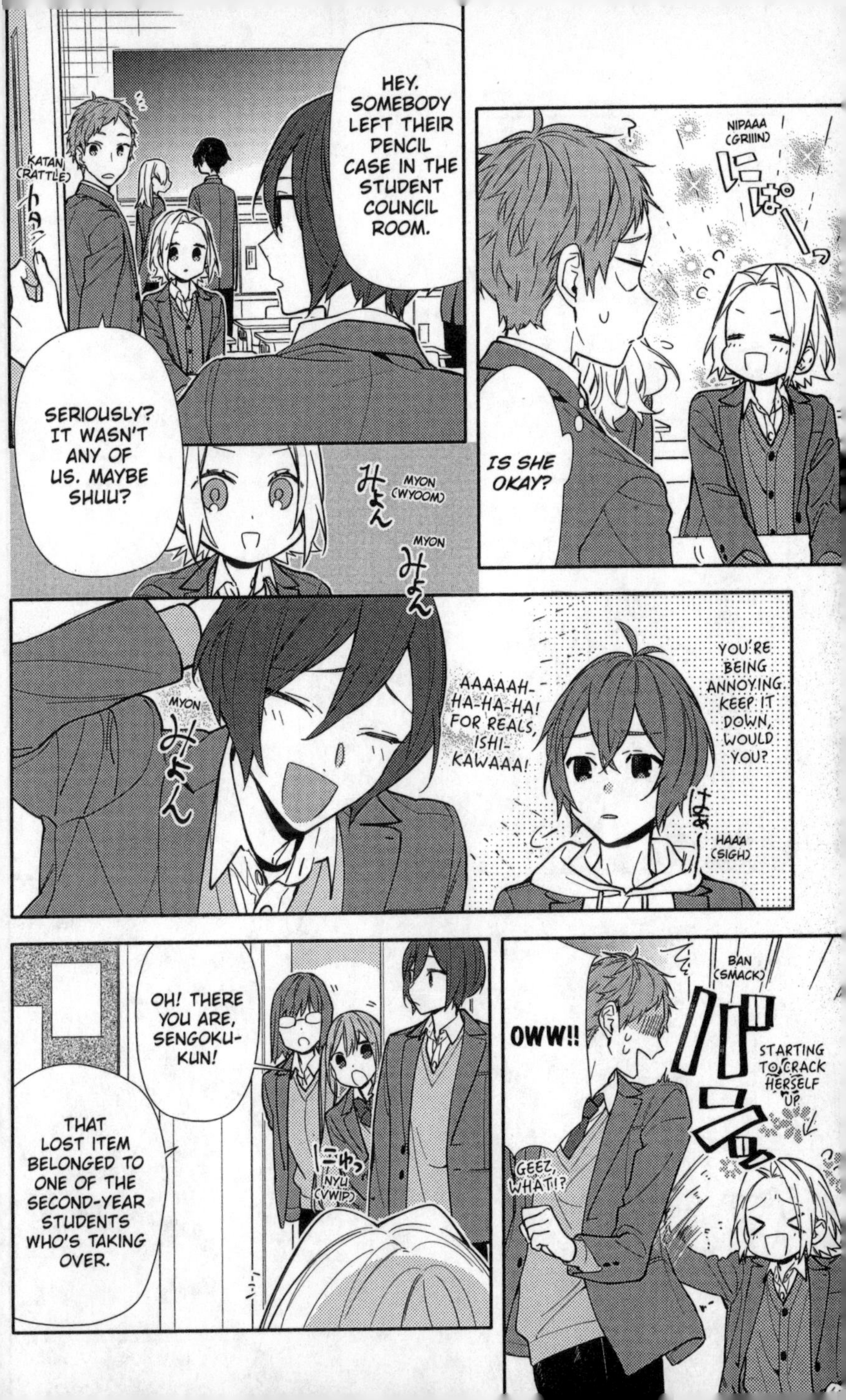
NIPAAA (GRIIIN)
にぱーっ
IS SHE OKAY?
HEY. SOMEBODY LEFT THEIR PENCIL CASE IN THE STUDENT COUNCIL ROOM.
KATAN (RATTLE)
SERIOUSLY? IT WASN'T ANY OF US. MAYBE SHUU?
MYON (WYOOM)
みょん
MYON
みょん
YOU'RE BEING ANNOYING. KEEP IT DOWN, WOULD YOU?
HAAA (SIGH)
はぁ
AAAAAH-HA-HA-HA! FOR REALS, ISHIKAWAAA!
MYON
みょん
BAN (SMACK)
OWW!!
STARTING TO CRACK HERSELF UP
GEEZ, WHAT!?
OH! THERE YOU ARE, SENGOKU-KUN!
にゅっ
NYU (VWIP)
THAT LOST ITEM BELONGED TO ONE OF THE SECOND-YEAR STUDENTS WHO'S TAKING OVER.

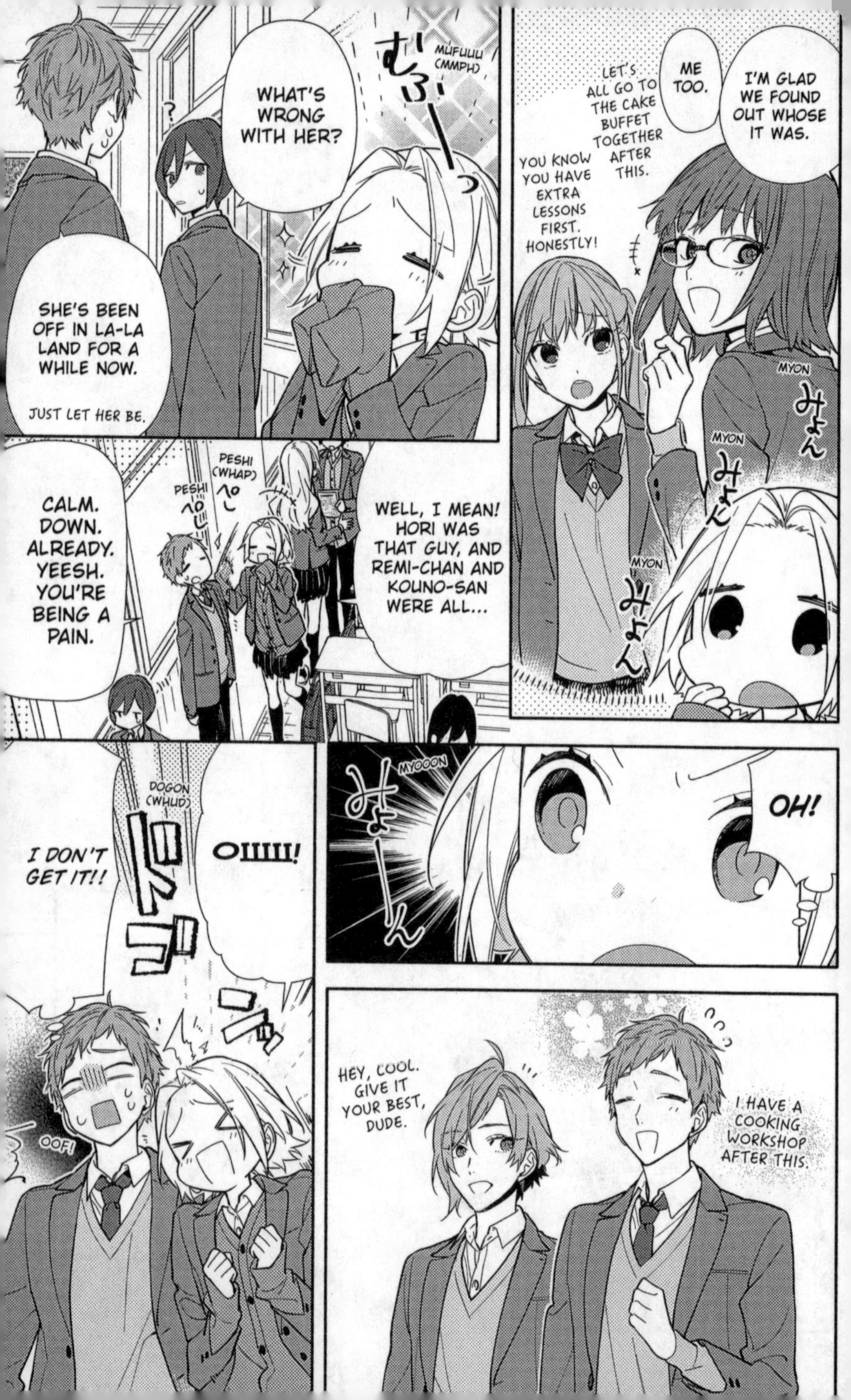
I'M GLAD WE FOUND OUT WHOSE IT WAS.
ME TOO.
LET'S ALL GO TO THE CAKE BUFFET TOGETHER AFTER THIS.
YOU KNOW YOU HAVE EXTRA LESSONS FIRST. HONESTLY!
MYON
みょん
MYON
みょん
MYON
みょん
MUFUUU (MMPH)
むふーっ
WHAT'S WRONG WITH HER?
?
SHE'S BEEN OFF IN LA-LA LAND FOR A WHILE NOW.
JUST LET HER BE.
WELL, I MEAN! HORI WAS THAT GUY, AND REMI-CHAN AND KOUNO-SAN WERE ALL...
PESHI (WHAP)
ぺし
PESHI
ぺし
CALM. DOWN. ALREADY. YEESH. YOU'RE BEING A PAIN.
OH!
MYOOON
みょーん
I HAVE A COOKING WORKSHOP AFTER THIS.
HEY, COOL. GIVE IT YOUR BEST, DUDE.
OIIIII!
DOGON (WHUD)
ドゴーン
I DON'T GET IT!!
OOF!

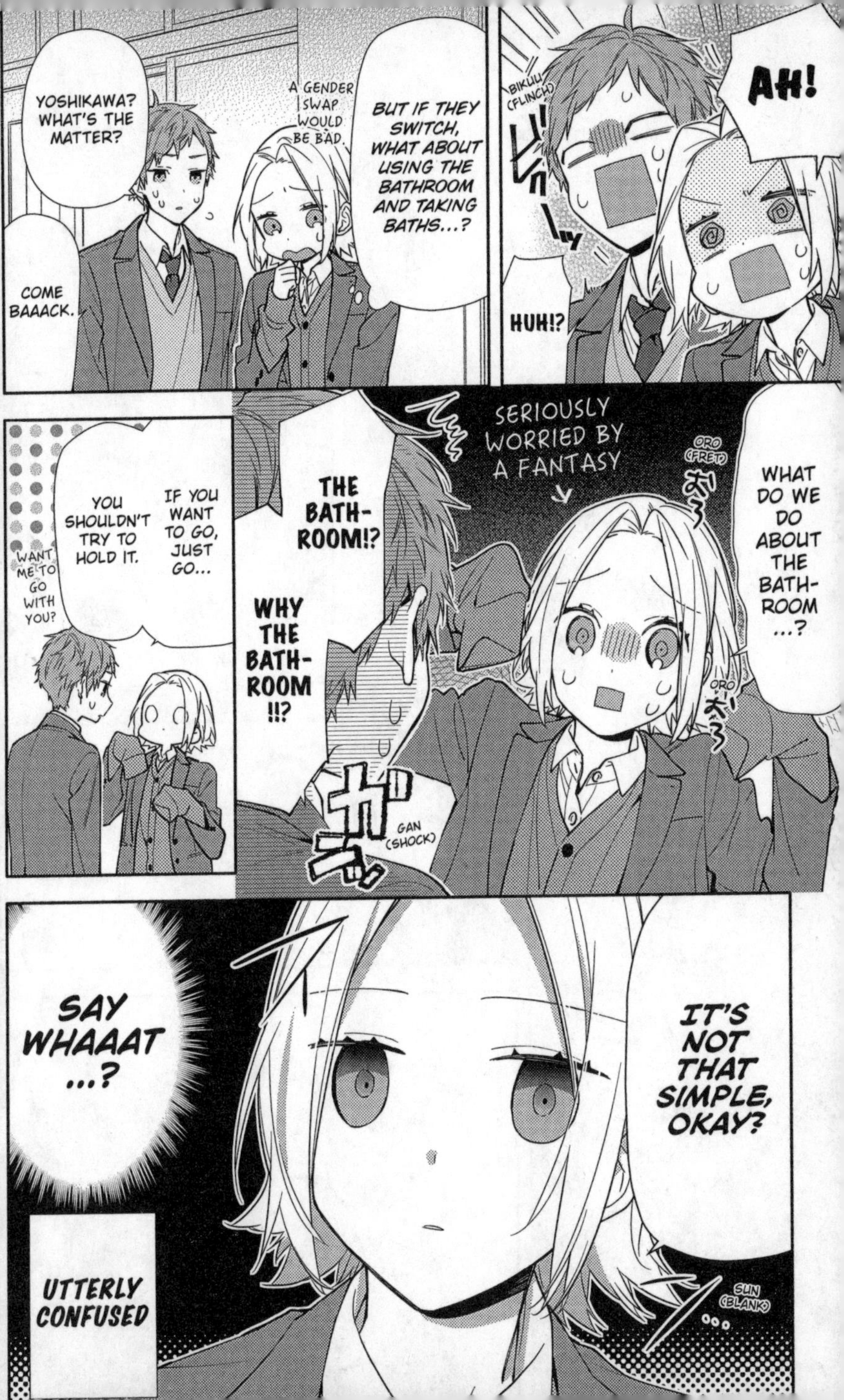
AH!
BIKUU (FLINCH)
HUH!?
BUT IF THEY SWITCH, WHAT ABOUT USING THE BATHROOM AND TAKING BATHS...?
A GENDER SWAP WOULD BE BAD.
YOSHIKAWA? WHAT'S THE MATTER?
COME BAAACK.
WHAT DO WE DO ABOUT THE BATHROOM...?
ORO (FRET)
ORO
SERIOUSLY WORRIED BY A FANTASY
THE BATHROOM!?
WHY THE BATHROOM!!?
GAN (SHOCK)
IF YOU WANT TO GO, JUST GO...
YOU SHOULDN'T TRY TO HOLD IT.
WANT ME TO GO WITH YOU?
IT'S NOT THAT SIMPLE, OKAY?
SUN (BLANK)
...
SAY WHAAAT...?
UTTERLY CONFUSED

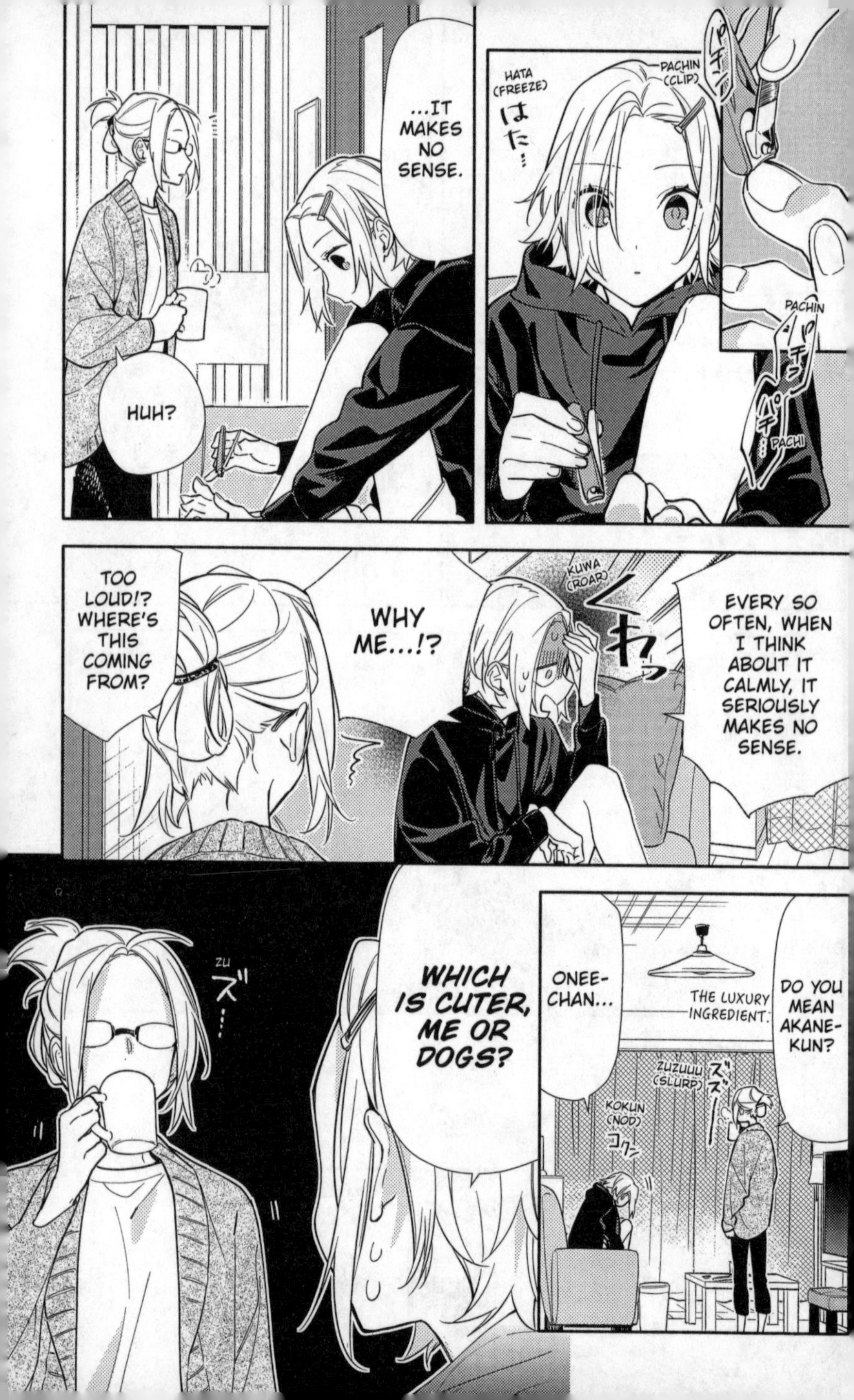
PACHIN (CLIP)
PACHIN
PACHI
HATA (FREEZE)
はた…
...IT MAKES NO SENSE.
HUH?
EVERY SO OFTEN, WHEN I THINK ABOUT IT CALMLY, IT SERIOUSLY MAKES NO SENSE.
KUWA (ROAR)
WHY ME...!?
TOO LOUD!? WHERE'S THIS COMING FROM?
DO YOU MEAN AKANE-KUN?
THE LUXURY INGREDIENT.
ONEE-CHAN...
ZUZUUU (SLURP)
KOKUN (NOD)
WHICH IS CUTER, ME OR DOGS?
ZU
ズ…

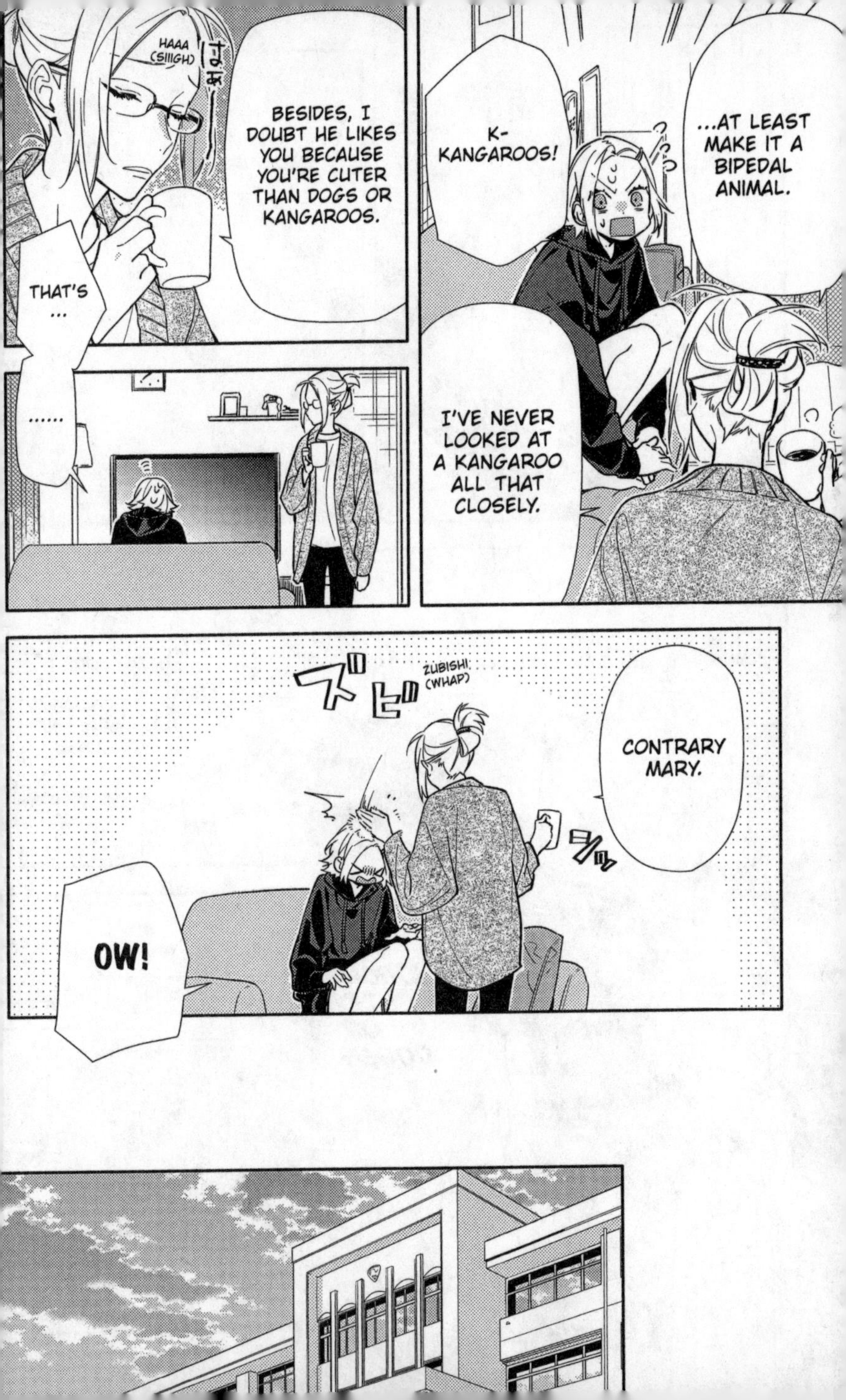
...AT LEAST MAKE IT A BIPEDAL ANIMAL.
K-KANGAROOS!
I'VE NEVER LOOKED AT A KANGAROO ALL THAT CLOSELY.
HAAA (SIIIGH)
BESIDES, I DOUBT HE LIKES YOU BECAUSE YOU'RE CUTER THAN DOGS OR KANGAROOS.
THAT'S ...
......
ZUBISHI (WHAP)
CONTRARY MARY.
OW!

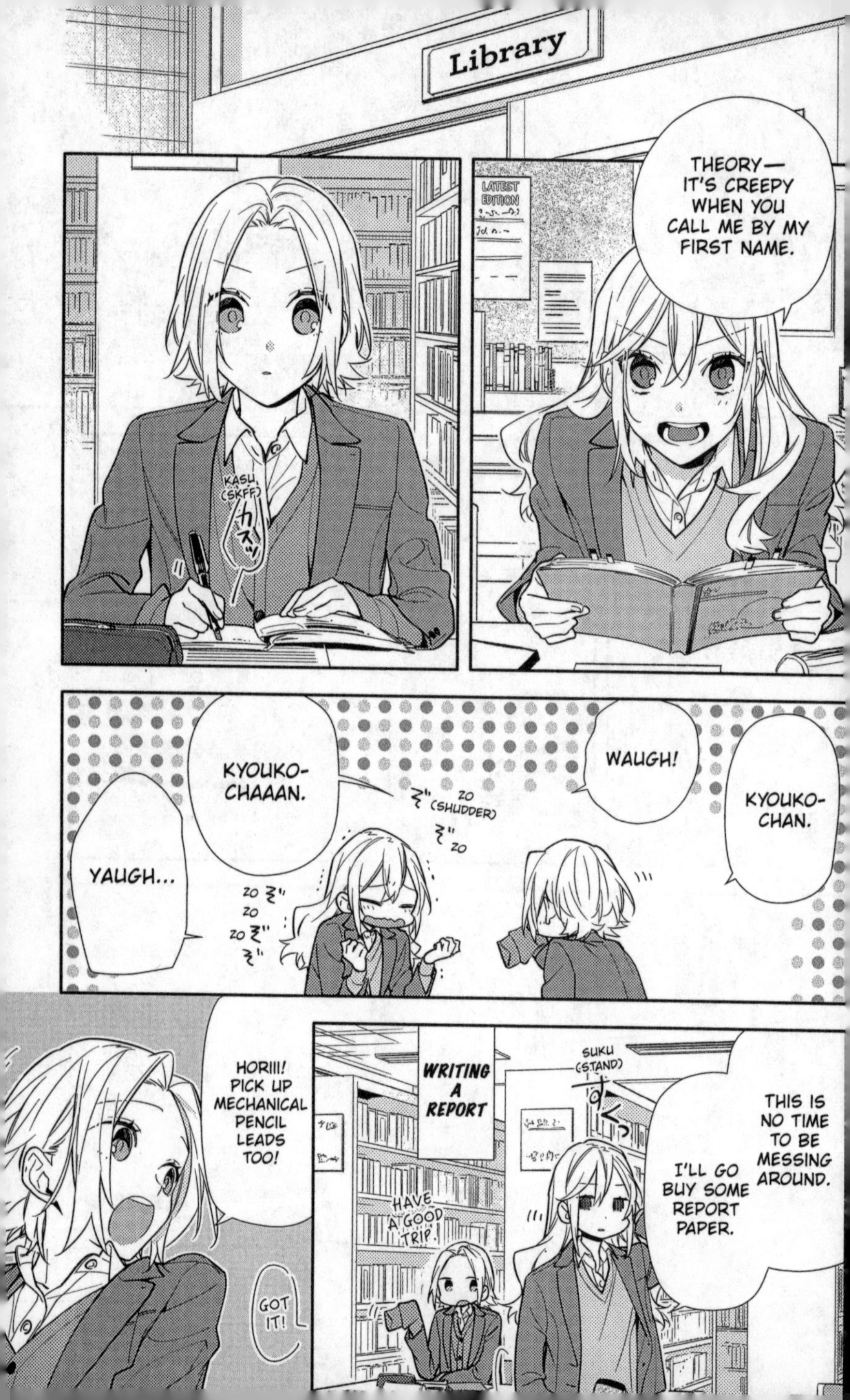
Library
THEORY— IT'S CREEPY WHEN YOU CALL ME BY MY FIRST NAME.
LATEST EDITION
KASU (SKFF)
KYOUKO-CHAN.
WAUGH!
ZO (SHUDDER)
ZO
KYOUKO-CHAAAN.
ZO ZO ZO
YAUGH...
WRITING A REPORT
THIS IS NO TIME TO BE MESSING AROUND.
I'LL GO BUY SOME REPORT PAPER.
SUKU (STAND)
HAVE A GOOD TRIP.
HORIII! PICK UP MECHANICAL PENCIL LEADS TOO!
GOT IT!

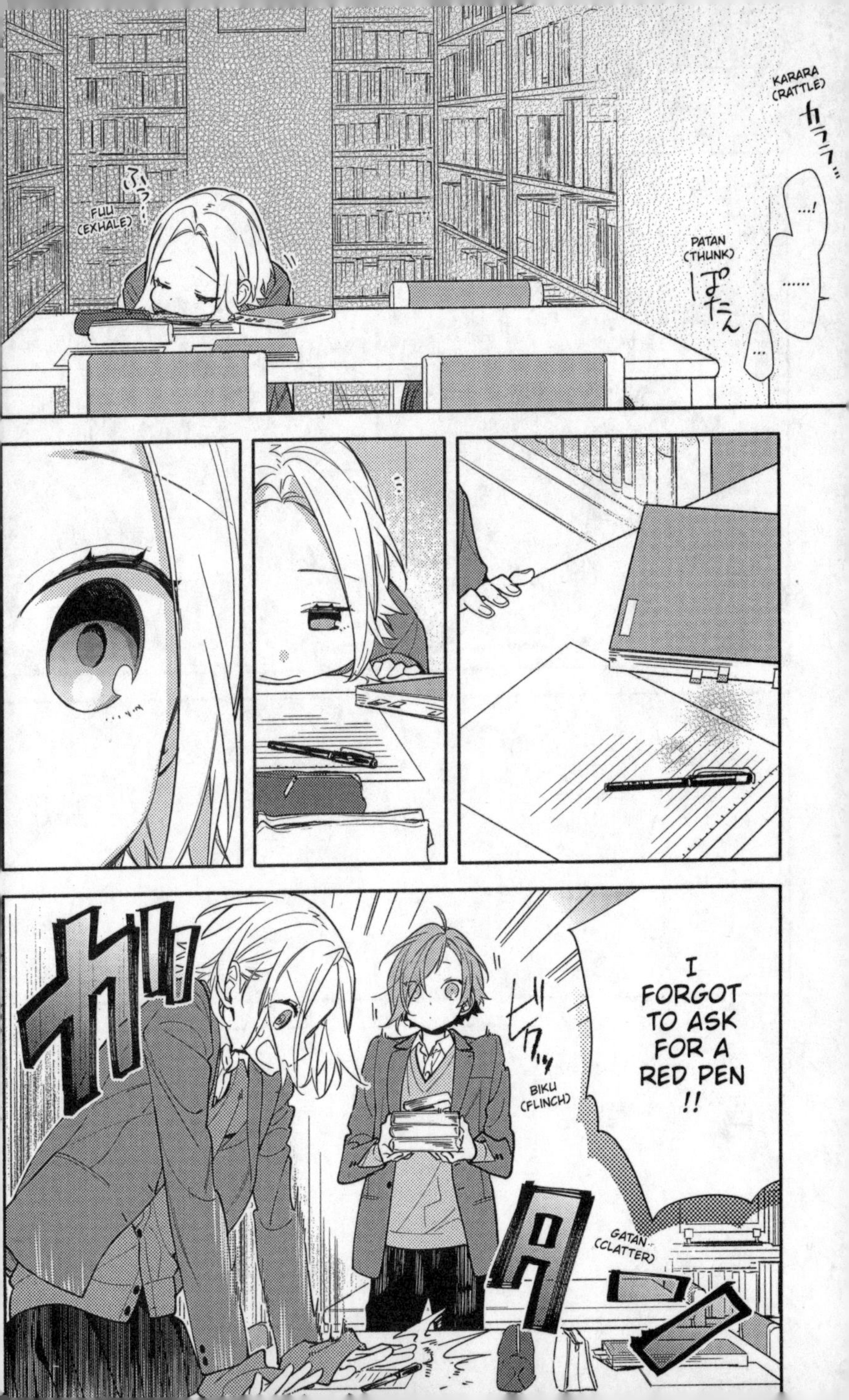
KARARA (RATTLE)
...!
......
PATAN (THUNK)
...
FUU (EXHALE)
I FORGOT TO ASK FOR A RED PEN!!
BIKU (FLINCH)
GATAN (CLATTER)

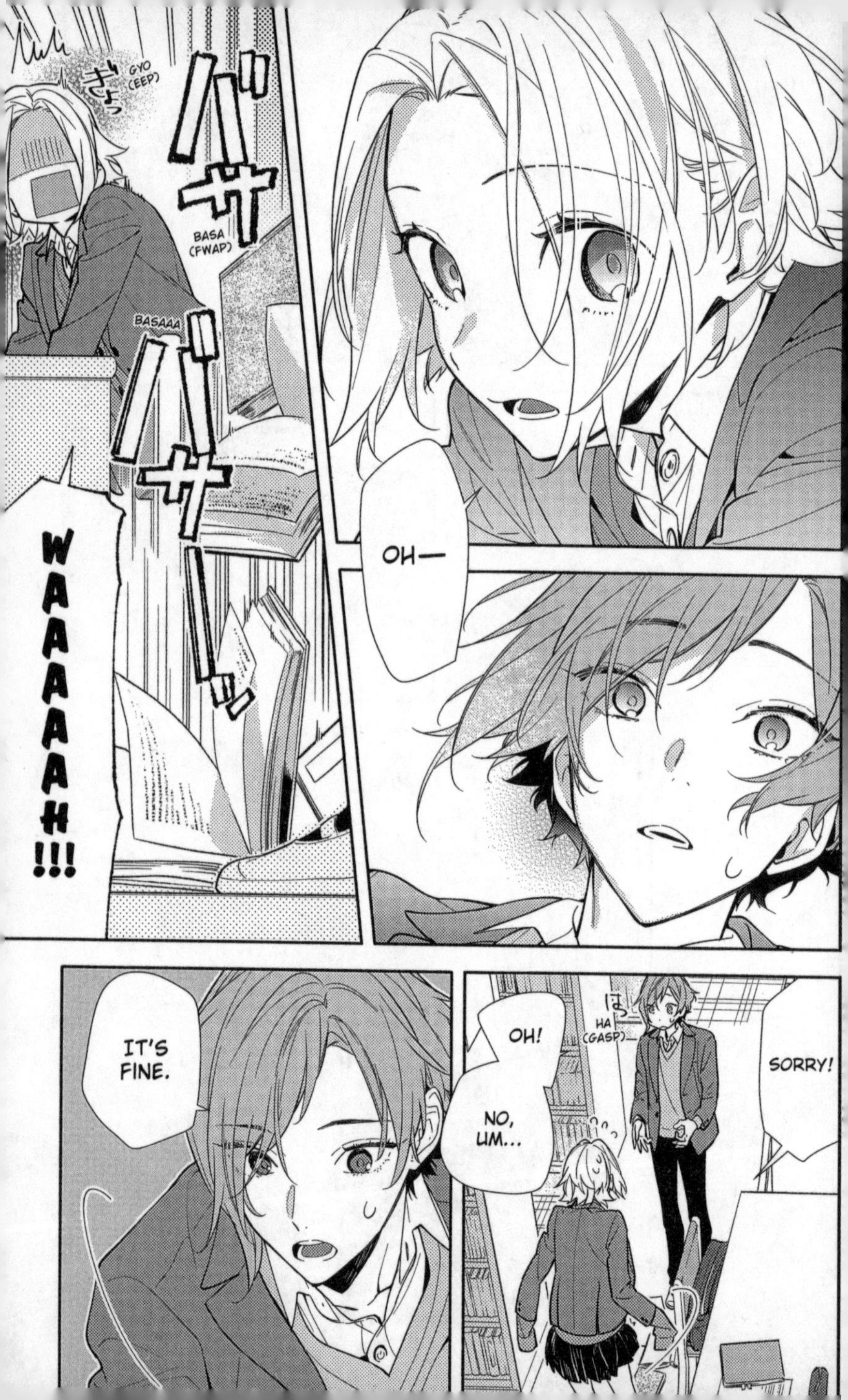

OH—
バサ
BASA (FWAP)
ぎょっ
GYO (EEP)
BASAAA
WAAAAAH!!!
SORRY!
はっ
HA (GASP)
OH!
NO, UM...
IT'S FINE.

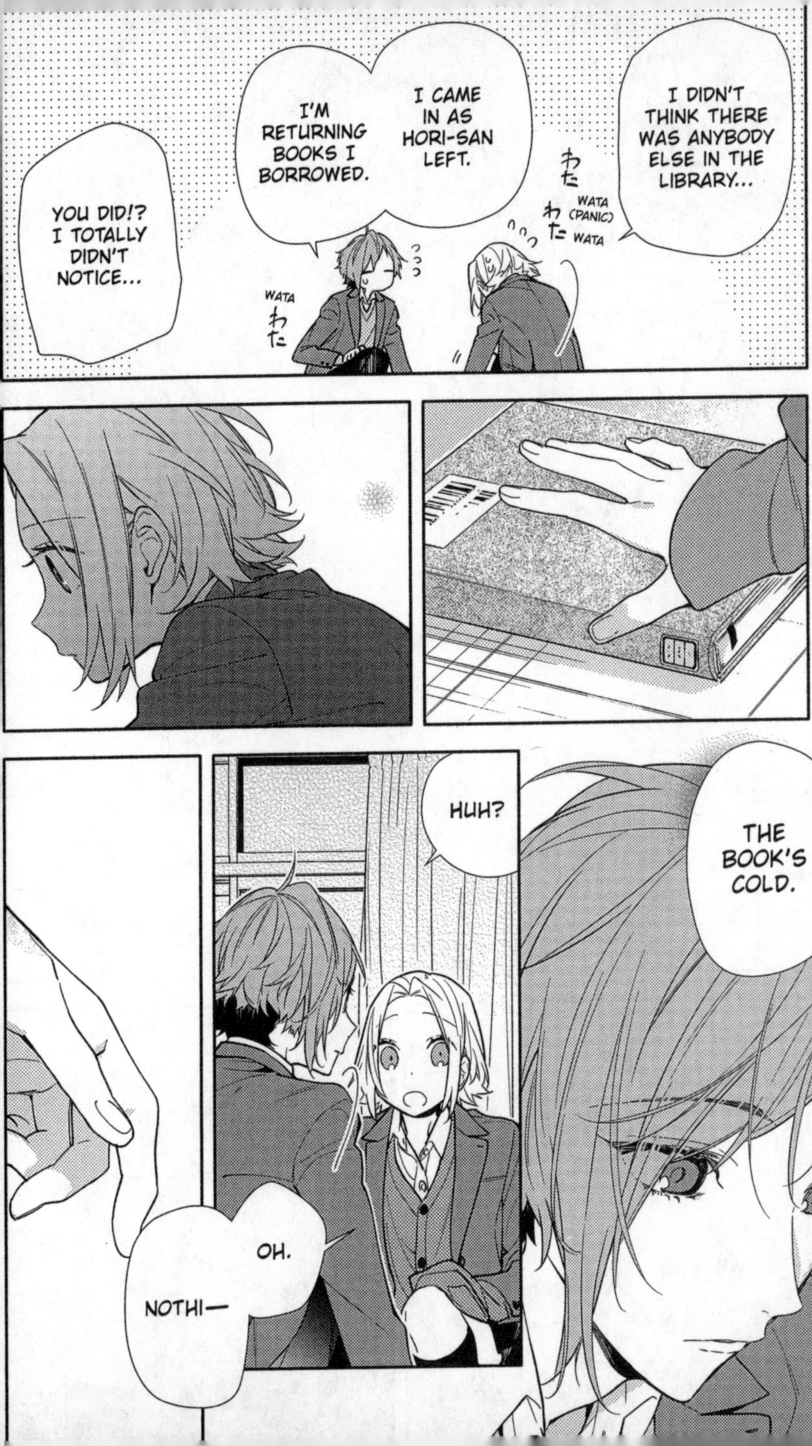
I DIDN'T THINK THERE WAS ANYBODY ELSE IN THE LIBRARY...
わた WATA (PANIC)
わた WATA
I CAME IN AS HORI-SAN LEFT.
I'M RETURNING BOOKS I BORROWED.
わた WATA
YOU DID!? I TOTALLY DIDN'T NOTICE...
THE BOOK'S COLD.
HUH?
OH.
NOTHI—

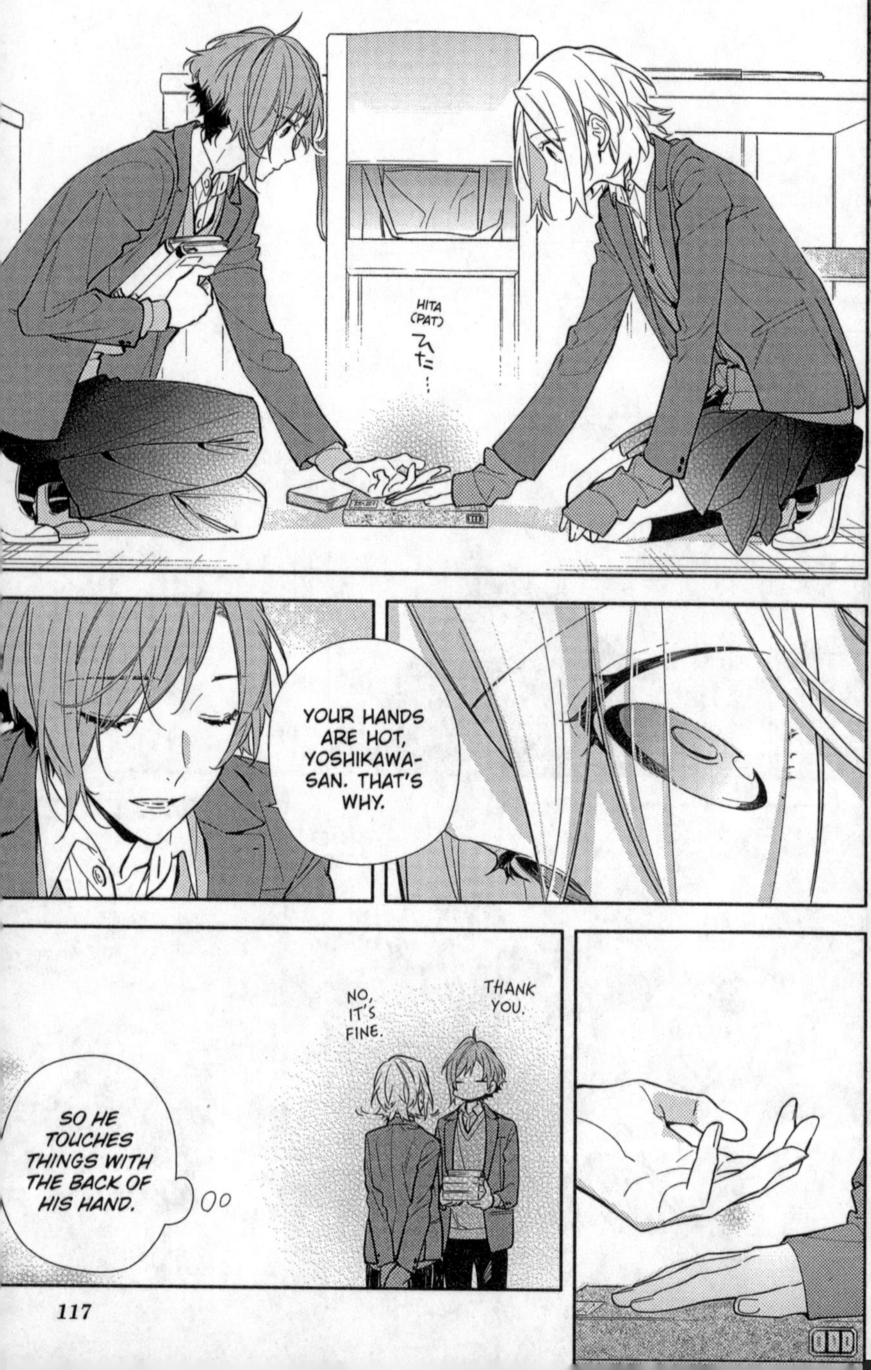
HITA (PAT)
ひた…
YOUR HANDS ARE HOT, YOSHIKAWA-SAN. THAT'S WHY.
THANK YOU.
NO, IT'S FINE.
SO HE TOUCHES THINGS WITH THE BACK OF HIS HAND.

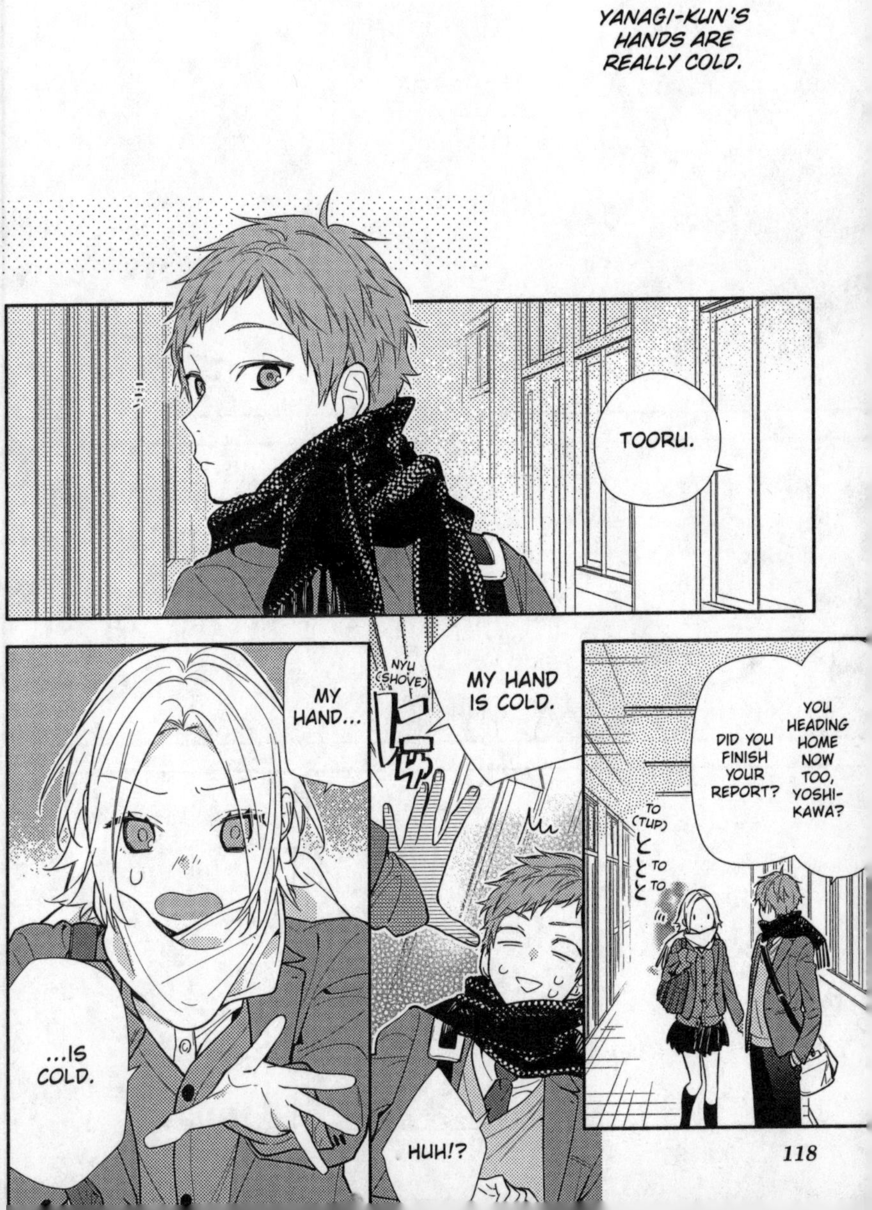
YANAGI-KUN'S HANDS ARE REALLY COLD.
TOORU.
YOU HEADING HOME NOW TOO, YOSHI-KAWA?
DID YOU FINISH YOUR REPORT?
TO (TUP)
TO
TO
MY HAND IS COLD.
NYU (SHOVE)
HUH!?
MY HAND...
...IS COLD.

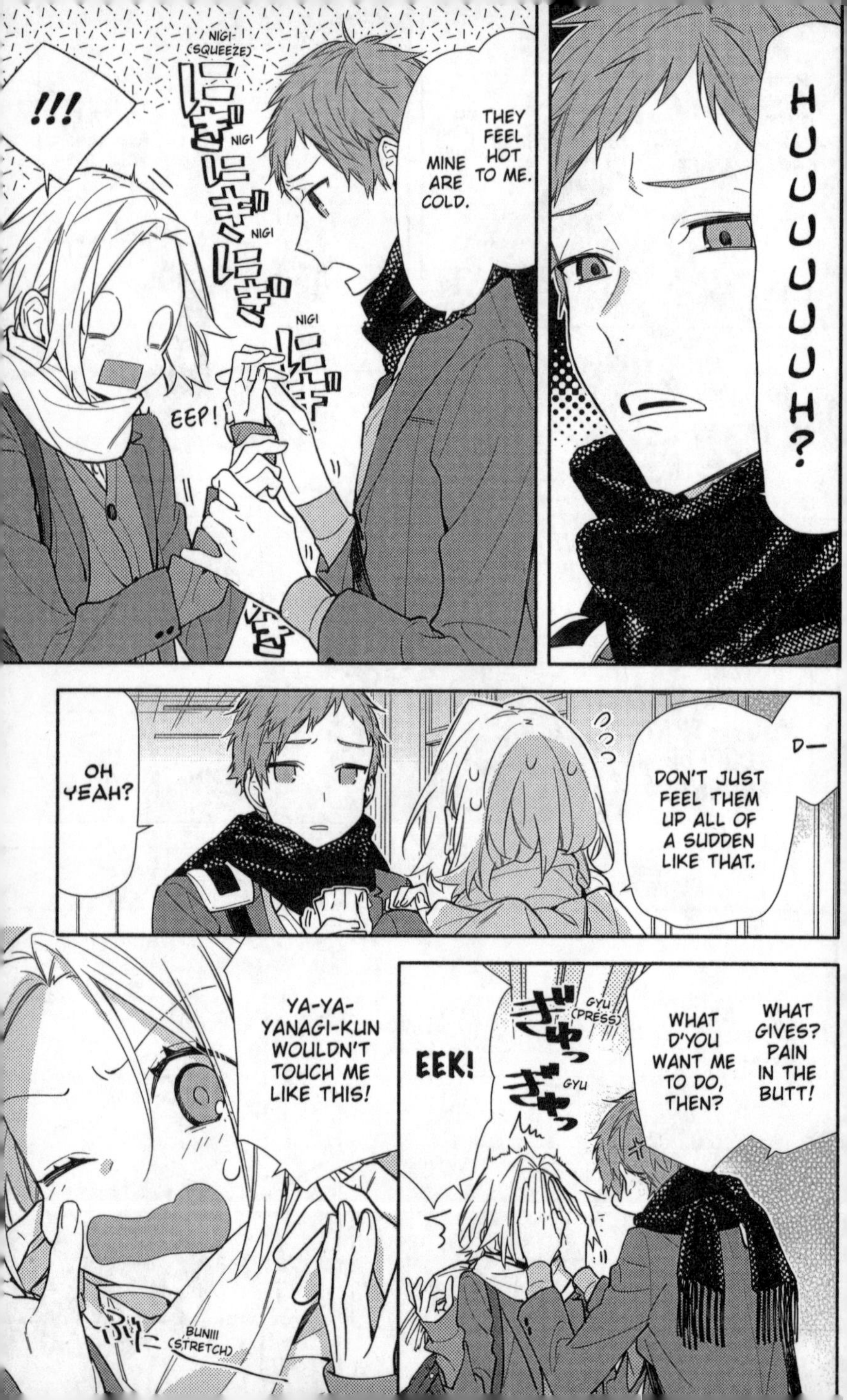
HUUUUUUH?
THEY FEEL HOT TO ME.
MINE ARE COLD.
NIGI-(SQUEEZE)
!!!
NIGI
NIGI
NIGI
EEP!
D—
DON'T JUST FEEL THEM UP ALL OF A SUDDEN LIKE THAT.
OH YEAH?
WHAT GIVES? PAIN IN THE BUTT!
WHAT D'YOU WANT ME TO DO, THEN?
GYU (PRESS)
GYU
EEK!
YA-YA-YANAGI-KUN WOULDN'T TOUCH ME LIKE THIS!
BUNIII (STRETCH)

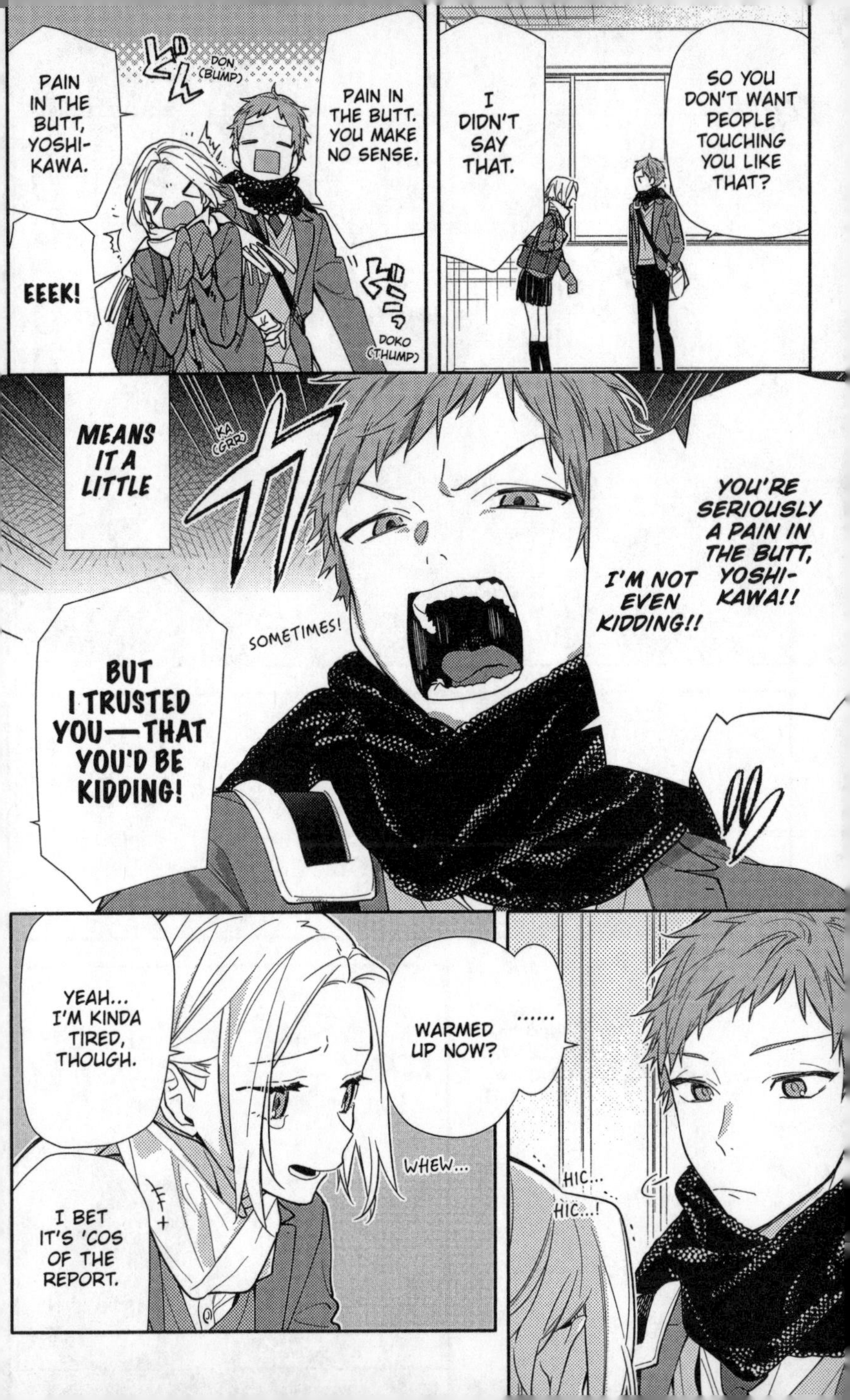
SO YOU DON'T WANT PEOPLE TOUCHING YOU LIKE THAT?
I DIDN'T SAY THAT.
PAIN IN THE BUTT. YOU MAKE NO SENSE.
DON (BUMP)
PAIN IN THE BUTT, YOSHI-KAWA.
EEEK!
DOKO (THUMP)
YOU'RE SERIOUSLY A PAIN IN THE BUTT, YOSHI-KAWA!!
I'M NOT EVEN KIDDING!!
KA (GRR)
MEANS IT A LITTLE
SOMETIMES!
BUT I TRUSTED YOU—THAT YOU'D BE KIDDING!
HIC...
HIC...!
......
WARMED UP NOW?
WHEW...
YEAH... I'M KINDA TIRED, THOUGH.
I BET IT'S 'COS OF THE REPORT.

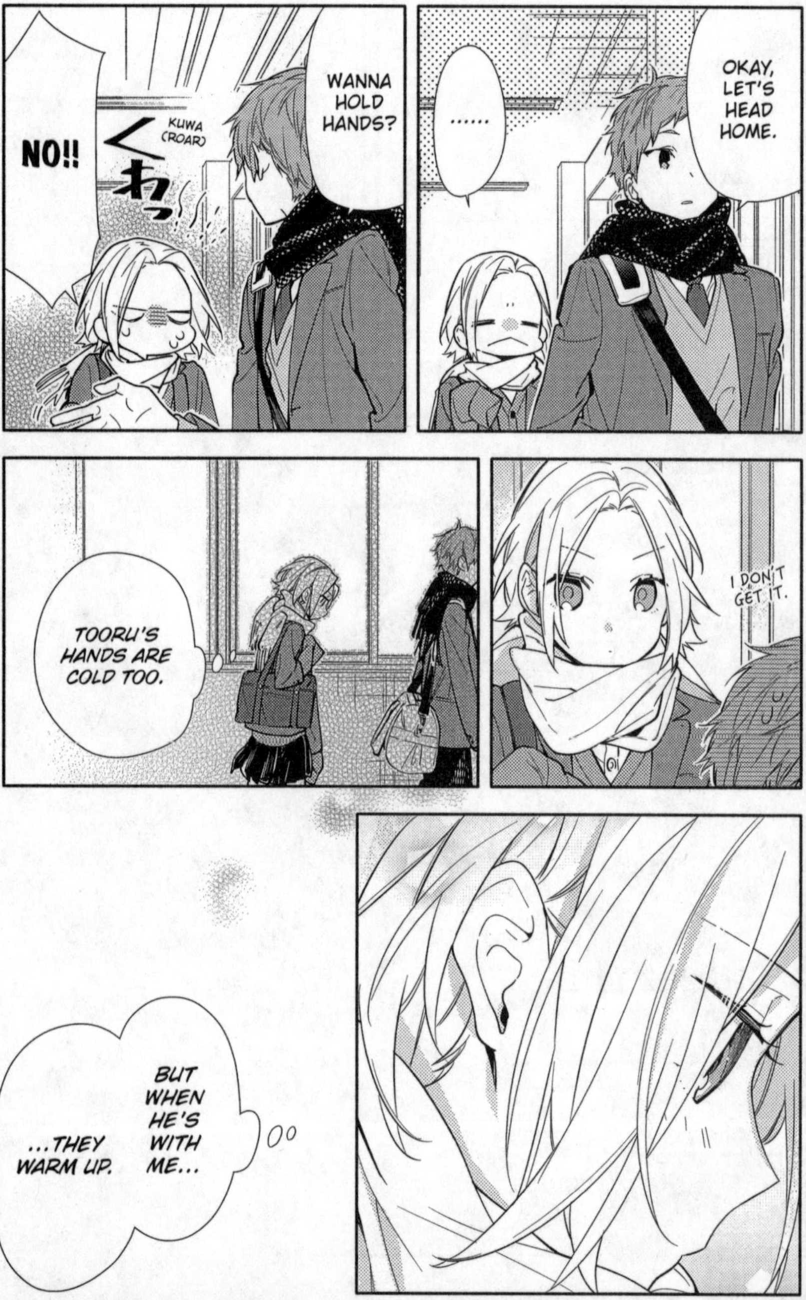
OKAY, LET'S HEAD HOME.
......
WANNA HOLD HANDS?
くわっ
KUWA (ROAR)
NO!!
I DON'T GET IT.
TOORU'S HANDS ARE COLD TOO.
BUT WHEN HE'S WITH ME...
...THEY WARM UP.

HORIMIYA

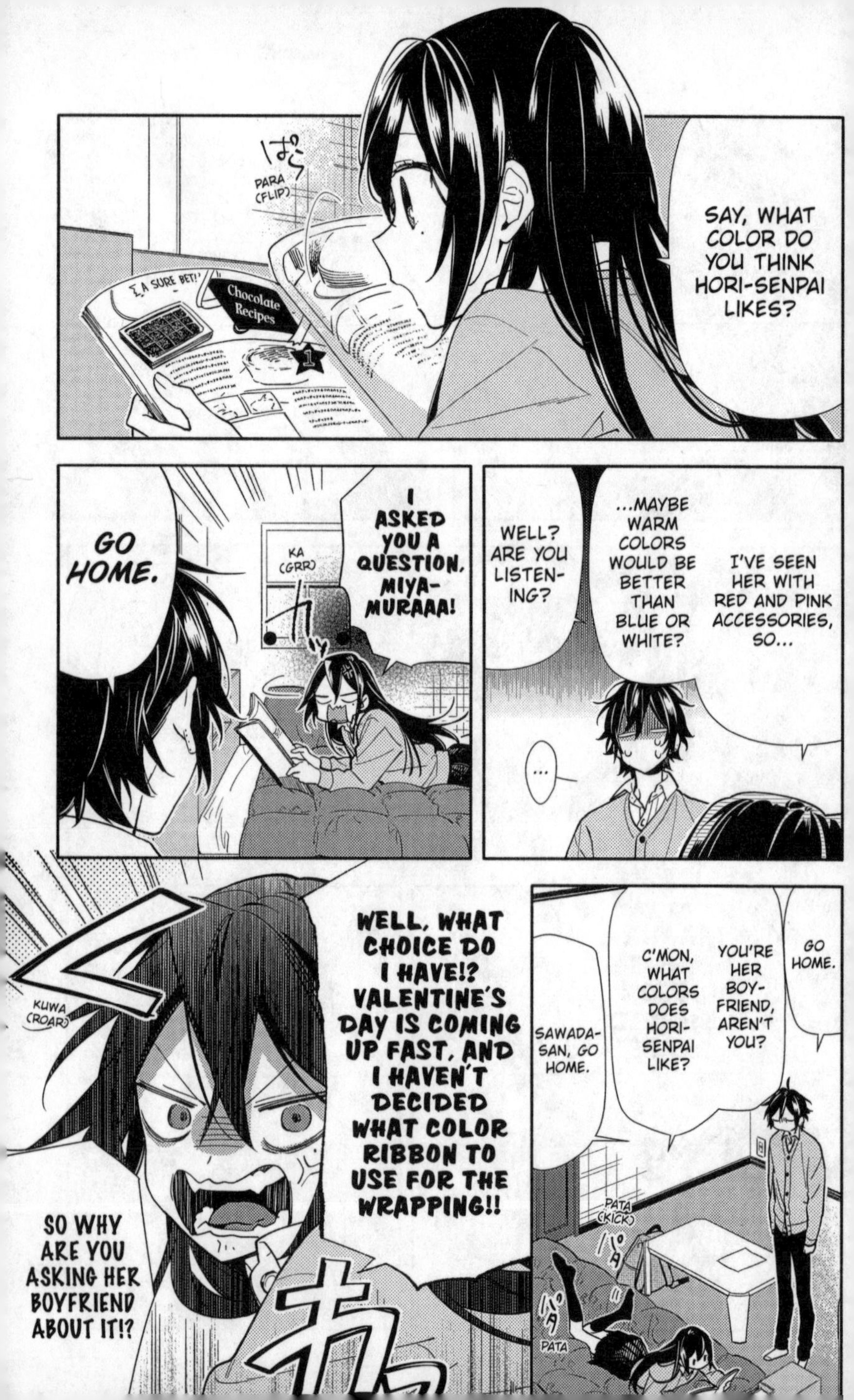
ぱら
PARA (FLIP)
SAY, WHAT COLOR DO YOU THINK HORI-SENPAI LIKES?
A SURE BET!
Chocolate Recipes
I'VE SEEN HER WITH RED AND PINK ACCESSORIES, SO...
...MAYBE WARM COLORS WOULD BE BETTER THAN BLUE OR WHITE?
WELL? ARE YOU LISTENING?
...
I ASKED YOU A QUESTION, MIYAMURAAA!
KA (GRR)
GO HOME.
GO HOME.
YOU'RE HER BOYFRIEND, AREN'T YOU?
C'MON, WHAT COLORS DOES HORI-SENPAI LIKE?
SAWADA-SAN, GO HOME.
PATA (KICK)
PATA
WELL, WHAT CHOICE DO I HAVE!? VALENTINE'S DAY IS COMING UP FAST, AND I HAVEN'T DECIDED WHAT COLOR RIBBON TO USE FOR THE WRAPPING!!
KUWA (ROAR)
SO WHY ARE YOU ASKING HER BOYFRIEND ABOUT IT!?

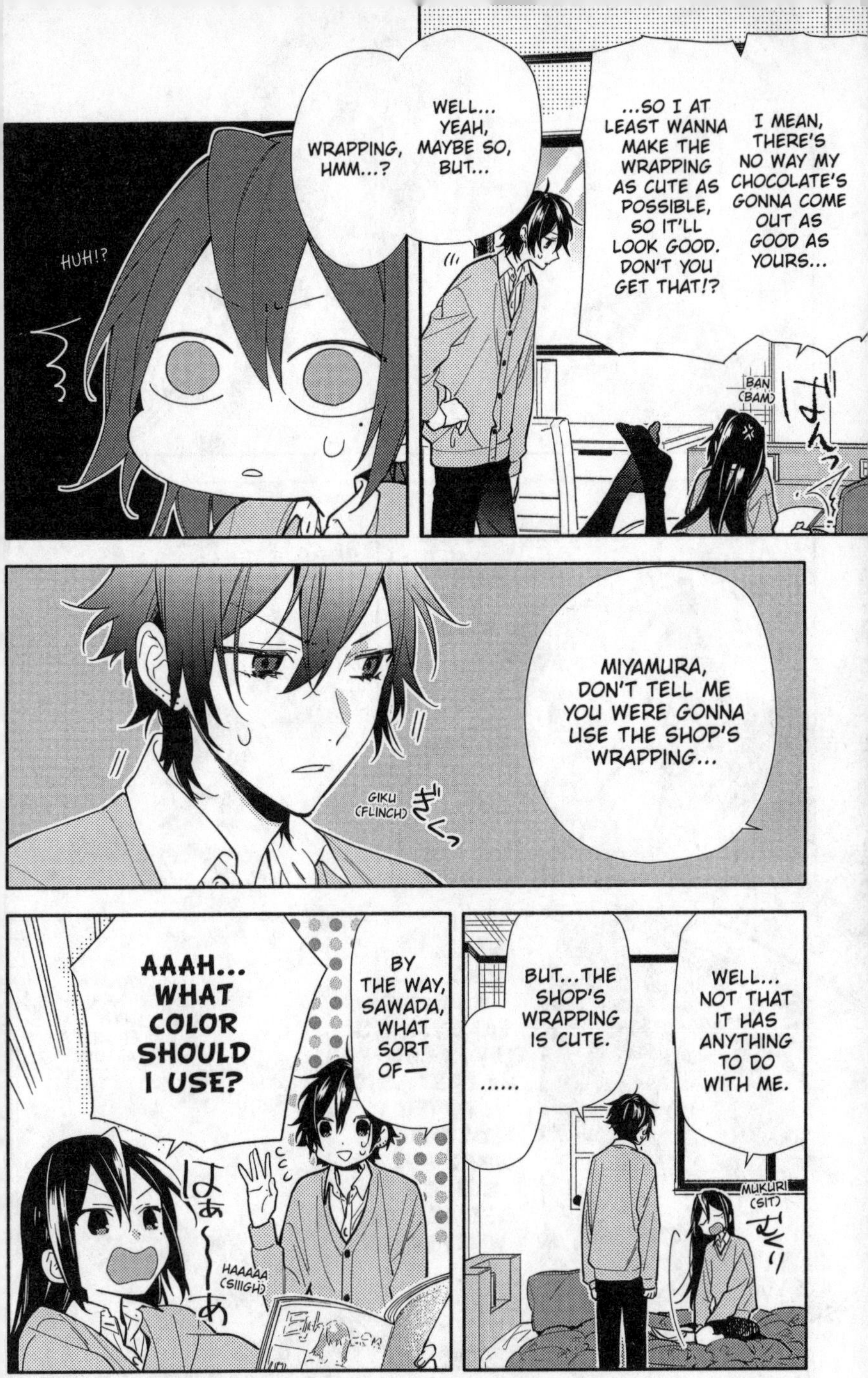
I MEAN, THERE'S NO WAY MY CHOCOLATE'S GONNA COME OUT AS GOOD AS YOURS...
...SO I AT LEAST WANNA MAKE THE WRAPPING AS CUTE AS POSSIBLE, SO IT'LL LOOK GOOD. DON'T YOU GET THAT!?
BAN (BAM)
WELL... YEAH, MAYBE SO, BUT...
WRAPPING, HMM...?
HUH!?
MIYAMURA, DON'T TELL ME YOU WERE GONNA USE THE SHOP'S WRAPPING...
GIKU (FLINCH)
WELL... NOT THAT IT HAS ANYTHING TO DO WITH ME.
BUT...THE SHOP'S WRAPPING IS CUTE.
......
MUKURI (SIT)
BY THE WAY, SAWADA, WHAT SORT OF—
AAAH... WHAT COLOR SHOULD I USE?
HAAAAA (SIIIGH)

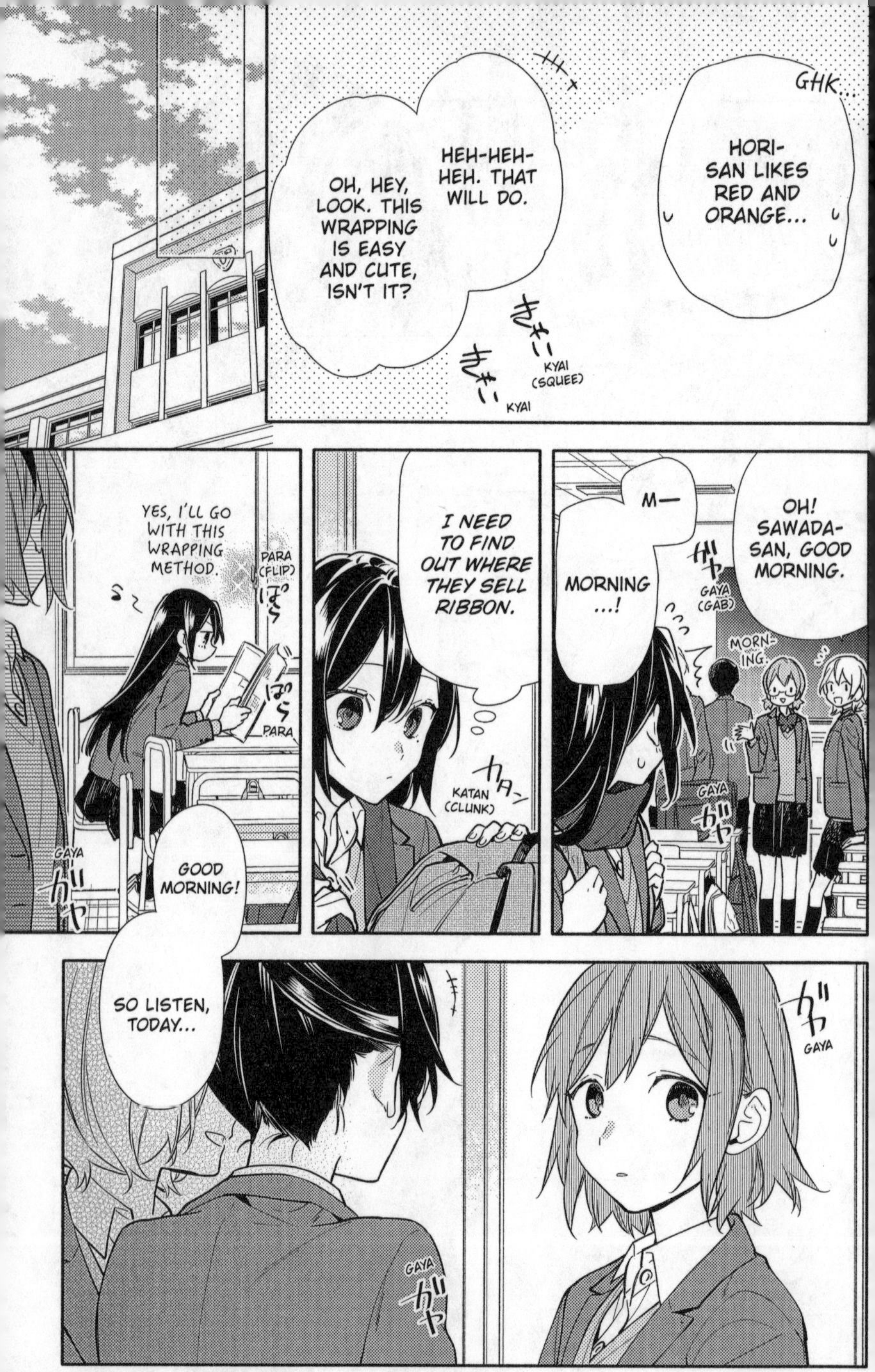
GHK...
HORI-SAN LIKES RED AND ORANGE...
HEH-HEH-HEH. THAT WILL DO.
OH, HEY, LOOK. THIS WRAPPING IS EASY AND CUTE, ISN'T IT?
KYAI (SQUEE)
KYAI
OH! SAWADA-SAN, GOOD MORNING.
M—
MORNING ...!
GAYA (GAB)
MORNING.
GAYA
I NEED TO FIND OUT WHERE THEY SELL RIBBON.
KATAN (CLUNK)
YES, I'LL GO WITH THIS WRAPPING METHOD.
PARA (FLIP)
PARA
GOOD MORNING!
GAYA
GAYA
SO LISTEN, TODAY...
GAYA

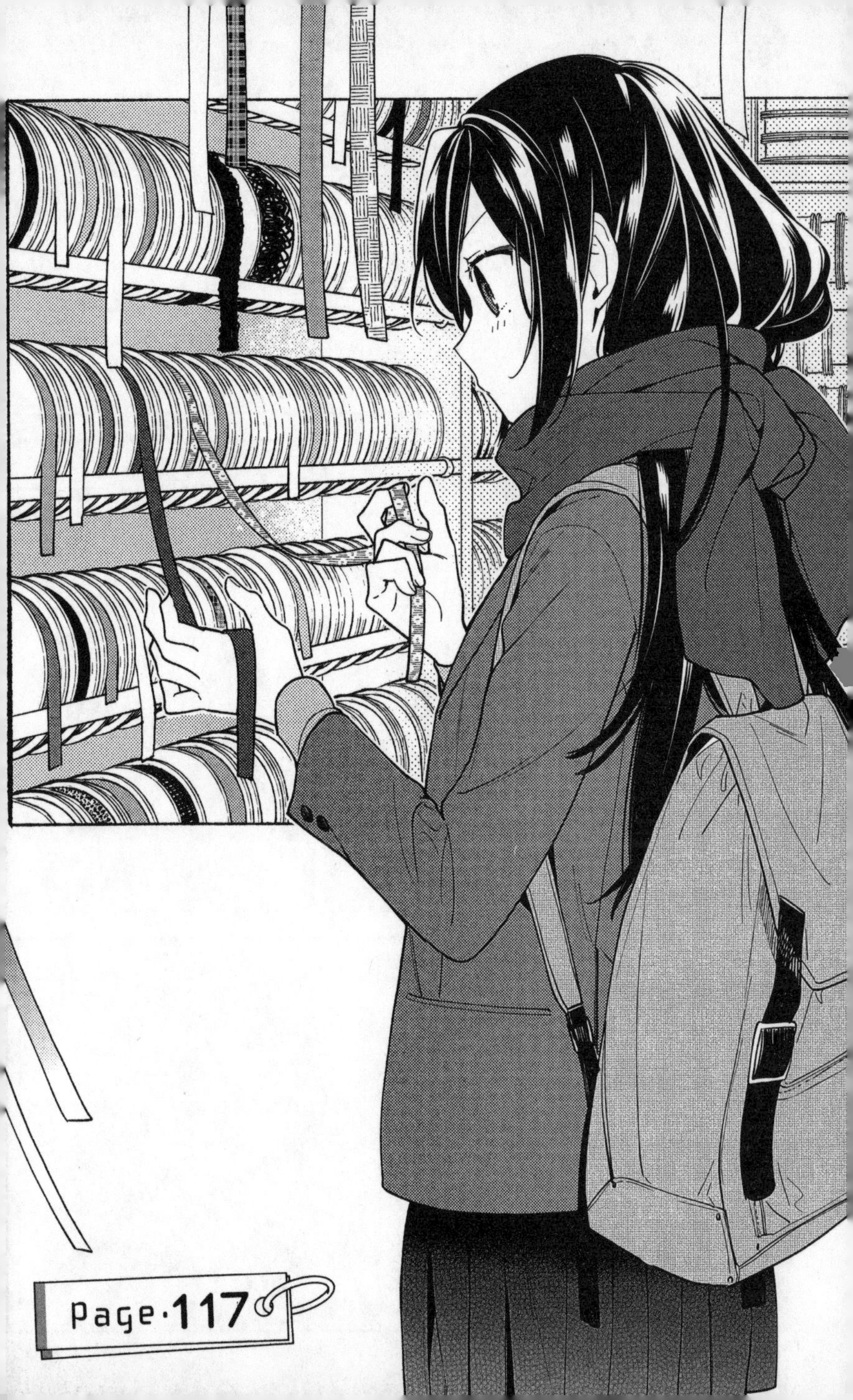
Page·117

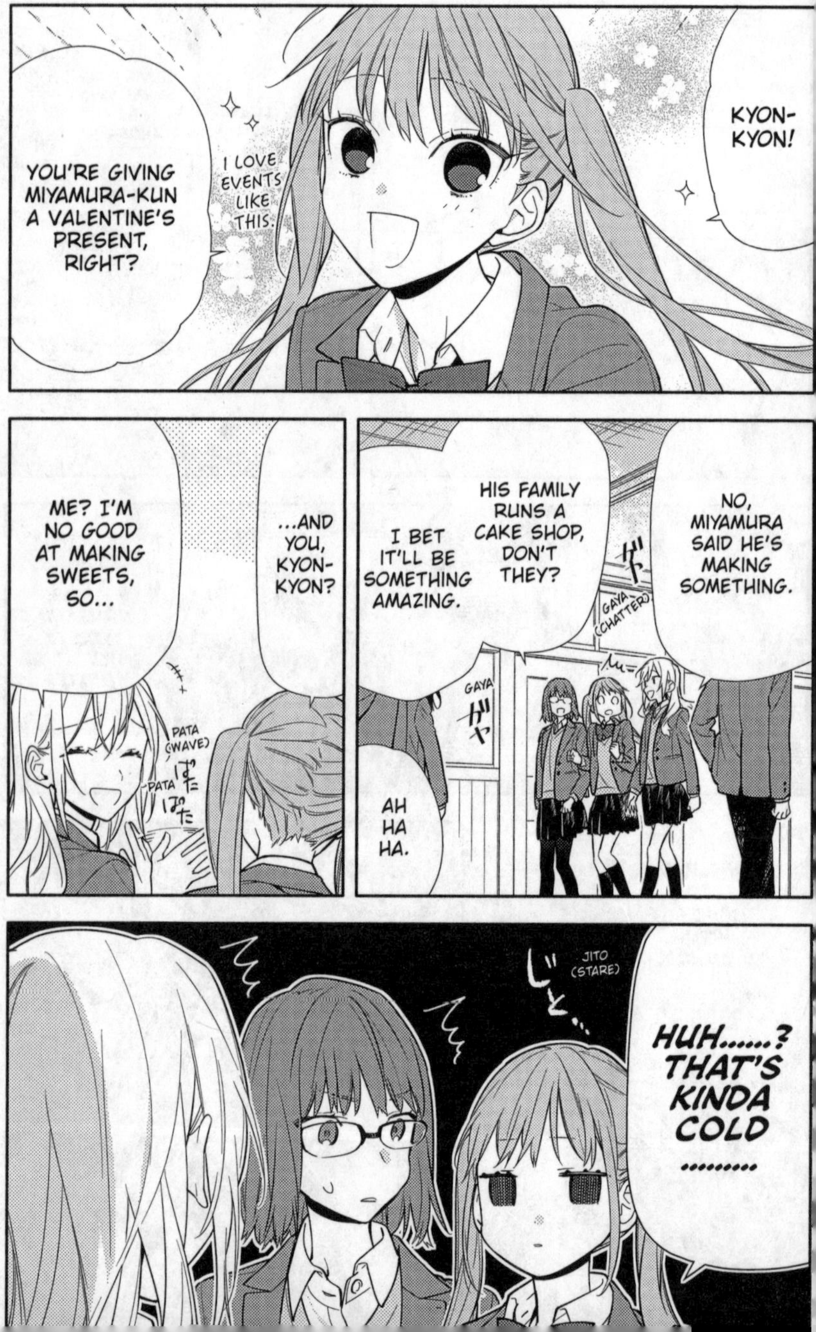
KYON-KYON!
I LOVE EVENTS LIKE THIS.
YOU'RE GIVING MIYAMURA-KUN A VALENTINE'S PRESENT, RIGHT?
NO, MIYAMURA SAID HE'S MAKING SOMETHING.
ガヤ
GAYA (CHATTER)
HIS FAMILY RUNS A CAKE SHOP, DON'T THEY?
I BET IT'LL BE SOMETHING AMAZING.
GAYA
ガヤ
AH HA HA.
...AND YOU, KYON-KYON?
ME? I'M NO GOOD AT MAKING SWEETS, SO...
PATA (WAVE)
ぱた
PATA
ぱた
HUH......? THAT'S KINDA COLD ....
JITO (STARE)
じと…

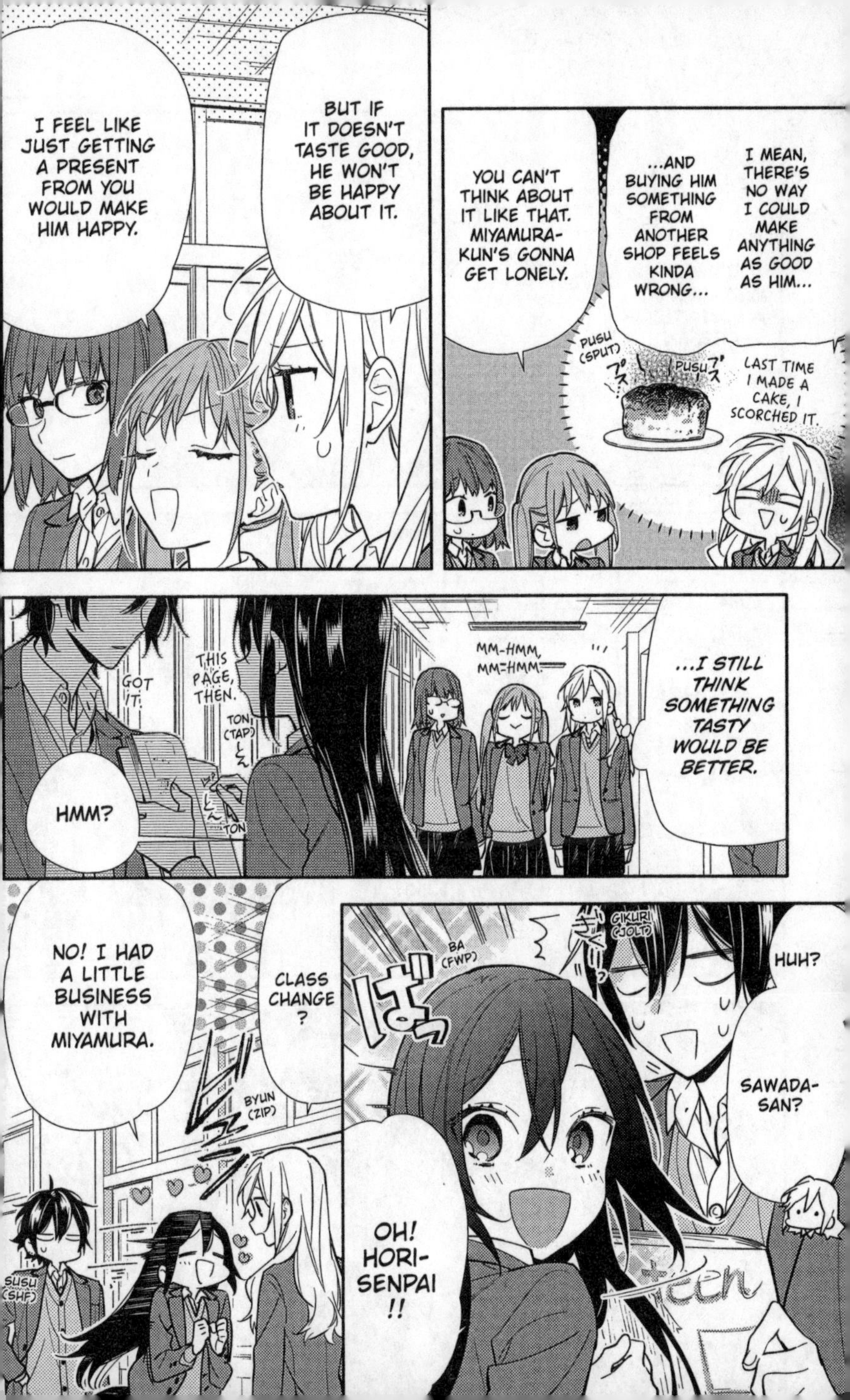
I MEAN, THERE'S NO WAY I COULD MAKE ANYTHING AS GOOD AS HIM...
...AND BUYING HIM SOMETHING FROM ANOTHER SHOP FEELS KINDA WRONG...
LAST TIME I MADE A CAKE, I SCORCHED IT.
PUSU
PUSU (SPUT)
YOU CAN'T THINK ABOUT IT LIKE THAT. MIYAMURA-KUN'S GONNA GET LONELY.
BUT IF IT DOESN'T TASTE GOOD, HE WON'T BE HAPPY ABOUT IT.
I FEEL LIKE JUST GETTING A PRESENT FROM YOU WOULD MAKE HIM HAPPY.
...I STILL THINK SOMETHING TASTY WOULD BE BETTER.
MM-HMM, MM-HMM.
THIS PAGE, THEN.
TON (TAP)
TON
GOT IT.
HMM?
HUH?
SAWADA-SAN?
GIKURI (JOLT)
BA (FWP)
OH! HORI-SENPAI!!
CLASS CHANGE?
NO! I HAD A LITTLE BUSINESS WITH MIYAMURA.
BYUN (ZIP)
SUSU (SHF)

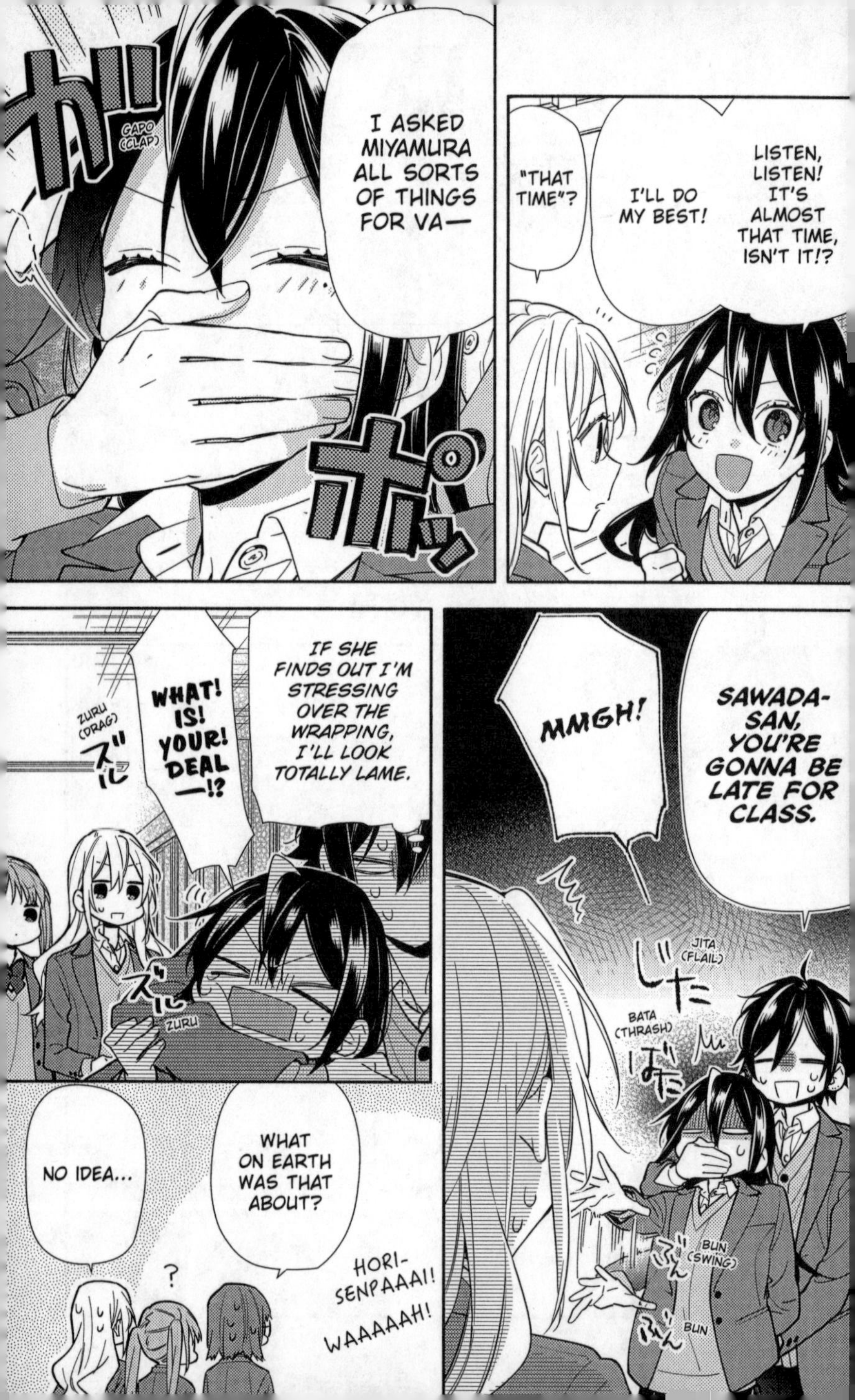
LISTEN, LISTEN! IT'S ALMOST THAT TIME, ISN'T IT!?
I'LL DO MY BEST!
"THAT TIME"?
I ASKED MIYAMURA ALL SORTS OF THINGS FOR VA—
GAPO (CLAP)
SAWADA-SAN, YOU'RE GONNA BE LATE FOR CLASS.
MMGH!
JITA (FLAIL)
BATA (THRASH)
BUN (SWING)
BUN
IF SHE FINDS OUT I'M STRESSING OVER THE WRAPPING, I'LL LOOK TOTALLY LAME.
WHAT! IS! YOUR! DEAL—!?
ZURU (DRAG)
ZURU
WHAT ON EARTH WAS THAT ABOUT?
NO IDEA...
?
HORI-SENPAAAI!
WAAAAAH!

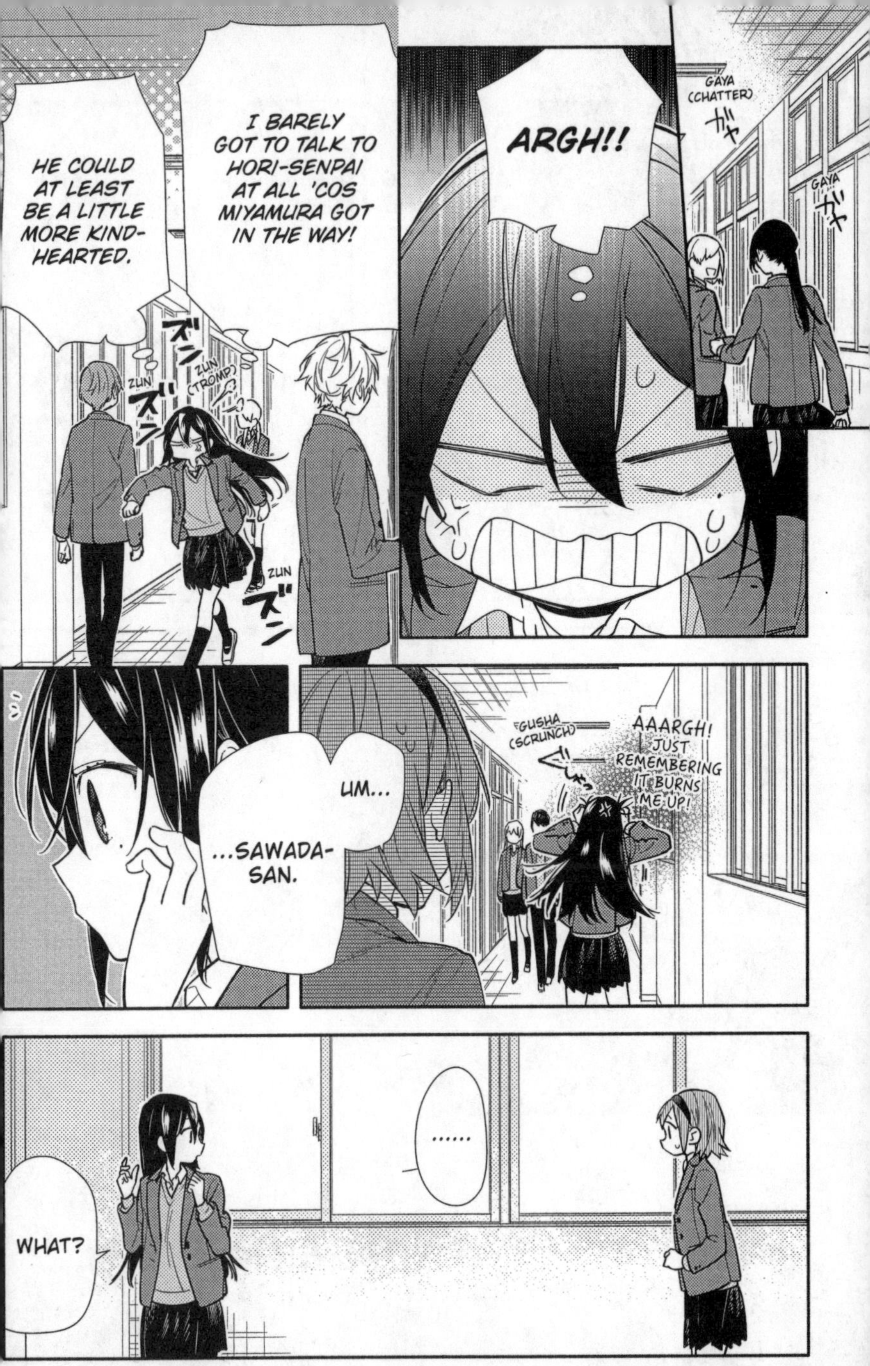
GAYA (CHATTER)
GAYA
ARGH!!
I BARELY GOT TO TALK TO HORI-SENPAI AT ALL 'COS MIYAMURA GOT IN THE WAY!
HE COULD AT LEAST BE A LITTLE MORE KIND-HEARTED.
ZUN
ZUN (TROMP)
ZUN
AAARGH! JUST REMEMBERING IT BURNS ME UP!
GUSHA (SCRUNCH)
UM...
...SAWADA-SAN.
......
WHAT?

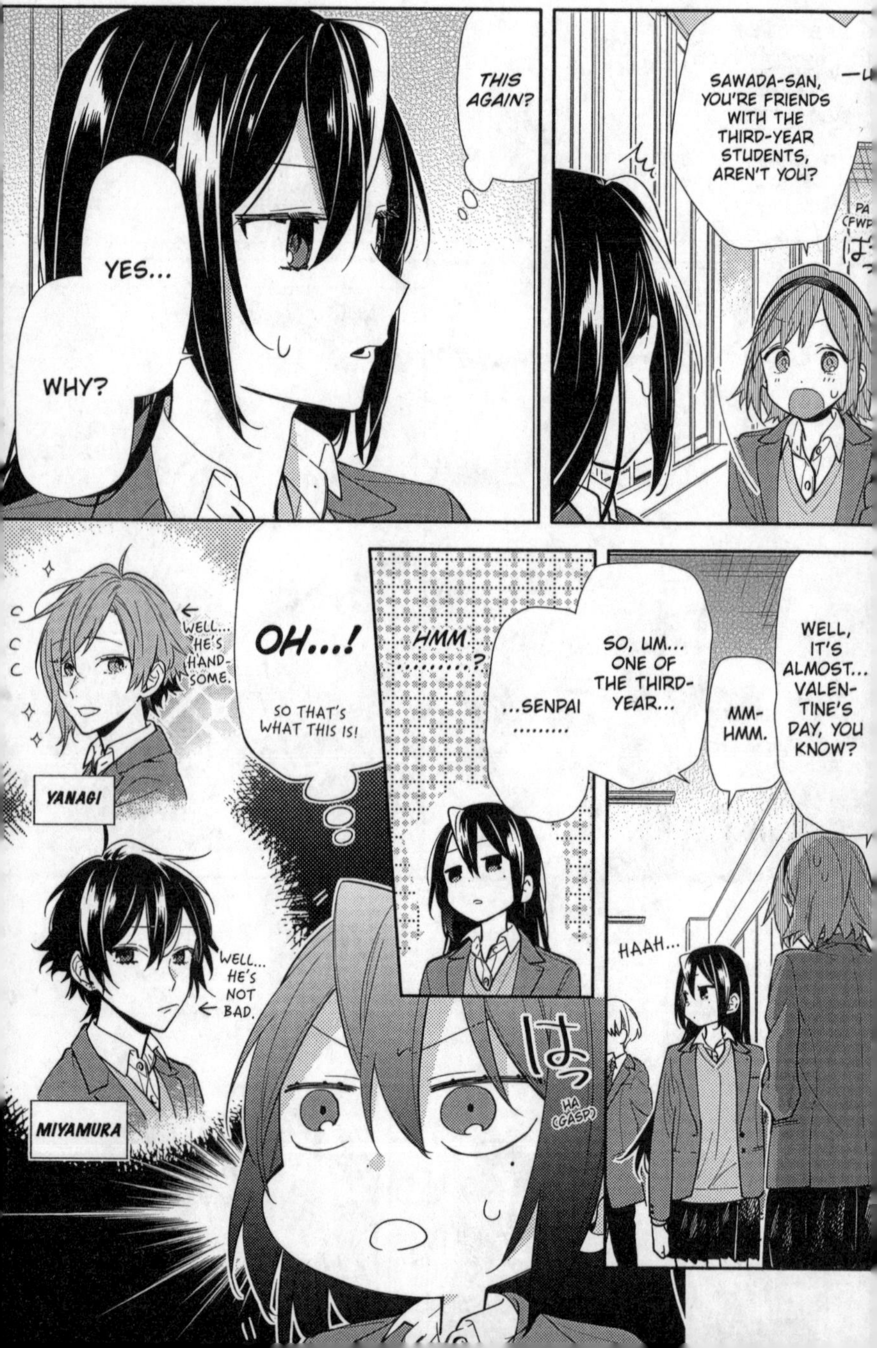
SAWADA-SAN, YOU'RE FRIENDS WITH THE THIRD-YEAR STUDENTS, AREN'T YOU?
THIS AGAIN?
YES...
WHY?
WELL, IT'S ALMOST... VALENTINE'S DAY, YOU KNOW?
MM-HMM.
SO, UM... ONE OF THE THIRD-YEAR...
...SENPAI ....
HAAH...
HMM ....?
OH...!
SO THAT'S WHAT THIS IS!
WELL... HE'S HANDSOME.
YANAGI
WELL... HE'S NOT BAD.
MIYAMURA
はっ
HA (GASP)

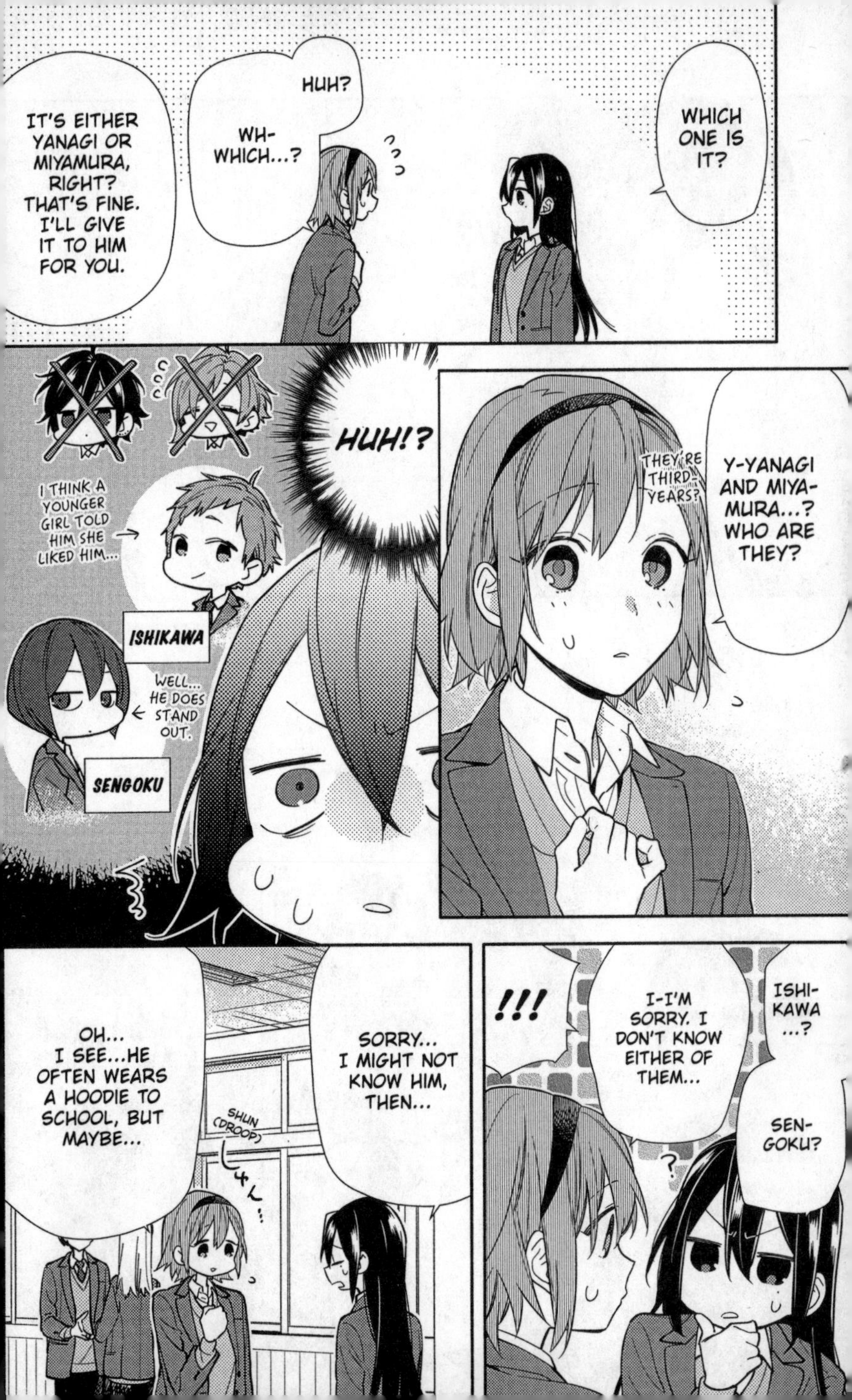
WHICH ONE IS IT?
HUH?
WH-WHICH...?
IT'S EITHER YANAGI OR MIYAMURA, RIGHT? THAT'S FINE. I'LL GIVE IT TO HIM FOR YOU.
Y-YANAGI AND MIYA-MURA...? WHO ARE THEY?
THEY'RE THIRD YEARS?
HUH!?
I THINK A YOUNGER GIRL TOLD HIM SHE LIKED HIM...
ISHIKAWA
WELL... HE DOES STAND OUT.
SENGOKU
ISHI-KAWA...?
SEN-GOKU?
I-I'M SORRY. I DON'T KNOW EITHER OF THEM...
!!!
SORRY... I MIGHT NOT KNOW HIM, THEN...
SHUN (DROOP)
OH... I SEE...HE OFTEN WEARS A HOODIE TO SCHOOL, BUT MAYBE...

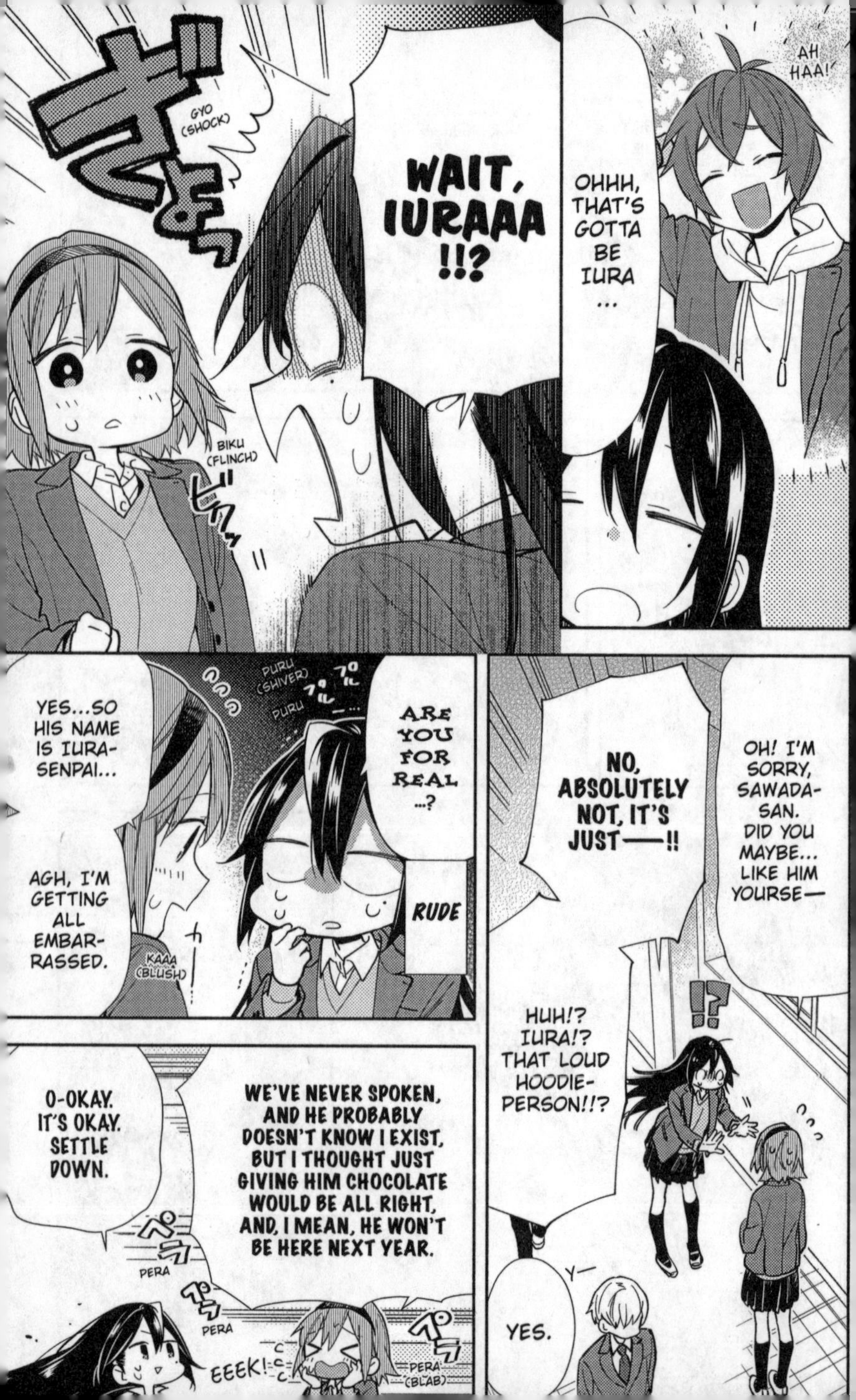
AH HAA!
OHHH, THAT'S GOTTA BE IURA ...
WAIT, IURAAA!!?
GYO (SHOCK)
BIKU (FLINCH)
OH! I'M SORRY, SAWADA-SAN. DID YOU MAYBE... LIKE HIM YOURSE—
NO, ABSOLUTELY NOT, IT'S JUST—!!
!?
HUH!? IURA!? THAT LOUD HOODIE-PERSON!!?
Y—
YES.
PURU (SHIVER)
PURU
ARE YOU FOR REAL ...?
RUDE
YES...SO HIS NAME IS IURA-SENPAI...
AGH, I'M GETTING ALL EMBARRASSED.
KAAA (BLUSH)
WE'VE NEVER SPOKEN, AND HE PROBABLY DOESN'T KNOW I EXIST, BUT I THOUGHT JUST GIVING HIM CHOCOLATE WOULD BE ALL RIGHT, AND, I MEAN, HE WON'T BE HERE NEXT YEAR.
O-OKAY. IT'S OKAY. SETTLE DOWN.
PERA
PERA
PERA (BLAB)
EEEK!

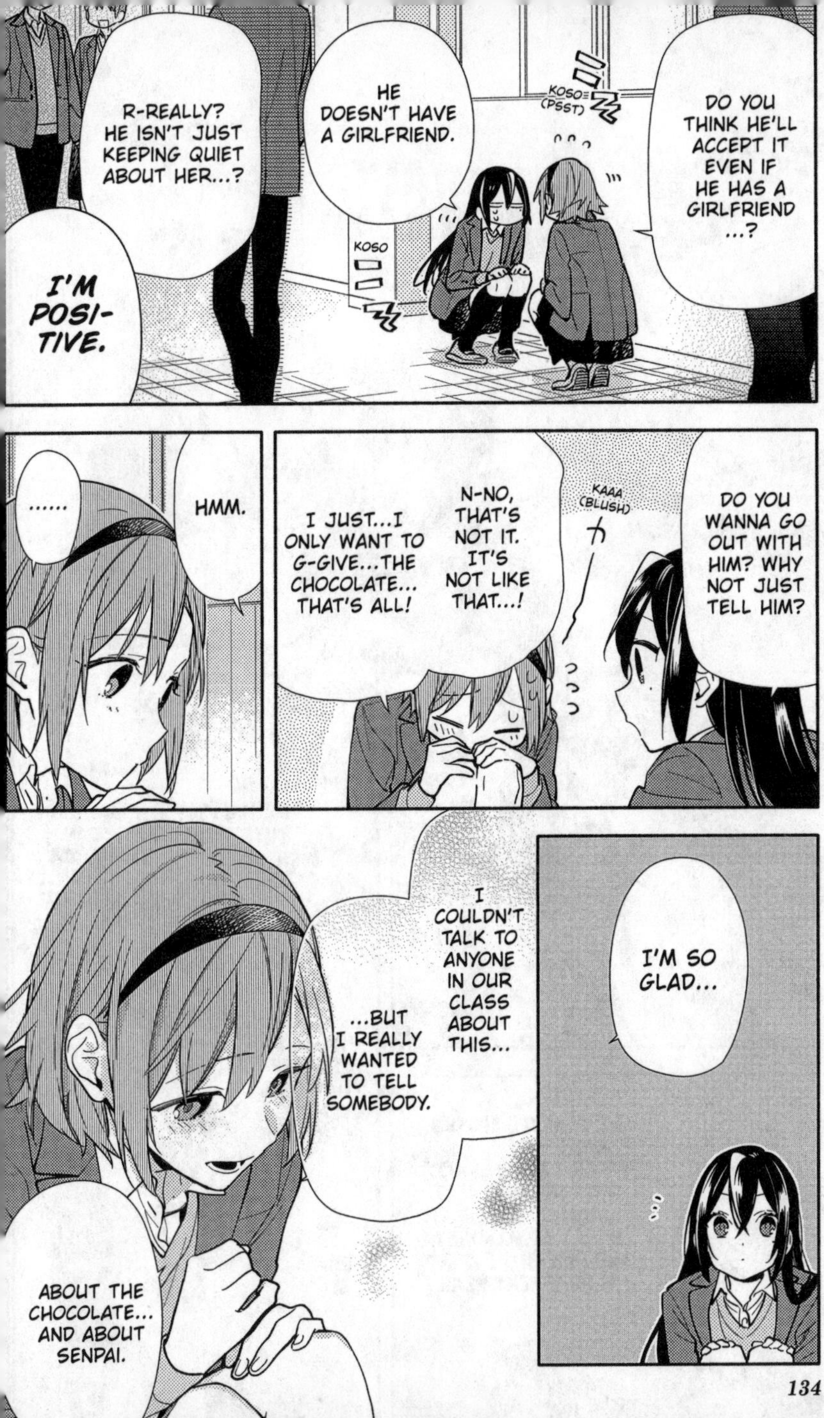
DO YOU THINK HE'LL ACCEPT IT EVEN IF HE HAS A GIRLFRIEND ...?
KOSO (PSST)
HE DOESN'T HAVE A GIRLFRIEND.
R-REALLY? HE ISN'T JUST KEEPING QUIET ABOUT HER...?
KOSO
I'M POSI-TIVE.
DO YOU WANNA GO OUT WITH HIM? WHY NOT JUST TELL HIM?
KAAA (BLUSH)
N-NO, THAT'S NOT IT. IT'S NOT LIKE THAT...!
I JUST...I ONLY WANT TO G-GIVE...THE CHOCOLATE... THAT'S ALL!
HMM.
......
I'M SO GLAD...
I COULDN'T TALK TO ANYONE IN OUR CLASS ABOUT THIS...
...BUT I REALLY WANTED TO TELL SOMEBODY.
ABOUT THE CHOCOLATE... AND ABOUT SENPAI.

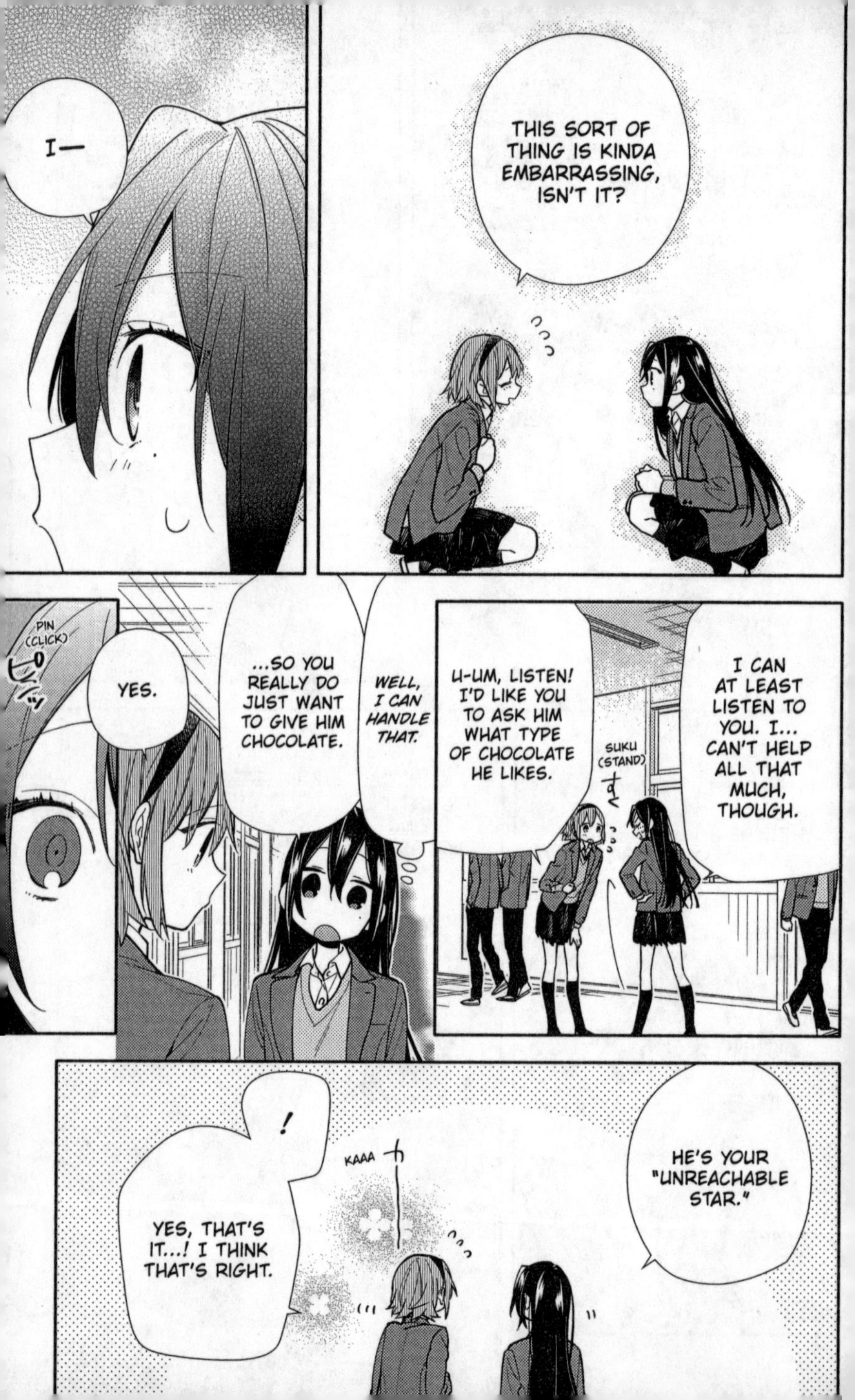
THIS SORT OF THING IS KINDA EMBARRASSING, ISN'T IT?
I—
I CAN AT LEAST LISTEN TO YOU. I... CAN'T HELP ALL THAT MUCH, THOUGH.
SUKU (STAND)
U-UM, LISTEN! I'D LIKE YOU TO ASK HIM WHAT TYPE OF CHOCOLATE HE LIKES.
WELL, I CAN HANDLE THAT.
...SO YOU REALLY DO JUST WANT TO GIVE HIM CHOCOLATE.
YES.
PIN (CLICK)
HE'S YOUR "UNREACHABLE STAR."
KAAA
!
YES, THAT'S IT...! I THINK THAT'S RIGHT.

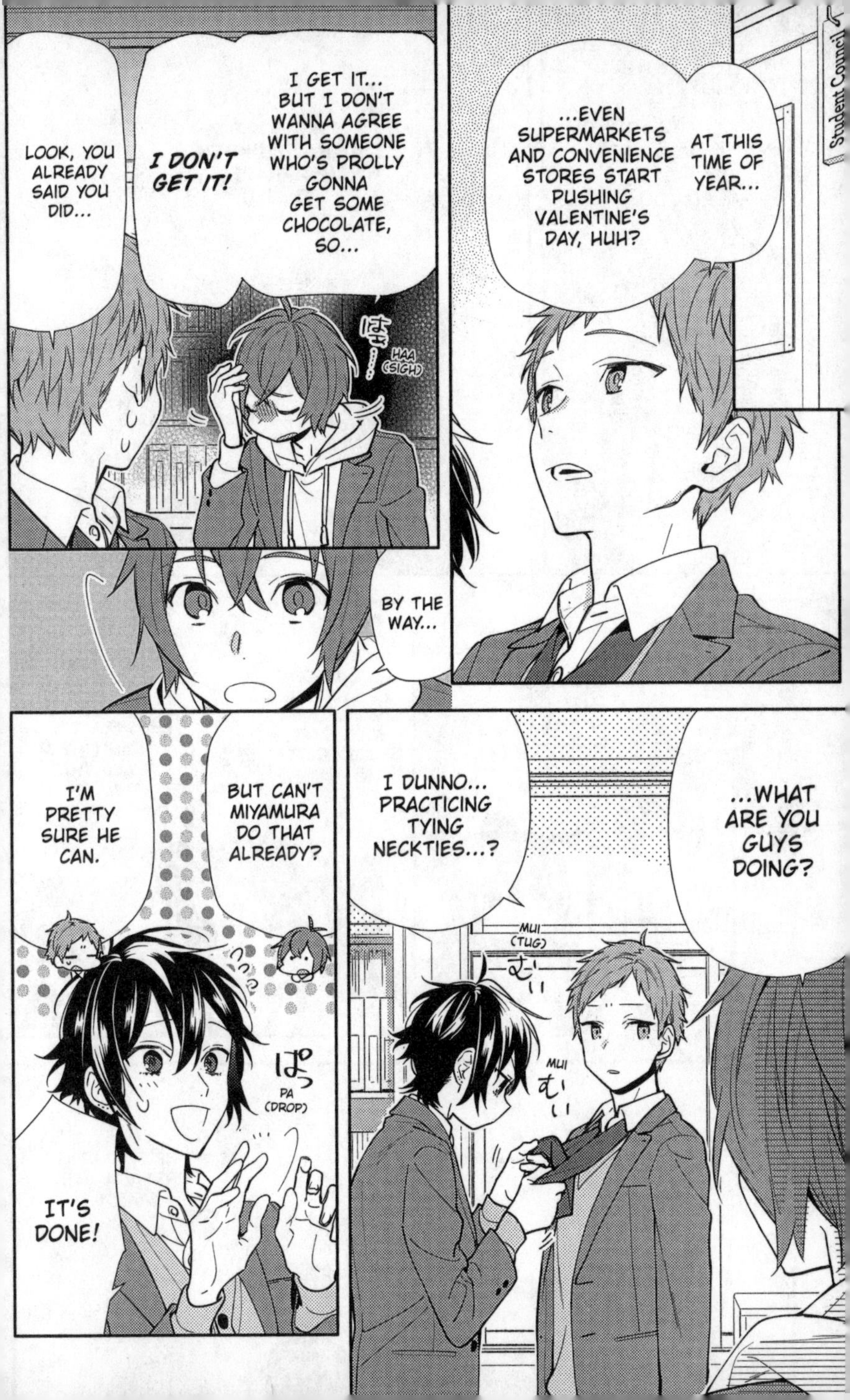
Student Council
AT THIS TIME OF YEAR...
...EVEN SUPERMARKETS AND CONVENIENCE STORES START PUSHING VALENTINE'S DAY, HUH?
I GET IT... BUT I DON'T WANNA AGREE WITH SOMEONE WHO'S PROLLY GONNA GET SOME CHOCOLATE, SO...
I DON'T GET IT!
LOOK, YOU ALREADY SAID YOU DID...
は…
HAA (SIGH)
BY THE WAY...
...WHAT ARE YOU GUYS DOING?
I DUNNO... PRACTICING TYING NECKTIES...?
MUI (TUG)
むい
MUI
むい
BUT CAN'T MIYAMURA DO THAT ALREADY?
I'M PRETTY SURE HE CAN.
ぱっ
PA (DROP)
IT'S DONE!

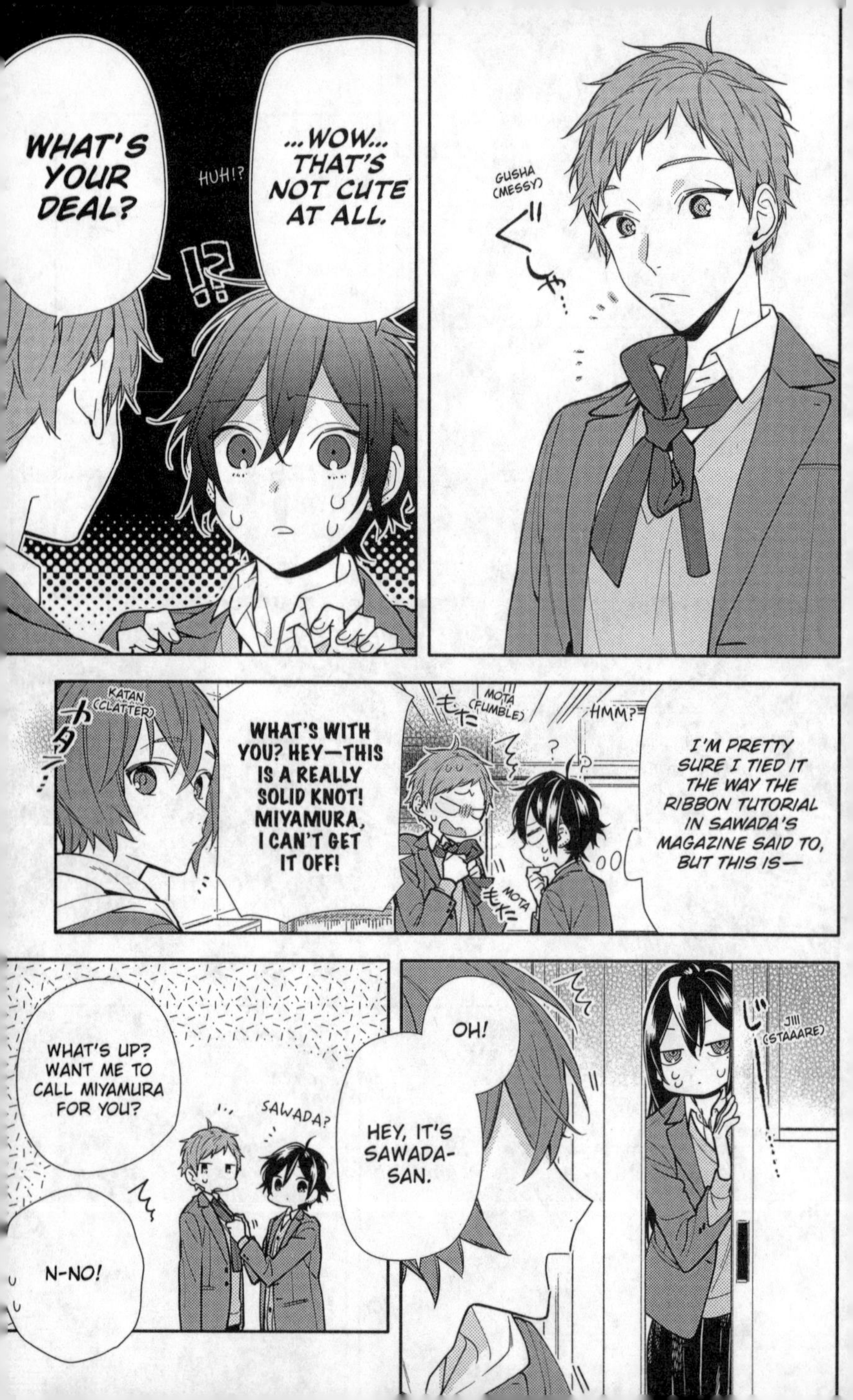
GUSHA (MESSY)
...WOW... THAT'S NOT CUTE AT ALL.
HUH!?
!?
WHAT'S YOUR DEAL?
I'M PRETTY SURE I TIED IT THE WAY THE RIBBON TUTORIAL IN SAWADA'S MAGAZINE SAID TO, BUT THIS IS—
HMM?
?
MOTA (FUMBLE)
MOTA
WHAT'S WITH YOU? HEY—THIS IS A REALLY SOLID KNOT! MIYAMURA, I CAN'T GET IT OFF!
KATAN (CLATTER)
JIII (STAAARE)
OH!
HEY, IT'S SAWADA-SAN.
SAWADA?
WHAT'S UP? WANT ME TO CALL MIYAMURA FOR YOU?
N-NO!

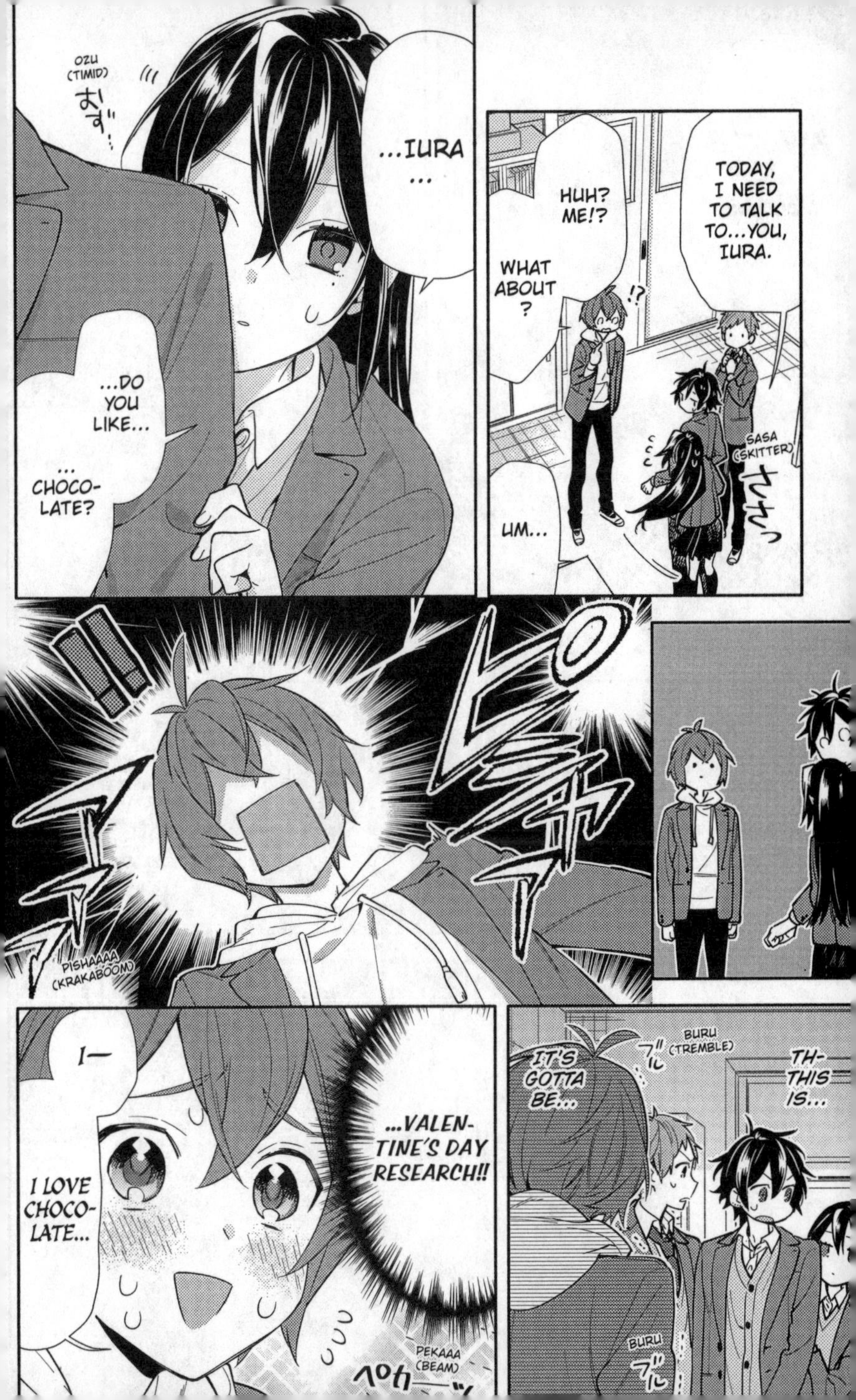
TODAY, I NEED TO TALK TO...YOU, IURA.
HUH? ME!?
WHAT ABOUT?
!?
SASA (SKITTER)
UM...
...IURA...
OZU (TIMID)
おずっ
...DO YOU LIKE... ...CHOCOLATE?
PISHAAAA (KRAKABOOM)
TH-THIS IS...
BURU (TREMBLE)
IT'S GOTTA BE...
BURU
...VALEN-TINE'S DAY RESEARCH!!
I—
I LOVE CHOCO-LATE...
PEKAAA (BEAM)

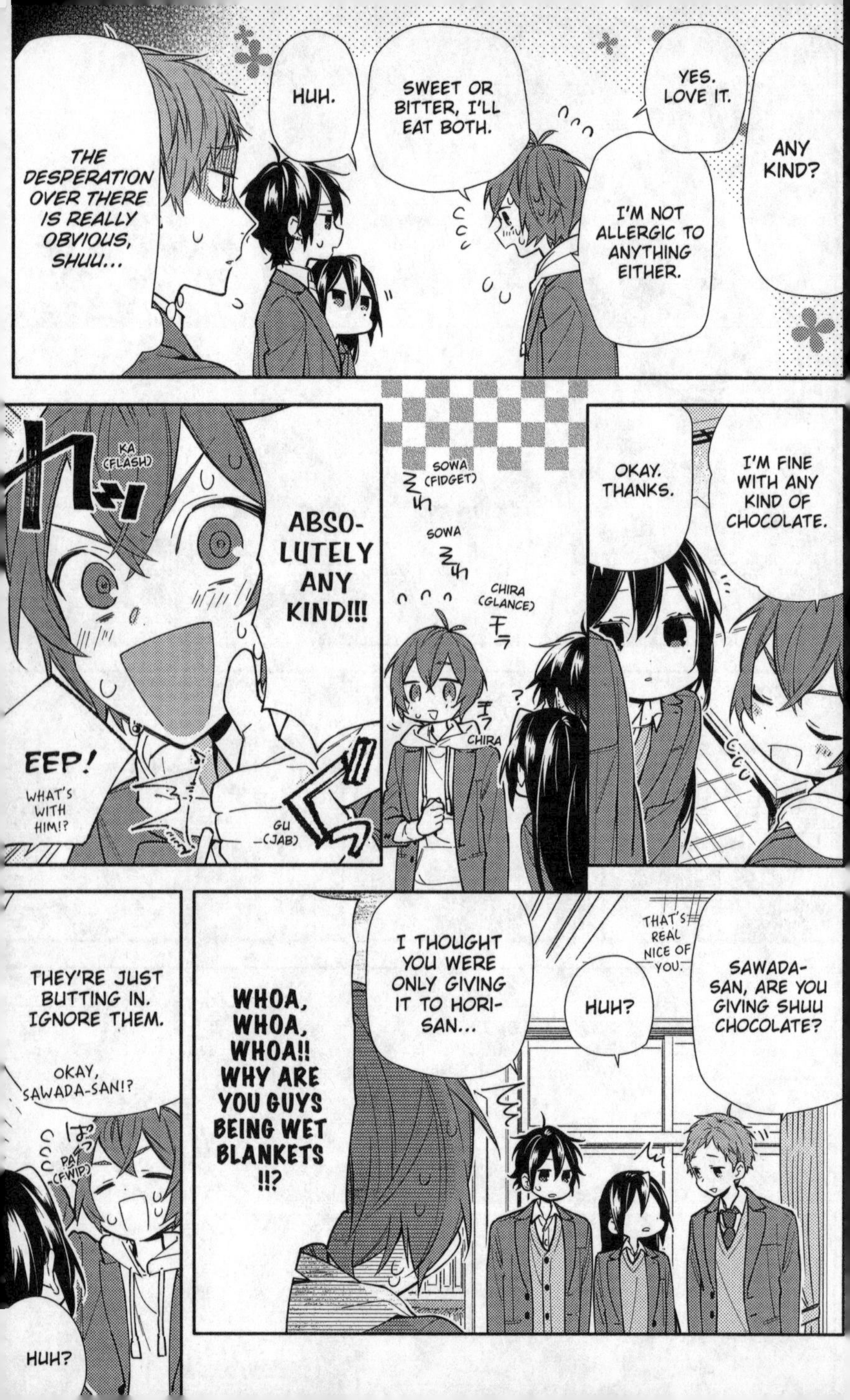
ANY KIND?
YES. LOVE IT.
I'M NOT ALLERGIC TO ANYTHING EITHER.
SWEET OR BITTER, I'LL EAT BOTH.
HUH.
THE DESPERATION OVER THERE IS REALLY OBVIOUS, SHUU...
I'M FINE WITH ANY KIND OF CHOCOLATE.
OKAY. THANKS.
SOWA (FIDGET)
SOWA
CHIRA (GLANCE)
CHIRA
KA (FLASH)
ABSOLUTELY ANY KIND!!!
EEP!
WHAT'S WITH HIM!?
GU (JAB)
SAWADA-SAN, ARE YOU GIVING SHUU CHOCOLATE?
THAT'S REAL NICE OF YOU.
HUH?
I THOUGHT YOU WERE ONLY GIVING IT TO HORI-SAN...
WHOA, WHOA, WHOA!! WHY ARE YOU GUYS BEING WET BLANKETS!!?
THEY'RE JUST BUTTING IN. IGNORE THEM.
OKAY, SAWADA-SAN!?
PAT (FWIP)
HUH?

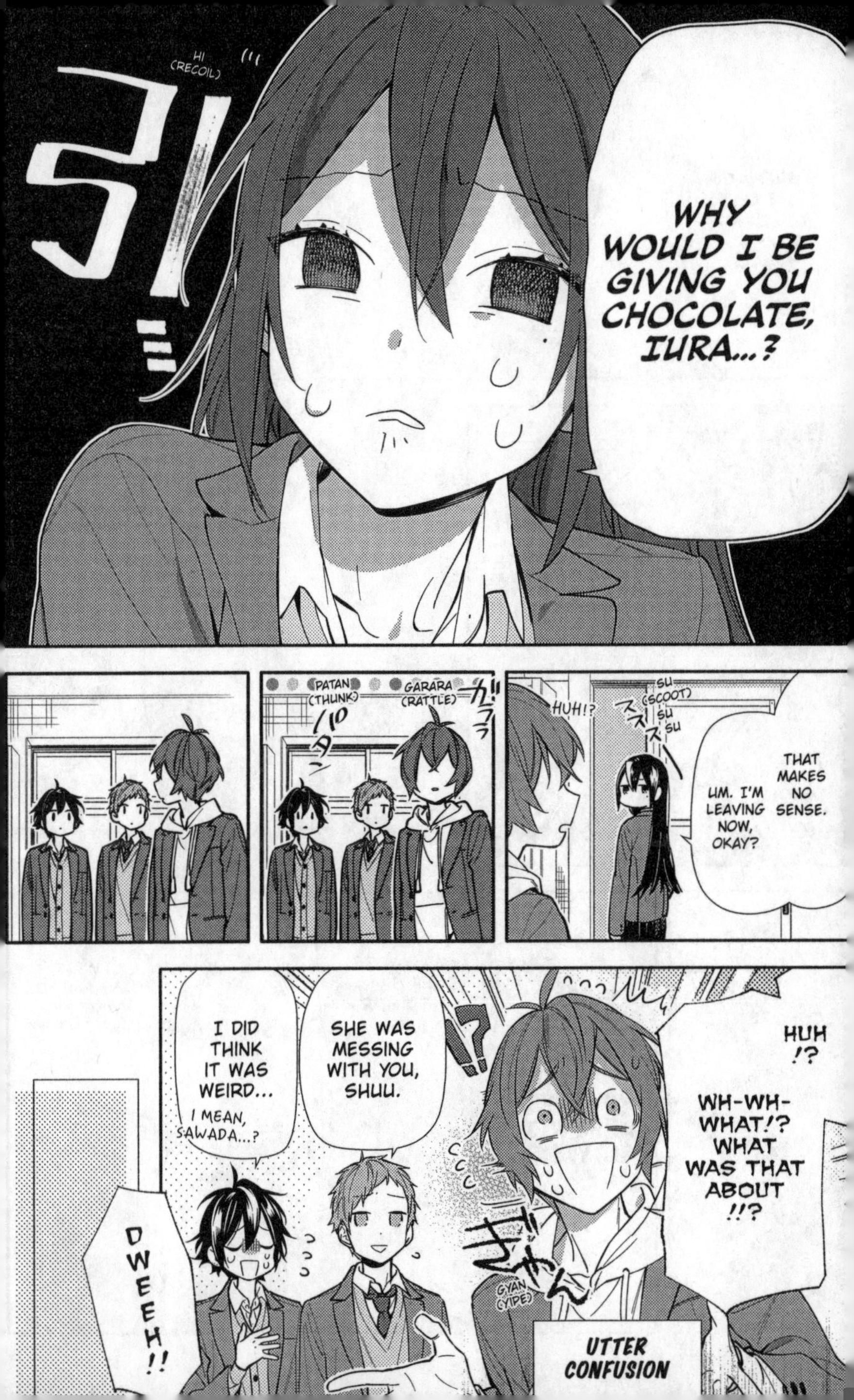
WHY WOULD I BE GIVING YOU CHOCOLATE, IURA...?
HI (RECOIL)
THAT MAKES NO SENSE.
UM. I'M LEAVING NOW, OKAY?
SU (SCOOT) SU SU
HUH!?
GARARA (RATTLE)
PATAN (THUNK)
HUH !?
WH-WH-WHAT!? WHAT WAS THAT ABOUT !!?
GYAN (YIPE)
UTTER CONFUSION
SHE WAS MESSING WITH YOU, SHUU.
I DID THINK IT WAS WEIRD...
I MEAN, SAWADA...?
DWEEH!!

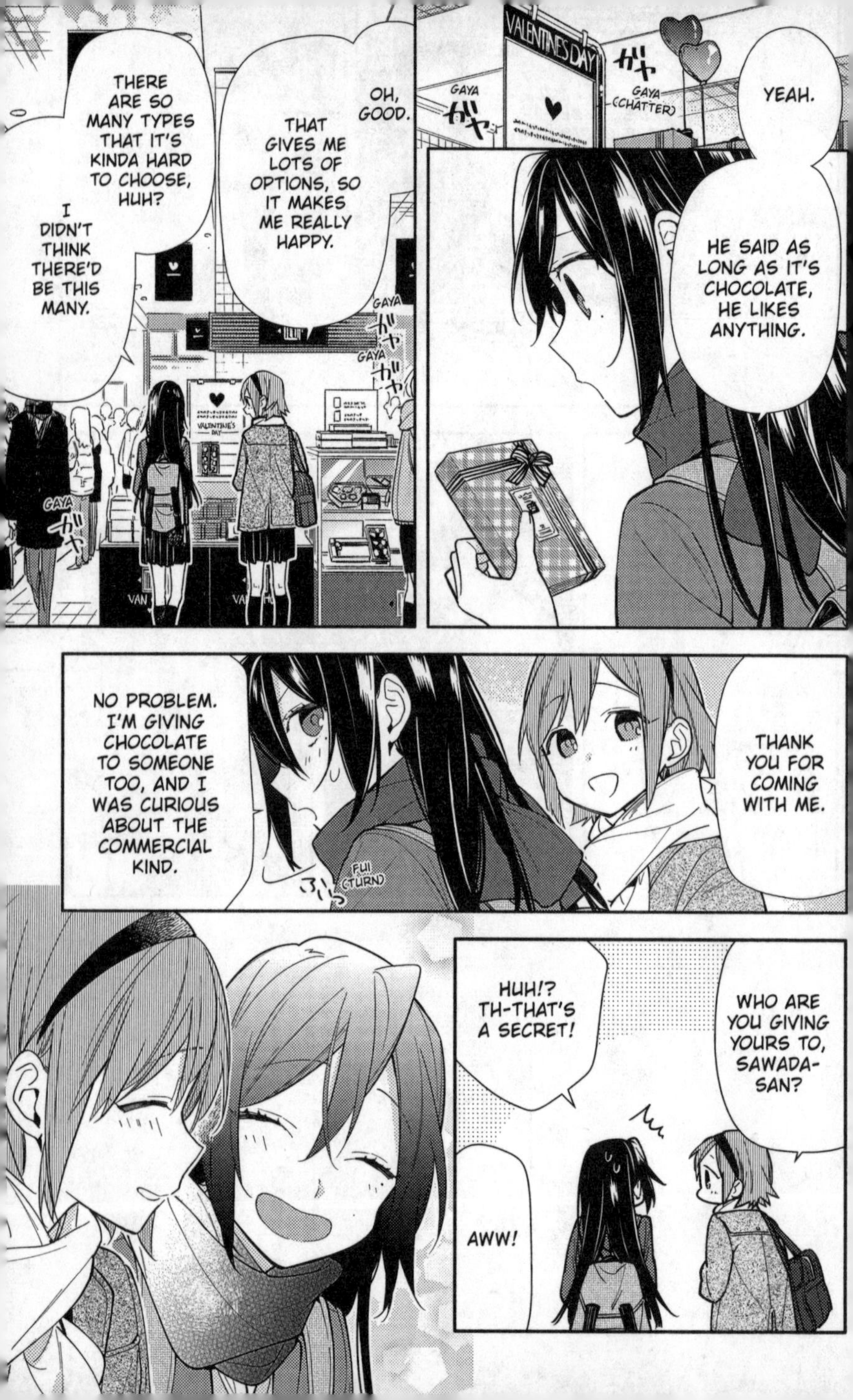

VALENTINES DAY
ガヤ GAYA
ガヤ GAYA (CHATTER)
YEAH.
HE SAID AS LONG AS IT'S CHOCOLATE, HE LIKES ANYTHING.
OH, GOOD.
THAT GIVES ME LOTS OF OPTIONS, SO IT MAKES ME REALLY HAPPY.
THERE ARE SO MANY TYPES THAT IT'S KINDA HARD TO CHOOSE, HUH?
I DIDN'T THINK THERE'D BE THIS MANY.
VALENTINE'S DAY
ガヤ GAYA
ガヤ GAYA
ガヤ GAYA
THANK YOU FOR COMING WITH ME.
NO PROBLEM. I'M GIVING CHOCOLATE TO SOMEONE TOO, AND I WAS CURIOUS ABOUT THE COMMERCIAL KIND.
ふい FUI (TURN)
WHO ARE YOU GIVING YOURS TO, SAWADA-SAN?
HUH!? TH-THAT'S A SECRET!
AWW!

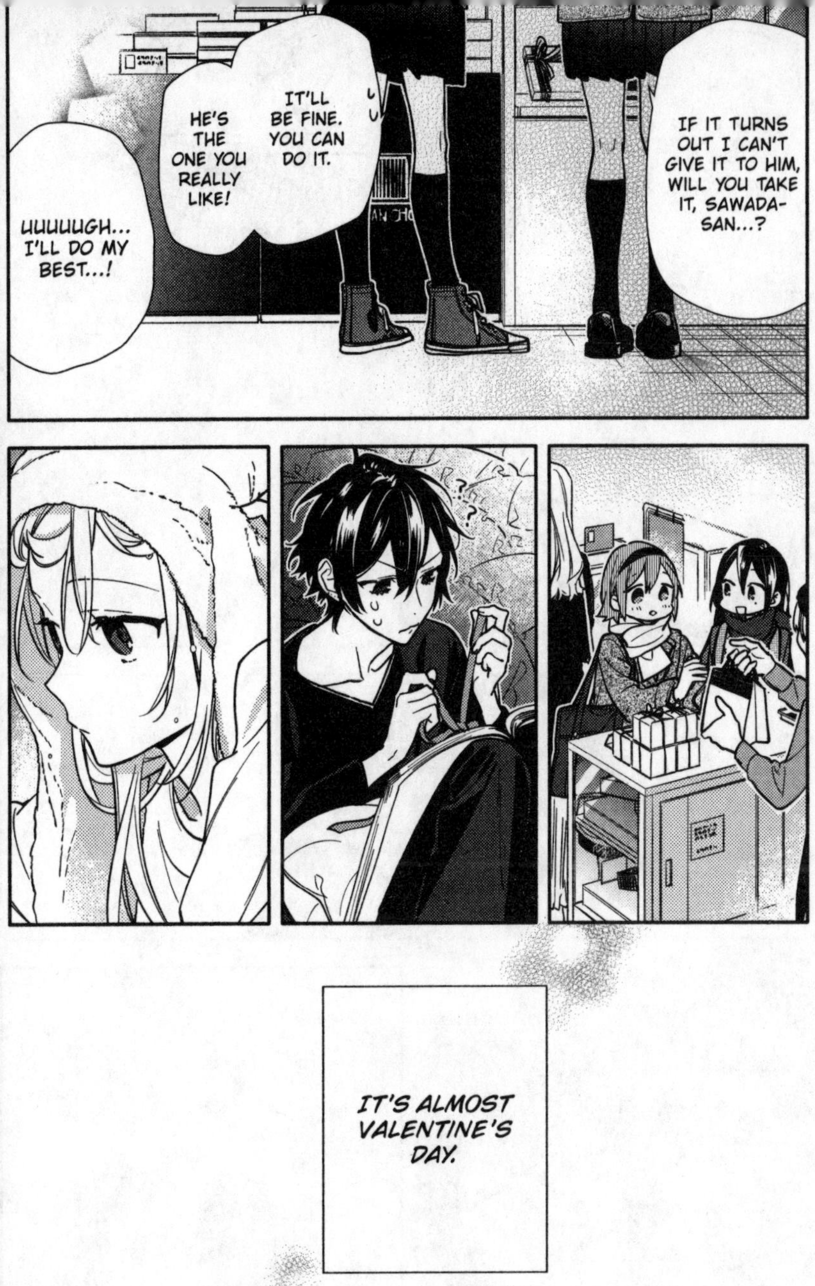
IF IT TURNS OUT I CAN'T GIVE IT TO HIM, WILL YOU TAKE IT, SAWADA-SAN...?
IT'LL BE FINE. YOU CAN DO IT.
HE'S THE ONE YOU REALLY LIKE!
UUUUUGH... I'LL DO MY BEST...!
IT'S ALMOST VALENTINE'S DAY.

HORIMIYA

HORIMIYA

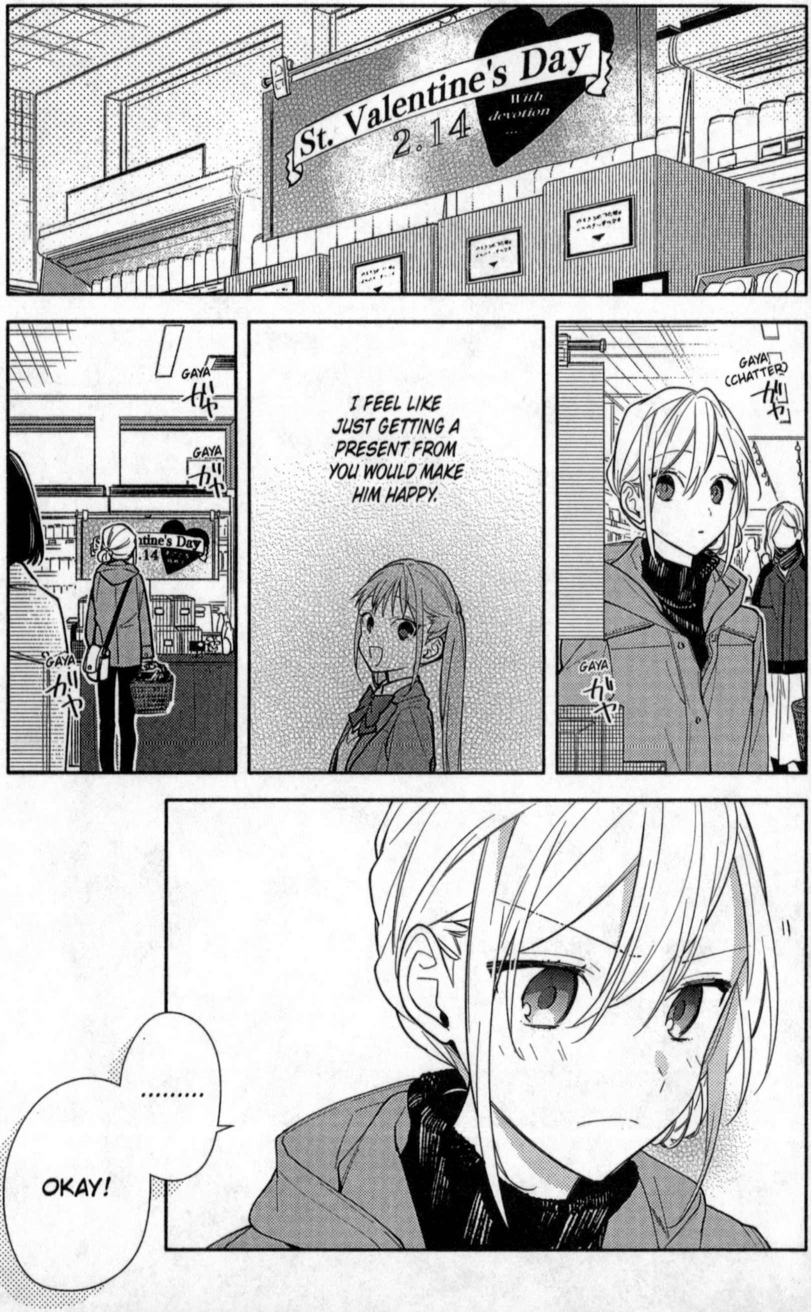
St. Valentine's Day
2.14
With devotion ...
GAYA (CHATTER) ガヤ
GAYA ガヤ
I FEEL LIKE JUST GETTING A PRESENT FROM YOU WOULD MAKE HIM HAPPY.
GAYA ガヤ
GAYA ガヤ
GAYA ガヤ
....
OKAY!

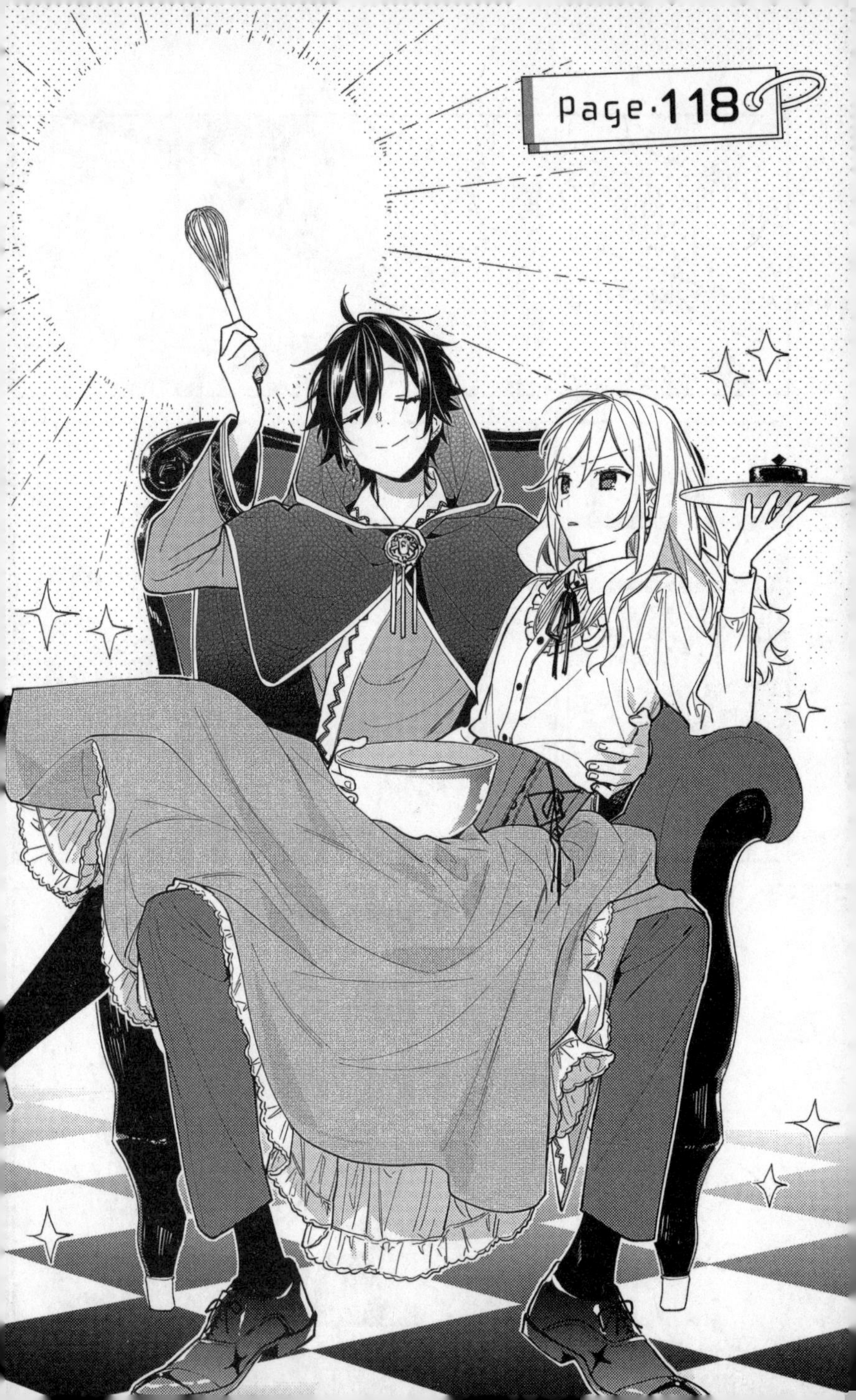
Page·118

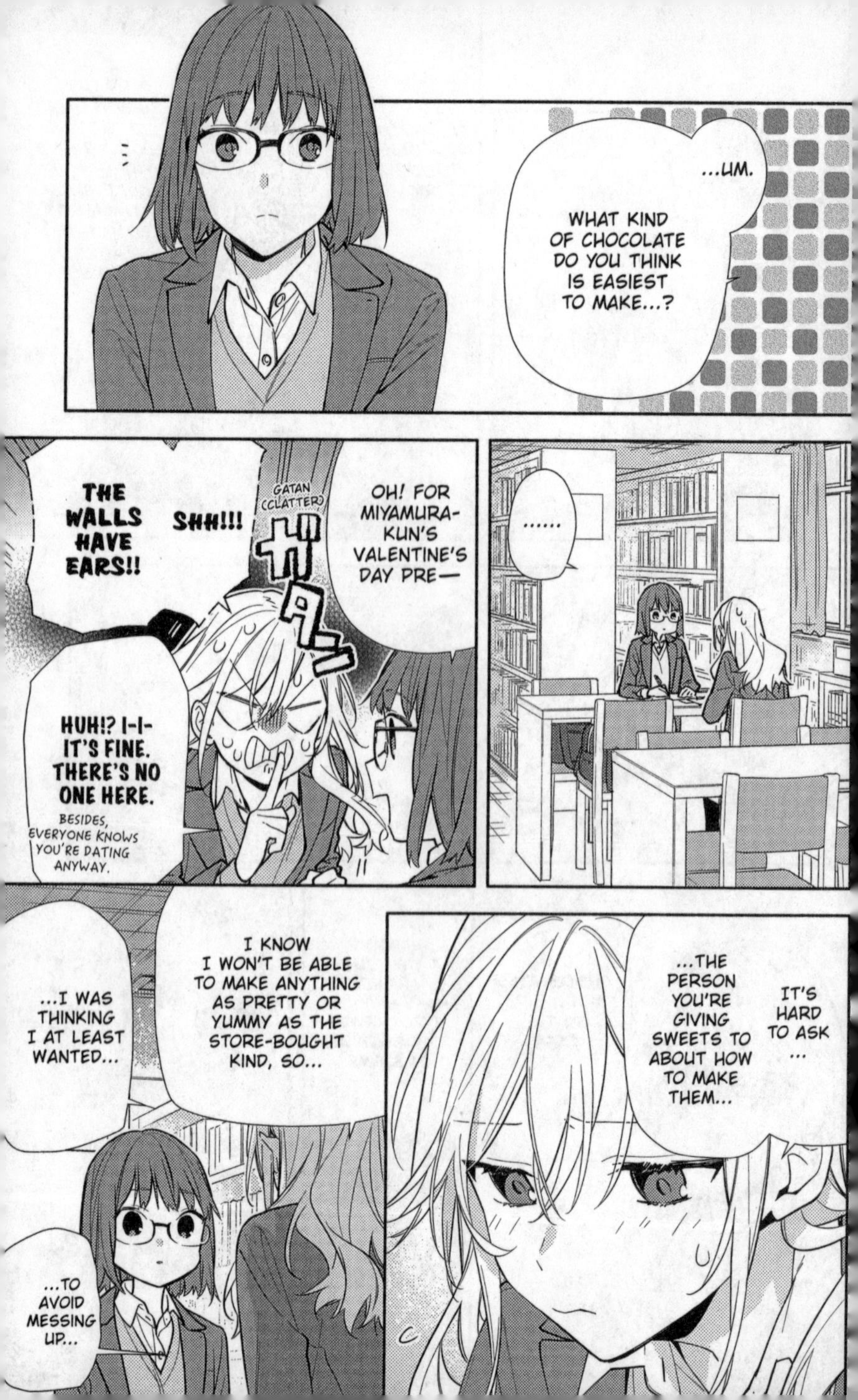
...UM.
WHAT KIND OF CHOCOLATE DO YOU THINK IS EASIEST TO MAKE...?
......
OH! FOR MIYAMURA-KUN'S VALENTINE'S DAY PRE—
GATAN (CLATTER)
SHH!!!
THE WALLS HAVE EARS!!
HUH!? I-I- IT'S FINE. THERE'S NO ONE HERE.
BESIDES, EVERYONE KNOWS YOU'RE DATING ANYWAY.
IT'S HARD TO ASK...
...THE PERSON YOU'RE GIVING SWEETS TO ABOUT HOW TO MAKE THEM...
I KNOW I WON'T BE ABLE TO MAKE ANYTHING AS PRETTY OR YUMMY AS THE STORE-BOUGHT KIND, SO...
...I WAS THINKING I AT LEAST WANTED...
...TO AVOID MESSING UP...

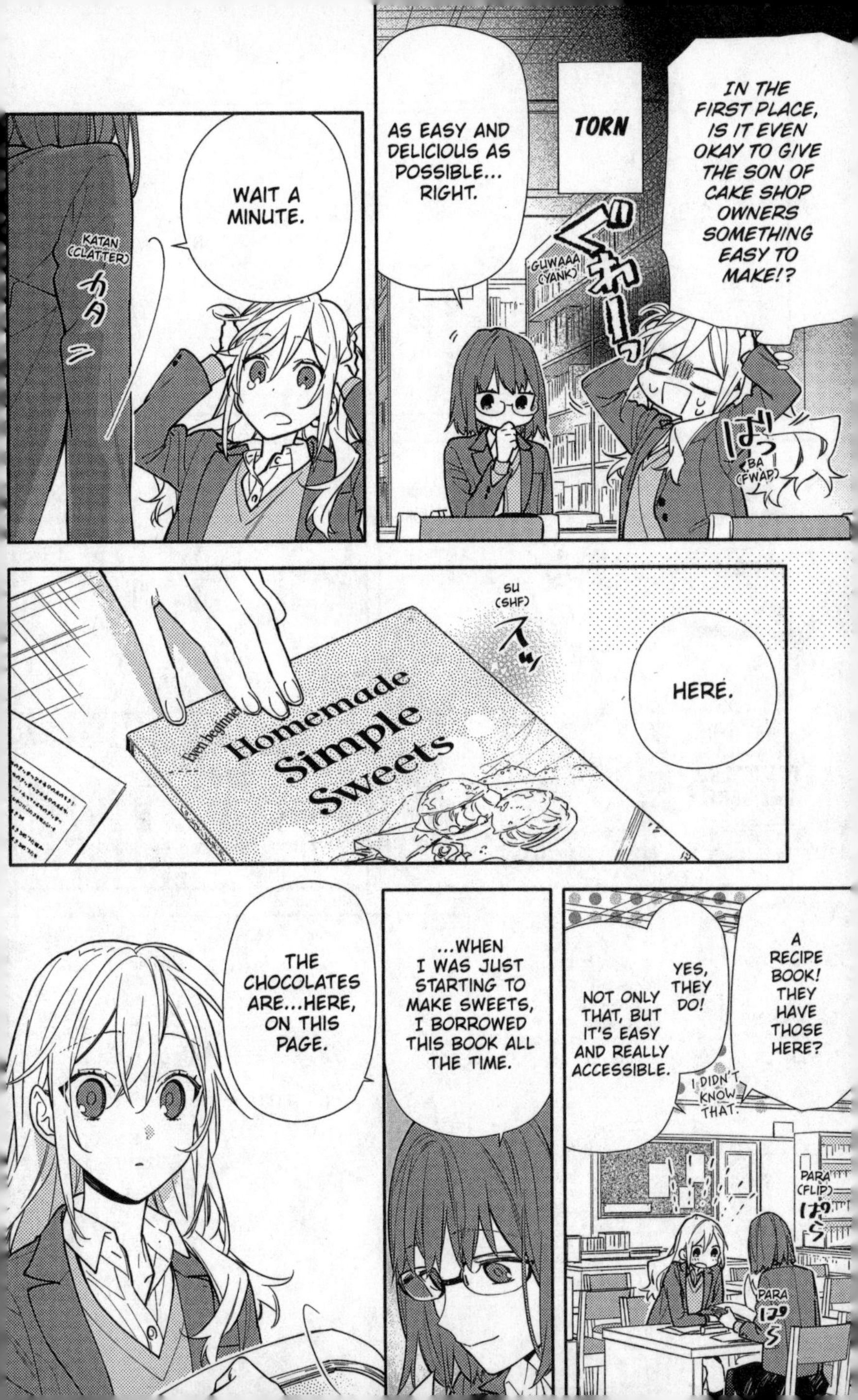
IN THE FIRST PLACE, IS IT EVEN OKAY TO GIVE THE SON OF CAKE SHOP OWNERS SOMETHING EASY TO MAKE!?
TORN
GUWAAA (YANK)
BA (FWAP)
AS EASY AND DELICIOUS AS POSSIBLE... RIGHT.
WAIT A MINUTE.
KATAN (CLATTER)
HERE.
SU (SHF)
Homemade Simple Sweets
A RECIPE BOOK! THEY HAVE THOSE HERE?
YES, THEY DO!
NOT ONLY THAT, BUT IT'S EASY AND REALLY ACCESSIBLE.
I DIDN'T KNOW THAT.
PARA (FLIP)
PARA
...WHEN I WAS JUST STARTING TO MAKE SWEETS, I BORROWED THIS BOOK ALL THE TIME.
THE CHOCOLATES ARE...HERE, ON THIS PAGE.

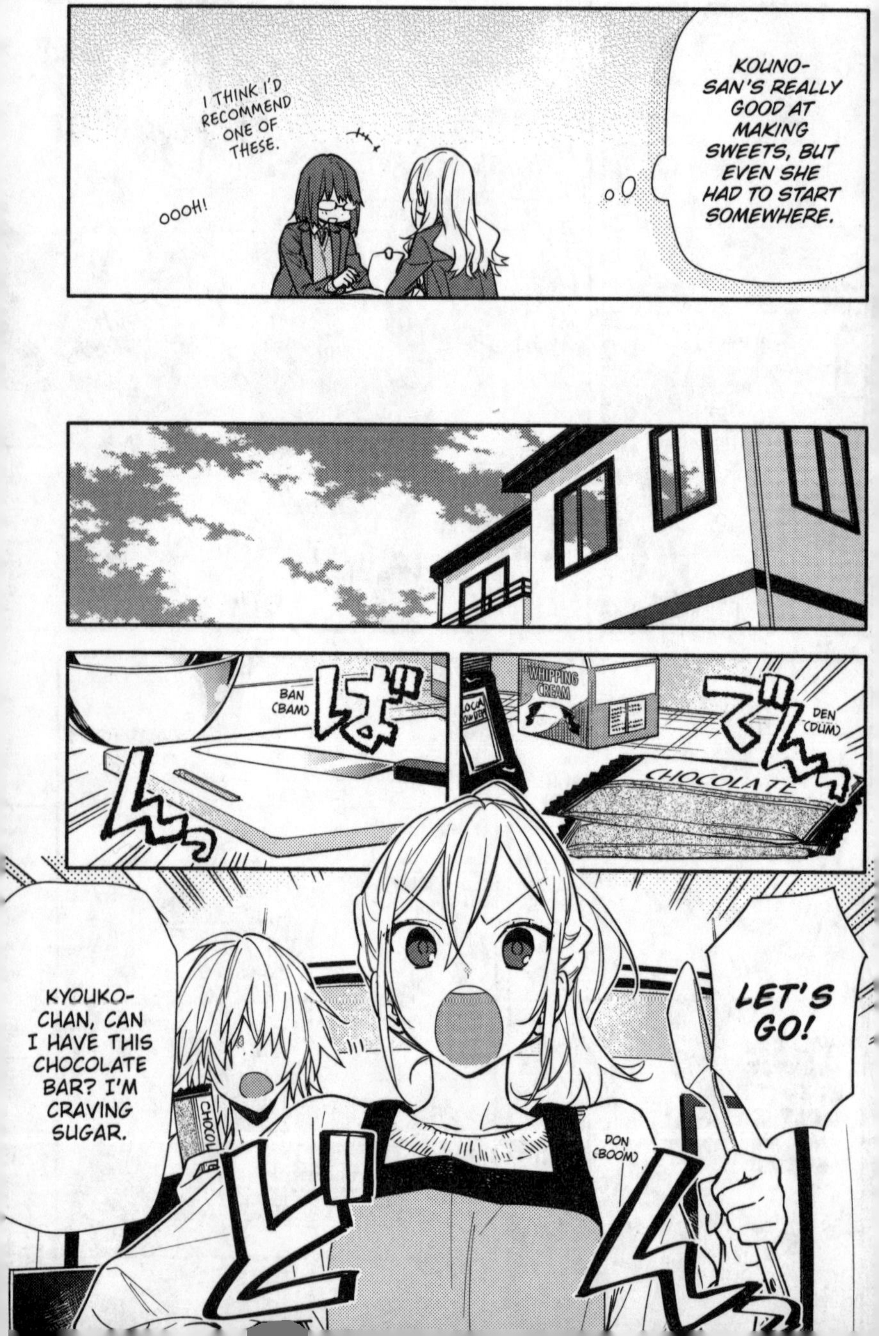
KOUNO-SAN'S REALLY GOOD AT MAKING SWEETS, BUT EVEN SHE HAD TO START SOMEWHERE.
I THINK I'D RECOMMEND ONE OF THESE.
OOOH!
WHIPPING CREAM
CHOCOLATE
DEN (DUM)
BAN (BAM)
LET'S GO!
DON (BOOM)
KYOUKO-CHAN, CAN I HAVE THIS CHOCOLATE BAR? I'M CRAVING SUGAR.

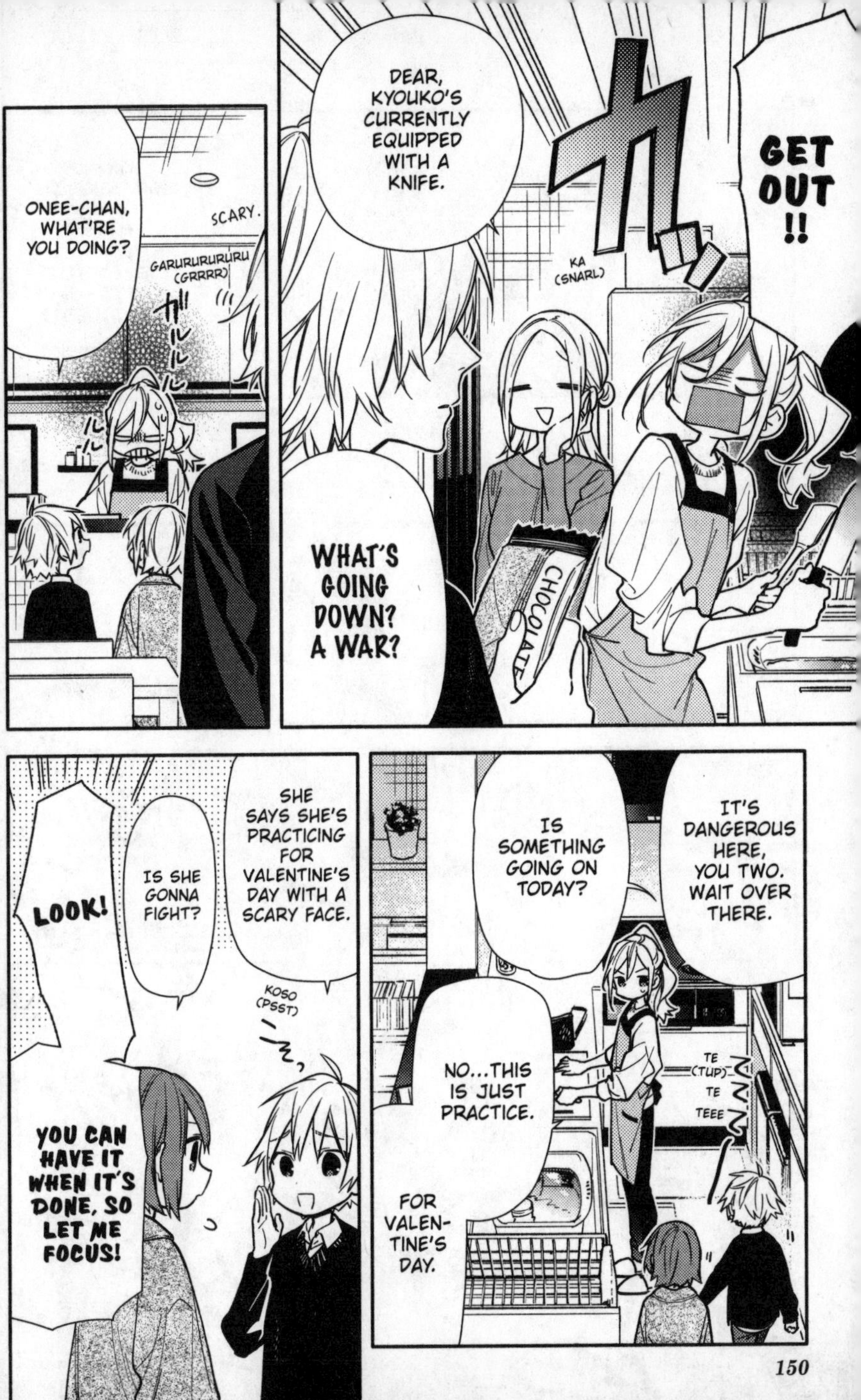
GET OUT!!
KA (SNARL)
DEAR, KYOUKO'S CURRENTLY EQUIPPED WITH A KNIFE.
WHAT'S GOING DOWN? A WAR?
CHOCOLATE
SCARY.
ONEE-CHAN, WHAT'RE YOU DOING?
GARURURURURU (GRRRR)
IT'S DANGEROUS HERE, YOU TWO. WAIT OVER THERE.
IS SOMETHING GOING ON TODAY?
TE (TUP) TE TEEE
NO...THIS IS JUST PRACTICE.
FOR VALEN-TINE'S DAY.
SHE SAYS SHE'S PRACTICING FOR VALENTINE'S DAY WITH A SCARY FACE.
KOSO (PSST)
IS SHE GONNA FIGHT?
LOOK!
YOU CAN HAVE IT WHEN IT'S DONE, SO LET ME FOCUS!

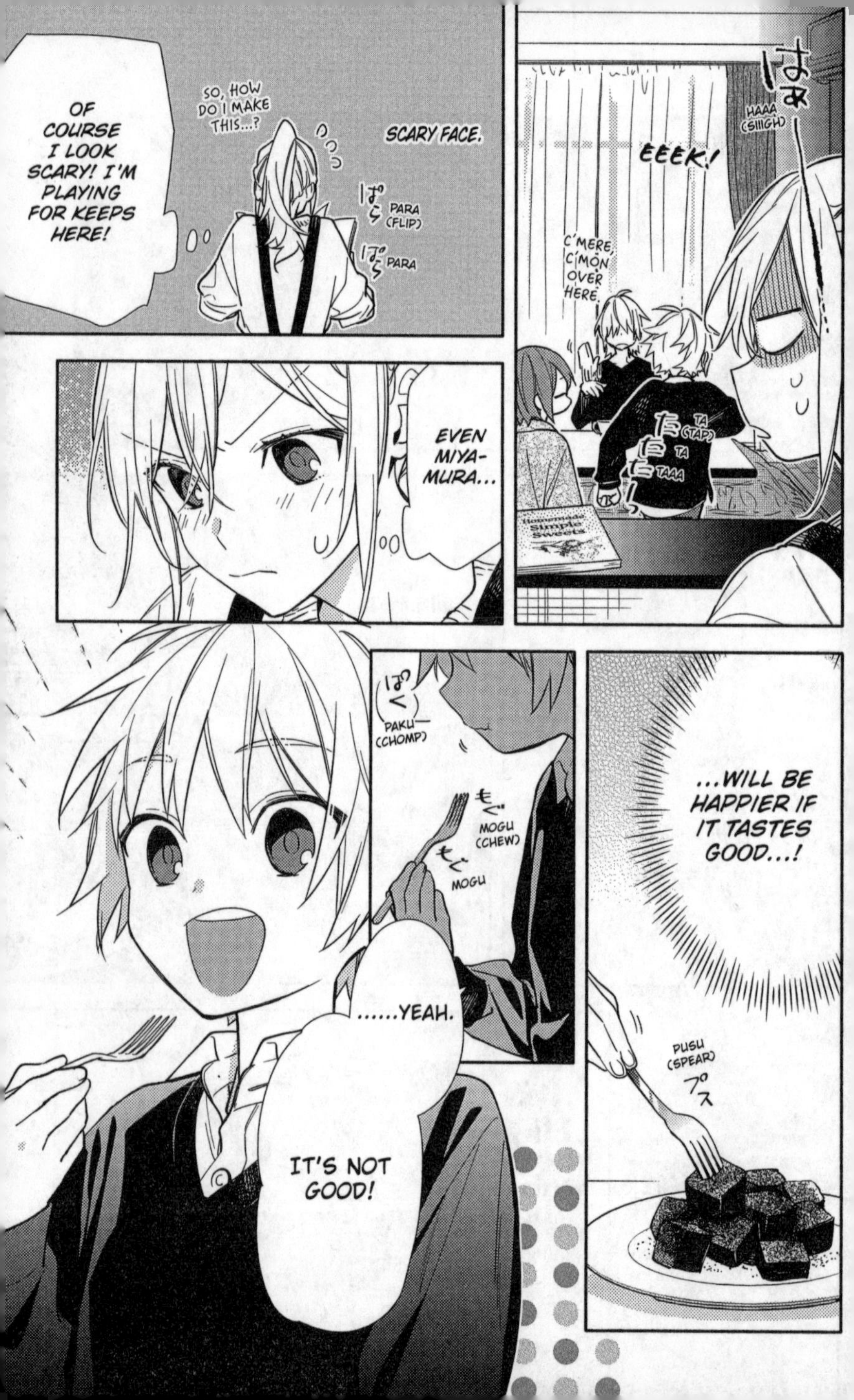
はぁ
HAAA (SIIIGH)
EEEK!
C'MERE, C'MON OVER HERE.
たたたー
TA (TAP) TA TAAA
Simple Sweets
SCARY FACE.
ぱら PARA (FLIP)
ぱら PARA
SO, HOW DO I MAKE THIS...?
OF COURSE I LOOK SCARY! I'M PLAYING FOR KEEPS HERE!
EVEN MIYAMURA...
...WILL BE HAPPIER IF IT TASTES GOOD...!
PUSU (SPEAR)
プス
ぱく
PAKU (CHOMP)
もぐ MOGU (CHEW)
もぐ MOGU
......YEAH.
IT'S NOT GOOD!

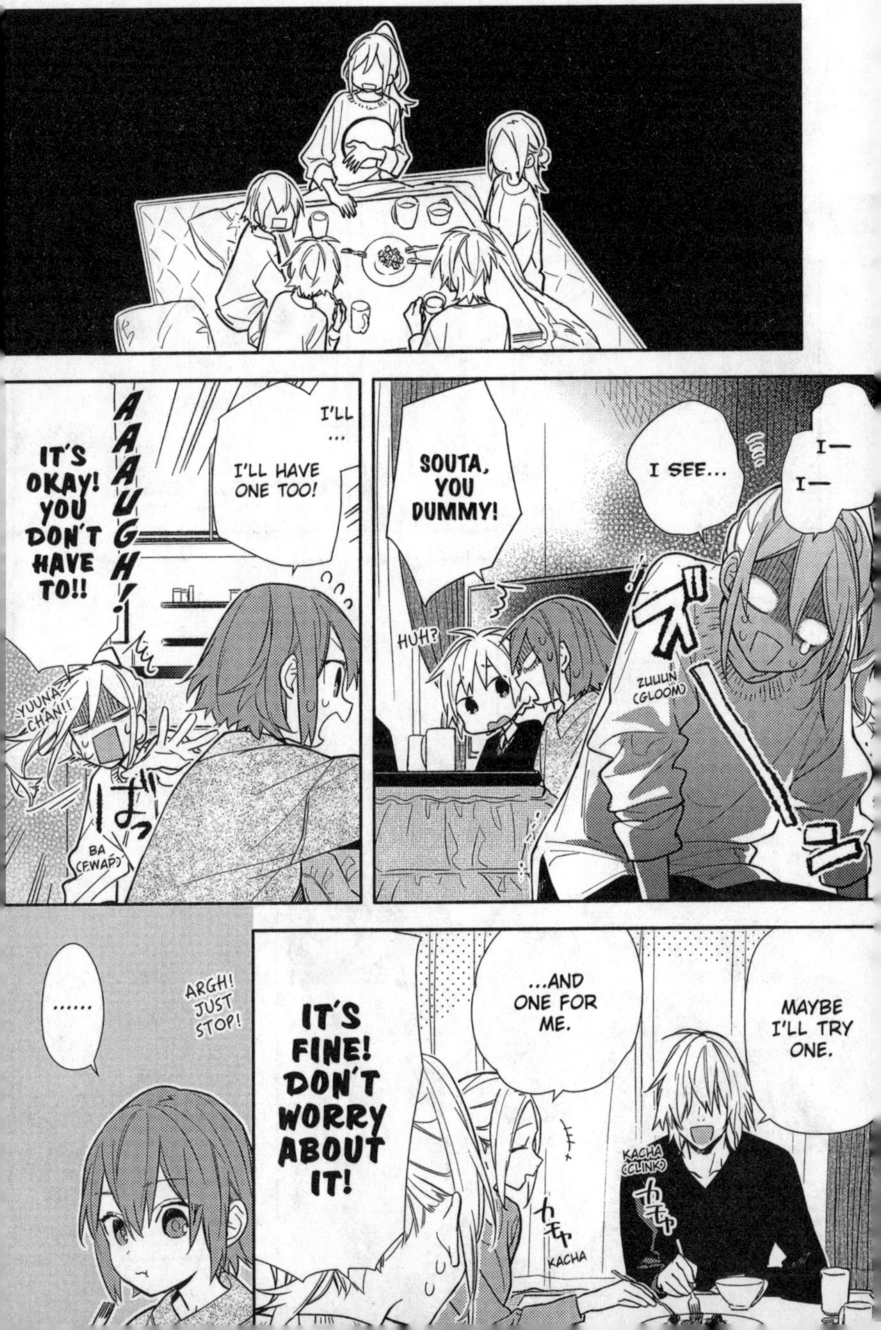
I—
I—
I SEE...
ZUUUN (GLOOM)
SOUTA, YOU DUMMY!
HUH?
I'LL ...
I'LL HAVE ONE TOO!
AAAAUGH!
IT'S OKAY! YOU DON'T HAVE TO!!
YUUNA-CHAN!!
BA (FWAP)
MAYBE I'LL TRY ONE.
KACHA (CLINK)
...AND ONE FOR ME.
KACHA
IT'S FINE! DON'T WORRY ABOUT IT!
ARGH! JUST STOP!
......

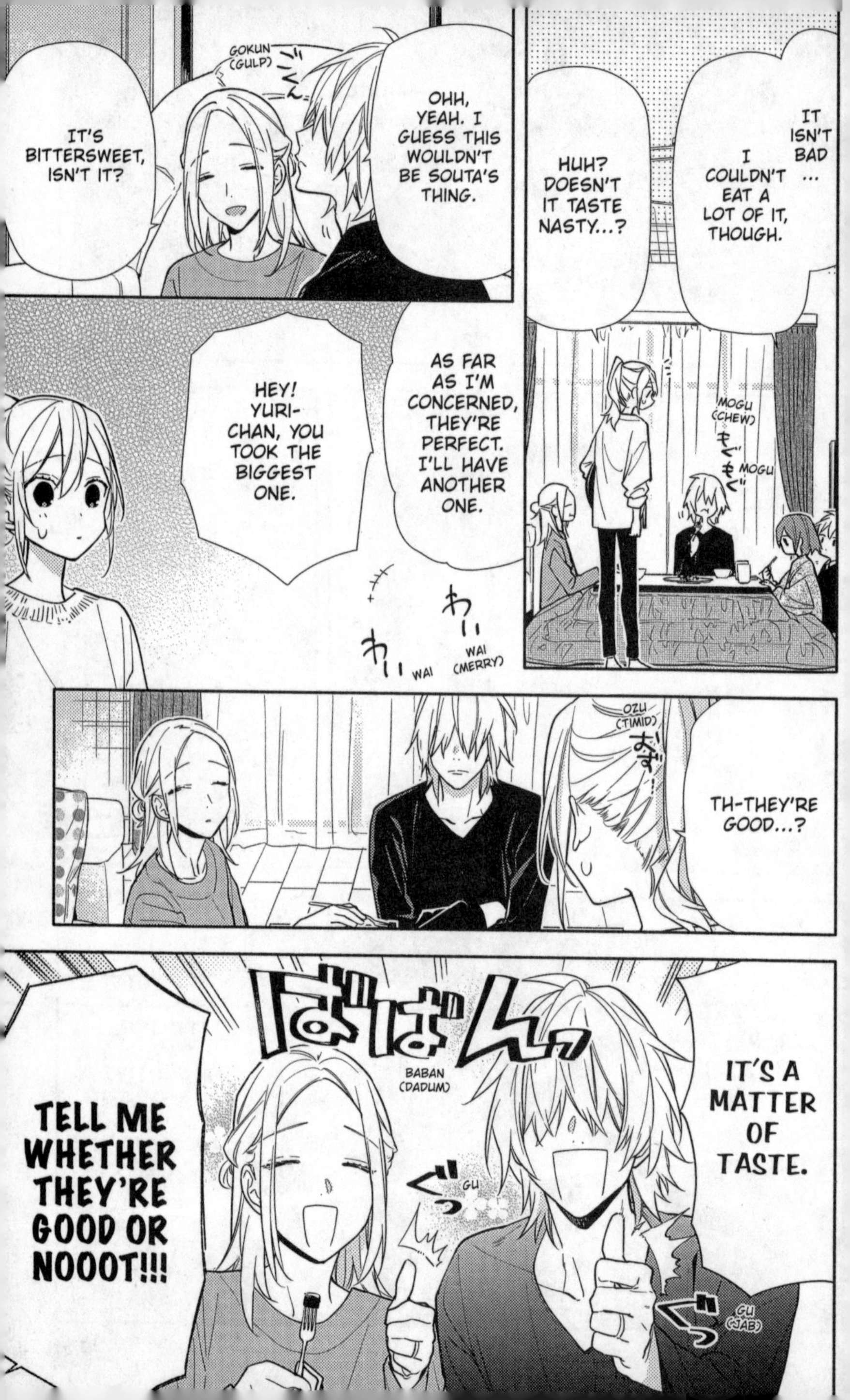
IT ISN'T BAD...
I COULDN'T EAT A LOT OF IT, THOUGH.
HUH? DOESN'T IT TASTE NASTY...?
OHH, YEAH. I GUESS THIS WOULDN'T BE SOUTA'S THING.
GOKUN (GULP)
IT'S BITTERSWEET, ISN'T IT?
MOGU (CHEW) MOGU
AS FAR AS I'M CONCERNED, THEY'RE PERFECT. I'LL HAVE ANOTHER ONE.
HEY! YURI-CHAN, YOU TOOK THE BIGGEST ONE.
WAI (MERRY) WAI
TH-THEY'RE GOOD...?
OZU (TIMID)
IT'S A MATTER OF TASTE.
GU (JAB)
ばばん
BABAN (DADUM)
GU
TELL ME WHETHER THEY'RE GOOD OR NOOOT!!!

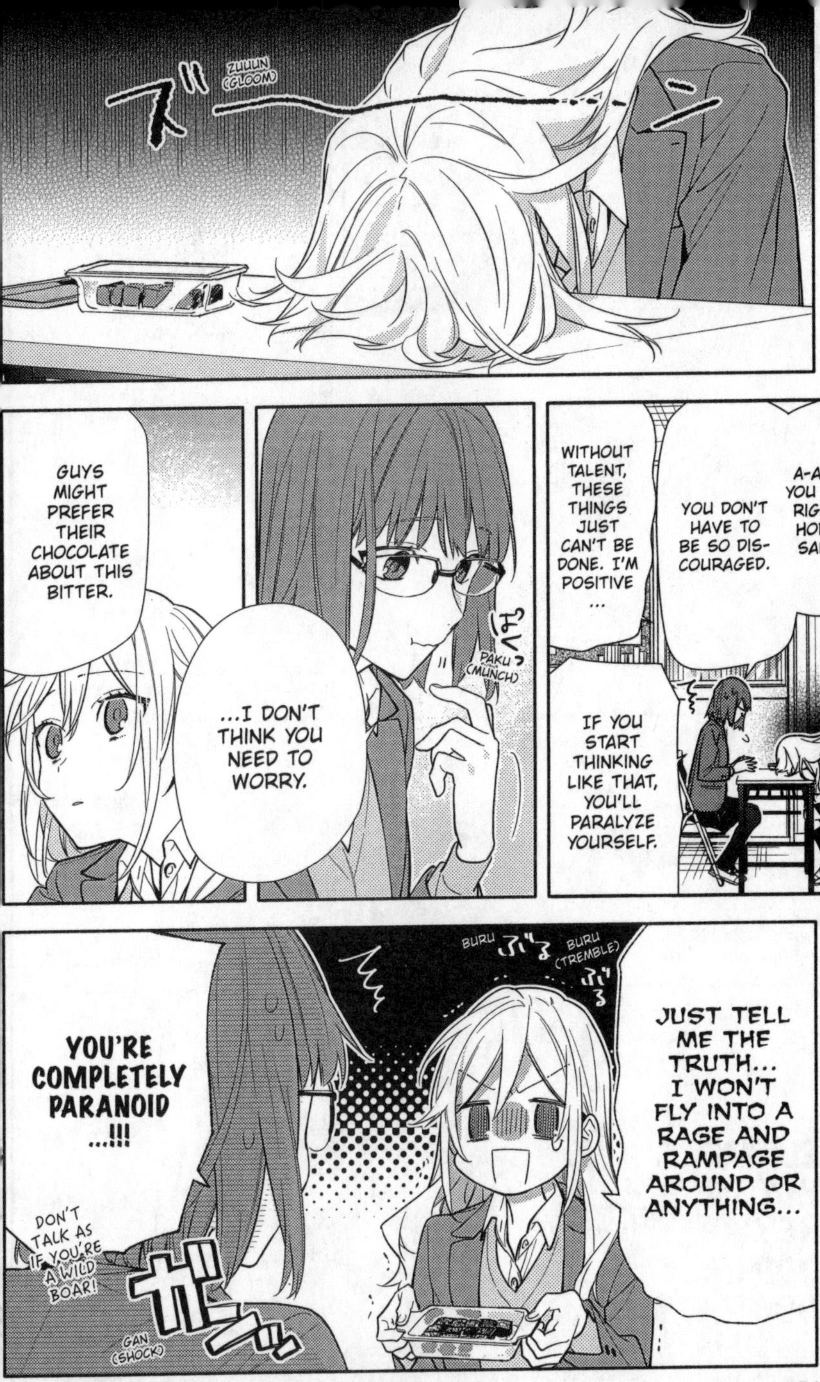
ズーン
ZUUUN (GLOOM)
A-ARE YOU ALL RIGHT, HORI-SAN?
YOU DON'T HAVE TO BE SO DIS-COURAGED.
WITHOUT TALENT, THESE THINGS JUST CAN'T BE DONE. I'M POSITIVE...
IF YOU START THINKING LIKE THAT, YOU'LL PARALYZE YOURSELF.
ぱくっ
PAKU (MUNCH)
...I DON'T THINK YOU NEED TO WORRY.
GUYS MIGHT PREFER THEIR CHOCOLATE ABOUT THIS BITTER.
ぶる
BURU
ぶる
BURU (TREMBLE)
JUST TELL ME THE TRUTH... I WON'T FLY INTO A RAGE AND RAMPAGE AROUND OR ANYTHING...
YOU'RE COMPLETELY PARANOID ...!!!
DON'T TALK AS IF YOU'RE A WILD BOAR!
ガーン
GAN (SHOCK)

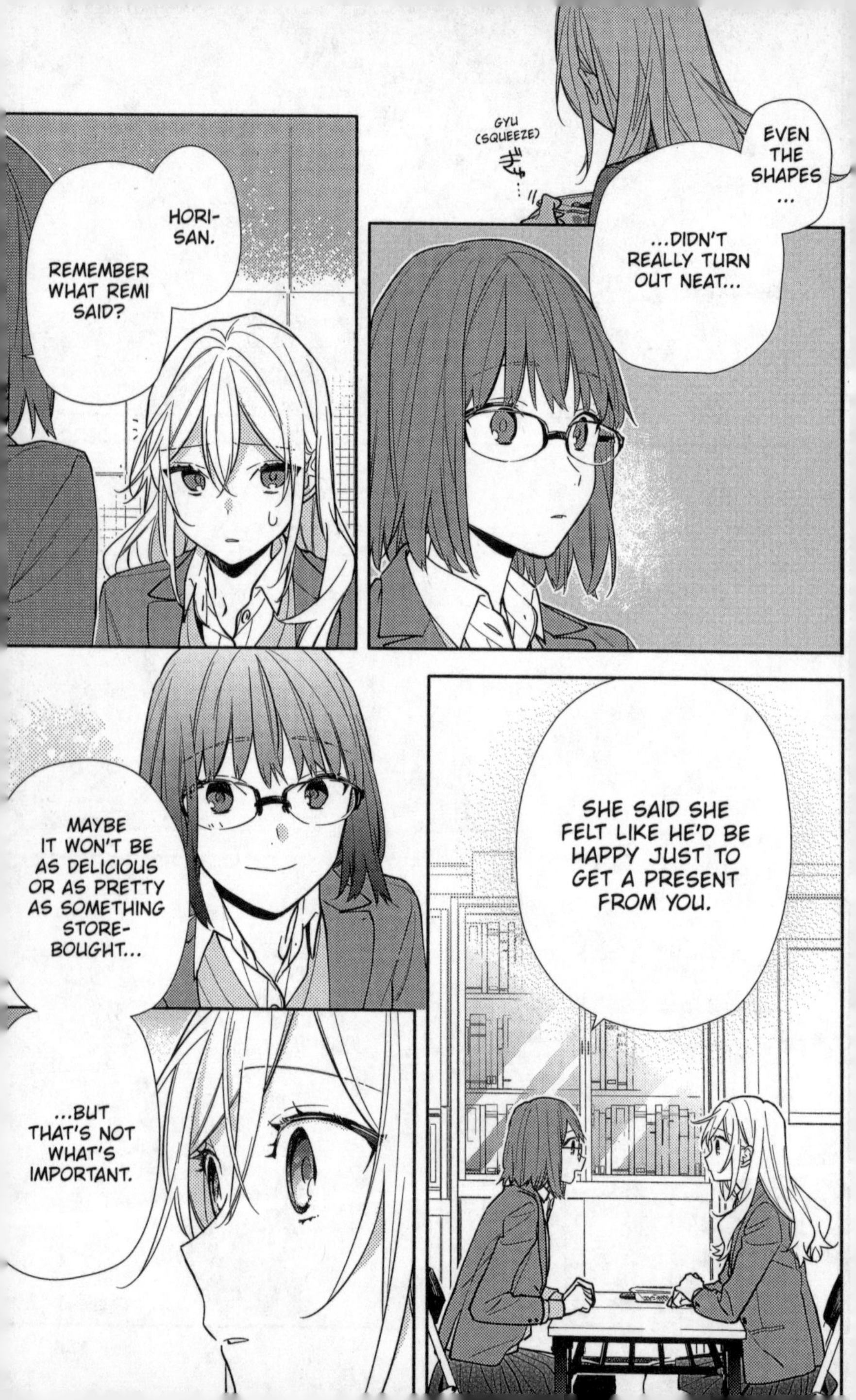
EVEN THE SHAPES...
GYU (SQUEEZE)
ぎゅ…
...DIDN'T REALLY TURN OUT NEAT...
HORI-SAN.
REMEMBER WHAT REMI SAID?
SHE SAID SHE FELT LIKE HE'D BE HAPPY JUST TO GET A PRESENT FROM YOU.
MAYBE IT WON'T BE AS DELICIOUS OR AS PRETTY AS SOMETHING STORE-BOUGHT...
...BUT THAT'S NOT WHAT'S IMPORTANT.

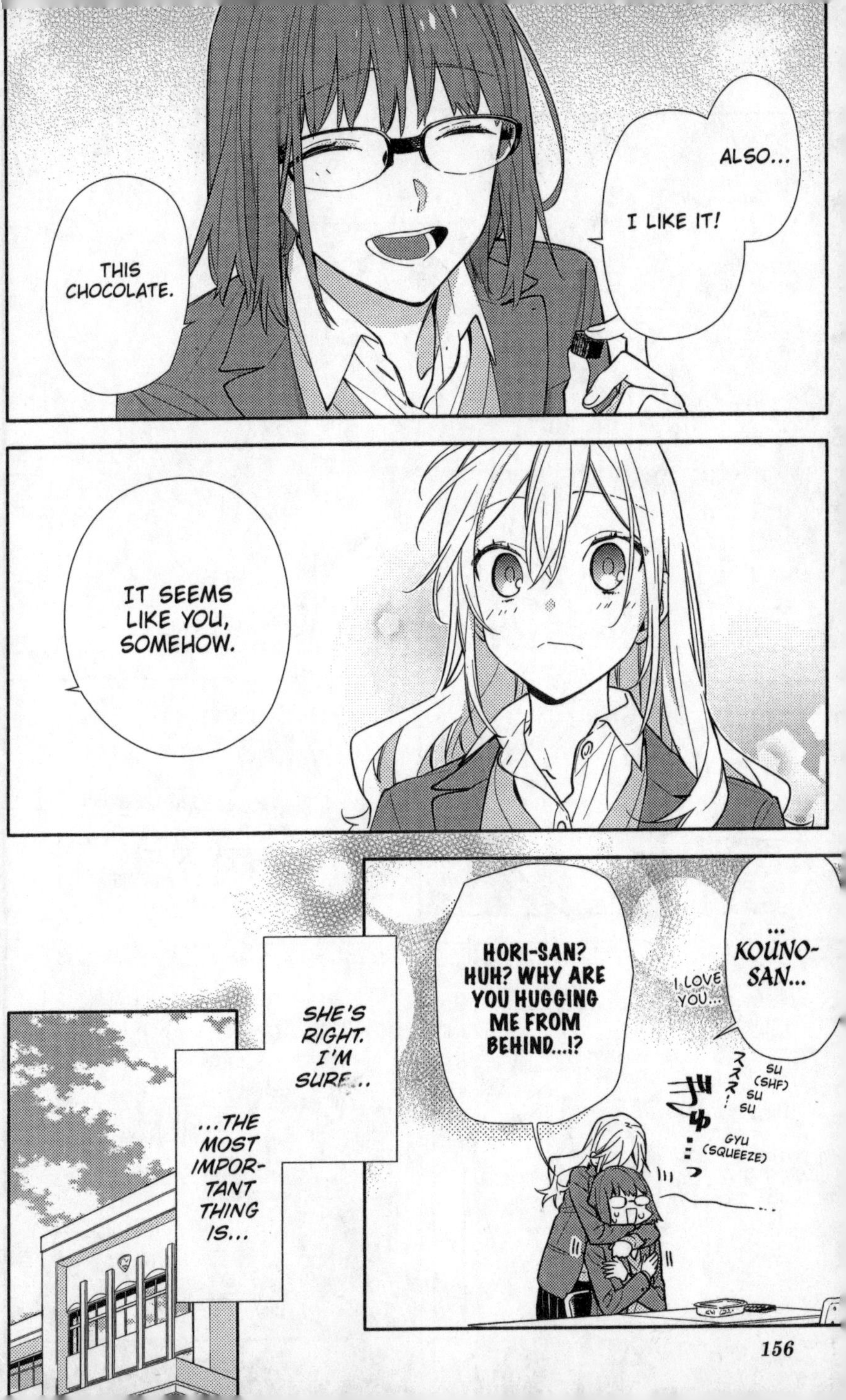
ALSO...
I LIKE IT!
THIS CHOCOLATE.
IT SEEMS LIKE YOU, SOMEHOW.
...KOUNO-SAN...
I LOVE YOU...
スス…
SU (SHF) SU SU
ぎゅ…
GYU (SQUEEZE)
HORI-SAN? HUH? WHY ARE YOU HUGGING ME FROM BEHIND...!?
SHE'S RIGHT. I'M SURE...
...THE MOST IMPORTANT THING IS...

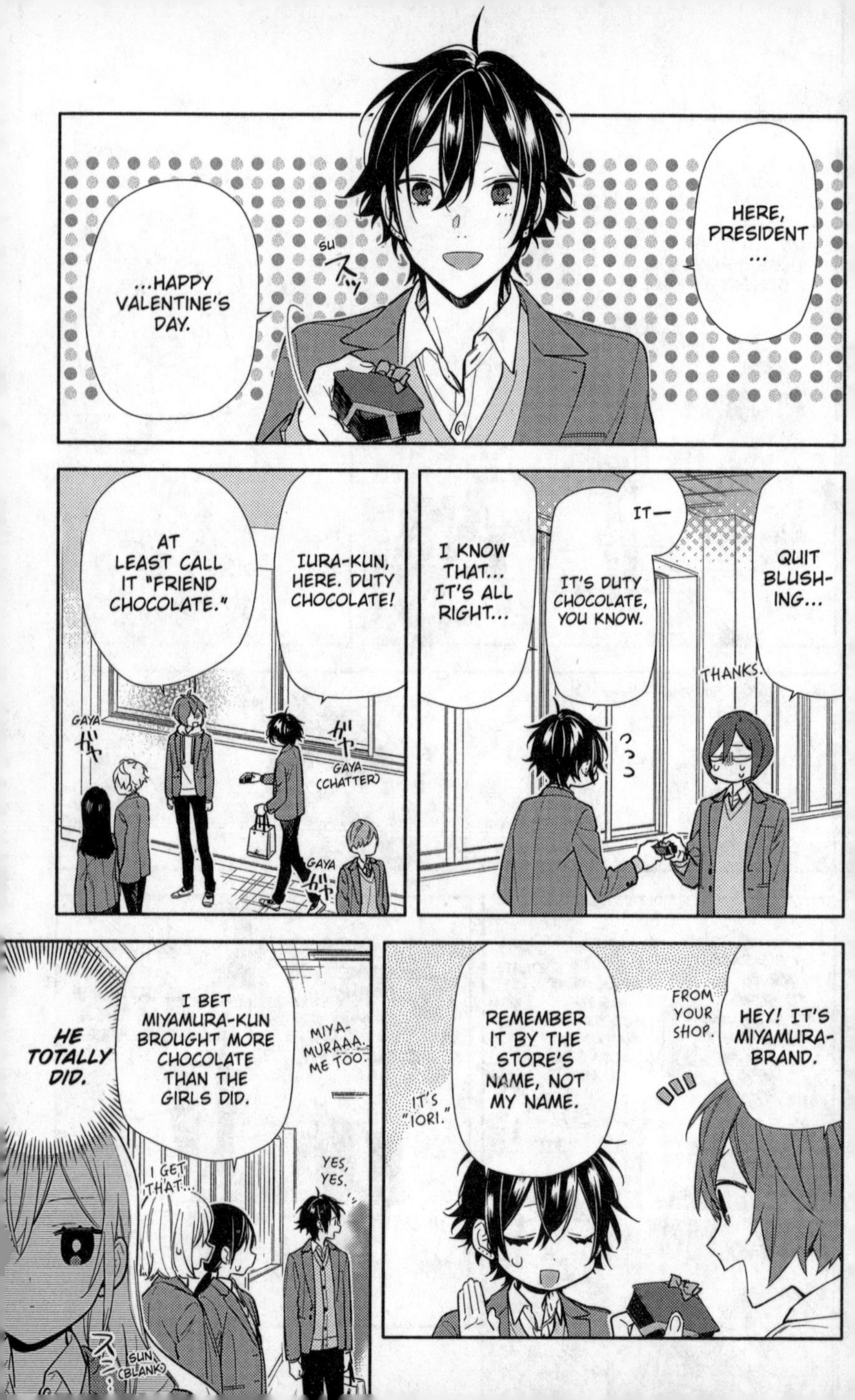
HERE, PRESIDENT ...
SU
...HAPPY VALENTINE'S DAY.
QUIT BLUSHING...
THANKS.
IT—
IT'S DUTY CHOCOLATE, YOU KNOW.
I KNOW THAT... IT'S ALL RIGHT...
IURA-KUN, HERE. DUTY CHOCOLATE!
GAYA (CHATTER)
AT LEAST CALL IT "FRIEND CHOCOLATE."
GAYA
GAYA
HEY! IT'S MIYAMURA-BRAND.
FROM YOUR SHOP.
REMEMBER IT BY THE STORE'S NAME, NOT MY NAME.
IT'S "IORI."
MIYA-MURAAA. ME TOO.
I BET MIYAMURA-KUN BROUGHT MORE CHOCOLATE THAN THE GIRLS DID.
HE TOTALLY DID.
YES, YES.
I GET THAT...
SUN (BLANK)

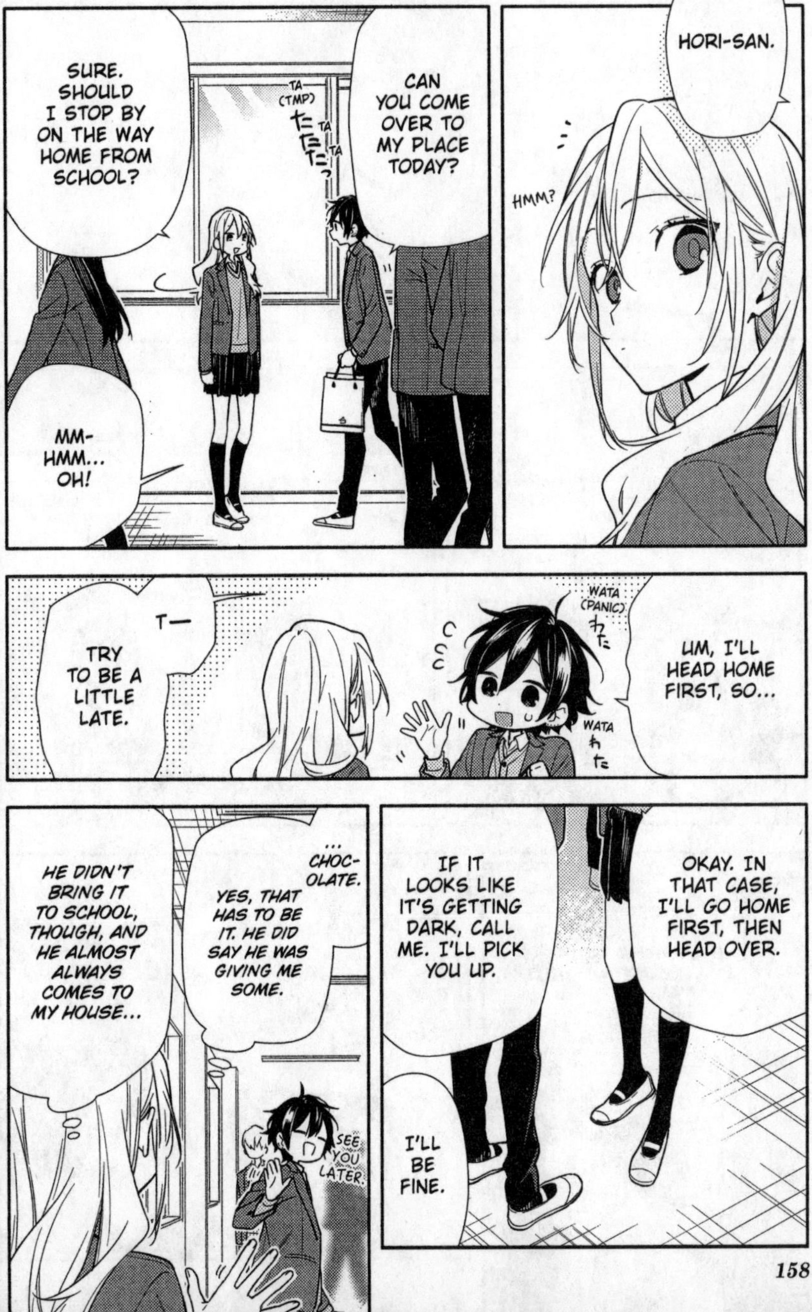
HORI-SAN.
HMM?
CAN YOU COME OVER TO MY PLACE TODAY?
TA (TMP)
TA
TA
SURE. SHOULD I STOP BY ON THE WAY HOME FROM SCHOOL?
MM-HMM... OH!
UM, I'LL HEAD HOME FIRST, SO...
WATA (PANIC)
WATA
T—
TRY TO BE A LITTLE LATE.
OKAY. IN THAT CASE, I'LL GO HOME FIRST, THEN HEAD OVER.
IF IT LOOKS LIKE IT'S GETTING DARK, CALL ME. I'LL PICK YOU UP.
I'LL BE FINE.
...CHOCOLATE.
YES, THAT HAS TO BE IT. HE DID SAY HE WAS GIVING ME SOME.
HE DIDN'T BRING IT TO SCHOOL, THOUGH, AND HE ALMOST ALWAYS COMES TO MY HOUSE...
SEE YOU LATER.

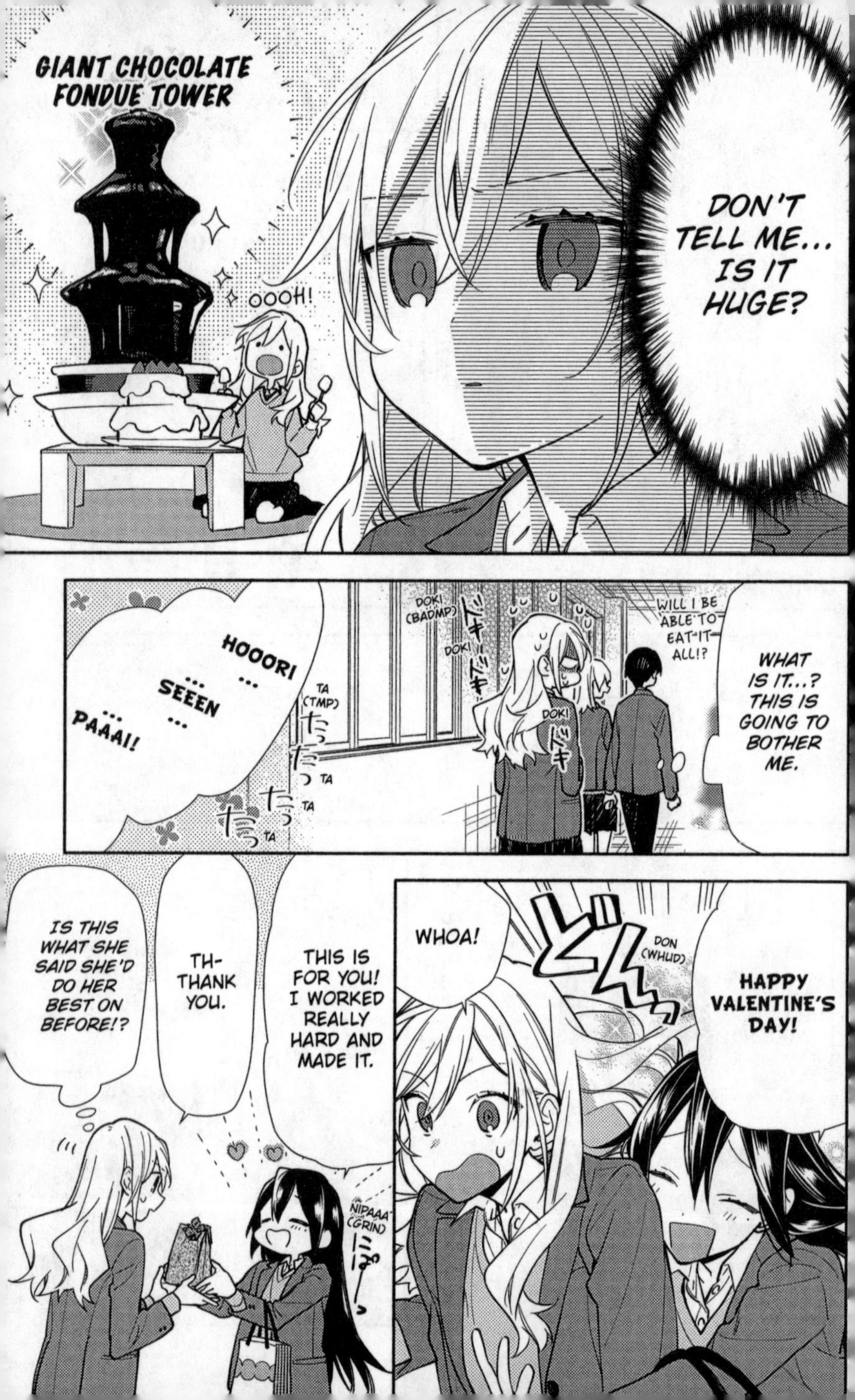
DON'T TELL ME... IS IT HUGE?
GIANT CHOCOLATE FONDUE TOWER
OOOH!
WHAT IS IT...? THIS IS GOING TO BOTHER ME.
WILL I BE ABLE TO EAT IT ALL!?
DOKI (BADMP)
DOKI
DOKI
TA (TMP)
TA
TA
TA
HOOORI... SEEEN... PAAAI!
HAPPY VALENTINE'S DAY!
DON (WHUD)
WHOA!
THIS IS FOR YOU! I WORKED REALLY HARD AND MADE IT.
NIPAAA (GRIN)
TH- THANK YOU.
IS THIS WHAT SHE SAID SHE'D DO HER BEST ON BEFORE!?

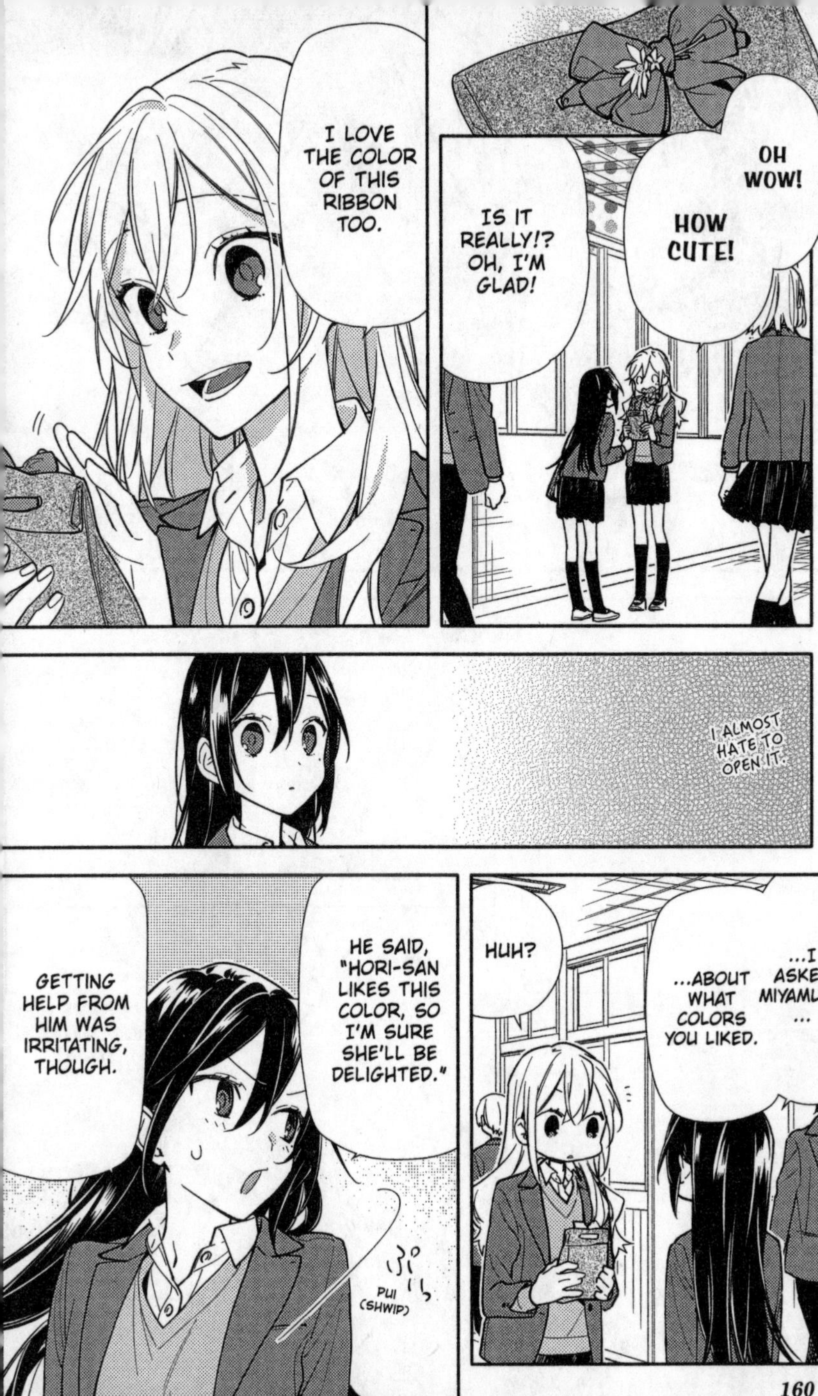
OH WOW!
HOW CUTE!
IS IT REALLY!? OH, I'M GLAD!
I LOVE THE COLOR OF THIS RIBBON TOO.
I ALMOST HATE TO OPEN IT.
...I ASKED MIYAMURA...
...ABOUT WHAT COLORS YOU LIKED.
HUH?
HE SAID, "HORI-SAN LIKES THIS COLOR, SO I'M SURE SHE'LL BE DELIGHTED."
GETTING HELP FROM HIM WAS IRRITATING, THOUGH.
ぷい
PUI (SHWIP)

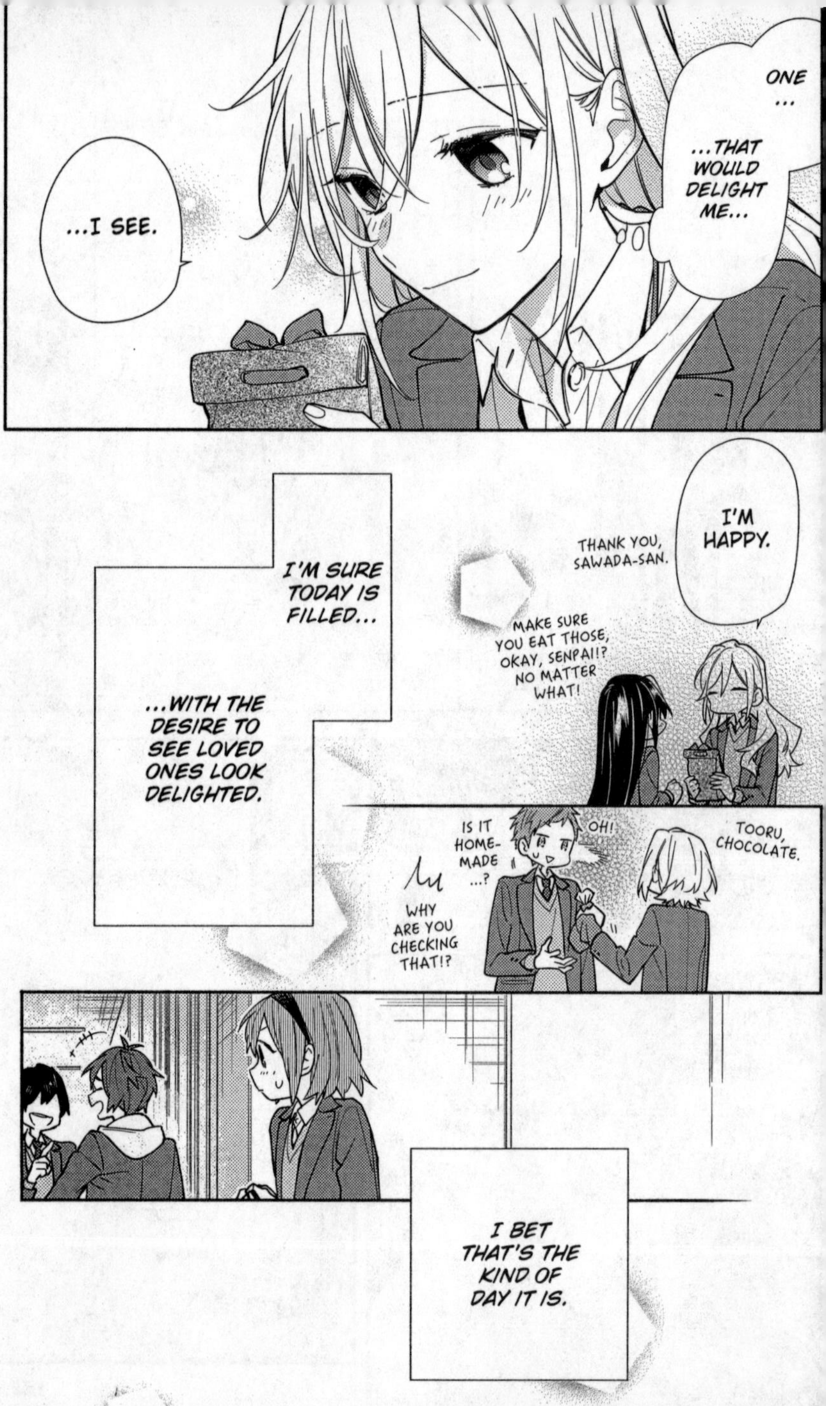
ONE...
...THAT WOULD DELIGHT ME...
...I SEE.
I'M HAPPY.
THANK YOU, SAWADA-SAN.
MAKE SURE YOU EAT THOSE, OKAY, SENPAI!? NO MATTER WHAT!
TOORU, CHOCOLATE.
OH!
IS IT HOME-MADE...?
WHY ARE YOU CHECKING THAT!?
I'M SURE TODAY IS FILLED...
...WITH THE DESIRE TO SEE LOVED ONES LOOK DELIGHTED.
I BET THAT'S THE KIND OF DAY IT IS.

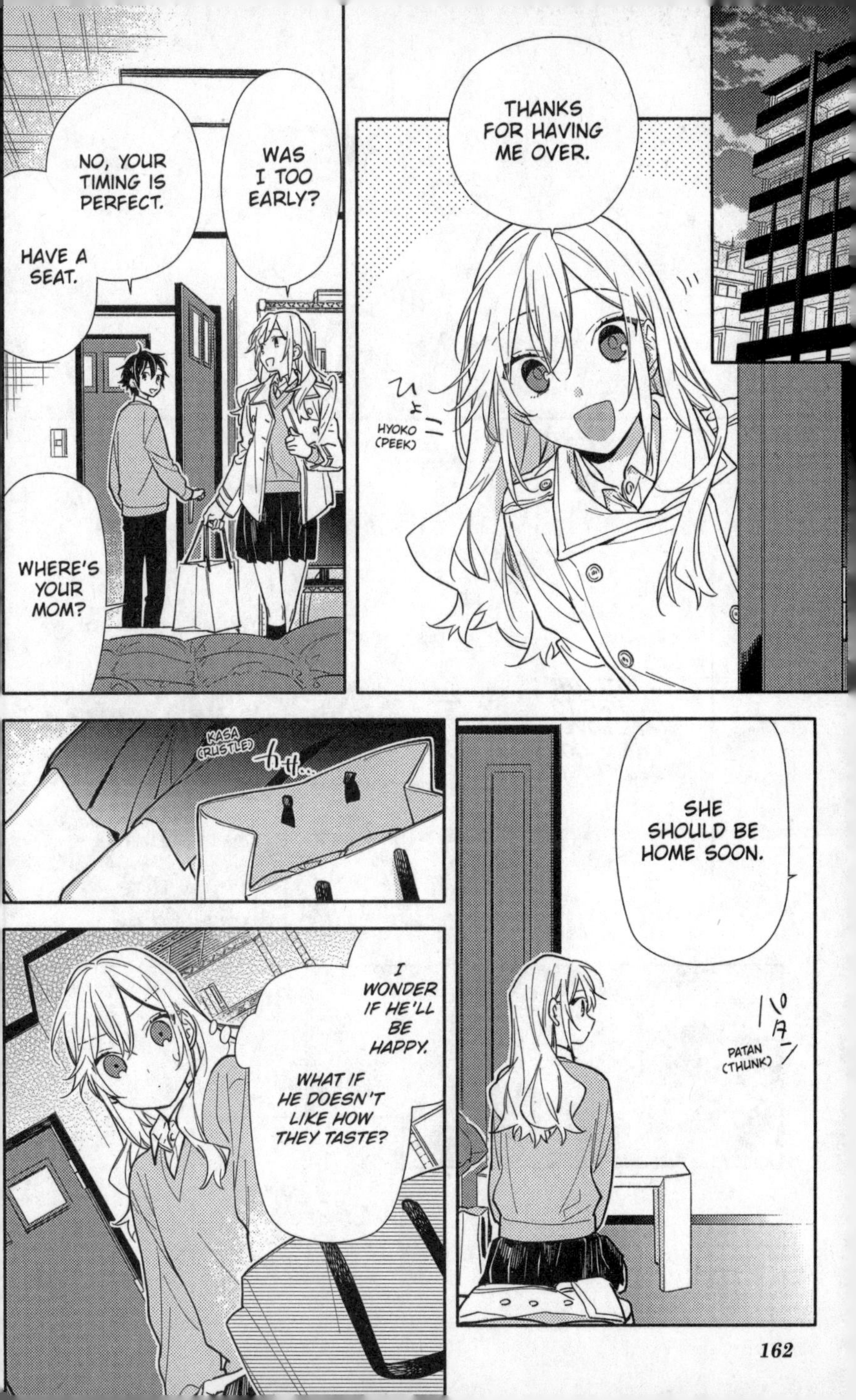
THANKS FOR HAVING ME OVER.
ひょ
HYOKO (PEEK)
WAS I TOO EARLY?
NO, YOUR TIMING IS PERFECT.
HAVE A SEAT.
WHERE'S YOUR MOM?
SHE SHOULD BE HOME SOON.
パタン
PATAN (THUNK)
KASA (RUSTLE)
カサ…
I WONDER IF HE'LL BE HAPPY.
WHAT IF HE DOESN'T LIKE HOW THEY TASTE?

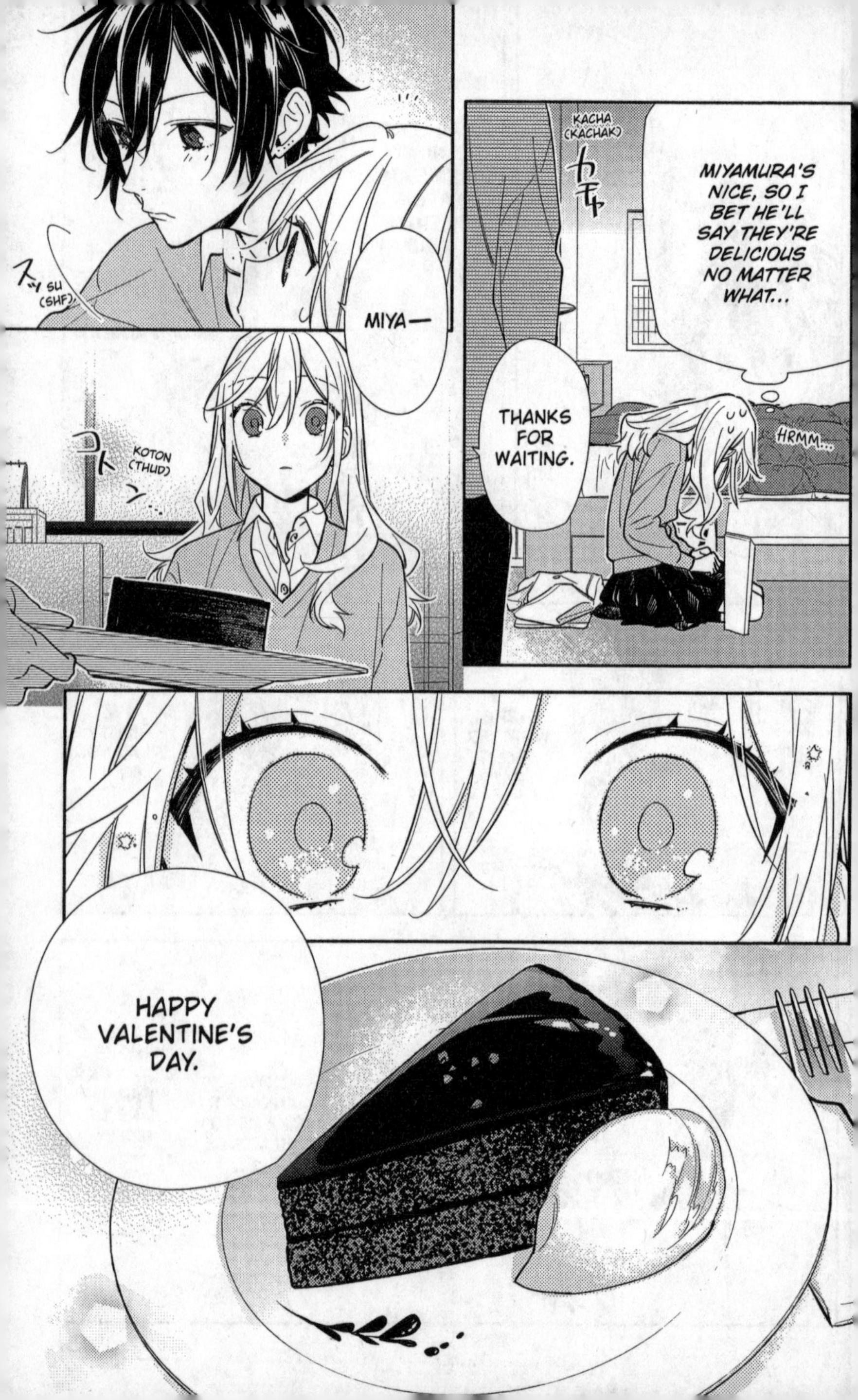
MIYAMURA'S NICE, SO I BET HE'LL SAY THEY'RE DELICIOUS NO MATTER WHAT...
HRMM...
カチャ
KACHA (KACHAK)
THANKS FOR WAITING.
スッ
SU (SHF)
MIYA—
コトン
KOTON (THUD)
HAPPY VALENTINE'S DAY.

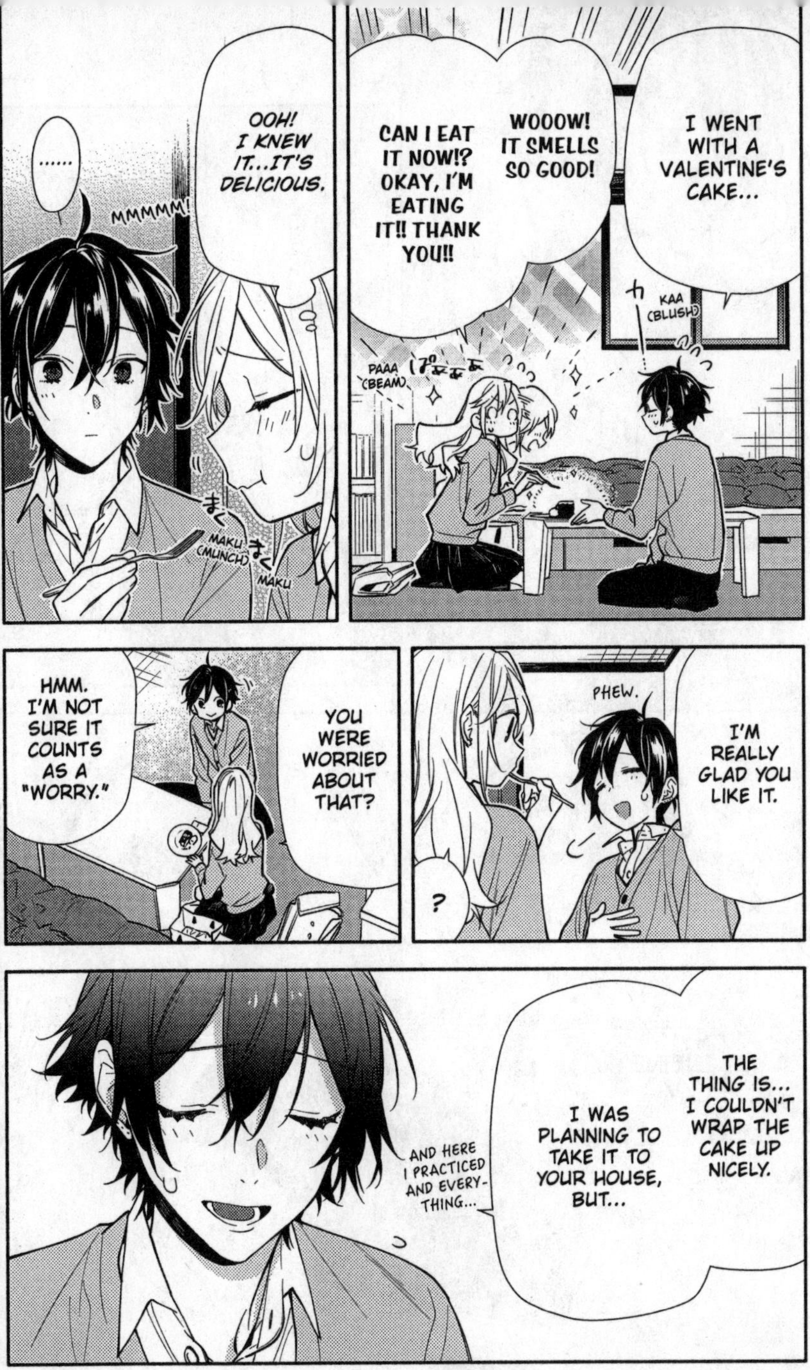
I WENT WITH A VALENTINE'S CAKE...
カ
KAA (BLUSH)
WOOOW! IT SMELLS SO GOOD!
CAN I EAT IT NOW!? OKAY, I'M EATING IT!! THANK YOU!!
ぱぁぁ
PAAA (BEAM)
OOH! I KNEW IT...IT'S DELICIOUS.
MMMMM!
......
まく
MAKU (MUNCH)
まく
MAKU
I'M REALLY GLAD YOU LIKE IT.
PHEW.
?
YOU WERE WORRIED ABOUT THAT?
HMM. I'M NOT SURE IT COUNTS AS A "WORRY."
THE THING IS... I COULDN'T WRAP THE CAKE UP NICELY.
I WAS PLANNING TO TAKE IT TO YOUR HOUSE, BUT...
AND HERE I PRACTICED AND EVERY-THING...

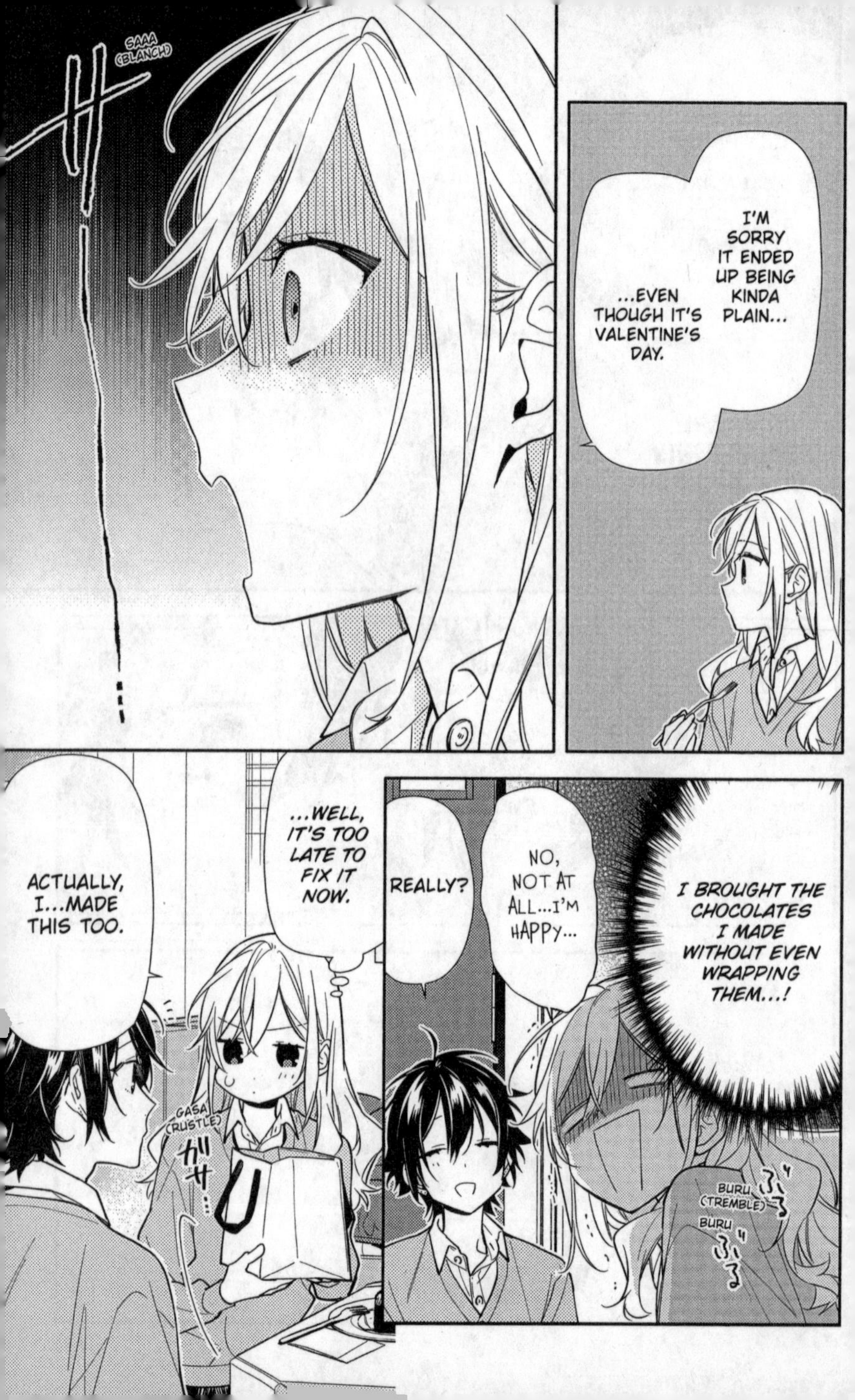
I'M SORRY IT ENDED UP BEING KINDA PLAIN...
...EVEN THOUGH IT'S VALENTINE'S DAY.
SAAA (BLANCH)
I BROUGHT THE CHOCOLATES I MADE WITHOUT EVEN WRAPPING THEM...!
NO, NOT AT ALL...I'M HAPPY...
REALLY?
BURU (TREMBLE) BURU
...WELL, IT'S TOO LATE TO FIX IT NOW.
ACTUALLY, I...MADE THIS TOO.
GASA (RUSTLE)

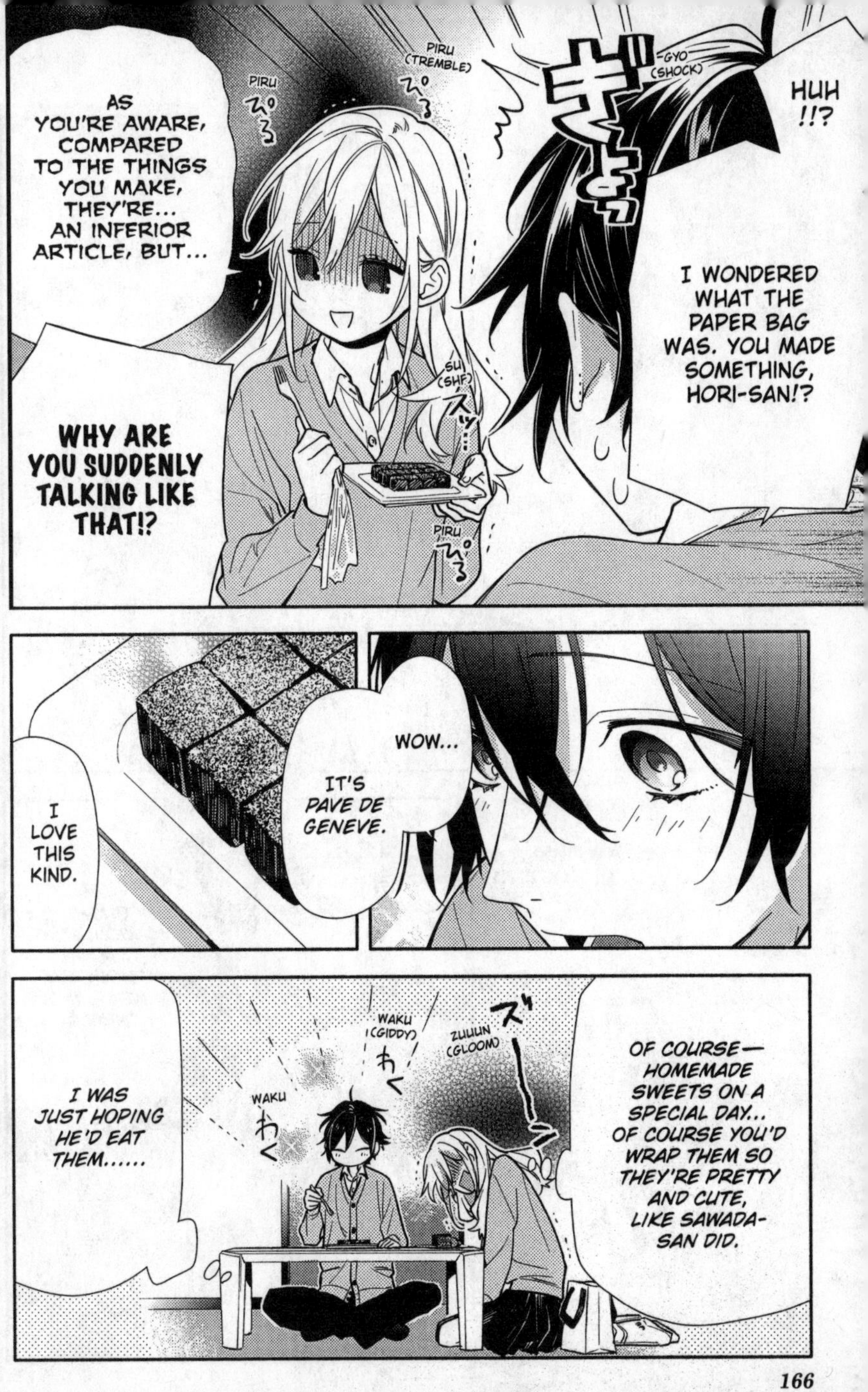
GYO (SHOCK)
ぎょっ
HUH !!?
I WONDERED WHAT THE PAPER BAG WAS. YOU MADE SOMETHING, HORI-SAN!?
PIRU (TREMBLE)
ぴる
PIRU
ぴる
AS YOU'RE AWARE, COMPARED TO THE THINGS YOU MAKE, THEY'RE... AN INFERIOR ARTICLE, BUT...
SU (SHF)
スッ…
PIRU
ぴる
WHY ARE YOU SUDDENLY TALKING LIKE THAT!?
WOW...
IT'S PAVE DE GENEVE.
I LOVE THIS KIND.
OF COURSE—HOMEMADE SWEETS ON A SPECIAL DAY... OF COURSE YOU'D WRAP THEM SO THEY'RE PRETTY AND CUTE, LIKE SAWADA-SAN DID.
ZUUUN (GLOOM)
ズーン
WAKU (GIDDY)
わく
WAKU
わく
I WAS JUST HOPING HE'D EAT THEM......

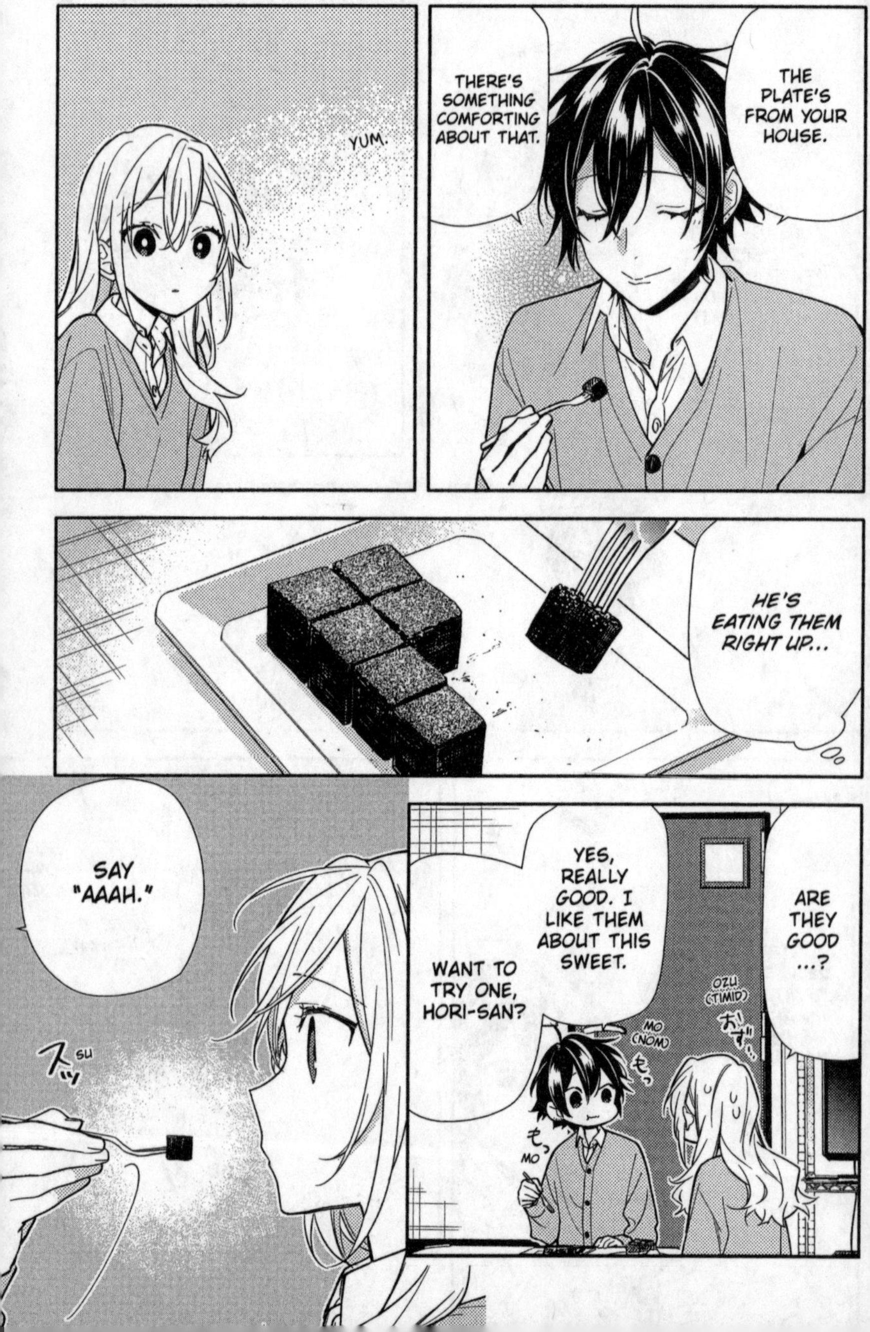
THE PLATE'S FROM YOUR HOUSE.
THERE'S SOMETHING COMFORTING ABOUT THAT.
YUM.
HE'S EATING THEM RIGHT UP...
ARE THEY GOOD ...?
おず…
OZU (TIMID)
YES, REALLY GOOD. I LIKE THEM ABOUT THIS SWEET.
も
MO (NOM)
も
MO
WANT TO TRY ONE, HORI-SAN?
SAY "AAAH."
スッ
SU

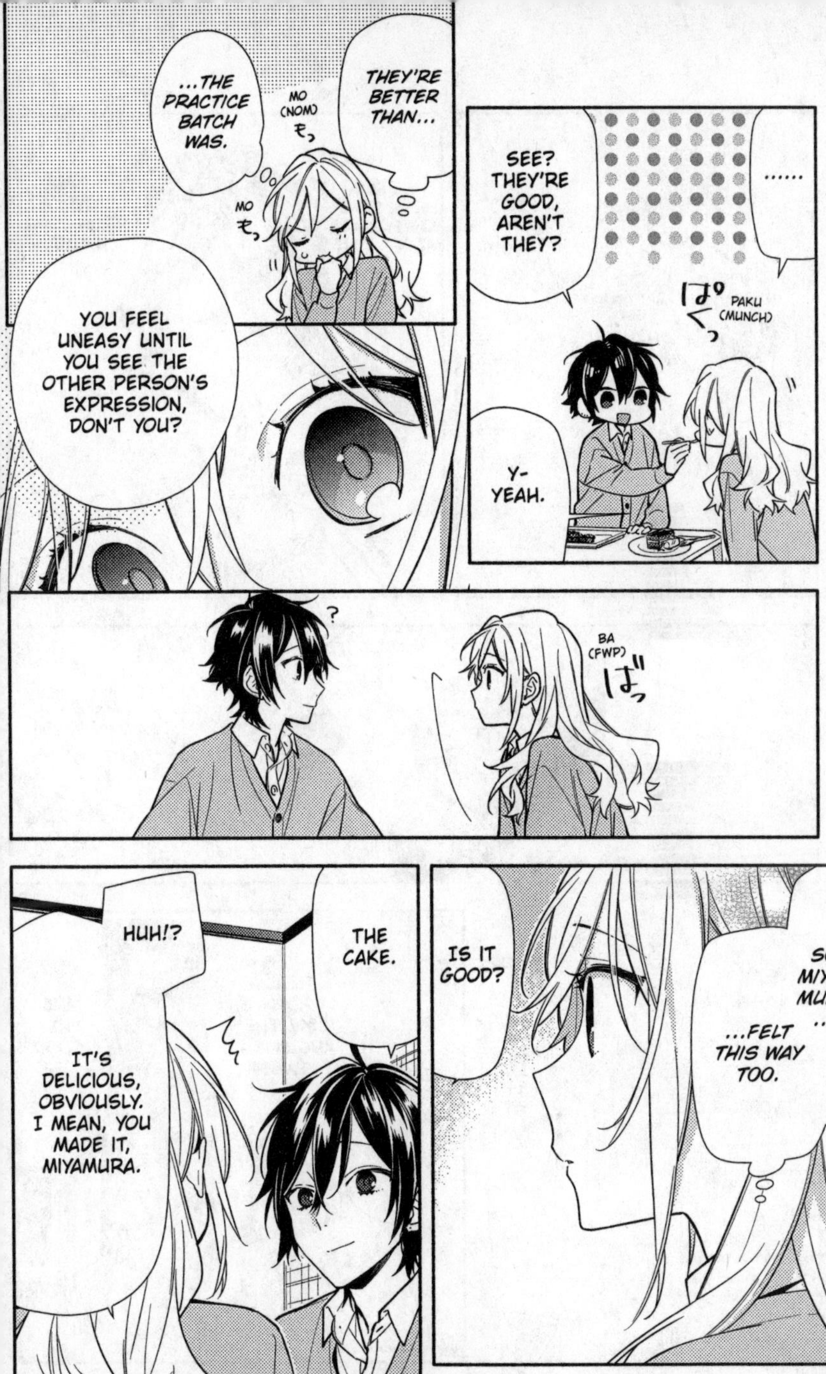
......
SEE? THEY'RE GOOD, AREN'T THEY?
ぱくっ PAKU (MUNCH)
Y-YEAH.
THEY'RE BETTER THAN...
もっ MO (NOM)
...THE PRACTICE BATCH WAS.
もっ MO
YOU FEEL UNEASY UNTIL YOU SEE THE OTHER PERSON'S EXPRESSION, DON'T YOU?
?
ばっ BA (FWP)
SO MIYAMURA...
...FELT THIS WAY TOO.
IS IT GOOD?
THE CAKE.
HUH!?
IT'S DELICIOUS, OBVIOUSLY. I MEAN, YOU MADE IT, MIYAMURA.

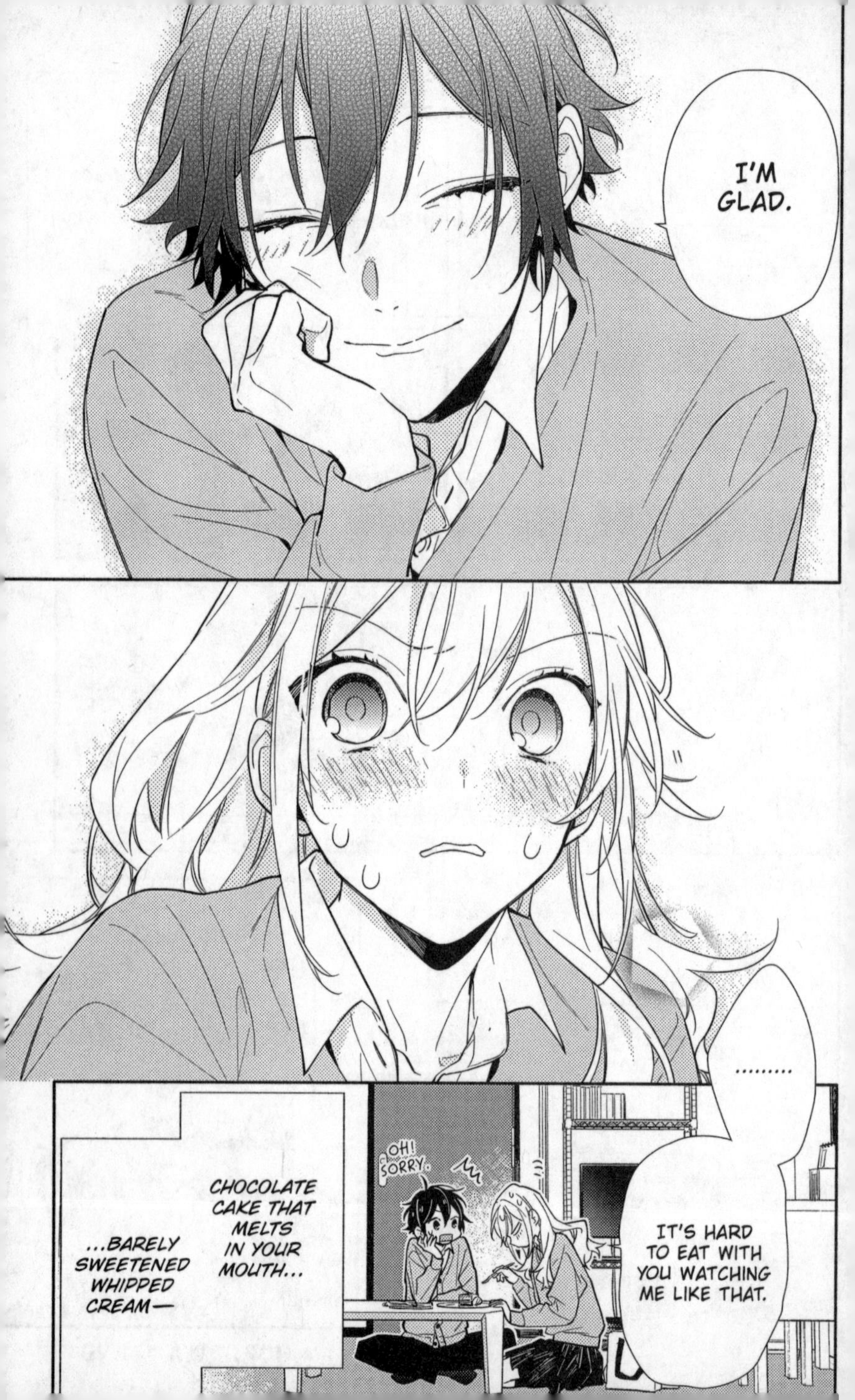
I'M GLAD.
....
IT'S HARD TO EAT WITH YOU WATCHING ME LIKE THAT.
OH! SORRY.
CHOCOLATE CAKE THAT MELTS IN YOUR MOUTH...
...BARELY SWEETENED WHIPPED CREAM—

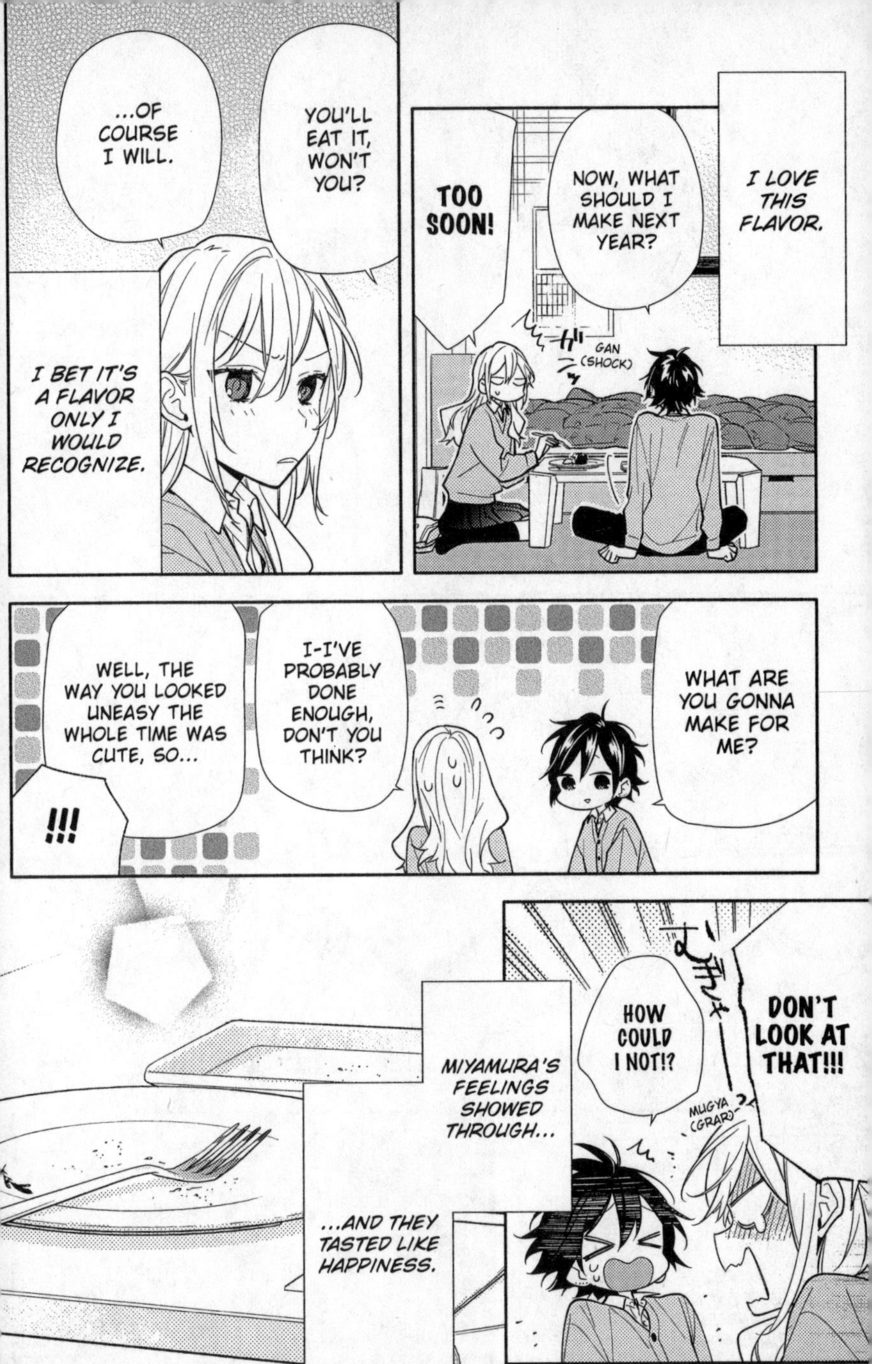
I LOVE THIS FLAVOR.
NOW, WHAT SHOULD I MAKE NEXT YEAR?
TOO SOON!
GAN (SHOCK)
YOU'LL EAT IT, WON'T YOU?
...OF COURSE I WILL.
I BET IT'S A FLAVOR ONLY I WOULD RECOGNIZE.
WHAT ARE YOU GONNA MAKE FOR ME?
I-I'VE PROBABLY DONE ENOUGH, DON'T YOU THINK?
WELL, THE WAY YOU LOOKED UNEASY THE WHOLE TIME WAS CUTE, SO...
!!!
DON'T LOOK AT THAT!!!
HOW COULD I NOT!?
MUGYA (GRAR)
MIYAMURA'S FEELINGS SHOWED THROUGH...
...AND THEY TASTED LIKE HAPPINESS.

HORIMIYA ⑮ END

To Be Continued...

HER AND HER VALENTINE'S DAY ①

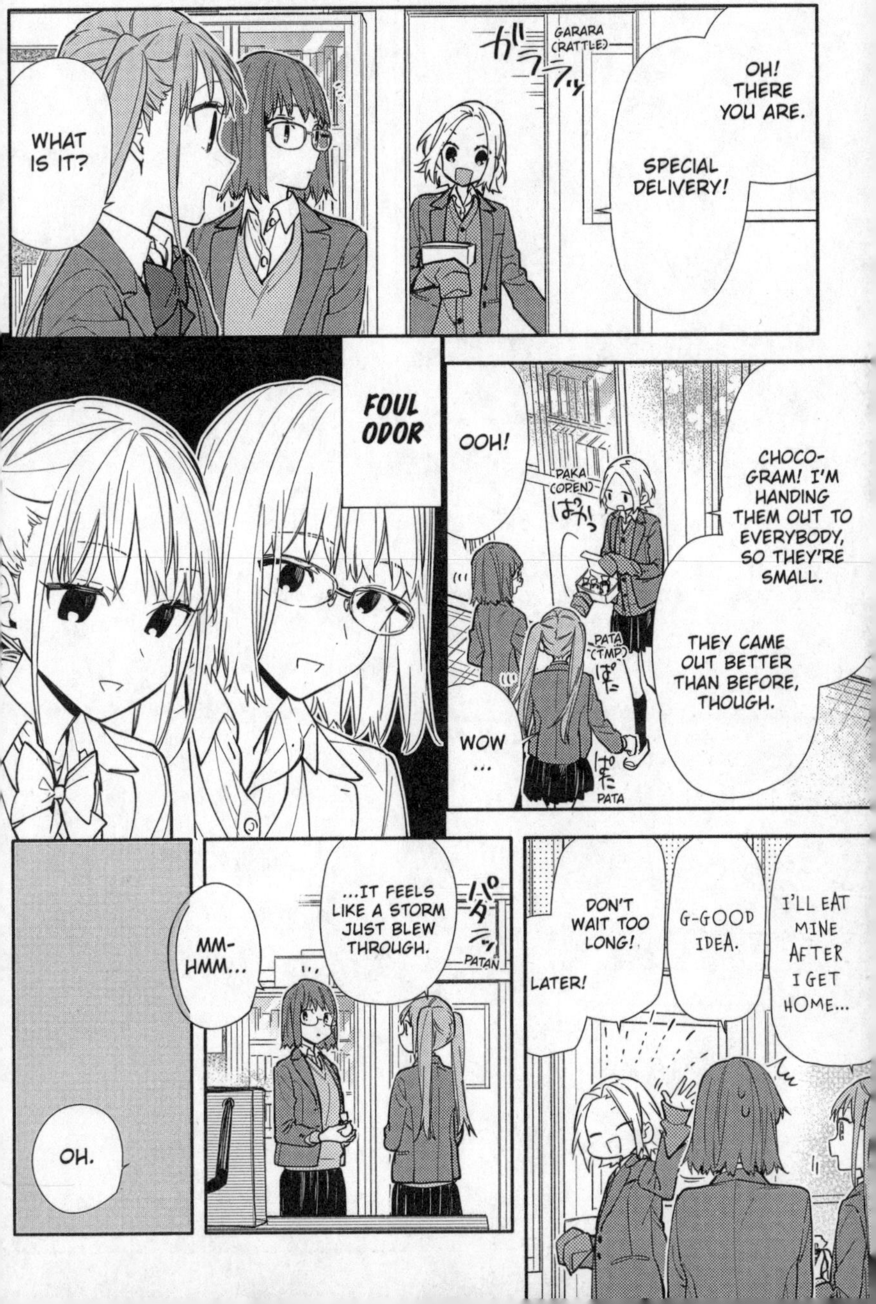
GARARA (RATTLE)
OH! THERE YOU ARE.
SPECIAL DELIVERY!
WHAT IS IT?
CHOCO-GRAM! I'M HANDING THEM OUT TO EVERYBODY, SO THEY'RE SMALL.
OOH!
PAKA (OPEN)
THEY CAME OUT BETTER THAN BEFORE, THOUGH.
PATA (TMP)
WOW ...
PATA
FOUL ODOR
I'LL EAT MINE AFTER I GET HOME...
G-GOOD IDEA.
DON'T WAIT TOO LONG!
LATER!
PATAN
...IT FEELS LIKE A STORM JUST BLEW THROUGH.
MM-HMM...
OH.

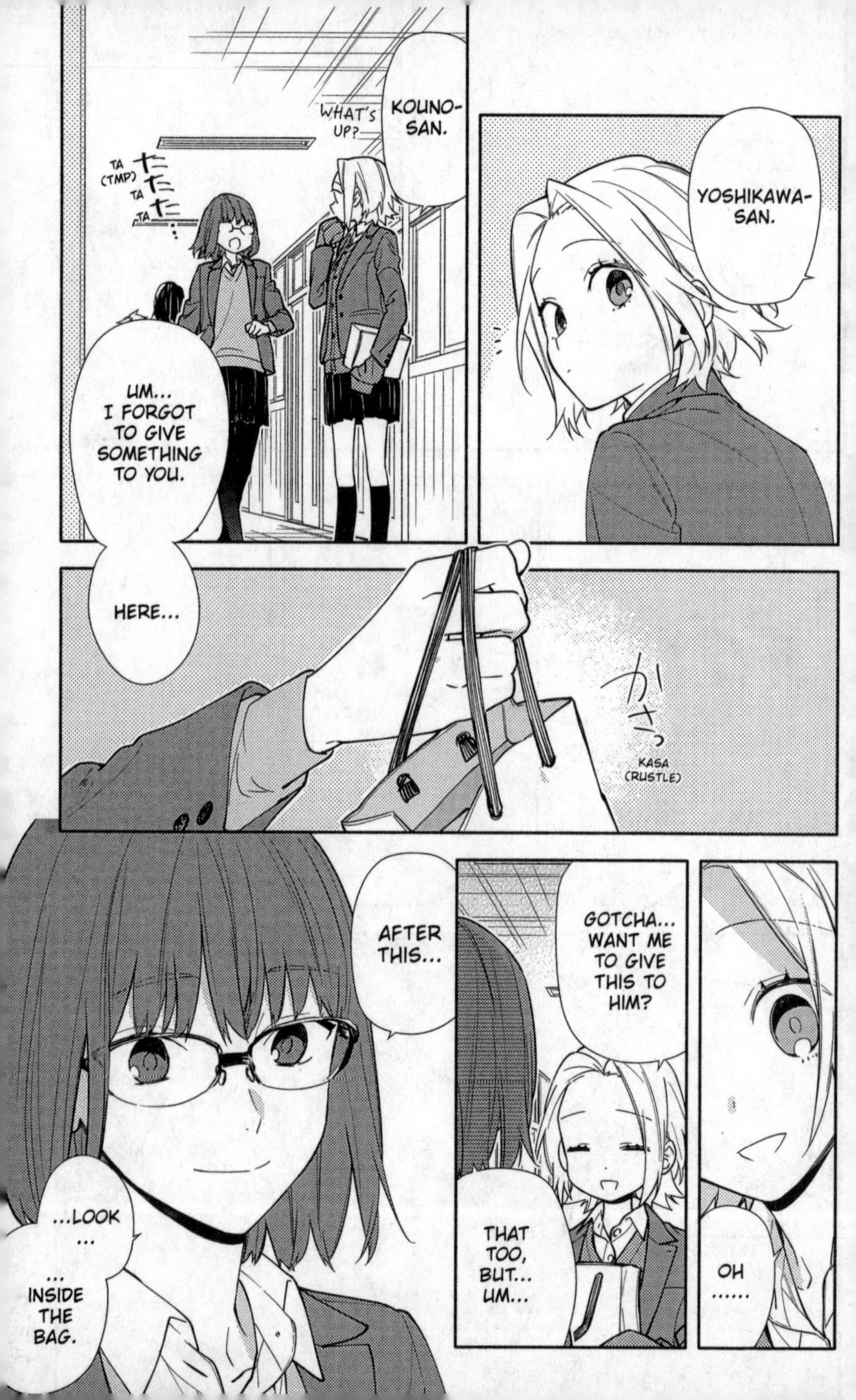
YOSHIKAWA-SAN.
KOUNO-SAN.
WHAT'S UP?
TA (TMP) TA TA
UM... I FORGOT TO GIVE SOMETHING TO YOU.
HERE...
KASA (RUSTLE)
OH ......
GOTCHA... WANT ME TO GIVE THIS TO HIM?
THAT TOO, BUT... UM...
AFTER THIS...
...LOOK ... ... INSIDE THE BAG.

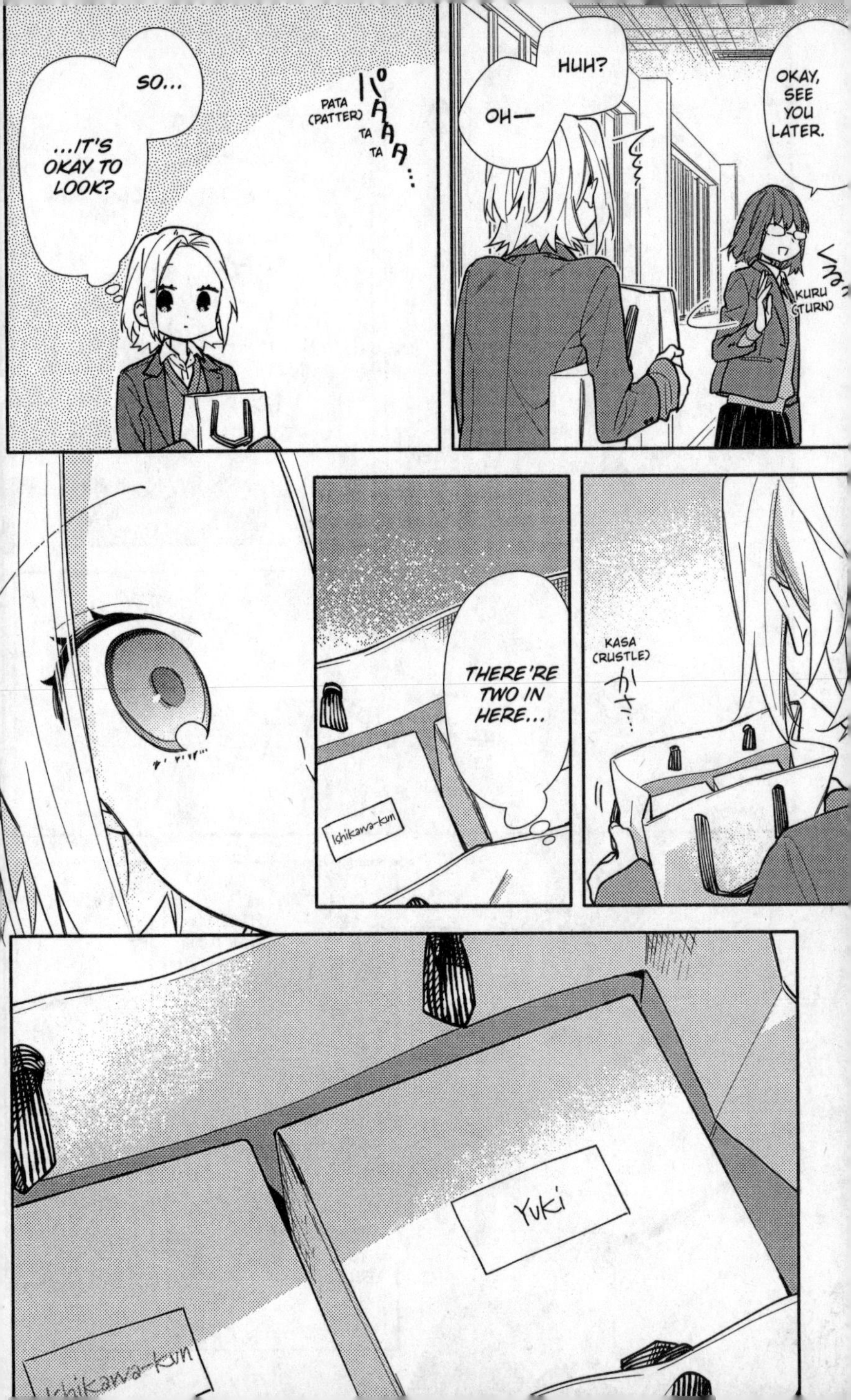
OKAY, SEE YOU LATER.
KURU (TURN)
HUH?
OH—
PATA (PATTER) TA TA
SO...
...IT'S OKAY TO LOOK?
KASA (RUSTLE)
THERE'RE TWO IN HERE...
Ishikawa-kun
Yuki
Ishikawa-kun

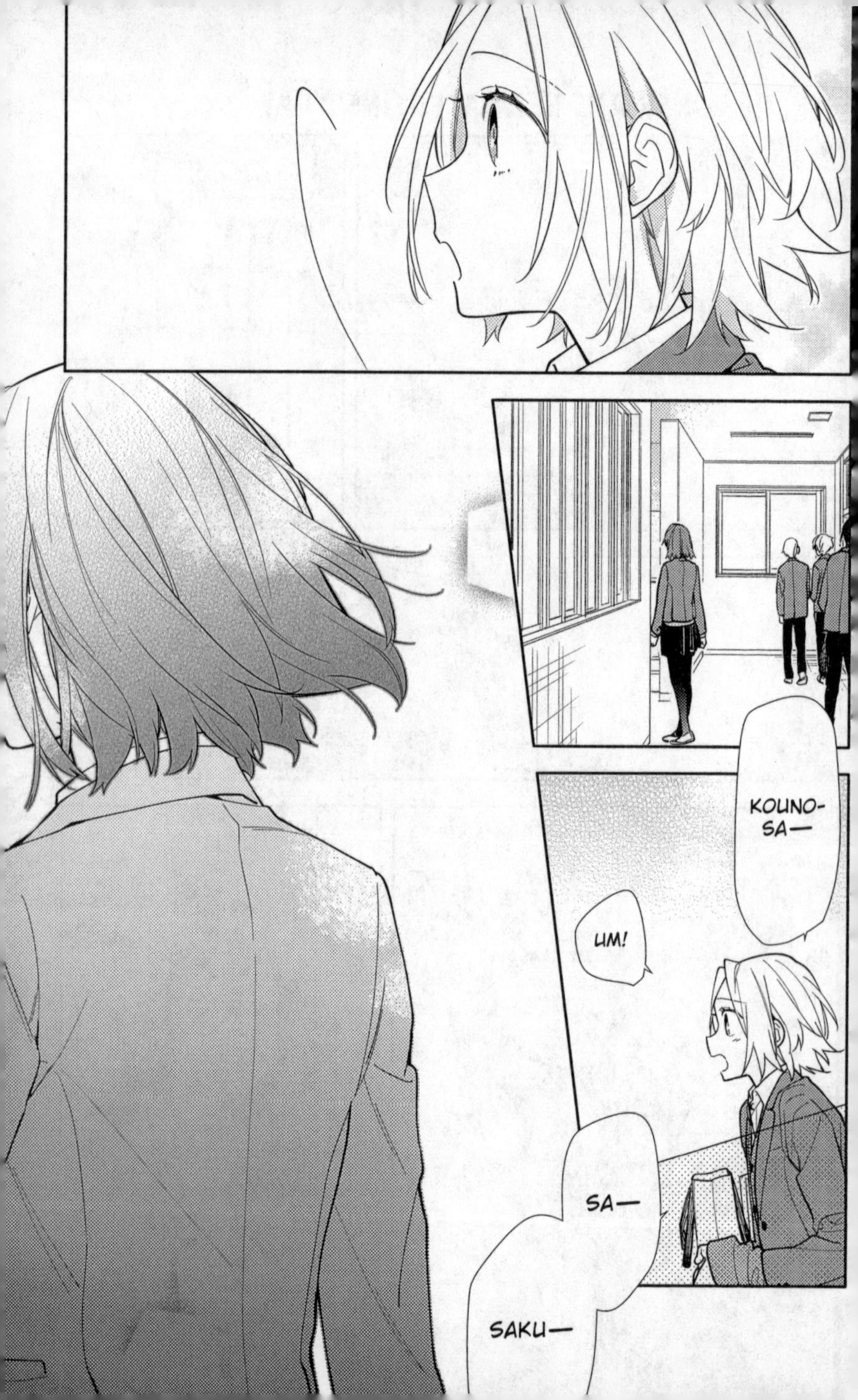
KOUNO-SA—
UM!
SA—
SAKU—

HER AND HER VALENTINE'S DAY ②

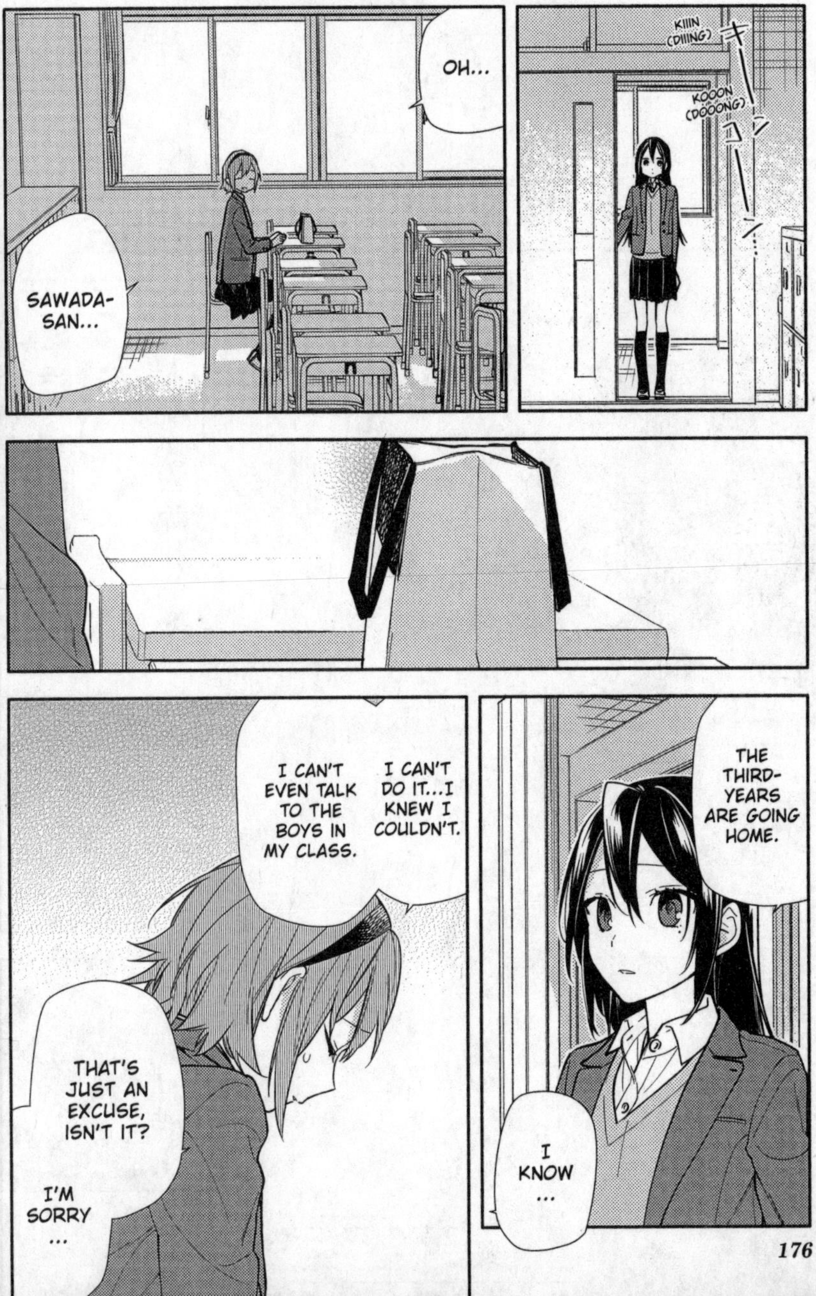
KIIIN (DIIING)
KOOON (DOOONG)
OH...
SAWADA-SAN...
THE THIRD-YEARS ARE GOING HOME.
I KNOW...
I CAN'T DO IT...I KNEW I COULDN'T.
I CAN'T EVEN TALK TO THE BOYS IN MY CLASS.
THAT'S JUST AN EXCUSE, ISN'T IT?
I'M SORRY...

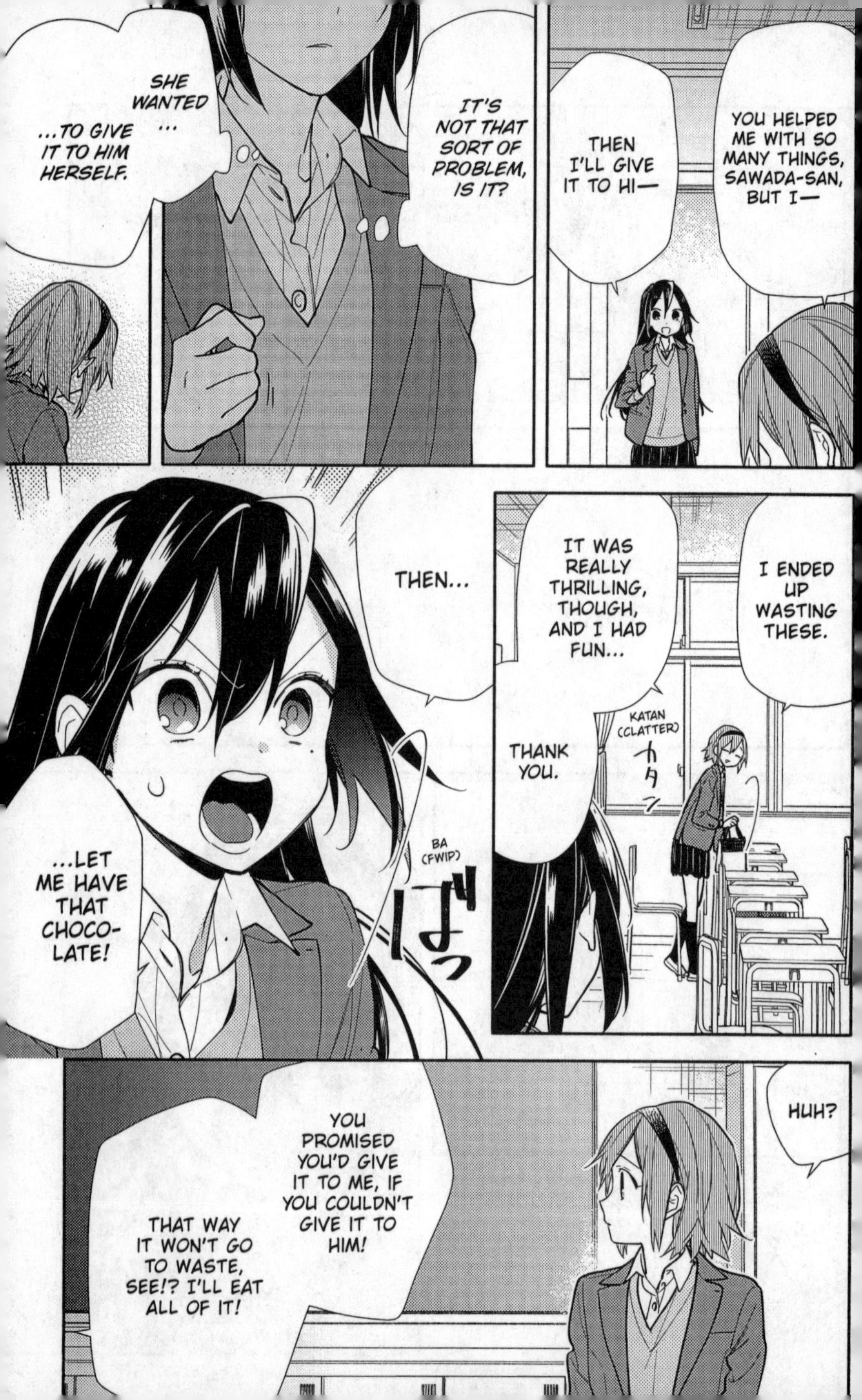
YOU HELPED ME WITH SO MANY THINGS, SAWADA-SAN, BUT I—
THEN I'LL GIVE IT TO HI—
IT'S NOT THAT SORT OF PROBLEM, IS IT?
SHE WANTED ...
...TO GIVE IT TO HIM HERSELF.
I ENDED UP WASTING THESE.
IT WAS REALLY THRILLING, THOUGH, AND I HAD FUN...
KATAN (CLATTER)
THANK YOU.
THEN...
BA (FWIP)
...LET ME HAVE THAT CHOCO-LATE!
HUH?
YOU PROMISED YOU'D GIVE IT TO ME, IF YOU COULDN'T GIVE IT TO HIM!
THAT WAY IT WON'T GO TO WASTE, SEE!? I'LL EAT ALL OF IT!

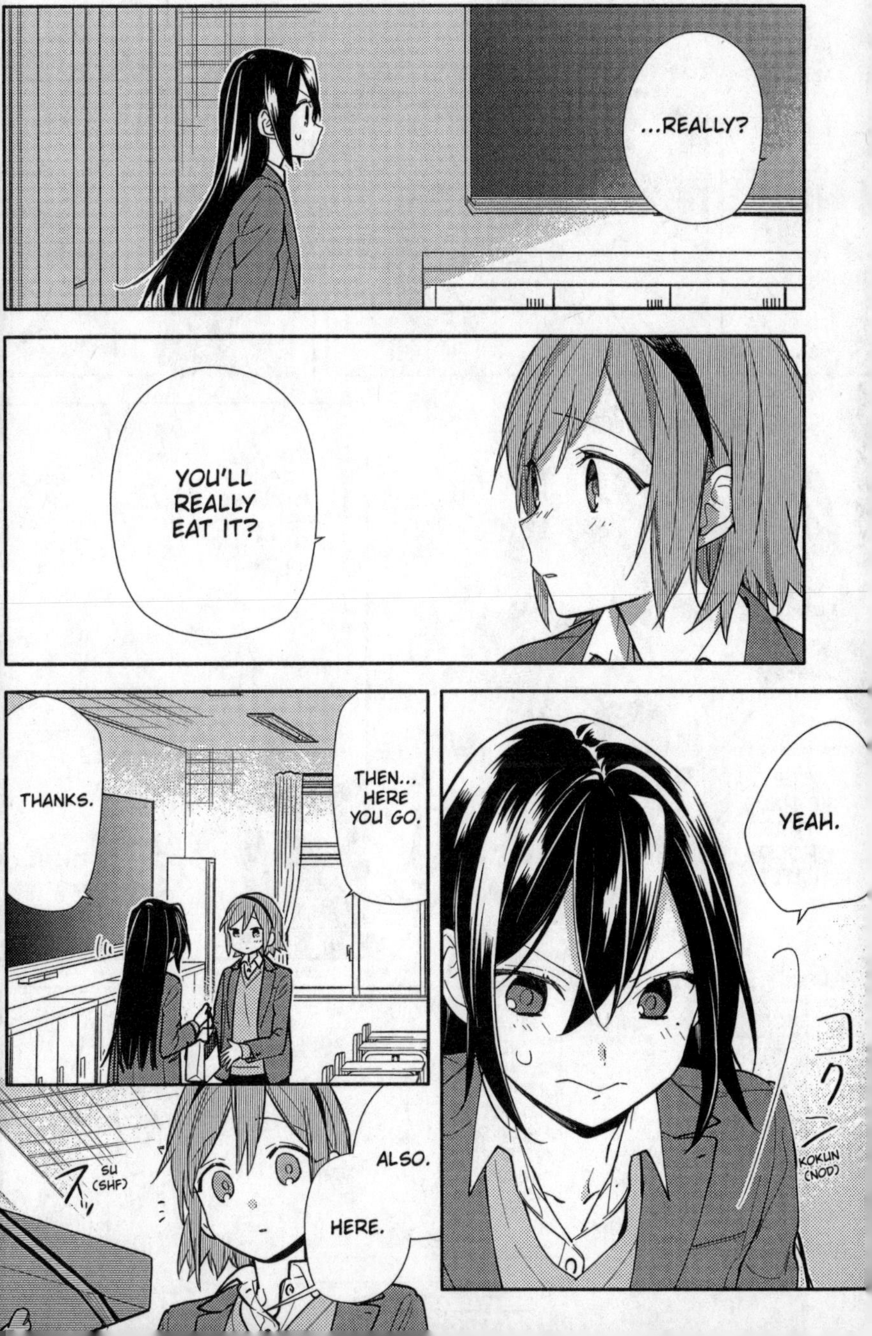
...REALLY?
YOU'LL REALLY EAT IT?
YEAH.
KOKUN (NOD)
THEN... HERE YOU GO.
THANKS.
ALSO.
HERE.
SU (SHF)

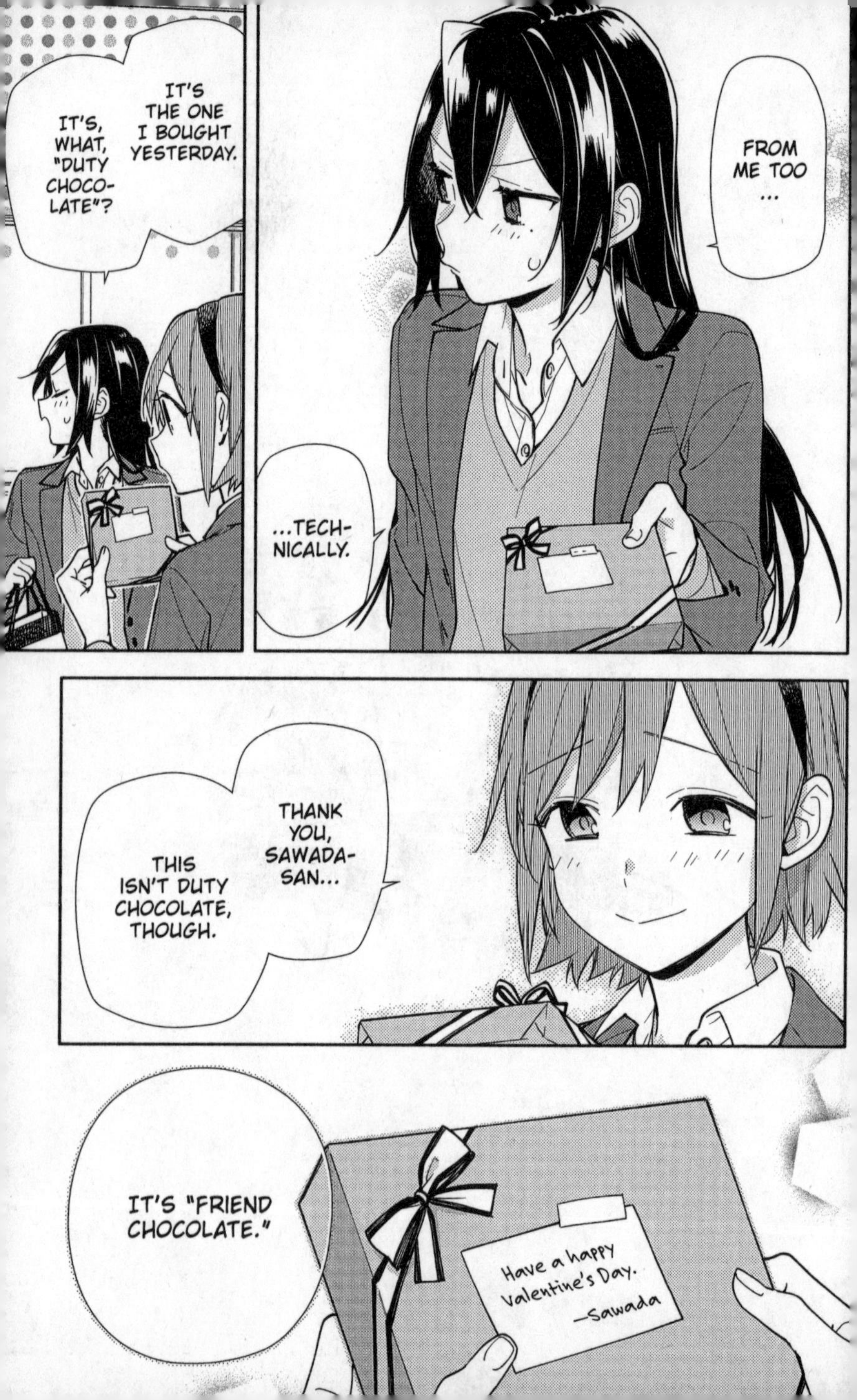
FROM ME TOO ...
...TECHNICALLY.
IT'S THE ONE I BOUGHT YESTERDAY.
IT'S, WHAT, "DUTY CHOCO-LATE"?
THANK YOU, SAWADA-SAN...
THIS ISN'T DUTY CHOCOLATE, THOUGH.
IT'S "FRIEND CHOCOLATE."
Have a happy Valentine's Day.
—Sawada

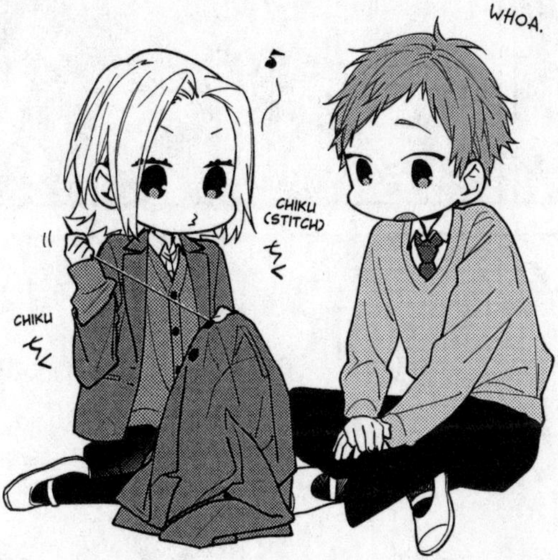
WHOA.
CHIKU (STITCH)
ちく
CHIKU
ちく

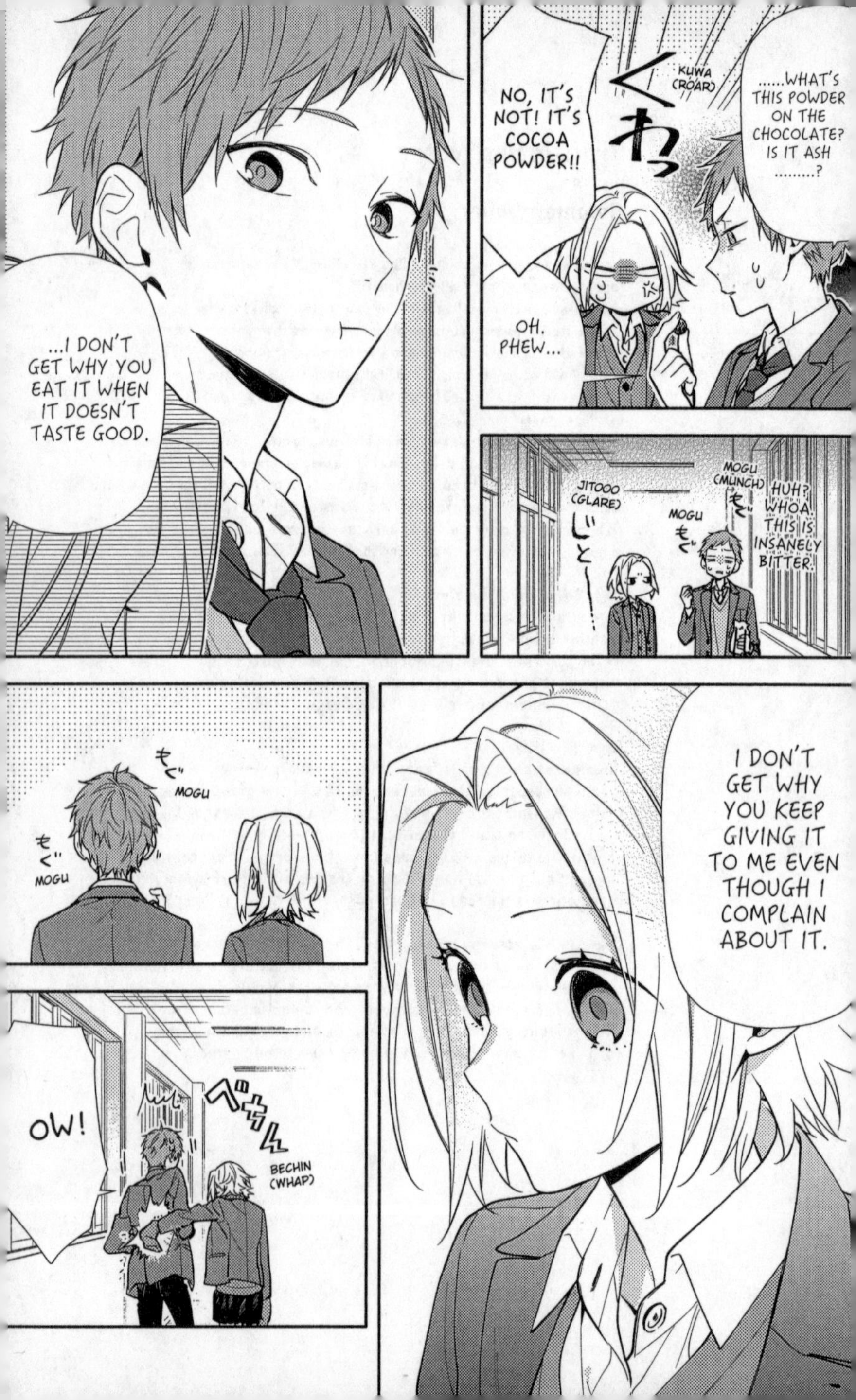
......WHAT'S THIS POWDER ON THE CHOCOLATE? IS IT ASH ....?
くわっ
KUWA (ROAR)
NO, IT'S NOT! IT'S COCOA POWDER!!
OH. PHEW...
もぐ
MOGU (MUNCH)
HUH? WHOA. THIS IS INSANELY BITTER.
もぐ
MOGU
じとー
JITOOO (GLARE)
...I DON'T GET WHY YOU EAT IT WHEN IT DOESN'T TASTE GOOD.
I DON'T GET WHY YOU KEEP GIVING IT TO ME EVEN THOUGH I COMPLAIN ABOUT IT.
もぐ
MOGU
もぐ
MOGU
べちん
BECHIN (WHAP)
OW!

Translation Notes

Common Honorifics

-san: The Japanese equivalent of Mr./Mrs./Miss. If a situation calls for politeness, this is the fail-safe honorific.

-kun: Used most often when referring to boys, this indicates affection or familiarity. Occasionally used by older men among their peers, but it may also be used by anyone referring to a person of lower standing.

-chan: An affectionate honorific indicating familiarity used mostly in reference to girls; also used in reference to cute persons or animals of either gender.

-(o)nii-chan: A familiar, somewhat childish way to refer to one's older brother.

-(o)nee-chan: A familiar, somewhat childish way to refer to one's older sister.

-senpai : A suffix used to address upperclassmen or more experienced coworkers.

-sensei: A respectful term for teachers, artists, or high-level professionals.

no honorific: Indicates familiarity or closeness; if used without permission or reason, addressing someone in this manner would constitute an insult.

Page 89 – School Regulations
Japanese high schools have strict dress codes that usually prohibit or limit piercings, tattoos, and hair coloring. As the student council president, one of Sengoku's duties is to enforce school regulations such as informing students when they are breaking said regulations.

Page 90 – Nay, 'tis
Miyamura actually says "*akan*" in the Japanese version, which would be recognized by Japanese readers as part of the Kansai dialect. Kansai is the name of the large plains area west of Tokyo upon which the cultural capitol of Japan, Kyoto, and the economic capitol, Osaka, were built. Since Japan's current political capitol, Tokyo, is built on the Kanto plain on the eastern side of Japan, Kanto is sometimes referred to as East Japan, while Kansai is West Japan.

Page 113 – It's creepy when you call me by my first name.
In addition to the honorifics listed above, the use of personal names can also indicate the social distance between people. Typically, very close friends, family members, and romantic partners will use a person's given name—classmates, distant acquaintances, coworkers, and strangers call them by their family name.

Page 123 – Valentine's Day
In Japan, this holiday is usually celebrated by couples spending the day together and girls giving boys they like chocolate. Unlike in the United States, a month later boys have the chance to return the favor on March 14, which is also known as White Day.

Page 157 – Duty/Friend Chocolate
While the chocolates given on Valentine's Day are oftentimes intended as romantic declarations to the giver's object of affection, some parties also use the holiday to show thanks and appreciation to coworkers, close friends, classmates, or family members. Duty chocolate is most often handed out to coworkers, bosses, or classmates as a general show of respect. Friend chocolate is usually given to close friends and family members to show appreciation or thanks.

Page 166 – *Pave de Geneve*
Chocolate cubes made of milk or dark chocolate, lightly dusted with cocoa powder. It is rumored that these chocolate squares were inspired by the cobblestones on a road in Switzerland. It is unknown whether the almost identical dessert called *namachoko* in Japan was truly influenced by the Swiss dessert or developed independently. However, given Miyamura's background as a baker's son, the dessert name is translated as *Pave de Geneve* instead of *namachoko*.

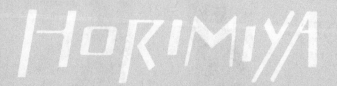

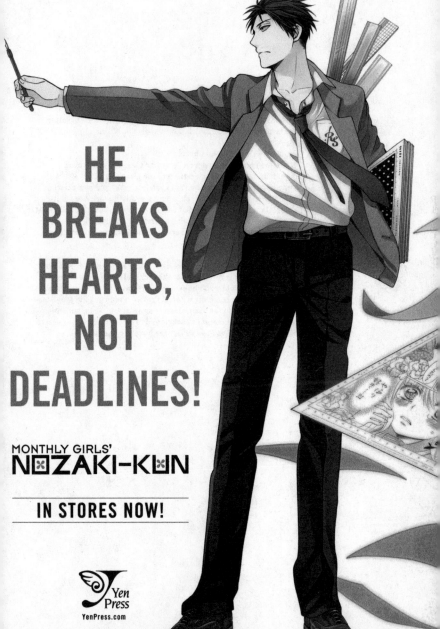

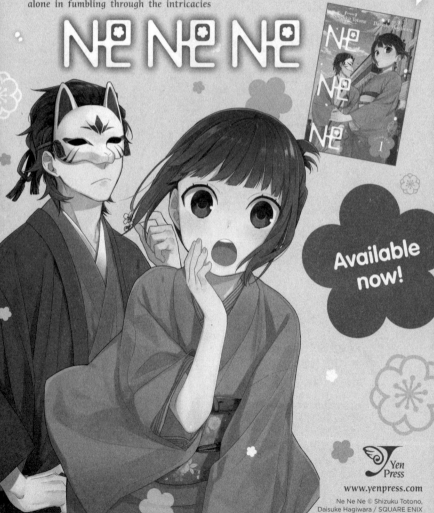

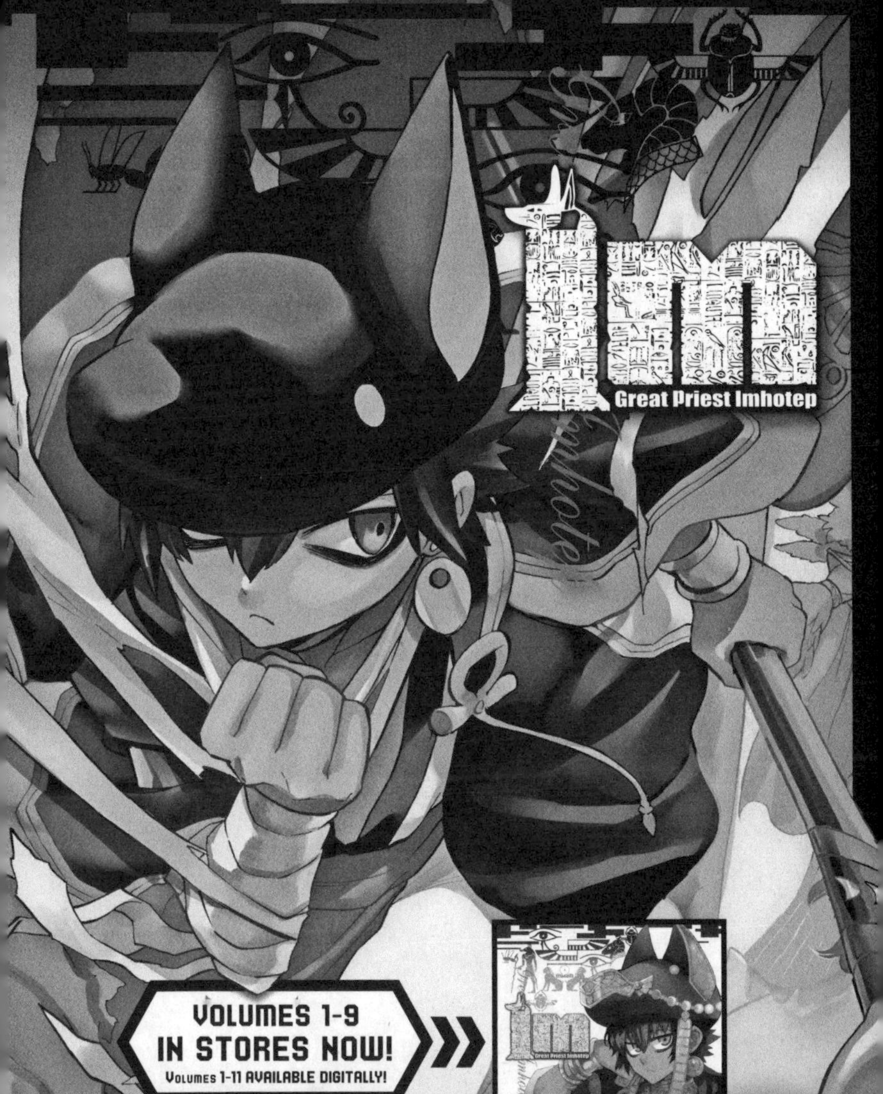
Im
Great Priest Imhotep
VOLUMES 1-9
IN STORES NOW!
VOLUMES 1-11 AVAILABLE DIGITALLY!
Im
Great Priest Imhotep
1
MAKOTO MORISHITA

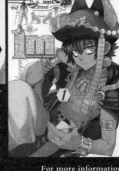

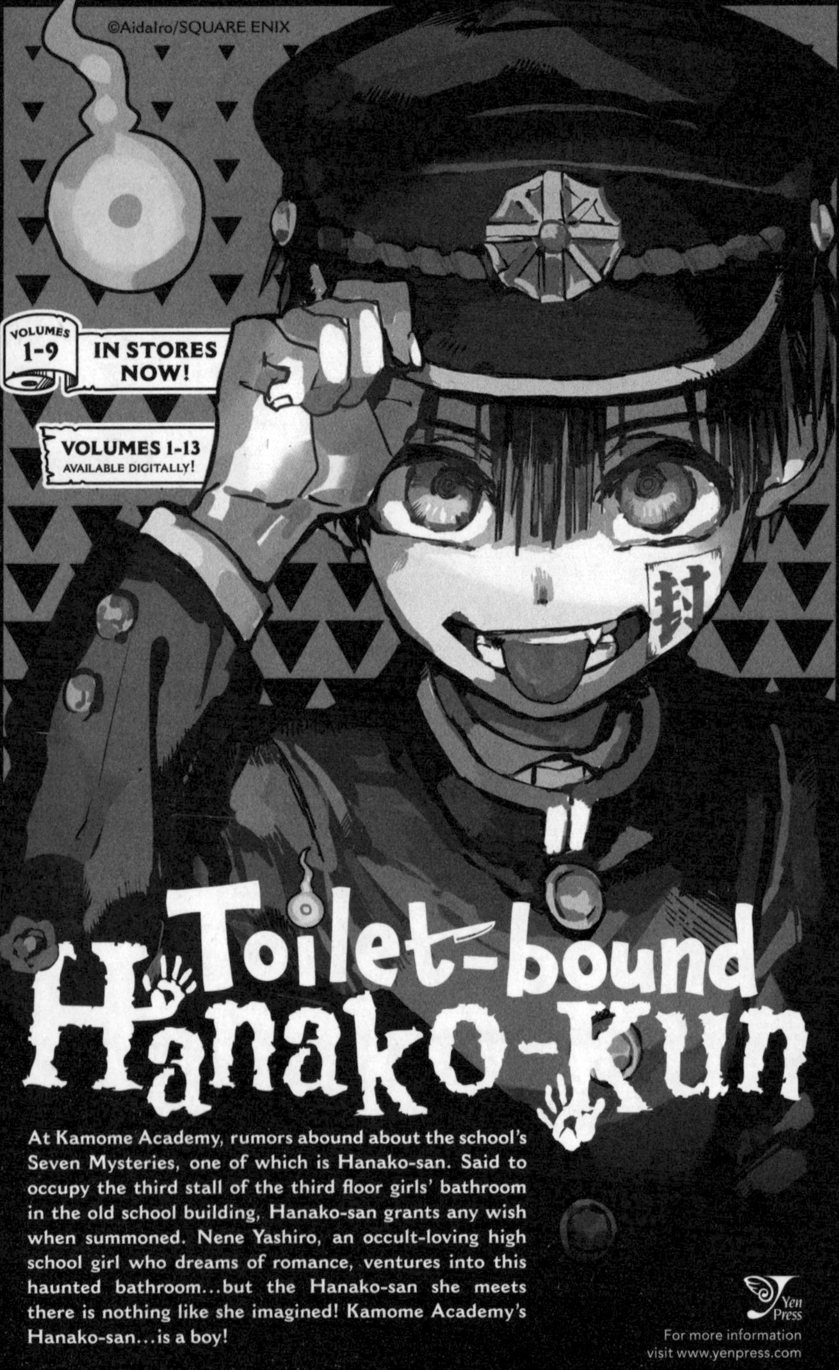
©AidaIro/SQUARE ENIX
VOLUMES 1-9 IN STORES NOW!
VOLUMES 1-13 AVAILABLE DIGITALLY!
Toilet-bound Hanako-kun
At Kamome Academy, rumors abound about the school's Seven Mysteries, one of which is Hanako-san. Said to occupy the third stall of the third floor girls' bathroom in the old school building, Hanako-san grants any wish when summoned. Nene Yashiro, an occult-loving high school girl who dreams of romance, ventures into this haunted bathroom...but the Hanako-san she meets there is nothing like she imagined! Kamome Academy's Hanako-san...is a boy!
Yen Press
For more information visit www.yenpress.com

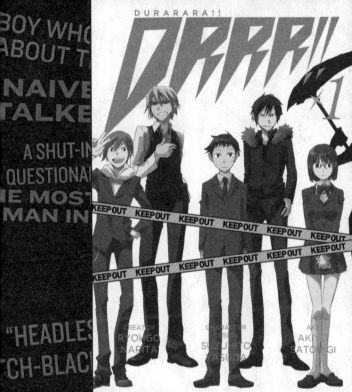

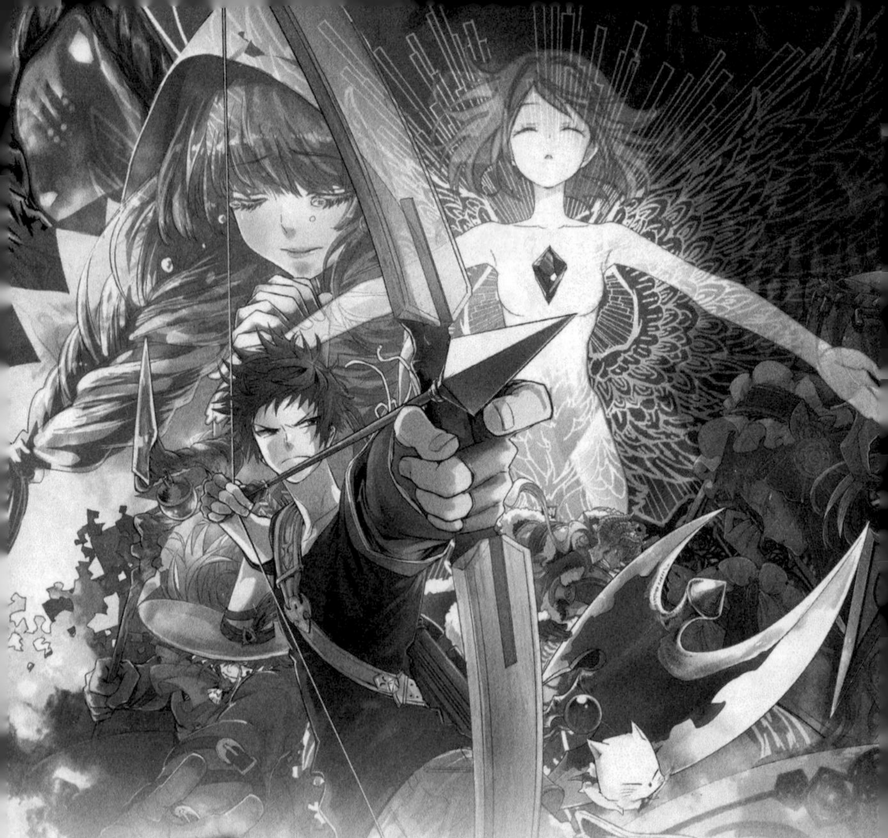

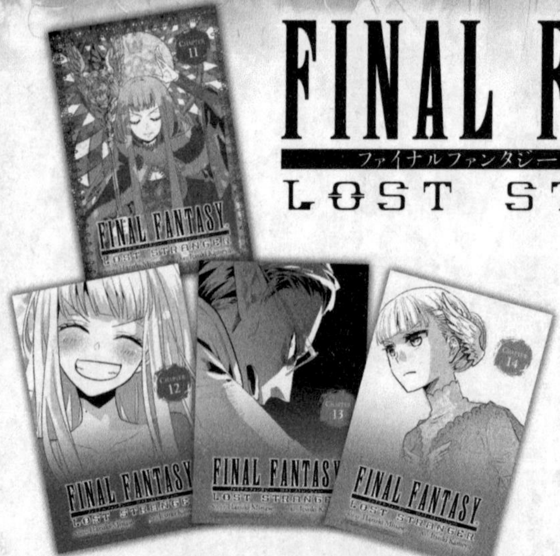

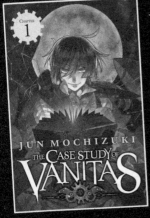

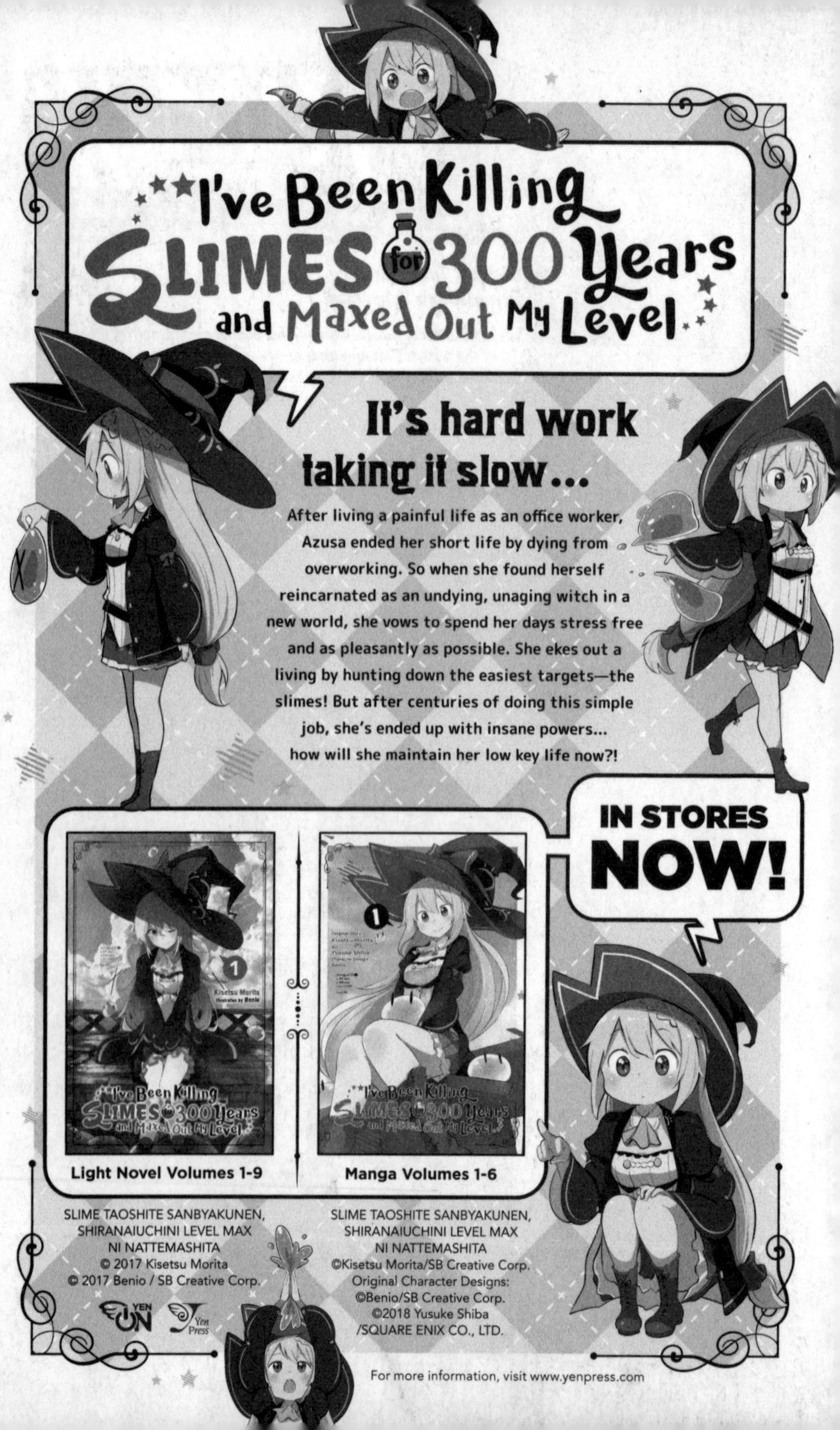
I've Been Killing SLIMES for 300 Years and Maxed Out My Level
It's hard work taking it slow...
After living a painful life as an office worker, Azusa ended her short life by dying from overworking. So when she found herself reincarnated as an undying, unaging witch in a new world, she vows to spend her days stress free and as pleasantly as possible. She ekes out a living by hunting down the easiest targets—the slimes! But after centuries of doing this simple job, she's ended up with insane powers... how will she maintain her low key life now?!
IN STORES NOW!
Kisetsu Morita
Illustration by Benio
I've Been Killing SLIMES for 300 Years and Maxed Out My Level
Light Novel Volumes 1-9
I've Been Killing SLIMES for 300 Years and Maxed Out My Level
Manga Volumes 1-6
SLIME TAOSHITE SANBYAKUNEN, SHIRANAIUCHINI LEVEL MAX NI NATTEMASHITA © 2017 Kisetsu Morita © 2017 Benio / SB Creative Corp.
SLIME TAOSHITE SANBYAKUNEN, SHIRANAIUCHINI LEVEL MAX NI NATTEMASHITA ©Kisetsu Morita/SB Creative Corp. Original Character Designs: ©Benio/SB Creative Corp. ©2018 Yusuke Shiba /SQUARE ENIX CO., LTD.
YEN ON
Yen Press
For more information, visit www.yenpress.com

HERO × Daisuke Hagiwara

Trans
Lette

This b   he
produc   ce
to act

HORII
© HEI
© 2020   an
in 2020 by SQUARE ENIX CO., LTD. English translation rights arranged with
SQUARE ENIX CO., LTD. and Yen Press, LLC through Tuttle-Mori Agency, Inc.

English translation © 2021 by SQUARE ENIX CO., LTD.

Yen Press
150 West 30th Street, 19th Floor
New York, NY 10001

Visit us at yenpress.com • facebook.com/yenpress •
twitter.com/yenpress • yenpress.tumblr.com •
instagram.com/yenpress

First Yen Press Edition: June 2021

Yen Press is an imprint of Yen Press, LLC.
The Yen Press name and logo are trademarks
of Yen Press, LLC.

The publisher is not responsible for websites
(or their content) that are not owned by the
publisher.

Library of Congress Control Number:
2015960115

ISBNs: 978-1-9753-2472-8 (paperback)
       978-1-9753-2473-5 (ebook)

10 9 8 7 6 5 4 3 2 1

BVG

Printed in the United States of America